Author Bio

Glen Fisher, despite a horrific childhood, has fought many demons to become the writer of this true story that addresses many issues surrounding children of dysfunctional families and how the system can get it so wrong.

Glen expresses himself through this book and also through art and poetry. His motivation for his various arts is to give hope and inspiration where there may be none.

Today Glen is a proud dad and grandad and advocate for Forgotten Australians.

Predators' Paradise

A Journey of Survival and Resilience

429 Refuge: still standing and condemned

By Glen Fisher

With Kate Shayler

This is an IndieMosh book

brought to you by MoshPit Publishing
an imprint of Mosher's Business Support Pty Ltd

PO Box 147
Hazelbrook NSW 2779

indiemosh.com.au

Cataloguing-in-Publication entry is available from the National Library of Australia: http://catalogue.nla.gov.au/

Title:	Predators' Paradise
Subtitle:	A Journey of Survival and Resilience
Author:	Fisher, Glen (1966–)
ISBNs:	978-1-922261-98-4 (paperback)
	978-1-922261-99-1 (ebook – epub)
	978-1-925959-00-0 (ebook – mobi)
Subjects:	Family & Relationships/Abuse/Child Abuse; Biography & Autobiography/Survival; True Crime/Sexual Assault.

Cover design artwork by Glen Fisher

Cover layout by Ally Mosher

Internal images from Glen Fisher's personal archive

I dedicate this book to:

Linda Kirby. You were the inspiration for me writing this book and you were my light.

The kids of Kings Cross especially to the children who lived in the refuge known as 429.

The children of Daruk, Yasmar, Minda and other children's homes.

Children who have been rejected by their family.

Children separated from their families by the system.

Every child who was raised in institutional care.

To half a million Forgotten Australians picking up the pieces of lives shattered by a system that failed them.

Table of Contents

Prologue

The motivation for writing this book was the death of a beautiful fifteen year old girl, Linda. Her life was stolen. Linda was one of many children who died on the streets before even reaching adulthood. Linda was my first girlfriend. She was raped and murdered and I still miss her.

Each day I remember Linda and the many little faces of children who died after lives of abuse and neglect. I was one of these living children and it's only by the grace of God that I am alive.

Most of the children moved from institutions of abuse to the streets of Kings Cross – Predators' Paradise. Their lives were destroyed by many evils: heroin, murder, rape, strip clubs, brothels, drug dealers, suicides to name a few. Predators roamed the streets looking for vulnerable children to prey upon.

Many of the abuses these children experienced began in their family home and were repeated in institutions, so by the time the kids had come to the streets they had been groomed and are vulnerable.

Corruption in the justice system at the time invaded the foot slogging levels and went all the way up the food chain to judges. Who was there to care for the children? Paedophiles. Death.

I aim to expose the corruption I saw in all its forms.

I have dedicated my present day life to getting justice for myself and other children who were vulnerable. I hope that by sharing my story I can give an insight into the journey of a survivor of sexual, physical and emotional abuse. I want readers to understand that an abusive childhood never leaves you, no matter how tight you hold it down inside.

No matter what we go through, we survivors, we Forgotten Australians are resilient and many of us have fought for many years to make changes not only to our own lives but for the many others who have survived abuse.

For the privacy of other victims in this book I have changed all names and the identifying information of some people but I refuse to hide the names of the abusers who have been convicted. I wrote the book myself and I had another Forgotten Australian, Kate Shayler, take it and help shape it into what you are reading now—a raw and honest account of my life.

I have used poetry to help me cope with PTSD, depression and the memories of abuse. I have shared some poems here. I have some of my files from YACS (Youth & Community Services) and institutional records. I have included direct quotes from these records to illustrate how my abuses were recorded and not dealt with effectively. Many entries have been whited out but the disturbing pattern of abuse within my family is clear.

The story may upset other survivors of abuse. I have kept this in mind but sometimes I needed to show the ugliness of what happened.

So many children raised in care suffer from mental health issues like depression, anxiety, PTSD and low self-esteem. Many end up in prisons, drinking or drugging or many died as children or are unwell. But we are a resilient lot and we lift each other.

A Poem: The Mouse

Four little Sparrows
Reside in this house.
One's now a Peacock
The other's a Mouse.

A Falcon and Eagle
Nest in there too.
The Mouse is so frightened.
What does he do?

If he moves to the right
The Peacock will tell.
The Falcon is active
Picks up on his smell.

The Hawk is luring,
Attacks whilst the Mouse is asleep.
After the attack
The little Mouse does weep.

He can't tell the Sparrows
They don't comprehend.
The Mouse is so frightened.
He longs for a friend.

The Peacock is laughing.
The Falcon grooms at his wing
The little Sparrows hover
They try but can't sing.

A Poem: The Mouse

The Mouse remains idle
In fear, in pain.
The Sparrows try to pick up the Mouse,
Too heavy the strain.

Two Lions enter
Right through the door
They pick up the Mouse
They promise no more.

To the jungle they take him
Alone and afraid
The Mouse now wonders
Should he have stayed.

Can a Mouse protect a Sparrow
From a Falcon or Hawk?
He returns but the Peacock
One move and I'll squawk.

The Eagle has separated
Left from the nest,
Takes with him the Mouse
To torment at his nest.

Though the Falcon was violent,
Likes to play with its kill,
The Hawk liked to torment,
Gave him a thrill.

The Eagle loved the power
He held over the Mouse.
Two beautiful Sparrows
Were left in the house.

Chapter 1.
Violence in Silence

My father took me with him to the park one day. I thought for a moment we might play but he had other ideas that didn't include me.

'Don't you move from that spot,' he demanded, pointing to a seat. Then he disappeared into the yacht club for a drink.

I was about five or six then and I got bored easily. I decided to walk along the water's edge. What's that I can see in the water? I reached down to get it and next thing I know I'm tumbling into the water, grazing my ankle on the rocks as I fall. I cut my self really badly. Worse than that though, I couldn't swim.

I keep going under the water, gulping for air. This was a new kind of terror. The more I panicked the worse my situation became. I knew I was drowning, taking in huge gulps of water. Drowning and bleeding.

Like Superman, an elderly man came from nowhere, jumped into the water and pulled me out! He saved my life. This was the first time I cheated death and it wouldn't be the last. After this kind man pulled me out of the water he put me into a taxi to be taken to The Royal North Shore Hospital where I got eight stitches in my ankle. Hospital staff couldn't locate my father to come and get me but the hospital had my records from previous visits, so they were able to return me home.

When Barry my father got home I was in a lot of trouble.

'Didn't I tell you to wait where I left ya! "Don't move," I said!' He's coming menacingly closer. 'You are so stupid.' I was regularly told by my father how stupid I was.

A scrawny little boy like me was easy for Barry to pick up and throw against the wall. That's what he did. As I slumped down, he and my mother started fighting about it. I should have stayed exactly where I was left in the park. He shouldn't have left me there … then the physical violence started and I crept my invisible self away. Our father was into martial arts, so he was fit and his hits met their targets.

Even after that episode, when we went swimming Barry used to swim up from underneath, grab my legs and hold me under. I'm sure he thought it was funny but every time he did it I'd panic and my fear made it that much worse. It was not funny Barry! I still get flashbacks of drowning.

My mother Margaret was a drug addicted drunk. Her first response to any stress, however minor, was violence. My father Barry was a violent manipulative drunk, but away from his family he appeared to be a well-spoken and charming man. They had four children and I am the eldest. A lot of mum's rage was directed at me. I was born when she and Barry were both quite young. My mother told me once or twice that Barry was not my real father. I am not sure if that is true, but I spent a large part of my life wondering. As I get older I start to see my father in the mirror and I don't like what I see: confirmation that I am his son. I spent most of my childhood walking on eggshells and trying desperately to be invisible to avoid the one constant in my life … violence.

At different stages I have found myself writing the words 'Mum' or 'Dad' in the book, but it doesn't ring true. I am not comfortable using those words and often I refer to them as Barry and Margaret. They don't deserve the titles.

Point Wollstonecraft was the first place I lived according to my Birth Certificate, dated 1st October, 1966. I don't know if this was a rehab place, a commune or a religious cult but I have very clear memories of being there. We used to meet out the front for breakfast each morning and then we'd chant for a session before the men went off to work on a truck, and my mother did arts and crafts. I remember the pastor's daughter had silk worms. For some reason we were kicked out of that place or maybe we just left.

We went to live in Neutral Bay on the north shore of Sydney after that. Today it is an affluent neighbourhood. Records show that my dad was working for a waste disposal facility. Maybe translated that means he was a garbo, so there must have been poorer areas in Neutral Bay too. My mother was a housewife, possibly suffering from battered wife syndrome as well as other mental health issues.

Margaret was no shrinking violet though. She was tall and thick set but not fat. She was a bit of a street fighter who'd grown up with three brothers two of whom were all violent drinkers, so she had learnt to handle herself. She showed no fear of Barry. In fact she was most often the aggressor in the frequent fights they had. Their fights involved slapping, punching, hair pulling, scratching hurling each about, throwing things at each other and kicking. I heard all the sounds and hid away for as long as I could.

After one huge fight between my parents my mother and I left on a train to go to Mackay, in Queensland. Uncle Joe, one of mum's brothers, lived up there with their parents. We seemed to be on the train for ages but we ended up outside my grandmother's place at three in the morning, waiting for her and her husband Robert to come home from the pub. Nanny drank heavily as did Robert, an ex-shearer. When they got home, very drunk, the adults kept drinking together while I fell asleep on the lounge room floor.

My mother's harsh treatment of me didn't change in company. When Nanny, this amazing old lady who I never saw sober, noticed how I was treated she would say, 'Margaret, give the kid a break!' The times when Nanny defended me are some of the few good memories I have from childhood. After a few days at Nanny's house we returned to Dad. He had calmed down by then.

Our house had so many steps leading up to it from the street, and a choko vine grew out the back. We had a dog, a Doberman, named Hindu. The back fence had a gate that led to the neighbour's yard and they were very close friends of my parents. I can't remember them at all. I do remember Barry and Margaret's oldest friends, Paul and Edna who were from Britain. They often visited us or we'd go on outings together. Sometimes Uncle Paul, as we were instructed to call him, would pick up all or some of us kids and off we'd go.

Welfare officers visited us regularly, child abuse and neglect being the reason for the visits. We were quite poor, on a low income and high rent and we often ran out of money and food. Mum was not coping with four children under five. The earliest welfare record I have, from when I was almost five reminds me that violence and fear were my constant companions along with hunger.

> *File 17/6/71: ... Margaret said that Glen was stealing from local shops and from neighbours.*

I don't remember stealing but I was probably starving. Welfare convinced the local school to try to take me in early, before the usual starting age. This experiment failed and I had to go back home and wait until I was the right age.

By the time Samuel, the youngest and most favoured child, was born in 1970, Margaret was beside herself with stress and it only got worse.

> *File 2/11/71: .... Mrs. Fisher asked if I could arrange ... temporary placement of her children ... her husband's temper tantrums were what mainly upset her and the children, and they were all becoming nervous wrecks.*

I had so many placements away from home that it's hard to remember which of them happened when.

> *File 3/2/72: ... She and Barry, her husband, were not solving any of their problems and she could not cope in any way, so that she knew now that she would have to be relieved of the children.*

It could have been that this time Child Welfare suggested a period of time in a Barnardo's Home, but our parents chose to put us in Lakeside Children's Hostel. We went there a few times as shown in my file but I don't remember it particularly. After each time in a home we were sent back into the storm that was our parents' life and ours.

When Dad got home from work each night they would go off to the sailing club, leaving us four kids at home. Michael was born in 1968, Tina in 1969 and finally The Golden Child in 1970. Like all kids, as soon as our parents left, we'd sneak from our rooms to play until all hours. We'd turn the radio on and dance and romp about laughing wildly, feeling our freedom. But our radars were always on high alert for the sound of Barry and Margaret coming home. We knew what time the pub shut so we had a pretty good idea when the fun needed to end. We'd make sure we were in bed, apparently asleep, before the next cyclone started.

Barry and Margaret would be totally pissed when they got back and they'd fight each other, starting with yelling then escalating to physical violence that often went through 'til dawn. I have vivid memories of the thumps, the shouting, the hoping I was invisible. Sometimes I would try to get between them to stop the fight but of course I couldn't. I was a puny little kid, terrified and undernourished. Fights were pretty much a daily occurrence.

If their fighting didn't resolve, the violence spilled over onto me sometimes. One time I was in a vehicle with my father, who had just been arguing with my mother. Suddenly my dad just lost it. He reached over, opened my door and pushed me out while the car was still moving. I skidded along the road feeling the pain as the skin on my shoulders burned on the tar. I walked back home and struggled up the many stairs to our place.

My mother looked at me as if to say 'Oh no. You're back are you?'

'Dad chucked me out of the car,' I told her. Margaret told me to get washed and left me to it. The scars from that day are still visible and they have the company of many others earned prior to the age of nine.

You might wonder why my mother didn't help me or show any compassion. The fact is I can't remember a single time that she hugged me, kissed me or even comforted me. She just didn't have it in her. I often wonder if she ever said, 'I love you,' to my siblings or ever showed them any type of affection. I am sure she did with Golden Child Samuel, although I can't recall it.

My mother was committed under the Mental Health Act for a time early in 1972. Where would us kids go? I was sent to a Barnardo's place and the others went somewhere else. Margaret was discharged in July that year and we were allowed to go home. Not all at once though. Margaret wouldn't cope with that. We came back one by one. I loathed being away from my siblings and I longed for us all to be together again.

Christmas day came as usual. Gifts were highly prized in our house. A memorable Christmas for me was when I sat eagerly waiting to see what I'd get. Mum handed me a gift and I ripped the wrapping off. The daily newspaper. What? Next my dad opened his present. A fire engine! How come he got a fire engine and I just got a newspaper? So drunk was my mother that she couldn't even get the presents right. She was mostly asleep that day or nodding off. She'd drink, start yelling and screaming at me and then she'd nod off.

Our frequent interactions with Child Welfare continued and most entries in my file are my mother referring to me as the cause of her problems. The Case Workers often expressed concern about this hatred. My mother herself told them that she feared for my safety when I was with her.

File 20/1/1972: … I am writing again to urge action be taken to remove all four children from this very disturbing home.

The mother Mrs Fisher has been committed under the mental health act … It is obvious that this woman, … lashes out with her children at home and causes them physical injury … When I visited the home on May 1971 Glen was observed by me to have a black eye … Mrs Fisher has admitted to battering the children and although she displays guilt about this, it is obvious that she cannot control her temper ... I strongly urge removal of all four children on the grounds of neglect and damage being sustained by the children both physically and mentally.

I was taken to Barnardo's Cottage for a time and my parents were told that if they took me away from there early, they would be taken to court. That is in my file but not my memory.

Another time three of us were taken to a home while the Golden Child stayed with our parents. In my file Mum said she wasn't ready to have me back but that Dad talked often about getting us back. Mum was attending group therapy at the time but it didn't solve anything as far as I knew.

File 28/4/72: ... I told her that ... she should not attempt to have [the children] return until her official period of being a patient at North Ryde came to an end in August. However, ... if she succeeded with Glen and Samuel ... the other two children in about four or five weeks.

I don't think that is correct because I can't see Mum giving Samuel up to anyone. The option may not have been hers to choose. Somehow we all got home again but on 21/6/72:

File: ...An unnamed caller phoned [Child Welfare] to report alleged neglect of Mrs. Fisher's children ... Continually swearing and screaming at her children ... often had scratches and cuts on their faces and bodies.

Mum told them she did yell at us but didn't hit us. The only child with problems, Mum claimed, was me, Glen, who was being bullied by someone at school. People at the local shops had seen me being hit by school kids. That was true. I was bullied for being different. My difference was that I was living in terror of violence twenty-four hours a day. (Today we know the reaction as a symptom of PTSD.)

Things could go well for a short time but then mum would be out of it again. Once she left to stay with a friend at Kirribilli, leaving us at home with Dad. We were no less terrified of him than we were of her.

There was a lady called Mrs. Stevenson who is referred to often in our files. Sometimes she would take us when things were particularly bad. Welfare describes her as 'kind and concerned.' I wish I could remember her. Anyway when Mum went off, Mrs. Stevenson stepped up. She got us off to school and we went to her after school. Then Dad would come and take us home when he'd finished work. Our Case Worker took us to see Mum on weekends because Dad wouldn't put himself out for us or Margaret.

That was typical of Barry. He was all about himself and his own wants and needs. Any decision he made was on the basis of what he wanted, regardless of how it affected anyone else. Although Barry was almost totally self-centred, there were times when he called the welfare people and said they needed to get us away from our mother because he was afraid she would kill us, particularly me.

My Dad had a job as the manager of a toy factory at Neutral Bay by this time. Records show there was a period of time when Mum wasn't doing drugs or drinking and we all seemed to be going all right. It didn't last.

File 5/4/73: ... X came to see me ... and told me that because of the disturbance caused by Mrs. Fisher either drinking or under the influence of drugs the various unit owners had ... notice to get out by the following Friday.

Welfare had asked the Housing Commission to give special consideration to our family being moved to the top of the waiting list to have a low rent house, in the hope that our parents would cope better without financial stress. The Commission refused. We seem to have stayed on a bit longer at Neutral Bay but then we were offered a brand new Housing Commission place in a new suburb in the rapidly growing Mt Druitt area. Pensioners Paradise! Welfare recorded that Dad was reluctant to give them our new address but Mum gave it to them. Mum had been going to go to school to discuss my bad behaviour but she decided there was no point as we were moving.

One of my last two memories of living at North Sydney is of my brother Michael falling or being thrown down the stairs. He was hurt so badly that he had to have a heap of stitches under his chin. Now we both had scars. This incident had a big effect on me. Michael was the closest to me in age and for the first eighteen years of my life he was my best mate. I ached to see him vulnerable and in pain like that. There was nothing I could do to help him.

We started our new life in Shalvey, Mt Druitt in 1973. This place was known as Pensioners Paradise because many families on unemployment pensions or low incomes moved there. Would this be safer and happier for us? For me, who Mum saw as the cause of all our problems, and for all of us? The house was one of the first built on Westward Avenue and it looked pretty much like the Pizza Hut buildings that popped up everywhere in the seventies.

As new houses started to appear, we watched our street slowly fill. Then surrounding streets began to fill with new houses and there were new people all around us.

Possibly to celebrate our move, Dad bought a new dog, a sausage dog, that he called Salami. I don't recall what happened to Hindu our Doberman. Dad always bought things that enabled him to show off and Hindu could do that. Tough man, tough dog. I'm not exactly sure what Salami was going to do for him. My father was still into martial arts. For practice he used to collect spare tiles from the newly built homes then he'd break them with his hands or feet. I felt quite uneasy and vulnerable seeing his ferocity and strength. He took it seriously and got to his Brown belt. He wore his outfit so proudly. He rode a motor bike and also had a little car that he worked with his mate Tony across the road.

Child Welfare or Youth and Community Services (YACS) as it had become, continued to check on us at Shalvey.

File 20/9/73: ... While the material aspect concerned is satisfactory there is a definite underlying current of instability in the family ... he (dad) has also been teaching these Karate blows to his children and child Glen has already been in trouble at school for imitating his father in the playground.

The school and welfare contacted Dad and told him about my performances. Dad insisted to them that he never practiced Karate at home and that I must have imitating something I'd seen on TV. Mum told the case worker that he'd stopped teaching us.

Dad didn't talk much but Mum was always talking and they soon started getting friendly with some neighbours who would pop in and out of the house. One time a welfare worker called in and mum had people in 'for coffee' so she spoke with the person on the verandah and said all was well. This could have been when she tried being an Avon lady. That didn't last long.

Sometimes it looked from the outside as though all was well with us when generally it wasn't. Mum was occasionally a happy drunk. Other people would come over and a party atmosphere developed. Mum put Abba on really loud and we'd all dance around wildly having fun. Those times are among my few happy memories.

Michael and I would go out and do really long walks around the place, feeling a bit of freedom and fun in a great adventure. We had some fun times on our bikes too. Concrete ramps were built for the roads that were being put all over the place. We didn't care about roads and we saw the ramps as playgrounds. We could hoon down them on our bikes or go running down or jumping. The speed we could build up was exhilarating and was pure fun that masked all our worries for a short time. Nearly all our fun was when our parents were not around. A lot of my time was spent in 'out of home care' so there wasn't a lot of time to enjoy my siblings.

Our parents' friends Paul and Edna had kept in touch when we moved to Shalvey. They had been friends for a long time. At some stage we had a duck named Sammy and we gave him to them. Edna had a huge birth mark on her face but apart from that they looked like ordinary everyday people. They would come to our place a lot with their two daughters who were a little younger than me.

Uncle Paul sometimes took us for drives in his van. On the first trip I was in the front seat. Uncle Paul pulled up and got a magazine out from somewhere. I could read a bit and I saw Ribald or something like that on the cover. Inside were pictures of naked people doing all sorts of sexual things that seemed lewd to me. I felt really uncomfortable.

Next thing I knew Uncle Paul pulled out his penis and a hanky. He played with himself. What's he doing that for? Then I saw why he needed the hanky.

'Wow,' I said, surprised as white stuff from his penis spilled into the hanky. 'What's that?'

'You will be able to do this one day,' he said.

I don't think I ever spoke about that, or if I did, no-one was taken aback by it. I was always uncomfortable with Uncle Paul. When both families went out together, Mum would often say to me, 'You go with Uncle Paul.' I would always beg and plead not to go with him. I'd do anything to be away from him. My pleading never worked and things got worse a bit later.

One day we were playing around in our back yard and us kids were all naked which wasn't unusual in our house. Uncle Paul's two daughters were in a tent.

'Go in with them,' Uncle Paul suggested. 'In you go. Get on them.'

Barry was walking about in the back yard, watching I suppose. I did what Uncle Paul said. I lay on top of one of the girls and that was that. Big nothing. What was that about?

Sometime after that came a life shaping event for me. I went to bed as usual at about eight o'clock. I went into a deep sleep, lying on my side. I was awoken with a jolt as the most horrible pain seared through my bottom and stomach. Terrified! Paul was lying behind me hurting me. So much pain. I wanted to scream but he slapped his hand over my mouth and held it there really hard. I could hardly breathe. My struggling seemed to excite him. He started to go really hard and even more violently. He was enjoying the fact that he was hurting me. It felt like that went on for ages but it was probably a few minutes of agony. What's happening? What is this?

When Uncle Paul was finished he just got up and left. I lay motionless, as if I was paralysed. I was so confused and angry and my stomach throbbed with the most incredible pain. I felt pain all over and fear crippled me.

Eventually I sat up, barely breathing, my pants still down. Liquid ran between my legs. The agony! I sat with my knees curled up for the whole night. I did not go back to sleep. I just didn't comprehend what had happened; I had no understanding of sex.

I got up in the morning and I went to the toilet. My mother looked off her face, asleep on the lounge. (Barry told me much later she was a heroin addict.) I sat on the toilet bleeding, crying, afraid. My mother swapped the rich for the bitch when we were just a young age. (This means swapped using drugs to drinking).

I never spoke up about that rape. I don't think, given the way my mother was, I would have dared approach her with it. My dad was just as bad and I never mentioned it to him either. I didn't know I could speak about it, maybe with a teacher or policeman. We didn't have the education given to kids today.

This incident probably happened at a time when I was being drugged by my mother to keep me out of her way. That would explain why Paul felt safe attacking me in my sleep. I would often be sedated and kept in my bedroom where my mother didn't have to see me, for days at a time. That was her least violent way to deal with me.

'Go to your room. Get out of my face. Fuck off!' That meant, 'Goodnight,' I suppose. 'See you in a couple of days.'

That rape is one of my worst memories and it is essential that I write it because it goes a long way to explain the rest of my life.

I never slept well after it. I waited for terror to strike again. The slightest noise and I was sitting bolt upright. If my door opened I'd lurch with fright. I always lay with my back to the wall, watching the door. Eventually I'd fall into some kind of a fearful sleep. I use to plead at night time for Mum to keep the light on, she would always tease me about it.

During the day I felt dull and anxious. I'd been quite a chatterbox but now I didn't talk much. I'd been a live wire but now I had no energy for anything but holding the pain and worthlessness inside myself. I'd gone from living in fear to living in terror. I spent many years blocking that incident out but it never went away.

'Leave the light on mum,' I'd beg. 'Please!' I wasn't going to stop begging until she agreed.

'What for?'

'Cause, I just like it on. It's better.'

'Oh all right ya weak cunt.'

'And shut the door. Please.' Again I wasn't giving up.

'What kinda bloody sheila are ya!' she'd mock. 'Gunna wet the fuckin' bed with door shut are ya!' She slammed the door shut.

Mum must have come and turned the light off later sometimes. My dad usually came home from Karate when I'd gone to bed. Being a bad sleeper I woke one night and saw a dark figure at the foot of my bed, watching me. For reasons I don't know Barry had come into my room but the light was off and I didn't recognize him. I tried to scream. I couldn't! I was paralysed again. I couldn't get a scream out. I couldn't breathe. I was petrified.

Barry turned on the light, saw me frozen there and yelled, 'Margaret! Margaret! Get in here. He's not breathing.'

My first panic attack. I was bundled into an ambulance that rushed me to Mt Druitt hospital. I don't remember that. Just the terror and panic. I wonder what story my parents told the hospital staff this time. I spent a lot of time going to hospital hurt. My mother kept my Blue Book, a record of health and milestones that parents had to keep back then. There are many entries about my being bruised or hurt from quite a young age along with explanations like 'Glen fell out of bed.' There is a reference to me having curvature of the spine, an issue with my tail bone and other illnesses. YACS files include this supposed spinal condition. I wonder how many issues result from the various abuses. My mother took full advantage of the possibility that I might have a spinal problem.

'Make the most of being a kid,' she'd taunt me. 'You're going be a cripple when you grow up. Won't be able to walk.'

I do have a funny tail bone which is odd to look at. I often wonder if this is the spinal disease they refer to.

All my fear at home went with me to school. I always went to school but I was bullied a lot. Kids noticed that I jumped at any sudden noise so they had fun by coming up behind me quietly and clapping. I would freeze up or jump out of my skin. The others would be jumping about pointing and laughing while I could do nothing but freeze and wait for some kind of calm. (Today this is recognized as a PSTD reaction.) I was so angry and humiliated but I couldn't act. Maybe that's why I can remember very little about school learning. That and because I was moved into 'care' so often. In some periods I was moved every two weeks or so, in and out of different places.

Margaret and Barry had friends who lived in the Mt Druitt community too and sometimes they'd let us go out with other families. Given Barry's enjoyment of pulling me under water, I'd rather have gone to the beach with almost anyone but him. Or Paul. So when my friend Deanne's father asked if I could go with them, I was really excited.

'No, you're not going,' Barry said firmly. Arrogantly.

'Please Dad. Let me go. Why can't I go?'

His replies were always the same, 'Because I said so.' End of conversation.

He had a mean streak that he applied whenever he felt like it. Simple things like if I wanted to go play with a friend he would say no. Only if I felt courageous would I ask why and his response was always the same. 'Because I said so!'

Deanne's family went off without me that day and I stayed home and hated my father. Driving to the beach with their big shady beach umbrella in the car, they smashed into a pole when a truck ran up the back of them. Deanne was killed by the umbrella impaling her. It was the only time my father's being an arsehole saved my life. I missed Deanne so much back then and I still think of her. She was the first of many friends I would lose to death over the coming years.

At first the Shalvey kids went to Dawson Public School by bus then we went to Wilmot Primary School when it was ready. At last the school at Shalvey was built, just a block away from our house, so we could walk there and back.

File 3/10/74: ... The Headmistress informed me that the children still attended regularly and appeared well cared for but as usual the main cause for concern was the occasional outbursts of bad behaviour which she feels sure are attributable to an upset home situation.

After this entry a huge amount of text has been whited out from my file. I received 300 pages from YACS of my files but any reference to anyone else like my siblings is blanked out. The next part that I'm allowed to see is;

File 15/10/72: ... Mrs. Fisher states that on the advice of the counsellor from Alcoholics Anonymous she placed the four children in Gateway House, Lewisham for two months ... a break from all forms of responsibility.

Then, after a long whiting out in the text an entry appears that I have not been able to confirm or deny though I have suspicions.

... It could be well imagined that he may well have interfered with his two sons which may account for their upset states of outbursts of temperament ... coupled with the fact that they will not discuss one word of the obvious turmoil with anybody.

I recall many incidents that involved sexual activity, for example my father was nearby on the day I was told to lie on Paul's daughters.

A painful incident that happened about this time supports suspicions about Barry.

Michael and I walked home together from school. As we walked up Westward Avenue, I noticed a police wagon parked outside our house. Chills went through my body. We were used to police being around the area but I had a bad feeling about it this time.

I had got to know two brothers who lived across the road from us and they were teaching me to play Two Up. Recently one of them had shot his brother dead. That day I sat on our verandah and saw the lifeless body lying in their front yard. I was repulsed and frightened but also fascinated and I just sat there staring, wondering how a man would want to kill his own brother. After a while they put a sheet over the dead man, the police put tape all around the yard and they came and went all day.

An observant police officer came over later and said to my mother, 'You probably should take your boy inside. He doesn't need to see all this.' It was a relief to be removed.

Police generally came when bad things happened and when I saw them parked at our place this day, I felt very uneasy. I ran the rest of the way home. I could see mum at our door talking to a policemen. As I ran past the paddy wagon, a voice from inside called out, 'Glen!'

It was my dad in there!

I stopped. Tears were rolling down my face by then. 'What's happening? Are you okay? What are you doing in there?'

Despite the way I was treated at home I had an incredible love and loyalty for my family. I was the eldest and I took the role of caring for my siblings and now I wanted to keep my dad safe too. I wanted him to like me.

Barry didn't answer my questions so I ran to the front door where mum was.

'Mum? Mum, why is dad in the police wagon? What did he do?'

She couldn't be bothered answering but I needed to know what was going on. 'Is Sissy ok? Is Samuel? What's happened Mum? Mum!'

She mumbled something dismissively and I dared not ask again. The two officers decided it was time to go so mum could attend to her kids. They walked toward the wagon.

I ran after them and pleaded, 'Please mister, let my daddy go. Please!'

The officer looked at me sympathetically. 'It's going to be okay son. Go inside now and help your mother.'

I watched as my father was taken away. I watched the wagon go all the way down the street. I was crying when I went inside and asked my mother one more time, 'Why did they take dad away Mum? What did he do?'

My mother spun around and slapped me off my feet. 'I don't need any shit from you Glen. Just fuck off and mind your own business!'

Our mother never told us the truth about this. She just said later that our dad had stolen something from the factory he worked at in North Sydney. Now I believe the charge was something much more sinister but will I talk about my thoughts on that in this book?

I scrambled up off the floor, ran outside and sat on the veranda. The two younger kids were okay, I could see, so I played with Michael until a car pulled up in the driveway. A heavy set woman got out, Barbara, who was a friend of mum's. She was my mother's sponsor from A.A. You got a clue that she didn't like kids by the way she thundered past us and went inside to talk with my mother for some time. She had an air of authority that was intimidating to us kids.

After a while Barbara came outside and demanded, 'Help get your brother and sister in the car.' It was snappy and loud and we thought we'd better jump to it. Michael and I were only wearing shorts and t shirts, no shoes.

'We're all going to my house for a while,' Barbara announced. Then before you knew it all four of us kids piled in the back of the little car and mum got in the front. Barbara drove us to her home in St Mary's.

'Yer done the right thing Margaret,' she told Mum on the way. Then, in a soothing tone, she added, 'Everything is going to be okay Margaret.' I didn't know what was going on but I knew instinctively that things were about to get worse for us kids.

When we arrived at Barbara's place she gave her next order. 'You lot go to the back yard. Don't come in unless you're told.' Seen and not heard. We knew all about that. It was probably the tension of the situation that made us start fighting noisily.

Barbara stuck her head out the door and barked, 'Shut up the lot of you. Give your poor mother a break for Christ's sake!'

We didn't need another warning. The other kids played like they always did then but I watched them and stole lots of glances inside, trying to make out what was going on. I didn't find out. We slept the night at Barbara's house.

In the morning, she ordered us kids into the car. Our dad had been taken to prison and that was a huge load on my mind. I still needed to know why.

'Where are we going?' I asked.

'Just get in the fucking car!' Barbara yelled. 'Your mother isn't doing too well and she doesn't need your shit right now!'

I guessed we were about to be removed from home again but we got into the car, still only dressed in t-shirts and shorts. We drove for what seemed like ages.

We arrived outside a huge building in a back street of Lewisham. Us kids were left in the car while our mother went inside with Barbara. The other kids played and argued and I kept looking at the building, willing mum to come out so we could go and get dad and go home. All the same I suspected that wasn't going to happen. I was frightened.

Unlovable me?

Chapter 2.
Bad Habits

Mum and Barbara went inside the big bricked place at Lewisham while we sat in the car. After what seemed like hours but was probably forty five minutes or so, Barbara came out and ordered us out of the car. Walking inside with us she told us, 'Your mother's having a nervous breakdown.'

She always had those. *So what's new?*

Inside we were greeted by two hostile looking nuns. One looked elderly and when she spoke she was just like Barbara, gruff and rude.

'Sit down there,' she said curtly. We sat.

Barbara and the nuns disappeared into a room where I assumed my mother was, probably putting on the performance of her life, revelling in the drama as usual. I could imagine her crying, making us kids a huge issue that she just couldn't cope with, especially me. Not little Samuel though. She could always cope with him. I sat watching the door attentively. Time stood still.

Eventually our mother came out with the two nuns and Barbara. She came up to us crying, seemingly distraught. She picked Samuel up, hugged him and showed him affection. Tina got a hug and some love too.

I had always tried to get my mother's love and approval but the harder I tried the worse it got. She reacted to my nice efforts with sarcasm and distain. The thought of saying 'I love you,' to Mum or Dad wasn't in my language and I rarely heard those words from either of them.

Mum turned and started walking away with Barbara. The other kids didn't catch on to what was happening. I did. I panicked. I jumped to my feet and yelled, 'Mum? Mummy? Where are you going? What's going on?' I had been removed from home so many times but this time it was all four of us. That raised my anxiety. It felt much heavier than the usual being left somewhere for a couple of weeks. It felt as if she was saying goodbye for a very long time, possibly forever. I chased after her, side stepping the nuns. I grabbed on to her.

'Where are you going Mum? What's happening? Don't leave us here. Please. Please Mummy. I'll be good. I promise I will.' Fuck, I said that a lot as a boy, usually when being belted or being told I couldn't do something the others could or being left in care. Please Mummy I'll be good.

Barbara stepped in, brushed me aside like I was a threat. She shielded my mother from me. 'Leave her alone! She's going through enough. She doesn't need this,' she roared at me.

The idea that we children were distressed didn't occur to any of them.

A very aggressive nun grabbed my arm hard and roughly and told me to go back to where the others were. My siblings were distressed now too. They wanted the same as I did.

'Look what you've done now, you stupid, stupid child! You've upset the other children!' the nun barked.

Barbara came to us and offered an explanation. 'Your mother is having a nervous breakdown. We are going to take her to a hospital to get some rest while you kids stay here. It'll just be for a few short days and then she'll come back and get you.'

I didn't believe her. It felt much graver than that. Mum walked hastily out the door with Barbara. The elderly nun grabbed me from the one who held me and she shook me hard.

'Look at what you have done! Look!' she shrieked. She points to my brothers and sister. 'You've upset them all.'

Perhaps I had upset the others by screaming the truth about what Mum was up to but I was fucking upset too. I didn't matter. What six year old has the insight to know that their own distress causes distress in their siblings?

If the nuns hadn't already read my YACS files, I'm sure my mother would have told them what a monster child I was and by my 'carry on' I had confirmed it. The stone cold hearts of those nuns thought a child could just let his mother walk out of his life and not care. Well I couldn't. In spite of all she did to me, Margaret was a constant, a devil I knew which seemed better than the ones here, dressed in black, who I didn't know. Funny hats and cranky faces on people who manhandle and belittle children.

Sure enough, the nuns made it known that my shit would not be tolerated. We were ushered outside to a yard that had huge walls. No way out. Red bricks. Everywhere, all around, red bricks.

Michael handled it much differently from me. That didn't mean he wasn't hurting. He just held it in, wouldn't or couldn't show emotion. Poor Tina though. She couldn't stop crying. I did my best to comfort her but I was not the person she needed most at four years old.

'Sissy don't cry. Please don't cry,' I pleaded. But she just couldn't stop. She cried day and night. I was really troubled that she was hurting and I couldn't fix it.

Samuel and Tina needed Mum even more than I did but they just had me now. And the nuns who were anything but compassionate.

This was the first time I felt the intensity of complete helplessness. I couldn't find out why Dad was going to prison. I couldn't make Mum like me enough to want me with her. I couldn't comfort the little kids or even myself. I kept trying to become Mum and Dad to my siblings. I was the eldest and very loyal to them. I remembered a song Mum used to sing to us. It was called The Field Family Song. Field was Mum's maiden name. The song was sung when Mum and her brothers got together. She had three brothers. One was a police officer named Dave, then there was Aaron, very violent drinker who taught Judo and finally Joe, a truck driver. When I met Uncle Joe once, he held a huge can of KB beer in his hand and his truck was parked out the front. Suddenly he punched me in the arm to see what I would do. Being used to being hit, spending so many days cowering on the floor trying to avoid the fists of drunks, I did nothing. Not even whimper. I felt proud that I could take a hit like that from my uncle. Michael was the same when he was hit by Uncle Joe. Didn't whimper at all.

The Field Family Song.

The Field kids are we.
The Field kids are we.
We're always up to mischief,
No matter where we be.

One day outside the school house,
A copper says to me,
Do you belong to the Field kids?
Then come along with me.

He grabs me by the collar
And tries to run me in,
But I get up my great big fist,
And punch him in the chin.

Oh The Field Kids are we.
The Field kids are we.
We're always up to mischief,
No matter where we be

So here at the orphanage I sang our song proudly in the back yard. We are Fields! We won't take shit from anyone. We are tough. That's how I wanted to feel but in fact I felt weak and very afraid, deathly afraid of the unknown. I was afraid that our mother had really abandoned us. Many times I'd heard her scream, 'I'll put you in a fucking home!' Had she finally made good on her promise?

The Field song had more verses and I sang it loud and proud as if acting defiantly would make me strong. I got the others to sing it with me to show that at least we were one. We would not be separated from each other.

Our first couple of days at Lewisham were pretty frightening and the nuns were especially scary. We kids were their only residents and quite a pest in their otherwise peaceful lives. They said I had to look after Tina who wasn't coping at all. No love or care would be given by the nuns, not even to Tina as she slowly dissolved in her tears. I spent most of my time with her and it was wearing me out, giving me stress. Nothing I did made my little sister feel better. She sucked her thumb constantly. She had a blanket that failed to comfort her but she clung to it anyway. And she had my arm.

The memory of her little face sitting there sucking her thumb, scared and bewildered, still hurts me deeply.

Our beds in the dormitory were a nice surprise to me. They were clean and nicely made. That didn't help to stop my sister and I from wetting our beds though. That was more fuel for the nuns' hatred of us. They derided me, calling me a baby and why couldn't I be like my brothers. They weren't bed wetting babies, were they!

One day they took us all to the movies to see Zorro and the Three Musketeers. Now I had a hero. Zorro! Tyronne Powers. There was an uncovered manhole in the grounds and I'd sit on the edge of it with my feet dangling in and whisper to him because I imagined he lived there.

'Don't know where Dad is Zorro. Can you find him and make your mark, zing, zing, zing on him? And can you make Mum come back for us. I hate it here.' I told him all my troubles and imagined him coming on his horse and saving us from all the evil nuns. I told him excitedly sometimes that Mum was coming to take us soon. Then I told him how sad I was that she hadn't. One day I got home from school ready to chat with my hero but some monster had put a heavy metal cover over the hole and I couldn't reach him. I was devastated.

I felt I was being treated as if I had done something wrong. All of us were. We were a dreadful inconvenience to the nuns. I was a curious child but if I ever asked a question, 'None of your business,' was the usual response. I had seen movies on TV at home and they'd always shown nuns as lovely, gentle people who help the sick and the needy. We mustn't have been needy enough.

Michael and I were taken to the school and enrolled. Were we going to stay here for a long time then? Not just a few weeks? I don't remember actually going to school there but maybe my memory only recorded family matters. It contains nothing about going home on weekends like the YACS File said would happen. I know I definitely didn't return home.

I remember us being in the back yard one day about two weeks after we'd arrived at Lewisham. Tina was sitting in her usual place still sucking her thumb with her blanket held close. Sitting with her, idly looking at the door we had first come in, 'What!' I sprang to my feet and ran flat out to Mum who had just come in with Barbara.

'Mum, are you here to pick us up? Are you Mum?'

The old nun shooed me outside as if I was a rabid dog. All right, I'll go but I'll watch you every second you're here Mum and you won't get away without us.

My brothers played on, having not noticed our mother's arrival. Sissy hadn't seen her either. I was certain our time here was up and Mum had come to get us. What a relief!

'Mum's here! We're going home!' I was so excited; I just blurted it out, exciting the other kids too.

We had a time of peace while we waited, laughing and chatting happily, knowing that this nightmare was about to end. Mum stayed inside for what seemed about an hour and when she came out I was up on my feet again. One of the nuns walked over to us and my heart was racing. I couldn't stand still. I sat down with Tina. We're going home. This is it. We're going home. The smile on my face stretched as wide as it possibly could. The nun grabbed Tina and took her inside.

Feeling the edge of a severe disappointment I jumped up again and yelled, 'What's going on?'

The nun turned back and said, 'Be quiet stupid boy! We've had enough of you. Just shut up.'

I sat down frustrated and confused but mostly afraid. To look at that old nun you wouldn't even dream of being afraid of her but her tongue could scar you as badly as any beating. As a kid I was hit a lot, yet the verbal abuse always seemed to scar me more.

The nuns knew how to upset me by constantly demeaning me, especially about the bed wetting. They didn't like that I was too curious either. I had questions whirling in my head all the time and I expressed them sometimes. My insecurity about having no control and the fear of the unknown made me desperate for any information I could get muster. I listened to conversations around me. I'd walk past the doors and stand outside to listen to what the nuns talked about. I needed to know what was going on. So being too curious and eaves dropping were added to my list of crimes against nuns.

They passed Tina to Mum. She clung to our mother like a limpet as they walked out the door. Mum didn't look back at us or even wave goodbye.

What the fuck! I am so angry as I write this memory. It still hurts watching Sissy leave with Mum while Samuel, Michael and I had to stay. Why?

I jumped up again and bolted towards my mother. So many emotions made my adrenalin pump and this time the nun had trouble containing me.

As she held me back I yelled at my mother, 'Mum, where are you going? When are we going home? Why are you doing this?'

She just kept walking. 'I'll be good. I promise. I'll be …'

I fell down totally defeated. It was all my fault. I was a baby, a bed wetter, an eaves dropper and stupid cunt when all I wanted was to be good and loved and wanted.

'Get to your feet you cry baby,' the nun growled over my yelling.

At last! At last Mum turned around and made this promise, 'Glen, I'll be back for you in a few days. It's going to be all right.'

I was so distressed and lonely I kept crying and yelling, 'I'll be good. We'll all be good, right now. Please. I promise.' It didn't convince her and she kept going. I felt some resentment towards Tina after a while. Why did she get to go with Mum? I know that feeling was wrong. She needed Mum more than all of us. That didn't help with my fears. I felt if Mum was going to return to get any of us it would have been the youngest brother, the Golden Boy.

A few days passed then my mother came back. I didn't let myself get as excited this time but I told my brothers, 'Mum's here. She is taking us home. I told you she'd come.' Michael didn't seem to pay attention. Was he angry with her? Did he stop himself being excited to protect himself from another disappointment or did it all just go over his head? He always handled stuff different from me. I spoke my mind while Michael stayed quiet. I yelled and screamed while Michael just ignored the scene. My head always had a thousand questions that needed to be answered and that bothered everybody.

Mum stood in the foyer to speak briefly to the nuns. One walked over and this time she grabbed Samuel and took him to Mum. Again I begged and pleaded using my usual promise. 'I'll be good Mum. I promise.' The result was the same as last time. Even Michael cried now. As she left Mum made the same promise that she had made before. Michael and I would leave in a couple of days. As she walked out with Samuel I still held on to the hope that our turn would come soon.

Simply by being left there Michael and I kept fuelling the nuns' idea that we caused our family problem and needed punishing. Our degradation continued. We were worthless.

File: ... the future of case work with this family will depend on whether the husband leaves home either through being sentenced to prison or leaving anyway.

Our mother didn't return. I could forgive every act of violence but being dumped hurt too deeply for forgiveness. I hated her.

After some time at Lewisham, Stewart House was one place we were sent for a two week holiday. It was beside the sea at Narrabeen. We walked on a beach each day with the other kids, mostly older than us, and ate fruit as we walked. What a treat! A juicy apple or a refreshing orange, banana or pear. We slid down the huge red slippery dip rocket at the front that seemed to be so high you could reach the sky when you climbed up it.

We were taken to a Barnardo's Home, up a huge drive way, flags out the front and a lot of other kids, many older than us. There are constant references in my files to Barnardo's. We seemed to be there for a very long time and all I wanted to do for the whole time was go home.

Everything was done to a routine in homes. We got up early, made our beds, did our allocated jobs then we went to school on a bus with kids who weren't in the home.

They were very religious and we had to go to mass and choir. We always sang 'Doe a deer' and we learnt scales. I was often called on to sing the higher notes that girls would normally sing because my voice hadn't matured yet and I was quite good. The demon child had the voice of an angel. I thought their rituals very strange and I hated this home.

One day, out of the blue, Michael and I were called out of choir practice.

'Michael, Glen, you have a visitor.'

We walked outside and our mother was standing there holding a picnic basket and a blanket. We couldn't run fast enough to get to her. 'Mummy! Mummy! You're here!' We didn't hug or kiss but we might have smiled and I might have shed some tears of relief.

The picnic might have been nice. I don't know because we spent the whole time begging to be allowed to come home.

'Well, the authorities won't let you come home yet,' Mum kept telling us. 'But I'll come back to see you again in a few weeks.' After more tears and begging she said, 'Look, you will be coming home in a few short weeks. You can bear that, can't you? Just a few short weeks?'

Did I believe her? Yes and no. I wavered between the two. I wanted so badly for it to be true but then she had let us down so many times before.

She did come back later. This time I was less enthusiastic. My pace slowed to almost a crawl when I noticed the picnic basket again. You don't bring a picnic if you're taking someone home do you? You bring smiles and say, 'I am here to get you boys home.'

We had our picnic. Again the whole visit was spent with me crying, pleading, begging, 'Please Mummy, let us come home. I'll be good. I promise I'll be good.' I cried like I had never cried before that day. I was acutely aware of all the times I'd heard her tell anyone who'd listen that I was the cause of all her angst.

'Glen I've told you, the authorities said you can't come home. Not yet. I'm not allowed to take you home.'

Before she left this time she said, 'Come on, let's sing our song.' The song was sung but it's hard to sing when your nose is blocked and all you want to do is bawl your head off.

As she went that day, when we were still crying, she said, 'All right, I'll go and talk to the matron and ask if I can take you with me.'

That was probably her way of getting away from us without saying outright, again, that she was not taking us home. That would have been kinder than leaving us in limbo, wondering all day whether matron would come and tell us we're going home. You wait and wonder all day.

I hated my mother for not taking us. Yet, inside I held on to a little glimmer of hope. At least she had come to see us. Twice. Right? So she hadn't forgotten about us like some other kids' parents had. Lots of the kids had no parents and no one ever came to see them. At least we got two visits.

Although I knew I hadn't done anything wrong, somewhere in my head I felt like being in the home was my fault, my punishment for something. People in charge, nuns in particular, reminded us that we had been dumped or that our parents didn't love us or want us. You belong to us because no one out there wants you. I was always in trouble for being too loud, too talkative, too anything, too everything.

I wanted to tell Mum to take my brother home because he wasn't bad but I didn't. I would be alone if she took Mike and I was so afraid of being completely abandoned. If Mum or Dad didn't come back for me, they'd surely come back for Mike and then they'd take me too. If I had any small blessing it was that Michael was with me. It made us very close. For my first six or so years Michael was always with me. We were very protective of each other, especially from adults or other kids in the homes.

Anzac Day was a big do at this home. We had to stand outside and salute to a flag while someone played a trumpet and spoke for what seemed like forever as we stood out in the heat. We sang songs and anthems but I had no idea what that was about.

We were in the convent, Stewart House and Barnardo's for the length of our father's prison sentence though we didn't know that at the time. When he was released he set himself up in a new life.

'Glen. Michael. You have a visitor.' Out of the blue we were called out of the dining room. It was a while since we'd seen our mother and I might have thought it was her.

No, it was our father. This visit went on for about twenty minutes as we sat behind the big buildings on the grass and my brother and I were very animated. We went through the same highly emotional begging we had done with our mother. I went through promising to be good if he took me home. We knew Barry had been arrested but we hadn't realised that he had been in prison the whole time we hadn't seen him. I am not sure we even knew what prison was, though given the life we lived and the people that were involved in my mother's life, it is likely we did.

After a long time begging our father, to my surprise said he would talk to the matron just like Mum had said. I didn't believe him but his reaction to our pain made me think he might be genuine. Maybe his own incarceration, and the guilt of knowing we were there because of his sins, aroused some sympathy.

Well, after our mother's performance I wasn't going to get my hopes too high. As Barry walked away I repeated, 'I promise I'll be good,' as if that would make him decide to get us out. Or at least try.

Soon after Dad came back with the Matron! 'You boys are going home with your father today,' she said.

We were as excited as two boys could possibly be. I literally couldn't stop crying tears of joy, of relief. We were not abandoned. Somebody wanted us. Rejection is a horrible thing.

I remember what we wore that day and for good reason. Leaving the home meant gathering all our property together. So the staff pulled out a couple of plastic bags. In them we found the things we had worn when we first came into Lewisham! We'd had bare feet, shorts and t-shirts. Now we had to take off the clothes provided by the institution and wear only what we had arrived in. So petty. Michael and I walked away with our father.

Barry took us down the road to Kentucky Fried Chicken where we had possibly the nicest tasting chicken I had ever had. I've thought of it as freedom chicken since then. I recall sitting there feeling elated.

Us boys are free,
Liberty! Hip hip hurray!
Been set free by our Dad.
Two boys admire this man
A criminal, so sad.

Dad wasn't supposed to get us out that day but he did. After our freedom chicken, he took us to Hornsby.

He told us that he had set up home with our old next door neighbour from Shalvey, Maureen Baker. I didn't remember her. She had three kids of her own he told us. I'm not sure how their relationship started but Dad had obviously split up with our mother. This was news to us. We were learning as we went along.

'When we go in, you go and sit with the other kids. Don't speak to Maureen and don't look at her. I'll take care of this.' This fight was his fight.

We walked tentatively towards the door and I noticed Barry looking worried. He had told us that Maureen would not want us there. What if she says, 'No'? I was terrified that we'd have to go back to the dreadful place we'd come from.

It was no surprise that Maureen did not look happy when she saw Barry standing in the doorway with us sort of hiding behind him. I disobeyed his order and I looked directly at Maureen. I wanted to see her face.

Maureen and Dad got into an argument almost straight away. Michael and I sat with the other kids. Maureen had two girls and a little blond haired boy, all younger than us. They started talking with us but my ears were trained on the argument, listening intently to every single word. I knew that with one move Maureen could say, 'No. Take them back where they came from.'

Barry and Maureen argued with raised voices for ages. Finally Dad said, 'I've got them out now.' He really put his foot down. 'I'm not leaving the boys in a place like that! They're staying.'

My dad was not a man who did nice things but this day he did. It is a moment that he fought for us instead of himself and I hold this memory with gratitude. He was rarely loyal and caring but on this day he was. It was the first time I felt admiration for him. He stood up for us.

Maureen backed down.

'Have they eaten?' she asked.

It soon became clear that Maureen was not like Mum. Maureen rarely challenged Barry and just basically did as she was told. She didn't fight him like Mum did.

So now we lived with Dad and Maureen and had three new siblings.

Maureen was a nice person then but I reckon that the years with my father changed her. She had left a marriage with a man who had plenty of money. In the following days I watched as her three children got picked up by their father in a Mercedes Benz and I watched them come home and talk about the fantastic things they'd done. I knew it is wrong to be envious but I was.

I was envious of every other family I saw. I liked watching The Little House on the Prairie on television, watching and wishing our life was like that. Parents who lived for their children, always found solutions and absolutely always showed love.

Our dad had stopped drinking and smoking. That probably meant we were safer with him and Maureen than with Margaret. Dad's temper was still volatile and he was very capable of doing permanent damage. It was a problem for me that with him trying to impress Maureen, it made him more a father to her kids than he ever was to us. I was deathly afraid of our dad.

Margaret got wind of our being out of the orphanage and living with Dad about two weeks after it happened. They spoke on the phone and mum insisted that dad return us to her.

I was sure dad wanted us to stay with him. One morning he took us two boys to enrol us at school. To me that meant we were here to stay.

'You won't be going to school today boys,' Dad said a few days later. He sounded sad. 'Your mother wants you back at Shalvey. Says I have to take you back or she'll call the cops.'

We knew Maureen didn't really want us there. Dad drove us back to our mother. Neither of our parents really wanted us. We were just pawns in their game.

Why the fuck did my mother say she wanted us? She could have got us out of the home more easily than dad had and earlier on too, but she chose not to. Now that our dad had us she decided she wanted us. We had to be given to her immediately. It shocked me to see how quickly dad did what she demanded and returned us to her. I imagine that because he'd just got out of prison he was very cautious in all he did.

Being with my real siblings would be good but I was still scared of my mother's violent words and actions.

When we arrived at the house at Shalvey there was no

welcome home or smiles. The only acknowledgement was Mum saying, 'You fuck up and you're back in that home.' We just walked in and got on with being there.

My mum could be two very different people. There was the happy party drunk I have some fond memories about. She'd put on music and us kids danced with her and stayed up to all hours. The Mr Whippy man, Mel and her brother Reg, some guy named Darcy were all her new best friends. They enjoyed the parties too.

At other times she was a bitter, angry women who rambled on for hours about how I wasn't really her son and that they gave her Michael, someone else's baby, at the hospital. Always just spewing venom that hurt far worse than any of the physical abuse thrown at us just as often.

The violence in our home up till now had been bad but a lot of that was with Mum and Dad fighting each other. Yes, we got hit often but the living in fear of it and witnessing repeated violence was tough. There are a few incidents I recall with Barry hurting me prior to his arrest.

Without Barry around, Mum was more likely to be the angry drunk who just picked on me day and night. The level of mean had escalated as did her new way to partying. Without Barry to go out with to get drunk, it all happened at home. Empty cartons filled the back yard, empty beer cans filled the bins and Mum now realised that her daughter could be her servant. Tina was in charge of all housework and worked her fingers to the bone, at the beck and call of Margaret.

The violence had a ripple effect. Scared of my own shadow, I was an easy target for bullies and I never fought back. What's more I was a bed wetter and that made me a target too. I would dream I was going to the toilet and every time I awoke the first thing I did was check my bed. Each time I found I'd wet the bed panic would set in. Another day began with dark prospects.

Almost every morning our mother would wake up hung over, reeking of alcohol, so that it was not nice to be close to her. She'd scream, 'Glen! Get me some coffee you fuckin brainless idiot!'

I can still hear her shrieking voice that sends chills through my body. At the sound of her, I'd bolt upright ready to follow her command.

Usually Tina would be doing the ironing or other house work our mother should have been doing. Sam just did whatever he wanted. I grew to resent Sam, not just because he received love we were never given, but because he played on it. If Sam asked me to do something I would usually tell him to get fucked. He would then yell out, 'Mum!' and I would comply.

Sometimes I pleaded, 'Please, just shut up! Don't call Mum.' It rarely worked.

Making breakfast one morning, (two Wheat Bix each but Samuel was allowed three because he was diabetic so he needed more), I put an extra Wheat Bix in my bowl.

'You're not allowed three!' Samuel accused.

'Get fucked,' I told him sleepily.

'Mum!' he yelled. 'Glen's got three-ee.'

I put one Wheat Bix back and once again felt a burning desire to smash into him. As an adult, to be fair to Samuel, it wasn't his fault. I guess if I'd been The Golden Child I might have been an arsehole too. I don't believe he was a diabetic. I think that was just an excuse Margaret used to give him more.

Whenever making coffee for my mother I used hot water from the tap, instead of boiled water. As soon as she took a mouthful she'd yell, 'That's the worse fucking coffee I've ever had!' Then she'd scream out for another kid to make it for her. Brainless was I Mum? That's only one of the repeated lines I heard daily. Weak cunt. Brainless. Baby. Barry usually stuck to 'Dumb'.

As I said, Barry didn't live with us anymore and there were a few friends of Margaret's who dropped in. One time I heard mum screaming loudly and that was followed by the usual thumps and bumps of a fight between my parents, only this time she was fighting Reg the brother of her friend Mel. I suspect my mother had been in some type of relationship with Reg. The fight went from room to room for about an hour. Suddenly glass shattered and Mum appeared with blood streaming from both arms.

'Get me too the bloody hospital. Now!' she demanded and an ambulance was called.

When she got back she showed us the stitches she had got. She displayed them like a trophy. They made me feel sick and afraid. There were around a hundred stitches in each arm. I have a very vivid memory of that and of the scars that she had on her arms for the rest of her life.

> *File 18/2/76: ... The mother is said to have jumped through a window of her home recently, following which the children were placed in Dalwood homes, but returned to the mother a week later. The mother then took an overdose of drugs and the children were placed with Mr and Mrs Field ...*

> *Mrs Fisher is said to be a drug abuser, and is said to have kept Glen heavily sedated with drugs for 48 hours during the holiday period while entertaining men in her home.*

So there we were, shunted backwards and forwards but always returned to our mother's drug fuelled rages. Each time we went home, nothing much had changed. We had to face it all again but we had no skills to do so.

> *File 20/2/76: ... She informed me that she had been endeavouring to calm down before administering discipline as she fears her previous position towards violent action.*

The YACS worker wasn't the only person who feared her violence. I was about to learn how far it would escalate. There are many notes in my YACS file that refer to our father trying to get YACS to remove me from my mum because of her propensity towards violence. Even my mother mentioned that she was afraid she'd go too far with me.

One morning we heard the Mr. Whippy truck in the distance. Margaret started to search frantically for money so she could buy her Bex Powders. She was addicted to both Bex and Vincent powders. She was ranting and raving as she scanned every surface for loose change. I was in the lounge room and she began to take her frustration out on me.

'You've stolen money off me, you little prick,' she screamed. 'I fucking know you have, haven't you!'

I wouldn't have had the courage to even sneeze in front of my mother, let alone steal money from her. The only things I ever did to take some type of revenge were to make bad coffee and occasionally shake her beer, hoping it would go off when she opened it. I didn't have the courage to stand up to her. And anyway my mother rarely had any money for me or any of us to steal.

Mr Whippy was on his way with Bex powders. My mother was ranting and raving at me. She started punching me. She picked up a carving knife from the kitchen and threw it at me. Luckily it just missed. Then she ran at me and started bashing into me again. I was curled up on the floor begging her to stop.

'Where's my money?' she shrieks. 'You fucking took it! I know you did.'

'Stop Mummy. Please. I didn't take it. No more please. I didn't. I'm sorry. I didn't. I'll be good.'

More often than not when I was saying this it was because I was being hit, not because I had actually done anything wrong. It was crazy how I was always saying sorry when I knew I hadn't done anything wrong. I didn't understand that by yelling I'm sorry I enraged her more. It would have been better to cop my beating in silence.

She stopped beating me and picked up the knife again.

'I'll cut your fucking fingers off, you weak cunt,' she snarled menacingly.

She grabbed me by the hair and tried to drag me down the hall, knife in one hand and her screaming terrified son's hair in the other.

Mel walked in. She might save me?

'Help me drag this thieving little arse to the bathroom,' my mother demands. 'I'm going to chop his fuckin' fingers off!'

'Please Mummy, stop. Mum I'm sorry. I'm sorry.'

Did Mel plead with her to stop too? Tell her to put the knife down? To let me go? Hell no. Mel helped her! I was petrified as they dragged me down the hall, carpet burns erupting down the side of my body, my knees and elbows. I was so terrified, I fought tooth and nail for the first time ever, to get free. I was only nine years old so it wasn't hard for two adults to get me into the bathroom.

'No Mummy. Don't cut me. Please!'

Mum holds the knife over my hands. So many tears falling. I can't breathe. It's that cry when you're so terrified that you can't even speak. You stutter. Is this a fucking dream? No it's fucking real. Mum and Mel hold my right hand over the sink and Mum is screaming like a demon. She's got a crazy, mad look in her eyes.

'Please Mummy, don't cut me.'

I can't breathe. She brings the knife down suddenly. She cuts the tips off two fingers on my right hand. She lets me go and I fall to the floor. She walks out. Mel walks out too but she pauses, looks back at me then follows my mother who still has the knife in her hand.

My blood pours out all over the place and I lie on the floor screaming. Mum is still ranting about Bex powders. Mel goes to the Mr. Whippy truck and gets them for her. I lie on the bathroom floor in shock, unable to understand how Margaret could do such a thing. It slowly dawns on me that I'd better try to stop the blood. I take off my t shirt and hold it on the cuts.

Eventually Mum calms down. 'Check that cunt's still alive will you Mel?' she says.

Mel looks at the skinny, pale kid on the floor, eyes swollen and blood all around and on him, pressing his bloody shirt on his hand. I pretend she isn't there.

Margaret comes in next. She seems to realise what she's done. The cuts are deep and there's so much blood. The shirt is soaked. I'm dazed. Not crying but absolutely sobbing, gulping huge breaths. Fear mingled with disbelief and a bit of wondering what she'll do next.

'Fuck, we have to get him to a hospital' Mum says to Mel. She calls a taxi and while we wait she plans her cover up story. Michael's coming too so she says, 'You boys tell them at the hospital that you were having a bloody sword fight, all right, in the kitchen.'

Aware she had gone too far, Mum sweet talks me on the way in a taxi to hospital. She always did that after an attack. Some of the nice Mum appears and for those twenty minutes or so I let myself believe she loved me. I lapped it up. I didn't know when the next attack would come.

I was given stitches in my fingers. I'm sure from the way the doctor looked at me that he knew this was a case of abuse. I didn't tell the true story of how I got the cuts because I did not want to go back to the homes. Yes, I was safer in the homes, but it was so lonely without my siblings. I wanted to be with my brothers and my sister. I'm right handed and the cuts were on the tips of my right fingers, so anyone with two cents worth of brains should have been able to tell that a child covered in carpet burn, visibly distraught and with two fingers cut open was the victim of child abuse.

I was treated for the carpet burn too. I recall something red being put on the whole side of my body. My fear of my mother had leapt higher than ever before. She had hurt me many times in many ways, but never as badly as this.

Shame on Mel for helping my mother and shame on the hospital staff who didn't call it what it was.

I hope Margaret never intended to really cut my fingers off that day. I hope that it was scare tactics to get me to get money from somewhere so she could get her Bex.

I went to the hospital many times as a boy. Whenever a doctor or nurse questioned Mum about how the boy got hurt my mother reacted aggressively and the questions would stop. She was viscously intimidating. I'm certain that if this happened today it would be reported.

As I wrote this I was overcome with emotion: anger, resentment, fury, even fear. Fear of myself, that inside I feel such fury when I revisit this and other events.

My mother had a brother Aaron. He was around six feet four and weighed about seventeen stone. He was a violent alcoholic and a Judo instructor. He had three kids and a wife who had Leukemia or another serious illness. Uncle Aaron taught Judo to his son, Little Aaron. They lived in Blackett in Mt Druitt and my file shows that both my mother's brothers took us in at various times.

Mum took us for visits to Uncle Aaron and one time we were staying there for a few days. Uncle Aaron drank even more than my mother, if that was even possible. They were inside drinking and us kids were out the back playing. Little Aaron and I had a fight. Suddenly Uncle Aaron came storming out with my mother.

'Get inside you boys,' he bellows. 'Get in the bedroom. Now!'

Mum is yelling at her brother, 'Bash the little cunt. He needs a man to give him a good flogging.' Yeah like a woman flogging me every day wasn't enough.

We went to his room and waited. Not for long. Uncle Aaron strode in, got out a belt and belted Little Aaron all over his body. He fell on the floor and cowered. He screamed, 'Sorry. I'm sorry!' Just like I did with Mum. I didn't think Uncle Aaron was ever going to stop hitting Little Aaron. He rained down blow after blow with all his might as he screamed and ranted at his son. It was like Uncle Aaron was possessed. Twenty or so welts started to swell on the boy then the belting stopped.

Uncle Aaron turned to me. I'd seen what he'd do so I protected my head from the blows with my hands. I thought he would never stop striking me and screaming at me. I thought I was going to die. He got my back, legs, arms and even got me on my balls twice.

Then he started again on Little Aaron. The same rage and power rained down and then it was my turn again. He probably hit us more than forty times each. We were black and blue and covered in welts the same shape as the belt. I hurt and hurt for several days. Once again I retreated into my shell. I was not safe anywhere. I hated my mother for insisting that a mountain of a man beat me. If that happened today both those adults would be in prison. Between Uncle Paul's raping me, Mum trying to cut off my finger tips and being belted by a huge drunk, I felt unsafe all the time.

Years later I met Little Aaron on the streets of the Cross. He was living in a care facility when I met him. I went with him to see our Nanny Field one time in Ryde. The place she lived in was not far from where Little Aaron lived.

After each YACS visit I was removed from home for short periods. Barnardo's, Stewart House or any one of a number of foster placements. After a week or two I would be returned to the family home. My files recorded every allegation my mother made about me, no matter how outrageous they were. She loved putting me down whenever she could.

File 3/3/76: ... Mrs Fisher expressed her concern at Glen wearing female apparel – his sisters. The lad squeezes into his sister's panties and has apparently done this on numerous occasions.

Bullshit! This didn't happen, it was just another way for our mother to belittle me or try to justify the continual violence. Just another way Margaret found to show that it was me not her fucking up the family. At least the violence against me is recorded there as well as my mother's drug abuse and drinking and Dad's being a sick fuck.

In total contrast to her hatred of me, Margaret's love for the youngest child was always visible. I felt very envious. YAC's noticed her favouritism and challenged Mum about it.

File undated: ... An enlarged photograph of Samuel indicating his favoured status has been taken from its position of pre-eminence in the home and Mrs. Fisher has been at pains to treat all the children equally.

I remember going on several camps with churches. One was called Bethsham. I remember being burnt really badly on my leg by a motor bike exhaust. I know that my mother treated this by putting butter on it. The burn blistered up really badly and got infected. I also remember going on a hike around a cliff top where I was really afraid of the height and being in a lot of pain.

File undated: ... Mrs. Fisher seen. She was in good spirits in contrast to last visit. She had stated that she had given the church away and no longer feels that God will save Glen. She has apparently made enquiries at the Polyclinic to obtain psychological counselling for Glen as I previously suggested.

Any time my mother was confronted by YACS about any of us being bruised or injured she went to great lengths to blame me. I was terrified of my mother and never acted out the way she describes. I often sat nearby as my mother described her demon child to anyone who'd listen. I wasn't the one taking drugs or getting drunk every night. I wasn't the one who lashed out with violent tantrums every day hitting anything that crossed my path.

Chapter 3.
Out of the Pot and Into the Fire

I think Mum had reverted to single woman, party mode while we had been away. Her house was now visited often by very nasty looking men. She was drinking much more heavily, her fits of rage were daily events and her violence had escalated to a seriously nasty level. The most common thing said to me was, 'I'll put you back in that home!' I was terrified of that.

Margaret hadn't really had a chance to be young and free in her teens because she had me at about nineteen years old and Michael not that long after. It could be said she was making up for lost time and then we came back from the homes and spoiled it all over again. She wanted her life to be a party.

I never looked forward to birthdays or Christmas because they usually resulted in disappointment, resentment and more drinking. My ninth birthday was memorable.

The theme was uncharacteristically 'Be nice to Glen' day. My mother gave me a green Hanimex bike. It was an unusually lavish gift, although I didn't give that much thought at the time. Our mother probably got the bike from a charity. That was how most birthdays and Christmases were catered for. Salvation Army Christmases. Gifts usually donated by whatever church our mother was going to at the time. Maybe she bought the bike but I doubt it.

It was not the sort of bike a boy would really want to own. Kids around our place were getting a new kind of bike, the BMX. The Hanimex had sissy bars, weird handles and it was bright green. Not cool. But I rode it around proud as a peacock. At about midday I was out roaming the streets of Mt Druitt on my bike when Mike arrived and said, 'Mum wants you to go home.' That wasn't unusual. I was often summoned by my mother. My nerves were twanging as I headed home. I replayed the last twenty four hours in my head, wondering if there was anything at all I might have done or said, anything at all that would get me in trouble or lose me my bike.

I rode home slowly. The sense of doom grew out of a day that had so far had been good. As I rode up Westward Avenue I noticed my father's motor bike in our driveway.

Dad was waiting in the lounge room with his long beard, protective biker gear, boots and his fake ass smile. He rode a motor bike that would make us call him a lounge room biker today. His smile made me uncomfortable. When someone is mean, you know how to handle it because you're used to it. But when someone is nice you feel uncomfortable. You can't trust it. You're waiting for the punch line. What was Dad's motive for the sudden onset of warmth? To upset Mum perhaps. Was that it?

'Hey mate! Nine years old, eh?' Barry said.

He handed me two gifts. The first was a wooden box with a handle like suitcases had. It turned out to be a tool box with miniature tools in it like a hammer, saw and other carpentry things. I especially remember the spirit level and the box. The second gift was a really slick looking wrist watch with a leather band and a purple face. It was even engraved on the back with my birth date and 'Happy 9th Birthday'. It was the most precious gift I had ever been given. The fire truck accidentally given to Dad was good but I don't know where that went.

We were not big on birthday gifts in our family, especially not a collection of costly ones. What was going on this year?

After he gave me the gifts Dad said, 'I've got another gift for you. I'm taking you out to the airport for the day. I've got a mate who's got an airplane. Guess what. We're going for a joyride! Yes! In the plane.'

I was really excited but I didn't believe him. He always said we would do things but we never did. I remember the time he promised to take me camping, we headed out on his motor bike, we slept one night under a bridge in a tent then the next day we rode to Doyalson to his mother's place. There ended our so called camping trip.

I got onto the back of his motorbike and we road to the airport for my birthday plane ride. I felt tough riding on the bike and people watched us as we came along. I think that's why Barry had the bike. He craved the attention.

Dad's mate was not at the airport so Dad tried to contact him. He wasn't able to. No surprise there. Suddenly without notice he says, 'How would you feel about coming to live with Maureen and I? We live up the Central Coast now, right near the water. Maureen's got her three kids and I think you'd really love it up there.'

I felt awkward. Fear in the pit of my stomach. He had been nice to me all day, bought me stuff and let me ride with him just so he could ask me that? I did not want to live with him. I was afraid to and I was afraid to say so. I was scared to hurt his feelings after all he had done for my birthday. What if he got angry! I didn't want to live with Mum or him. I just wanted to be with my two brothers and my sister. That was my answer. Thank goodness I thought of one.

'I really want to be with my brothers and sister.'

Dad didn't react badly. 'I thought that might be the case but I thought I'd ask you and give you some time to think about it.'

We rode home to Shalvey. I think Barry knew that if he got angry with me it would have made it harder to convince me to go to the Central Coast. He must have known I was already shit scared of him. I was having a hard time living with Mum so I did give it some thought.

Stay with Mummy and siblings.
Live life with a bottle. Afraid.
Go with Daddy who's twisted
The price would have to be paid.

When I got home Mum was drunk and she gave me a hard time about Dad buying me gifts. 'Here he is,' she said sarcastically.

'Little Lord Font Roy.' She'd say that so often but I never knew what she meant. 'You can share that tool box with your two brothers, you cunt. Don't think you're anything fuckin' special.'

'Be Nice to Glen' day was over. One parent with an ulterior motive and the other with a deep rooted hatred made it what it was. Confusing and irritating. Glen, the child I was, so desperately wanted someone to make me special, love me, and say nice things about me and to me. My parents couldn't do it spontaneously and my mother made a sport of doing the opposite.

Thinking I could change the topic as she kept drinking and becoming even more agitated, I told her what Dad had asked me. I hoped I might get Brownie points for telling her.

'Mum, Dad asked me if I wanted to move in with him and Maureen up at Gosford.' Before she could do a thing I added, 'I told him to stick it up his arse.'

Not true but I thought it might go down well too. At first she laughed a sick kind of laugh. Unbeknown to us kids, Dad had a serious charge hanging over his head so my mother had an ace up her sleeve.

After the laugh ended she roared, 'Over my dead body!' She left it at that for a while then as she got more pissed she began to rant and rave. 'I don't care what you do, you little shit. You can fuck off with your father for all I care. I never wanted you anyway. You're more work than ten kids!'

Sure, her words hurt but they weren't new or any different from what she told me every day. My confusion lay in what I should say next. There was not a thing that would make her like me or want me. From experience I knew that the harder I tried to make her like me, the worse her hatred became. I wanted to be loved and wanted, but most of all I wanted stability with my siblings.

Some days, when Mum was at her worst, I wondered if being back in the home might be better. It definitely would have been safer physically. The homes were so emotionally cold though. Apart from the obvious point of feeling rejected, you were treated like a criminal. The people who worked there were just doing a job. You were their job so you were no-one who mattered. A number! It's not living. That to me was just existing. With my mother it was surviving.

Margaret probably had some mental disorders. In my file there is a reference to her 'identity confusion'. Does that explain her aggression and her turning to physical fighting? I don't know but she tried to convince welfare that I had the same disorder when she told them that I liked to wear girls underwear! A complete lie.

Samuel was the only one of us who avoided Mum's wrath. He did that just by being who he was, not by trying very hard to be exactly who Mum wanted. As the eldest I seemed to cop more than my fair share of her rage. Michael and Tina were tormented too. I really loved those two but each day I resented Samuel more. It wasn't his fault that he was the Golden Child. Maybe I would have behaved as he did if I had been the favoured one. The fact is that we barely knew each other because we were separated early in his life and a sibling relationship didn't get a chance to even start.

Sometimes when our mother was drunk we were free to roam the streets of Mt Druitt. One time a boy pinched my bike. I was riding in circles and this kid, much older than me, came along and stopped me, put his hand on my bike and started chatting to me. Then he suddenly grabbed the bike and took off. I didn't know what to do or how to get it back. I went home and told my mother. She went off her head. No one messes with the Field kids. Mum used her maiden name now.

She trotted me down to the group of kids and said to the older one, 'You want to bully my son with the lot of you in it? Hey? You little fuckwit? You try fighting him one on one!'

The kid was twice my size and he readily accepted the challenge. I was nine and he was in high school. Needless to say I didn't want a bar of it. But we are Field kids and in my mother's head that carries a responsibility to be tough, the kind of kids who no-one dares mess with. Great. I was much smaller than most kids my age and well underweight. Inside me a tornado of fear whirled.

Before I knew it the gang circled the two of us and the kid my mother had challenged started punching the shit out of me. Mum was there egging me on to beat him up. I'd never fought anyone but Michael but our fights were nothing like this! Mum never stood around screeching at us to belt the crap out of each other.

I knew I was too small to fight this kid so I didn't. I was frightened and I was sick to death of being hit. I'd always been afraid that if I fought back it would make my attacker hurt me more. Fury was building inside me as the kid hit me over and over again. I hated everything at that point, especially adults. Maybe I'll try and fight back, I thought as he kept on pummelling me. I only got him once in the face and that infuriated him. Eventually it was over. Glen defeated.

Mum soon let me know what she thought of me. 'Ah, you pathetic cunt. You take after your bloody father! You're a Fisher. You're no Field!' she sneered. 'Yer no Field kid! You're a Fisher. Gutless like your arsehole father.' She kept yelling abuse at me in front of the other kids, then, talked with them for ages about how much of a little poofter I was. There was fight in me but I hadn't reached the age or the size where I could let it out yet.

When she'd finished with the boys she dragged me home by my long, scruffy hair, insulting me all the way. 'You fuckin' coward. Yer couldn't be a Field. Fields fight like machines. Not you though. You fought like a fuckin' girl.'

Sometimes she'd force me into the backyard to fight Michael. That wasn't fair. I was eighteen months older than him and I didn't want to hit him. Michael would try so hard to hit me, but I had longer arms so I would block every punch he threw. Michael complained to Mum, 'His arms are too long!' The fights Michael and I had when we were angry with each other were more like wrestling without intending to do serious harm.

When Margaret was drunk she'd try to teach us how to fight.

She forced us into this stupid stance, arms high up, face like a fucking rooster, tongue between your teeth to look scary. Later in my life I learnt boxing and I learnt that all things you should never do in a fight were the exact things our mother had taught us to do. My instructor said, 'Protect yourself. Don't leave your body vulnerable. Get your tongue away because if your opponent makes a connection with your face, you'll bite your tongue off.'

Alcohol was not Margaret's only demon. Drug fuelled rages or withdrawal also created havoc. I think she used whatever drugs she could get including sleeping pills, headache powders and perhaps illegal ones like marijuana as well.

> *File 29/4/75: ... Following a phone call ... Mrs. Fisher was visited on the 28th ... reported that Mrs. Fisher had taken an overdose ... sometime over the previous weekend and was not in a fit state to care for the children. All four children were in the home at the time. When the home was visited Mrs. Fisher was so influenced by the drug that little sense could be got from her. When asked if she wanted – & myself to take the children to see that they were looked after for the night she said that was what she wanted ... Mrs. Hayward of Lethridge Park, an approved remand home keeper cared for Glen and Tina for the night. The other two children were taken back to Mrs. Fisher and later sent to school.*

I can only see one reference in my file to mum overdosing but I think it happened a few times.

Mum overdosed herself at times but she dosed me up too when she had had enough of me. I lost days at a time asleep in my room. I can't be sure but I think that gave Uncle Pat more of a chance to rape me that time. YACS recorded the drugging of me in my file but I didn't tell them about the rape.

> *File: ... Glen was questioned regarding the incident where Mrs Fisher administered drugs to the lad in the form of sleeping tablets. Glen said that this incident occurred shortly after his birthday*

1.10.76. And said that he had slept for a week. This conflicts with his statement and that he feels that he slept for a couple of days, although the lad's concept of time would probably have been blurred.

Glen recalls the incident which apparently occurred a few months ago but was rather vague about the details surrounding the incident, although he recalls a number of young people being in the house.

When I was ten years old my father filed for custody and we were told to attend court. For the months leading up to the court case my mother said repeatedly, 'You're not going anywhere. Who does he think he is?' However when she got drunk she changed her tune. 'Fuck off! Can't wait to see you go to your father.' Then back again, 'You're not going anywhere.' It wasn't that she wanted me. The only person she hated more than me was Dad. Ever ready to get brownie points, I'd pile on and on about how there was no way I was going to live with him. I'd run away if he got custody of me.

On the way to court my mother was being so nice to me. 'I'm not letting Barry get you,' she said trying to sound warm.

'I don't want to go with Dad. I want to be with you and the kids,' said the boy pawn who wanted his mother to want him.

'Don't worry. You're not going anywhere.'

I knew deep down that her warmth wasn't real but I bathed in its dim light while I could.

We spent the morning in court, and I mostly hadn't a clue what they were talking about. There were men in suits and an old judge with all the power sitting on his throne. I was so bored. It seemed to go on forever. Each time I looked over at Barry and Maureen they smiled.

Finally after what seemed like a lifetime the judge said to my parents, 'I have decided I am going to have a talk with the boy in my chambers. I need to know what he actually wants.'

He kept looking at me and he must have been able to read

my face. It was pleading, *Please, please, don't separate me from my siblings again.* He must have known that I wanted to speak but was too afraid to even fidget.

We broke for lunch. I was led into a room to speak with the judge. He seemed genuine when he asked me what I wanted and why. He spoke very gently and listened to everything I said. Inside I wanted to say, *I am terrified of Barry. I am terrified of both my parents. I can get away from my mother sometimes when she's in a rage but not always. She hurts me. Barry isn't angry every day like mum is but you can't tell when he's going to suddenly just snap into a fury. I'm really seriously afraid of them both.*

Sadly, that was what I would like to have said but I don't think I did. At the heart of what I did manage was that I just didn't want to go to a new family. I didn't want two new sisters and a new brother. I loved the ones I already had. I told the judge that when we were separated and put in a home, it was very hard for me. As mad as our home was, it was my family. My dad, to be fair to him, had changed since he had been released from prison and stopped smoking and drinking but he was still scary.

'All right then Glen,' the Judge said gently, 'when we meet back in the courtroom after lunch, I'll send you back with your mum.' He gave me a warm smile, not something I was used to seeing from adults.

I met up with mum for lunch and she said, 'Glen, I think you should at least go have lunch with your dad. He's come all this way to see you, to get custody of you. I think you should just go to lunch with him.'

So Maureen, Dad and I went to lunch. Dad was being extra nice to me and that made me even more anxious. I knew it was fake nice and I hated him as much as I always did for being fake nice. At this time Barry wasn't as unpredictable as he had been when he was drinking but he was still capable of going off at the drop of a hat and his nasty mind games were as bad as ever. He had done enough in those early years for me to remember that he was as capable as Mum of losing the plot and resorting to violence.

After lunch we went back to the court room.

'I have made my decision,' the judge said. I was relaxed. I knew what he was going to say. I looked at Dad. *Oh you poor man. What a waste of your time.* The judge continued, 'After listening to all the evidence I have decided to send young Glen to live with his father on the Central Coast. I think this is best for everyone.'

So there, Barry. Wait! No! What? No, you said I could stay. I don't want … it won't be best for anyone! I sat frozen, death staring at the judge. What's happened? He didn't look at me. He looked down at the paper work he read from. When he finished reading, he stood up and everyone else stood up until he'd left the room. What the hell just happened?

I hoped I'd heard him wrong but I knew I hadn't. I broke down and cried and cried. Being taken away from my brothers and sister was the surest way to hurt me and the judge had done it! The judge who I trusted and thought understood me. He was tearing me away from Michael, my best mate who I had spent my life with and who I loved most in the world, along with Tina.

While my father, Maureen and I had gone to lunch that day at court, Margaret had approached the judge and told him that she didn't want me. She preferred that I go with my dad. I didn't know that at the time. I came away from the court crying and screaming at the judge, 'You said I could go with my mum. You said it. You did. To me!' I was probably incoherent but I kept on. 'I don't want to go with Dad. I want my brothers and my sis.' I had no idea at this time of the shady deal my mother made with the judge whilst we are at lunch.

I was forced into the car with Dad who wasn't impressed with my behaviour. As we drove off I saw my mother playing the part of someone who has been ripped off. She played the victim. The nasty judge had taken her beloved son away. The car window was down and she said, 'I'm sorry. You'll be okay.' I watched her performance as we drove away, the distance between us expanding quickly. I thought that all along Mum had fought to keep me with the other kids. That must mean she really did love me. It was only later in life that I heard about her betrayal.

It didn't take long for the mood in the car to turn sour. Maureen obviously wasn't impressed with me coming with them. Dad wasn't impressed with my song and dance about not wanting to go with him. His pride was severely wounded and I would pay. Later no doubt

Barry rarely reacted like normal people would. Normal people would have belted me then and there if they were the belting type. Barry always made me wait and wonder. I could be sitting next to him two months after offending him and he would suddenly backhand me and say, 'That's for (whatever I did two months ago).' It would take a minute to figure out what had just happened. My face would go numb while Dad ranted and raved. My nose still has a part that sticks out where one of his backhanders ripped it from the bone. His surprise attacks got so bad that I was deathly afraid to sit next to him, especially in the front seat of the car. I would sit so that my elbow was on the knee nearest to him and my hand was on my chin, to try protecting myself from surprise backhanders that might have accumulated in him.

I blamed Dad and Maureen for separating me from my mother and the other kids. Let's get it clear that I didn't give two fucks about my mother but I loved my brother and my sister. I still do. Why couldn't Barry have just told me the truth about Mum's talk with the judge? It would have made me a lot less resentful of him.

My mother didn't want me but she didn't want Barry to have me either. I guess her hatred of me outweighed her hatred of him at that stage. Who knows why? Anyway, there I was going to the Central Coast with Barry and Maureen while my siblings and mother lived in Mt Druitt, a long way from the Central Coast.

Chapter 4.
The Central Coast

The Central coast was a nice area to live except for the fact that I had to be there with Barry. We lived at Yattalunga, between Green Point and Davistown, close to the water. The house was one of the oldest in the area and it was really just a shack.

I grew to like Maureen and I think I felt a bit safer with her and her kids around. She had a bit of a nasty streak but she was under Barry's thumb and did whatever he told her. I think she was basically a good mother. At least here there wasn't the constant smell of cigarettes and alcohol which were the dominant smells at my mother's place.

Dad and Maureen's shack was at the bottom of a hill and it had to have a deep ditch dug out the front to stop it flooding. Sometimes the floods were so bad that the moat would fill up and one time we were flooded so badly, the only way out would have been in a boat if we'd needed to go. The roof was corrugated iron that made the house unbearably hot in the summer. The yard had an old chook pen, my dad's Great Danes everywhere and a huge red belly black snake living under the house. The snake never bothered us.

We had an outside toilet that was emptied by a man in a truck. The dunny was home to hordes of red back spiders. The bathroom was outside too and we had no hot water. We used an urn in the bathroom to heat the water for showers or a bath. It took more than an hour to heat right up so there were no spontaneous hot showers. In fact we mostly had cold showers, not too bad in the summer but in the cold weather they were terrible.

Once again I had to start a new school. I was enrolled at Brisbania Public School in Davistown. Given the bullying at my old school, starting a new one didn't seem so bad. I went to that school for two years, doing Years 5 and 6. I was intelligent and I could read and write. All the family 'stuff' got in the way of my doing as well as I could have. I don't want to talk much about the school I went to other than to say the teachers were far worse than the kids when it came to bullying. They were a big part of the reason kids thought it was okay to pick on me. Mr Peg and Miss Goford loved to slam her hands down hard on the desk and my reaction was to be expected. Goford, if you ever read this, shame on you. How can you do what you did and sleep at night? I was caned so many times by Mr Peg! Miss Goford was the nastiest bully I'd come across to that point, aside of my parents. Being the brunt of bullies at home and at school was a heavy burden.

I once was in class when Miss Goford saw a piece of paper next to me. On this piece of paper were the words I love Michael, Tina and Samuel. My siblings names. Just so happened we had a Samuel and a Michael in our class so she belittled me in front of the school.

My father had the same approach to food. At Mum's we got two Wheatbix for breakfast. At Dad's a bowl of Corn Flakes. Lunch from Mum's was two Vegemite sandwiches in a brown paper bag. Same at Dad's. Mum made meat and vegies for dinner and at Dad's it was chops and chips or fish he'd caught at the wharf.

My father had a nasty habit of preparing food he knew I didn't like, such as steak and kidney, brussels sprouts and cabbage and he would stand over me screaming at me to eat it. I just had to force it down in fear that he'd do something worse. We had little food in the house so you might think I'd gobble down anything on my plate. But kidneys, brussels sprouts and cabbage? No, I hated them and Barry managed to pile them into a single meal.

I remember once having home work on maths. Dad stood over me screaming at me that I was so fucking stupid. I knew how to do the sums but him standing over me and abusing me made me too nervous to do anything but sit and tremble.

People probably saw me as a puny, smelly, badly dressed, skinny little kid. I was starving all the time. I was so hungry every day that I use to steal kids lunches. I would ask to go to the toilet when we were in class and I'd go through kids bags and stuff my mouth and pockets with whatever I could. I was amazed at how much some kids got to eat. I was never in a position to eat whatever I wanted and leave what I didn't want. When I got caught stealing I was bullied. I would have picked on me too. I smelled of stale urine because of the bedwetting and not being able to shower properly.

Our shack looked pathetic and sad next to all the nice houses being built around us. People built their homes on stilts so they could avoid the floods and gradually all the snakes seemed to all come to our place. I'm surprised we never got bitten. Snakes were even more plentiful than spiders. There were lots of posh houses in the area and those kids went to the same school as me. David was one of the kids at my school who lived in Davistown, a fifteen minutes walk from my house. Our mutual poverty bonded us as friends.

I think that under Maureen's care I didn't wet my bed at first but it didn't take long for it to start again with all the pressure my father had me under. Whereas my mother would just yell at me for bed wetting, my father was far more harsh. He'd berate me from the minute I woke up.

'You wet the bed on purpose!' he'd roar. 'Get out there and wash yourself.' He'd march me outside for a cold shower while he hovered over me, screaming about what a baby I was. What a girl! What a poofter!

As if I'd wet the bed on purpose just to endure his punishments every morning! A freezing shower under a barrage of abuse from a maniac that prevented me washing properly. I barely stood under the water as it was so cold. I just got wet enough to wash the front of my body and let the water mingle with tears.

Whereas when I lived with Mum we all knew if she had a problem, with Dad we didn't. He kept things from us. I remember one night Maureen came home very drunk. Barry helped her inside quietly so we kids wouldn't see. He kept a lot from us including the fact that in a car crash he caused the death of someone and was charged with manslaughter. I remember hearing Barry and Maureen discussing the court case about the man dad had run over. I'd developed the habit of prying at Lewisham, of listening to adult conversations and peering around corners. It often got me into trouble but at least I knew most of the time what was going on.

I think Barry did try to make a good enough life but his biggest problem was his complete selfishness. He had changed while he was away, at least in the way he presented himself. He dressed more respectably, took better care of his health and was less erratic and volatile. He had a calmness about him but even that was scary. I couldn't trust it. I think he was trying to impress Maureen and her children.

One day after I got back from school Maureen was out so I walked into the bedroom I shared with Len, Maureen's youngest child. Barry walked out of the room as I came in and he was naked. Len was lying in the fetal position on his side, facing the wall. It was as if he was frozen. He had no pants on. I sensed instinctively that a very bad thing had happened to him. The scene terrified me and I walked quickly away, barely able to breathe and without doing a thing for Len.

As an adult I've had to learn not to feel guilty about that. I was an abused, terrified, powerless child. I won't say anything in this book unless I know it's true and I know what I saw that day. I have many snippets of memories that I can't be certain of and that is very distressing. Len wasn't much of a talker but after that incident he hardly ever spoke.

Mum sent the other kids up for Christmas that year. We had Maureen's three kids and my three siblings. I loved that we were all under the same roof. We were excited about Christmas when we went to bed early on Christmas Eve. We had a Christmas tree with decorations on it and later that night, eaves dropping again, I heard Maureen and Barry wrapping presents and putting them under the tree.

We got up pretty early on Christmas morning. Barry stood next to the tree and us kids came close to look at all the presents. I counted them, knowing there would be nine: one for each kid and one each for Barry and Maureen. I counted eight. I counted again. Still only eight. I looked for my name. Was it on the big box? No. The little one? No. Which one was for me then? I was so excited. Maybe one of the presents was for two of us to share.

Dad picked up each present and gave it to the kid whose name was on it. Michael, Samuel, Tina, Tegan, Helena then Len. Maureen gave Dad his gift and he gave one to her. I got nothing and there were no presents left under the tree. I was so hurt! Anxiety rose but I looked around behind the tree to see if mine was hidden. No. Barry kept looking at me and I could tell from that look that he knew I was hurting.

'Where's Glen's present,' Tina blurted out. 'He hasn't got one yet.'

The other kids were looking at me now. Inside I was hurting deeply but I was determined not to let it affect me outwardly. If someone had spoken one word to me I probably would have burst into tears.

It wasn't about getting a gift. It was about being included in the group of people worthy of some thoughtfulness, worthy of someone taking the time to think about what a ten year old boy might like. Barry was playing another of his cruel mind game. When we'd go out to a party at the Doyalson RSL for example, I'd want to join in activities for kids but with just a look from him, I knew I wasn't allowed to. I could just watch. Depriving me of pleasures seemed to bring him joy.

After watching me watch the other kids open their gifts, Barry gave me an order. 'Glen, go to the chook shed and get the eggs for me, please.'

He seemed agitated. I wanted to ask, *Where's my gift?* I couldn't muster the courage. I knew Barry would twist that to make me look like a selfish, greedy brat.

I obeyed my father, thinking, *it isn't enough to give me nothing but you have to humiliate me in front of my brothers and sisters.* I felt especially embarrassed in front of my real siblings who looked up to me as the big brother.

I walked out to the shed, my head hanging down. I had a quick glance in the nesting box. No eggs. Back inside I declared, 'No eggs today.'

Barry repeated his order aggressively so off I went again to look for eggs, properly.

'I looked properly and there aren't any eggs,' I told Barry, a bit cheekily this time. I knew where the eggs usually were and I knew there were none.

Suddenly Barry exploded. 'Go out to the fucking shed and have a good look!'

Out I went again with my heart pounding with fear and anger. I could not find a single bloody egg anywhere. When I went in again Barry went completely off his head.

'Are you fucking stupid?' he screams. All the kids sit rigid, terrified about what might happen next. Tina's big eyes look into mine. I walk outside again and Barry tells Sis to go with me. That's how stupid I am: I need my little sister to help me find the eggs. I know exactly where the chooks lay their eggs every day and there are no eggs there.

I cry now because I'm afraid and humiliated. I don't get it. What am I missing? Does everyone but me and Sis know what was going on?

We go together to the shed and I walk to the nesting boxes. Nothing. Definitely nothing. Sis can't find any either. I turn to look at Tina and I see a foam surfboard leaning against the wall. The darkness of the room made the surfboard hard to see but there it was. I had always wanted one, a fiberglass one, but was this for me? It wasn't fiberglass but it was still a surfboard. Is this what Barry's performance was all about?

I don't feel good now. I don't know if it's mine. If it is mine it's a horrible way to give it to me. It's wrong and hurtful and unloving. It was almost a punishment.

Yes the board was for me, but it was obviously bought to let Barry show off to the other kids what a great dad he was. He probably knew I would never actually get to ride it. It was another thing he could deny me. Barry never took me to the beach that was only about fifteen kilometres from our house. A couple of times we went to the beach at Avoca, my board was never brought to use.

I thought about running away every day. But where could I go?

Every day I went past Green Point Baptist Church on my way to school. That is how I found out about Boys' Brigade. I started going to that and kept going because it was fun and it was my safe place. Barry loathed church and wouldn't go anywhere near one but I was allowed to go to Boys Brigade on Thursday nights. Maureen started going to the church. The minister, Geoff, told Maureen she had thirteen demons and that she had to leave my father. After I was told about the demons, I started thinking I could see them too and I became more and more frightened in the house. The real demon was Barry. The fear of demons had been planted in my head by Maureen's beliefs and I began to see shadows in the dark that I was sure were demons. I was already afraid to get up in the night and trot out to the toilet outside. At night time huge spiders use to build webs between the house, toilet and bathroom.

Maureen decided to leave Barry and take her children with her. One night when Dad was out, we crept out to the phone box nearby. Maureen was frightened. As we looked across to the house she asked me, 'Can you see that figure through the window in the house Glen?'

'No, I can't see anyone.'

'Look! There! In the front room.' She sounded almost hysterical. 'There's someone in there.'

The more she said it the more I began to see things, evil figures like shadows moving about in the house. These memories stick with you for life.

I don't know the full story about why Maureen left but in hindsight taking her kids away from my father was the best move she ever made. I hope that she and her kids went on to have a normal life. If you read this book please know I am grateful and I would love to meet you again. We shared a few years together and your kids became my only friends in that troubled period of my life.

With no other options, I stayed with my dad after Maureen left with her kids. I think I did Years 5 and 6 in primary school. At about age twelve I couldn't take living with Barry and his cruelty any more. Barry wasn't home a lot of the time but when he was he was particularly nasty. Thank goodness he left very early in the morning and would sometimes not return until late at night. I was so scared alone in that house. Dad had great Danes that he and Maureen use to breed and show. I would sit alone at night in that old house and hear noises. I would have one of the dogs sitting in the lounge room with me. One night Zulu, the bigger of the two dogs, was growling at the door.

'Who is it? Is someone there?' I called timidly. No-one answered. I was grateful to Zulu who might have scared someone away.

I was missing my brothers and sister a lot and this is when I began my running away from home period.

The first time I ran away was just before Christmas. I went to Mum's. I hitch hiked to the station. It was easy to get a ride, maybe because I was so small and young looking. My lifts would often be protective sorts of people who'd ask where I was going and when I said I was running away to my mum, they'd give me my train fare and sometimes buy me food. I'd jump on the train, sometimes without a ticket and get myself to Mt Druitt. Then I'd walk up to Mum's. She had moved from Shalvey to Bidwell, a one hour walk from the station.

As I travelled I thought about another disastrous Christmas I had with my family the year before. I got a mini bike, one of those fat wheeled second hand ones. Most kids I knew rode Honda 75 Red Devils or the old greys. Rodney, a friend who bullied me at school for a short time, had one. Most of the kids whose parents had money had motor bikes. I had asked Dad over and over again for one. Last year he had managed to get me one but if I had turned up to ride the thing with the other kids on their 75 ccs or their 125s, they would have laughed and mocked me. My bike actually worked for a while although it took an hour to get it going and you could walk faster than the bike could run. I rode it around a bit on Christmas day but I accidentally ran over Tina's Slip 'n Slide and tore it. I was in huge trouble. Barry took the bike off me and shut it in the garage. I spent the rest of the day in my room. That was the only ride I had on the mini bike. I guess I can at least be grateful that he got it for me, but like other gifts he gave me they were second hand and I was never allowed to use them. They served Barry well though. Something else to show off about.

I brought two girls from school home once. Edwina and another girl. Showing off as usual, Barry tried to get the bike going but it refused to start. To save face he got the horse out for us to ride but he spent the first twenty minutes riding it while the girls just watched. It was sickening. He was showing off to the girls and his behaviour around them was embarrassing. I had already struggled with making friends and my Dad's trying to impress them was humiliating. I think the girls could see what a jerk he was though. He fell off the horse that day and broke his collar bone. Karma's such a bitch.

Barry got me a second hand record player that had no speakers once too. It didn't work. He found old wooden boat with a huge hole in it and he promised he would fix it so we could go fishing. He never did. Promises. Promises. I didn't want to spend another day with him. I hated him and always will.

Anyway, having run away from Dad's I arrived at Mum's on

Christmas Eve. She was drunk but she welcomed me a bit more warmly than usual. She had got all the kids two gifts each from the Salvation Army who delivered them all in a box. She was trying to wrap them all, so I sat up with her and helped her while I told her I didn't want to go back to my dad's. I knew at least this year I would get to wake up for Christmas with my brothers and sister.

One of the gifts Michael got was a dartboard. He knew there wasn't a gift for me and he selflessly gave me the dartboard. That's the kind of giving that I think matters at Christmas. It's not about impressing neighbours or friends. I remember playing darts with Michael on Boxing Day. Aunty Edna and Uncle Paul were there too so playing darts with Michael was a good way of keeping away from Uncle Paul. Michael lost a game, got cranky and as I walked away, he threw a dart into the back of my leg. I do remember as a child wondering if I should find the courage to tell Mum about Uncle Paul. But the words "I'll send you back to that home, played around in my mind". I felt they were much more important to Mum than I was.

Other kids might have got cared for by their mums but I didn't. I knew if I told Margaret, she'd make Michael and I fight each other, using fists and punches. That's how Mum dealt with trouble between us. We fought anyway over that dart. We wrestled around the yard until we'd had enough and went to do something else. All brothers' fight I think but we hardly ever did. I loved my siblings especially Michael and all I ever wanted was to be with them.

Tina and I were arguing about something that Christmas day and Mum sent us outside to do gardening. We did what she told us but I hit a rock with the shovel and it flew up and collected my sister in the side of her mouth. She needed stitches and she still bears the scar. I was even less popular than usual. My mother didn't see it for the accident it was.

'You're going back to your dead shit, useless father, you little cunt,' she said. 'I'm not having you here chucking rocks about the bloody place.' She drove me back to Barry. Tina told her repeatedly that it was an accident but she had her excuse now to send me back. She drove me up with her new, drunk boyfriend Henry.

'Please don't make me stay with him Mum,' I pleaded as always. 'I'm sorry. I'll be good. Please! I don't want to go back to Barry.' My words fell on deaf and drunk ears. Barry was not glad to see me.

It was time for me to go to high school. Would I be bullied now that I was getting away from Mr. Peg and Mis Goford?

I started Year 7 at Erina High School but I didn't go much. I was put in Class 7E but not because I was dumb. I was not dumb. Most kids in that class came from the same primary school as me and most of us were always in trouble rather than in class learning with good teachers. I hadn't had enough schooling to learn much at all. But that didn't mean I was dumb.

The bullying started up again and it was relentless. I started wagging school. I'd pretend to catch the bus then sit around the wharf fishing and swimming all day.

The first time I ran away properly I went to Gosford Station and got the train to Newcastle without a train ticket. The train inspector caught me and took me to wait in his cabin until he could hand me over at Newcastle Police Station. I wasn't going to any police station so when the train stopped at a red light between stations, I jumped off and ran for my life. At first I went to a local school where I walked up to some kids and asked, 'Hey, who's the toughest kid in this place?'

It was silly for me to have asked that question. I was hoping the kid might be a troubled kid like me and he might help me find somewhere to sleep. He didn't. He was confused if anything.

I walked to a shopping centre, not really sure what I'd do there but it was somewhere to go. After roaming through the shops for a while I sat down aimlessly. A lady came along and asked, 'What are you doing? Where is your Mum? Shouldn't you be at school or at home?'

'I ran away from home,' I told her. 'I'm never going back.'

She was so kind. She listened to me while I told her my problems. I told her how my dad kept hurting me and I begged her, 'Please don't send me home.' I was twelve by then but I might have looked about eight.

The lady seemed quite overwhelmed. 'Well, I can't just leave you here. You'd better come home with me,' she said smiling. 'I'll take care of you.'

She took me home to her place. She recognized that I was young and in danger.

'I won't dob you in,' she said. 'I promise.'

She cooked me a delicious meal then put me to sleep in a nice warm bed. I asked repeatedly, 'Can I stay here with you? I'll be good. I promise.' I was afraid she would ring the police when I went to bed but she promised that she wouldn't and I believed her. Now I had a new mother and I believed that she would let me to stay with her and take care of me.

When her husband came home he apparently insisted that she call the police. I was woken up by the police shining torches in my eyes. When I realised what had happened I was so angry and upset with that lady. I thought I could just live with her for as long as I liked but she had betrayed me. I thought that this lady could just keep me and raise me. I knew my dad didn't care enough to look for me.

The policeman held me by the back of my pants while I let go with a verbal barrage. 'You promised I could stay with you. You wouldn't tell the police. I hate you, you liar! I hate you.'

She was clearly distraught. She was crying and saying, 'I'm sorry. I'm so, so sorry.'

As an adult I understand her position. She was very kind and caring but she was caught between a rock and a hard place. She had to report me to the police but as a child I felt betrayed.

My file shows that they took me to the police station but I think the police doctored the record to protect that kind lady and themselves from any trouble. When the lady took me home she was probably breaking the law. She did what any decent person would do and rang the police. She had probably wanted to stop my parents worrying and to let them know where their kid was. I was way too young to understand. She probably couldn't conceive of a family like mine.

The police sat me down and said, 'Mate, tell us your name and we'll send you home to your dad.'

'No! You don't understand. I'm not going back! Please don't send me back.' The prospect of being returned to Barry scared me more than anything. I preferred to stay in my prison cell and I did for quite a while, not breathing one word about who I was or where I was from. I refused to give them any information at all. Just before running away dad had screamed at me for something and I was so tired of being afraid. I was tired of living life fearing of a backhand of cruel words.

'Come on son. Just give us your name and address. You're not in any trouble. We just want to take you home.'

'I don't want to go home! Don't take me back to him. Please don't take me back! You can't. I'm not going back to that psycho! You don't understand,' I told them desperately. 'I'm not safe at home. He'll hurt me! That's why I ran away.'

'All right. We get that. You don't want to go back to your dad. We'll be able to get you into a place called Warrami. It's a home in Newcastle. That okay?'

I thought I understood. (I didn't know I'd be charged with a criminal offense.) They brought me a soft drink and assured me that, if I told them the details they wanted, I would not be returned to my dad but I'd go to a home. I could see the officer felt sorry for me. I pictured homes like Stewart House or even Barnardo's. I didn't know what their kind of home was.

They charged me with the offence 'Uncontrollable. Exposed to Moral Danger.' (What an irony! Putting a boy who is exposed to moral danger into an institution where he will be exposed to moral danger by associating with criminals imprisoned for rape, murder, armed robbery etc.) Back then kids who ran away or did crimes like car theft or rape or murder would all be treated the same in the justice system. Running away was seen as a crime and kids were locked up for it.

The police drove me to Warrami at Broad meadows. I thought I'd be going to another orphanage or foster care place or something like that. It would be my first time in a criminal institution. I had not committed any crimes. I just had to get myself away from Barry. I had no idea what going into an institution for kids who broke the law would be like. I didn't know homes like that existed. Why would I? The orphanage was the scariest place I'd ever been sent to but it wasn't like Warrami.

The police tried to contact my father in Yattalunga and, when eventually they did, they told him that if he went to Warrami to retrieve me, I would be set free without charge. He never came. So I was kept in Warrami and the charge was laid.

Soon after I got to Warrami I was sent to the Governor's office to get the big spiel. It was a woman and she said something like, 'This is my institution and if you toe the line you will have no trouble. But if you mess up you will be in all sorts of shit.'

What had I got myself into?

'Can you ring me mum and see if I can live with her?'

'I can't do that! You've been charged with a crime!'

'What have I done? I didn't do any crimes! It was me who asked the police to bring me here,' I explained.

'You ran away from home mate. That's a crime in NSW. You're a prisoner not an orphan. You can't leave until the judge decides on your sentence.' Did she see my distressed face? 'It's likely, given that you have never been in trouble before, that you will be sent home, as long as your parents agree to take you. Otherwise you will be made a ward of the state and you'll be inside until you are eighteen.' Fuck!

That reality hit home. I understood that I could spend the next five years in a home for running away from violence. It felt so unfair.

Would my mother let me come home? If not, would Barry?

I didn't want to be here and I hated the idea of going back to Barry. I literally felt safe nowhere as a child.

Please Mum. I'll be good. I promise.

Or maybe a nice family could adopt me. But I was twelve or thirteen, past the age that people want kids to adopt. Would they ever want to adopt a troubled kid? I was so angry. I was stuck at Warrami.

Warrami had a pool in a court yard with a big brick wall around it. Each of us had our own room with our own shower and toilet. All day I'd heard boys talking about boy's homes like Mt Penang and Daruk where kids get raped and beaten. I didn't feel safe when I went into my little room the first night. I was frightened but after they locked me in I felt safer. I came to like it.

The room had a toilet, shower, basin and a bed. On the wall of each room was a two way radio. After each of us was in a room, a lock shut us in for the night. I felt safe then but out of place.

After getting up in the morning we all came outside and then I could see there were lots of kids here and most were bigger than me. They were between the ages of twelve and sixteen. They looked aggressive, tough and many had tattoos on their arms. An aboriginal kid named Allen came up to me with his mate Troy. Allen's tattoo, a knife, was on the inner part of his arm.

Rusty and Troy were the first kids I spoke with.

'What are you in 'ere for?' Allen asked me.

'Running away from home,' I told him.

'Phh. That all,' they scoffed. They had both been charged with much more serious crimes and were prone to violence.

We all had a little book where points we earned for good behaviour were recorded along with points for bad behaviour. It was like an account book. The more points we got the more privileges we'd be given. You could get 'in the red,' minus points, by being bad. No privileges then. The boys charged with more serious crimes took to the book scheme so they could get to the Privilege Room. I didn't care what happened in my book. I thought it was a bit silly.

We got boiled lollies as rewards each day. The more points you got the more lollies you got. At the end of the week the person with the most points got to spend the weekend in the Privilege Room with a television and other things. I never got to see that room.

There was a huge dining room where we all went to eat and as I looked around I noticed again that the kids here all looked very big. A fight broke out between two of them. They punched into each other fiercely and tables and chairs flew everywhere. The others kids egged them on. The officers eventually broke it up and the offenders were taken away.

Where the hell had I ended up? In a very scary place! If I thought I was afraid at home, I was possibly even more afraid here. Though the sources were different, the fear itself was the same. The language I knew well: Violence. I gradually found out that many of the kids here had come from violent places while others had grown up stealing cars and doing all sorts of crimes. All I'd done was run away from home.

There were all sorts of scams played on new kids like me. On the wall there was a big red button called the Dingo Bell.

'Hey mate, you press that big red button when yer hungry and they bring ya some food!'

'If ya wanna get out, just go and tell the officer you're sorry for what yer done, say you wanna sign the sorry book an' they let you go home!'

I was smart enough to know when things were not true. My inbuilt radar from living with my parents meant I treated everything with suspicion. I never got caught out by those kids. Other runaways did. They were very upset at being in Warrami and they were easier to convince about the sorry book. Other kids would laugh as the innocents went up to officers saying how really sorry they were and asking to sign the sorry book and go home.

Many of the boys spent a large amount of time talking about their crimes, break and enter, car stealing and so on. Some kids couldn't seem to talk about anything else. Their crimes were like badges of honour. I could tell you how to steal a car but I had never done it. I could tell you how to do a lot of things that I had never done because I learnt it all from these inmates. That kind of talk was forbidden and officers called it 'neg raving.' Negative talk. The boys also talked about the homes they'd been sent to by the judge after their court cases. Reiby, Daruk and Mt Penang were the main ones. I learnt a lot from listening to them. I learnt the word 'remand.' I was on remand, kept in custody until a judge sentenced me. I didn't have a crime against me. Why was I here?

I met a boy who was going to court on the day I met him.

'Why? What did you do?' I ask.

'I ran away from home and I am charged with uncontrollable.'

Four boys went to court that day, each for their own reason. They all came back upset.

'I got a general,' the runaway boy said. 'They're sending me to Daruk.' I could see the fear in his eyes.

'What's a general?' I asked.

'A general means you get four and a half months to three years inside. Depends on the officers in the home when they're gunna let you out. They can keep you 'til you're eighteen if they want to.'

Another kid who was charged with car stealing got two years.

I couldn't have imaged being locked up for all that time! I got really upset and cried as soon as they locked my door that night. You would never ever cry in front of other boys unless you wanted to be bullied and vulnerable. I paraded around like a tough confident kid but that was just a mask that I hoped would protect me. I learnt not to cry years ago with my parents, especially my mother.

I hated every day I spent in Warrami and I was scared. I'd run away from being hurt all the time only to land into the most barbaric of systems where violence was a language every one spoke. I saw so many things, learned so many things in my stay and none of them was good. Kids talked constantly about stabbing each other with knives they'd make that looked pretty lethal. Fights were truly vicious especially when packs of boys fought. There'd be punching, kicking, biting, whatever they could think of. Sexual innuendo was there in just about everything boys said, especially the older ones.

One day I had to see a doctor for a health check so they took me to Newcastle Hospital. An officer escorted me and he left me in a room by myself while he did something else. I thought to myself, *I need to get out of Warrami. I hate it.* So, I just walked through a few doors and down the stairs and I was free!

I was going to take off but two things stopped me. One was that I remembered a kid in Warrami telling me that because he had absconded from custody, he was going to be sent to a worse place for two years. I think that place was called Grafton, a home I would later learn was even more barbaric than Daruk. All the kids were frightened of going there.

The other reason for not taking off was that everyone talked about how in Daruk and Mt Penang they raped little boys and beat them up and made you march everywhere. The word rape scared me as I recall the pain of Uncle Paul. All this was going through my head as I stood out the front of the hospital trying to figure out where to go. I thought if I ran away then they would definitely send me to Daruk when they caught me.

I walked back inside and as I sat back down, the officer came in.

'Where've you been?' he asked angrily.

I was terrified. I'd been caught.

'To the toilet,' I whispered.

'If you need to go to the toilet, you tell me and I'll take you,' he yelled. 'Right?'

'Yes sir.' I replied sheepishly. I felt a little power in knowing I could have escaped and that I had pulled the wool over his eyes. It was a small victory.

I am not sure exactly how long I was in Warrami. I was very apprehensive about the judge, given the previous betrayal when the last one sent me to my father's place. Boys in Warrami all had stories about how unjust judges' decisions could be and how if they were in a bad mood, watch out. There were some judges who thought that all kids who came through their system ought to be locked up and the key thrown away.

On the day of my court case my mother came to visit me. 'Please Mum, please take me home,' I begged yet again. 'I promise I'll be good. Don't let them lock me up. Please. You don't know what it's like in here Mum. They're criminals. They've done real bad things.'

She replied, 'I can't take you.'

Barry was there too.

I thought the judge was an arsehole. He treated me like I had killed someone. 'I am considering that a sentence in a boy's home might be a good thing for you,' he announced. 'A year or two there and you'll learn to behave yourself.'

Behave myself? What had I done wrong? I was possibly the best behaved child in the whole of Australia. I was too fucking scared to be anything else. But that wasn't the impression he'd got from my dad or my mother. I was a rough, uncontrollable rat bag with criminal intentions. I admit I was hyperactive but I wasn't bad. I'd definitely changed after Uncle Paul raped me. I'd retreated into my shell, too afraid to speak up. But I was not bad.

Finally the judge said, 'I find you guilty of the charge Uncontrollable. I am giving you eighteen months.' He paused and rephrased. 'I am giving you an eighteen month bond. You are released to the care of your father, Barry. Blah Blah blah.' He carried on but all I heard for some time was that word 'guilty,' echoing around in my head and eighteen months. Why couldn't they just talk straight so kids could understand them?

I'd dodged a bullet but now I had to face the bloody great bomb of living with Barry again. What's more I had a criminal conviction. I was in the system and on notice.

Chapter 5.
Runaways

I was back from Warrami and living with my dad who was the same selfish arsehole he had been before Maureen.

The blue surfboard, put away as soon as the other kids left that Christmas, was now sitting up in the spare room. It was never used, not by me anyway. I never even put it in the water. It was just a trophy to show off to visitors. It was torture to me.

'Can I take my board down to the jetty?' I'd ask Barry. It was only a ten minute walk from our house.

'No you can't,' he'd reply nastily. 'It's a surfboard. Get it? Surf. To ride on waves not paddle about at the jetty!'

We only lived five minutes drive from Brisbane Waters! Whatever the fuck he reckoned the board was for, it was mine, wasn't it? Why couldn't I use it the way I wanted to?

Barry was always looking for women and he joined Parents Without Partners. He had a few girlfriends he met there but they were all short term relationships. He used to take me everywhere he went on his motorbike. Often it was to his current girlfriend's place and I think maybe I was a kind of trophy, to show what a good man he was. He'd put on all his orange protective gear with thermals underneath in case he came off. I'd be on the back in school shorts and shirt. All right, I had a red and blue striped helmet but no other protective stuff. He'd be safe and I'd be minced meat. Dad was friends with a lady from Wyong for a time so sometimes we'd be riding home at four o'clock in the morning, ducking in and out of traffic, mostly huge trucks and me freezing to death on the back.

We went on a few camping trips with various girlfriends. Barry was so pre-occupied then that I actually had some good times camping. I could explore or swim or do whatever I liked usually with other kids from Parents Without Partners.

It was at one of the women's homes in Wyong when I was in the bath with Dave, her son, when Barry walked in. He started talking to us both about how to masturbate and about our penis sizes. It felt an odd conversation to be having at twelve years old I felt confused and embarrassed.

My father was on and off with different women so he was always searching. I wanted to play footy but he enrolled me in a ballroom dancing and disco classes instead. More women in dancing I suppose. It was always about him. Dancing lessons served me well later on when the break dancing craze hit the streets but it wasn't what I wanted to do as a kid.

Michael came to live with us not to long after I got out of Warrami. I'm not sure how that came about but I liked the idea of us being together. I had an ally. Sure enough, after a time of being polite, Dad started to verbally abuse Mike as well. We decided to run away together.

We hitched hiked to Gosford station, aiming for Wyong. We made it to Gosford Station then caught a train to Wyong. It was a hot summer day and we happened to pass a swimming pool.

'Let's go in! Look at all them school kids goin' in. We can just hang 'round with them.'

We didn't exactly blend in though and pretty soon a cop grabbed Michael! A teacher must have seen us and dobbed us in. When I saw them collar Michael, I kept hiding under the water. I was more or less over my fear of being underwater by then, as long as my father wasn't there. I swam to the top to look where Michael and the cop were. Michael was pointing straight at me. In his defense he was only eleven and when the police asked where I was he innocently pointed to me.

The cops sent us to the remand section at Mt Penang for the night. Just for the night thank goodness but that was scary enough.

The bars on the windows were bent to the shapes of sports figures whose job was to prevent us escaping. It wasn't a good night for me because I'd heard all the bad stories of this place. Lucky for us we were kept separate from the inmates at Mt Penang.

The next day we were in Gosford Court. Michael and I sat in the office all day. We tried to act tough but I think we might have been quaking inside with Mt Penang or Daruk on the cards. We were set free without any conviction! I didn't care much. I was so tired of being my father's scapegoat and object to rage at for no reason that had anything to do with me.

On the school holidays I would go to my mum's or the other kids would come to us. Not too long after we had run away we were sent to stay at Mum's for a week.

Mum had a new boyfriend Henry. He was a short, stout man about five and a bit feet tall, nearly the same height as me at age of twelve but he must have weighed twice as much. (Mum was about five foot ten.) We were told to call him Dick, not Henry. The two of them were always fighting and mum was always fighting with the people in the adjoining town house.

Henry liked to drink and he was an angry little drunk. He and Mum came home from the pub one time and there was the woman from next door, gardening out the front of her place. Mum hated her. Not just because her husband was a cop. Mum and Henry were both very drunk and Henry did a bad job of parking the car. As mum got out she said something snide to the neighbour who decided to bite back.

'Your husband would have to stand on a stool to fuck you, wouldn't he Margaret!'

She had a small shovel in her hand and mum jumped the fence to take her revenge. This is probably the time when the police came and arrested my mother.

Margaret often got involved in physical fights, especially at The Clock, the pub at Bidwell. Us kids spent many days sitting outside that place while she spent the day drinking. There was a cockatoo in a cage and sometimes we played and talked with him. All sorts of drunks would come up and speak to us kids. When we got home mum often screamed at the neighbour's through the wall.

'They're sending me to prison,' she'd tell them. This could have been after the shovel incident but I'm not sure.

The police knew our place. I remember one time they came for Michael. They dragged him out screaming and as they went he grabbed the phone. They pulled him and he pulled the phone socket out of the wall. We weren't popular with the cops.

When Mum and Henry were drinking at The Clock they'd sometimes give us two dollars and send us to the Emerton Pools. It cost twenty cents to go in and the extra dollar bought a lot of lollies. You got two for a cent or a twenty five cent bag. I'd buy four bags and share them evenly amongst us kids.

When the pool closed we'd trot back to the pub and sit there until the pub closed, or until mum was thrown out or they decided they'd drunk enough. We'd all pile in and Henry somehow got us home without crashing. The guy could hardly see over the steering wheel, let alone drive. I was often afraid when my dad drove angrily and erratically but Henry was pretty frightening too. He did actually have a car accident once with my sister in the car years later.

After any stay at mum's place ended, Henry and Mum would sometimes drive us back up to dad's.

Back at Yattalunga Michael and I became good friends with a kid at school called Kyle. He was a real knock about kid and he used to run away from home too. He came to see me at our place once after he had run away from home so I let him stay in one of the back sheds. The bush made it feel like we had twenty acres. There was a creek on the block and it drained into the Brisbane Waters.

The five main sheds just outside our backyard had been knocked down but there were four more next to each other. Dad's horse lived in the first one and there was one shed hidden deep down in the bush, far enough away from the house to not be seen. It was like a little cubby house. It was my sanctuary, a place I could retreat to when things were tough. It was one of my many jobs to carry down bucket after bucket of water to the shed. Other jobs would be to do all the gardening in dad's vegetable garden and mow all the lawns. Once when I ran away I stayed there, about two hundred metres from the house, and no-one found me. I'd also been camping near the shed with a friend called Tyson. Wild pigs came into our back yard too so we could get into the shed if we needed protection. We took one of our dogs with us to the bush shed. We made a shelter for him with a blanket for a door to keep him safe from pigs. Oil lanterns that we found lying around came in handy too. Camping out there was better than being with Barry. We often had camp fires because the smoke would scare the pigs away.

Anyway, this time Kyle was staying in the shed. Michael and I left for school and Dad left for work. When we got off the bus from school that afternoon, there was our dad raging furious out the front of our place. Someone had stolen his car, a Mini Moke.

As Dad was telling us his car had been stolen, his car went flying past our house with Kyle at the wheel! Of course, we didn't mention that to Barry. He would have gone ballistic. Kyle must have waited for us to leave that morning then rocked up to our place and 'borrowed' a few things. Michael and I took that as a personal insult.

Somehow Dad got the car back, Kyle got arrested and a few days later he was back at school. Michael and I were so pissed off with Kyle. I was going to confront him but he managed to hide from me all through the lunch break. I'd had a physical fight with Kyle in Woodwork in Year 7 and we'd landed on a lathe. My school record says that I had been expelled from woodwork for putting a kid's head in the lathe but that not what happened. I had to report to Mr Chapman, the Principal, and he doled out the punishment which was to sit every day outside his office and type with the secretary while the woodwork class was on. I missed out on Woodwork.

I was ready for my second fight with Kyle. A kid in my class told me he had punched on with Michael at lunch time and Kyle was now in Mr. Chapman's office in trouble. My blood boiled.

No-one messes with my brother! Kids teased me all the time and I never lifted a finger to help myself but a person puts a hand on my brother and I'm ready to fight them. I stormed out of class, charged down to the principal's office, barged in and attacked Kyle.

While I was doing my thing, Mr. Chapman did his. He announced, 'I am ringing your father and the police.'

I ran out of the office and ran through the school looking for Michael. I didn't want my dad or the police here so I decided right then that I was running away. I found Michael in a classroom.

'Come on Mike. I'm running away. You comin'?' He followed me out the door.

I knew this time when we ran away we'd eventually be caught and I'd be sent to Daruk or some other dreadful place. Michael would be sent back to Mum's or Dad's because he'd had one or two court appearance less than me, so he still had a bond up his sleeve.

We caught the train to Kings Cross. We went to the Snooker Room and we played the Kiss pinball machine. We'd heard about this place from other kids.

Somehow we ended up in Manly later on and we met a guy called Black John. He lived at Manly wharf and targeted runaway kids to do crimes and stuff for him. I told John the story of our Dad's abuse and why we ran away. John initially said we should go up there and beat up our dad. I agreed. John suggested that we go with him, break into Dad's place and steal heaps of stuff. We agreed. Dad loved his stuff.

We went up late at night and camped at the wharf all night. Michael broke into a nearby house and stole some food for us: ice-cream and so on. We knew that the people who owned it only came up for the Christmas holidays. Michael had a lot more courage than I did when it came to doing these things. I just loved being with my brother and hated being with either of our parents. I think living and surviving with our mother in Mt Druitt forced Michael to learn his own ways to survive.

In the morning we moved from the wharf to the bus shelter just up from our house and watched for Dad to leave for work. His job was at the Erina Squash Courts and he left for work at around four every morning. From the bus stop we could see him going about his business getting ready for work. We watched as he drove off.

We didn't have to actually break in because the house had no handles or locks on the back door. We just walked straight in. The spare room was like an Aladdin's Cave. Dad kept his treasures like tents, cameras, all his camping things, all types of stuff in there. We carried out as much as we could and got a bus to Gosford station then a train to Circular Quay. Still loaded up, we took a ferry to Manly. I absolutely loved going on the ferries at Circular Quay to Manly. It felt liberating standing on the front of the ferry as it crossed the water.

At Manly wharf Michael, always ready for action, took out an airbed of Dad's, blew it up and took to the water with it. We'd lived near the ocean for a while now so we weren't scared of sharks like many people seemed to be. I got in too and we swam about for ages.

Being on the run I had a feeling of uncertainty mixed with a sense of adventure. Normally I didn't think about consequences and I just enjoyed the moment but this time I knew that I'd be caught and I'd have to actually deal with the consequences. I was so over living with my dad's bullshit that I was willing to go to any lengths to free myself of him. Meanwhile, being free with Michael was a great feeling.

While my brother floated about on the camping bed in the sea I talked with John. He told me to ask people for money so we could get food and he said he'd go and sell Dad's stuff.

'No! We're not sellin' his stuff!' I said.

Although we'd stolen it, I felt protective of his property. I took it to hurt him, to let him know I could stand up to him but I knew we'd get it back to him eventually.

Manly wharf had an amusement place, Coney Island I think,

on the side of the jetty. It was a haven for the scores of runaways who'd escaped the abuses of home and become street kids. As I walked out to the road to ask a stranger for some coins, I was spotted by police in a wagon. They pulled up at the wharf and the street kids scattered in seconds, knowing the police wouldn't bother chasing them. I hadn't got the street smarts yet so I didn't run. John separated from me and the police came straight up to me.

'What's your name sonny?'

I was a runaway and I guess I looked like it. I looked way younger than my thirteen years too. I handled their questions like a smart ass kid. Cheeky, angry answers.

'Me name's Mickey Mouse. What's yours!'

'I want your real name.'

'What about Popeye then?'

'Look, sonny, you should be at school so what are you doing here?'

All the usual questions and all I wanted to do was run. I didn't run. What would be the use? While they were busy arresting me, Michael was splashing about in the water without a clue. I was handcuffed like the hardened criminal I must have been and driven to Manly Police Station. They took me inside and, rather than place me in the cells, they put me in the docks where you wait to get bailed. I was so tired. I lay down and I fell asleep. The last week had been long with nowhere much to sleep and no food in my belly. I was defeated. I just curled up in a little ball of skin and bones and fell asleep.

I must have stayed asleep for a while because when I woke up the first thing I heard was Barry's voice at the counter. I hadn't said a thing to the police about Michael but there was my father, telling them that Michael was with me.

They talked for a while when I heard Barry say, 'No, don't charge him.

Just see if you can find the ring they took.'

I didn't know what the ring was but it obviously mattered to him. It might have been a wedding ring. I remember a gold ring with red stones from somewhere. The police went out to the wharf again and got Michael.

It wouldn't be long before we would make that choice to run away again. Apart from the time I was sent to Warrami, I was always sent home after running away. It had been eight months since I'd been released. Would they send me to a home like that again?

One morning Barry told Michael and I to mow the lawn. That was a mammoth job. We got out the mower but we couldn't get it to start. We were too scared to tell Barry but eventually I had to. He was lying on the bed.

'Mower won't start Dad,' I said, trying not to sound wimpy.

He sat bolt upright and exploded. 'Get out there now and mow the lawn!' he bellowed.

We kept trying to start the mower and I became increasingly anxious as it refused to fire. If he didn't hear it running soon, Barry would come out in a fit of rage and all hell would break loose.

'Fuck this Michael. I'm running away.'

When Dad wasn't looking I crept into his room, got his red biscuit tin where his collection of fifty cent pieces were and I took the whole thing. There was thirty dollars' worth of coins. We were off.

We headed to Saratoga to see a girl I liked. Lorraine was her name. She hung around with us until she had to go inside. We didn't know what to do with ourselves then so we slept at the jetty. We walked to Green Point in the morning thinking we'd go to see my mate Tyson. He wasn't home so we decided to break into houses along the shore. Michael did the breaking in while I kept watch. All we took were jars of coins.

Thirsty work that, so when I saw Tyson's garden tap I put my mouth over it to get water. I could feel something in my mouth that wasn't water. I spat it out and saw it crawling away. A funnel web! I can't believe it didn't bite me. It happened so fast. Spiders crawl into dried up taps and I never put my mouth over an outside tap again.

I'd already had some disasters at Tyson's place. He collected snakes and I had helped him many times. One time I was running through the house chasing Tyson and I ran straight through the glass door he'd closed to slow me down. I wasn't hurt but Tyson's Dad freaked out, not only because I'd broken the door but he was worried I'd hurt myself. Tyson had the best dad in the world and Tyson seemed to have everything a boy could want. I was shattered when he told me one day they were leaving Gosford to move to Blaxland in the Blue Mountains.

We spent some of the money Michael got from the houses at Green Point and we ate chocolate I'd nicked from a shop too. We still had about thirty dollars. We ended up back in Saratoga. I had such a crush on Lorraine that I just wanted to be there.

As we walked along we came across a man named Clarry who restored and sold second hand pushbikes. He had a sign up and that's how we found him. We looked at the bikes and for the money we had there'd be enough to buy one shit old bike and have a bit left. I thought if we had bikes it would be easier to run away and travel everywhere.

Clarry agreed to make some adjustments to a bike, so while he was doing that, Michael and I concocted a plan to steal a second bike. We thought he had so many he wouldn't miss that one. I rode out the front with this stupid old bike distracting Clarry, as Michael jumped the back fence, taking another bike. We met down the street.

So now we have our transport sorted out. Who runs away from home on a pushbike? Our house on Davistown Road was a three hour walk to the station. That road was the only route to each town along the coast. We had to make sure we rode past Dad's house in the dark so he wouldn't see us.

We decided that instead of turning left towards Green Point we'd go the other way towards Avoca Beach. It would be a long ride but there were no houses along the way, just darkness and bush. We'd been this way by car before but at night, on push bikes, it seemed endless and scary. It was totally black and every tiny sound was amplified.

Then, 'Ah fuck. Me seat's bloody fallen off.'

'See if we can stick it back on.'

We seemed doomed when we couldn't.

'I'm not goin' back. I'll bloody ride standing up if I have to.'

I had to. Both bikes eventually fell apart so we dumped them on the side of the road and started walking.

We arrived at Kincumber Pub. Back then the Pub stood alone in the middle of nowhere. Out the front there was a pinball machine and a Space Invaders machine. We had about one or two dollars left so I played the pinball machine while Michael played Space Invaders. All the game machines had a little wire that stood up in the coin slot. If you put the coin on a piece of string, with chewing gum or a special kind of knot, you could put it some of the way then pull it back up, getting free credits. I learnt this off a street kid at Manly. You could keep playing and the machine registered that you had paid each time and gave you a free credit. If you held the cash return and broke the string you could also get your two bob back.

'I'm starving,' Michael said after a while. He thought he had a good idea for getting some money. He didn't share it with me.

'Give us fifty cents an' I'll get a Cherry Ripe,' he said. 'We can go halves.'

I played the machine while Michael asked the man behind the counter for a Cherry Ripe. As the guy took the money from Michael, he opened the till. Suddenly Michael grabbed all the notes and ran. We were in the middle of nowhere and there was nowhere to go. What the fuck was he thinking? It shows how little we cared about anything anymore.

If Michael had warned me about his plan I would have told him not to do it but I think we'd reached a point where we had both been pushed too far. We didn't give a shit about authority or anything but being free and together. We wanted to impress each other too. This was not Michael's finest hour as a master criminal though.

'Hey! Stop that little prick,' the man behind the counter yelled. 'He's taken the till!'

I took off as soon as I saw what Michael had done. Two men chased us. Michael was pretty quick on his feet but they managed to catch him and wrestle him to the ground. I was still free. I watched them take him inside but I didn't go anywhere. There was no way I was leaving my brother alone. I was trying to think of what to do. *A plan, I need a plan.* I was panicking. Distressed, I ran down the road and sat there anxiously thinking. What the fuck do I do? There was bush for miles around and the road was the only way in or out.

I ran back to the pub. I could see Michael through a window, sitting on a chair, his head hung down and he looked defeated. The door was closed and a man blocked the way so he couldn't get out. The publican called the police. I thought of ways to free Michael. Pick up a rock and chuck it through the window. No use. Even if I got him out, where could we go? It was at least five kilometres back to Davistown Road and probably further to anywhere in the other direction. Eventually I did the only thing that seemed sensible. I knocked on the door. When it opened I demanded, 'Let my brother go!'

No luck.

Then I screamed wildly, 'Let my brother go!'

The guy grabbed my arm and tried to drag me inside. I busted free and backed off, hoping he'd follow me out and Michael could run out the door. The man wouldn't be drawn away. I was terrified but Michael seemed quite relaxed. He always did that when he waited to see what adults decided to do with us. I was way more distressed than he was.

'Please mister,' I pleaded, changing tack. 'Please let him go. We won't come back an' you've got yer money back. Please.' I was frantic. I was the big brother. I should look after the little brother.

Inevitably the police arrived and arrested both of us. This time they take us to Gosford Police Station. I was charged with

Uncontrollable. Michael was charged with Stealing and Uncontrollable. We were taken to Mt Penang for the night and the next day we went to court at Gosford. Court sent us to Yasmar, a remand centre for kids. I'd been to Warrami so I had some idea of what to expect but Michael hadn't.

Yasmar was where you waited for the court to decide your fate after you'd committed a 'crime.' You might 'graduate' to a reform homes or you might be given a bond or a sentence to a less severe home. Yasmar had a Junior side and a Senior's side and a huge brick wall surrounded it. It was a cold, desolate place. The court house was ruled by a woman Judge named Sue.

We were marched into the Rec Room and I felt some anxiety creeping up. There was a TV on the wall, a pool table and some chairs in this room and a lot of boys were hanging out there. Next to the Rec Room was a dining room. A corridor ran down past dormitories with polished wooden floors and it led to the ablution area.

Days were regimented by officers whose approaches to us boys varied from mean arseholes to dirty predators. Mr Watson and Mr Neat were officers who loved their job because of the power it gave them over us. Mr Neat smoked a big cigar, had a huge belly and a deep voice.

Early each morning you'd be woken up by him yelling, 'Wakey wakey. Hands off Snakey!' Or 'Rise and shine.' The loud orders and the stench of cigars was a horrible way to wake up at six every morning.

Kids were here for all sorts of crimes: rape, murder, robbery, car stealing, break and enter. It seemed that a large number of the kids were in on charges of Uncontrollable, like us. Running away from home. There were a lot of brothers in Yasmar. Sometimes the elder brother would be sent to the senior side of Yasmar but they kept Michael and I together for the first part of our stay.

There were demountable rooms at the end of the ablutions area. There was an oval surrounded by high brick walls. At the end of the property near the highway was a metal fence about ten feet high that would be easy to get over if you really wanted to.

Many of the kids liked to fight. They were tougher than us but we had well developed survivor instincts because of the violence we'd grown up with. We could stand up for ourselves when we were together. But it was a different kind of violence in Yasmar. The officers could be worse than the kids. Officers could be instigators of violence between boys or perpetrators of violence themselves. We learnt to adapt.

When Mr Neat bellowed every morning, I'd jump out of bed quickly, follow the order to make my bed with hospital corners, grab my towel and toothbrush then run out naked, except for the towel, into corridor and stand in a line as instructed. Our clothes were folded in neat piles in front of us. Our names were read out.

'Jones!'

'Here sir.'

'Blackburn!'

'Here sir.'

We no longer had first names.

'Fisher'

I hated that name and probably always will but it was tough luck because every kid and officer would call us Fisher from this day until we left.

We marched in line down to the ablutions block. Groups of eight or ten of us had two minute showers before the next group came in. Officers monitored and yelled the whole time.

'In.'

An officer walked past each cubicle, putting shampoo on each boy's head.

'Wash.'

'Rinse!'

'Out!'

We moved to the sinks and listened for, 'Teeth!'

That is what happened on a good day.

'Stand up but don't stand tall,' was an expression often used. It meant if someone puts his hand on you, you need to fire up.

Don't ever back down. But, don't strut around like you're tough either because that will make you a target. Try to fly under the radar.

I grew out of bed wetting around this age but there were a couple of incidents of it in Yasmar. It was a sure way to make yourself a target. When it happened to me the officer made me hold my wet sheet out in front of me like a sail, arms fully stretched as boys went past for their showers. There was no flying under even the highest of radars there. I copped so much flack over it.

If a kid woke at night needing to piss, the ablution area was a very scary place. The officers, or older boys on instructions from officers, would rape little boys. You could hear them screaming at night. It happened more on the senior side and I didn't witness any sexual abuse on junior side. I saw boys and officers going to ablutions together on the senior side and there were always rumours going around about what happened.

After morning showers we'd dress and go back to our dormitory. We went to school every day and I did all right there.

At last our day came to go to Gosford Court and I was nervous. I'd seen kids come back happy to be free but others had come back shattered or broken because they were about to start a sentence. To be honest I had come to terms with the fact I would definitely get a sentence. What would it be? I hoped that Michael would get off free, although he had two charges.

Escorts took us to court. One was a huge ex wrestler but they were all big burly blokes. Funny guys but scary too. The escorts held the back of our pants so we couldn't run away. They sat with us all day at court.

It looks better if you arrive at court with nice clothes, bought especially for the day by parents who stand beside you and declare that they love and support you. Michael and I had escorts beside us as we stood there wearing what we'd had on when we were arrested.

Barry was there all dressed up in nice clothes. He stood before the judge and made out that we were rotten, evil kids that a good, socially conscious citizen like him just could not control or tolerate. It made me angry as he stood there all holier than thou, making out that we were demon children. I wished we had been able to speak up about how he treated us.

We didn't get to tell our side of the story or to speak at all. We didn't run away without a very good reason. We hadn't run away because Barry treated us well and we didn't like being treated well! We hadn't run away to be criminals. We had run from a criminal to be safe.

My sentence was a General, four and a half months to three years in a home. They could hold me until I was eighteen if the officers thought I needed it. It would depend on my behaviour. Michael got a General term for running away but he got a longer sentence because he'd grabbed the money at Kincumber Hotel and run away. It was his first offence. I think Michael had learnt to live on his wits by living with our mother longer than I did. He had to fight hard for everything. Even Barry seemed to favour Tina and Samuel.

If what he had done back then happened today he would have been sent home with a warning or slap on the wrist. He was sentenced and I thought, *At least we'll be together.*

In my YACS records there are constant references to my two younger siblings being dad's favourites and Samuel our mum's. Now I felt sad for Tina who would be the sole brunt of all Mum's hatred and anger. I knew my mother had to take her frustration out on someone and it certainly wasn't going to be the golden child.

As we were led away from court I spat at my father. I hated and loathed him. I hated and loathed both my parents. I'm sure that made me look more like the demon child they made me out to be.

Michael and I were returned to Yasmar while the authorities worked out where to send us next. The powers that be had decided that separating brothers was better than keeping them together where they either got into trouble or were a power base. The authorities didn't understand that all my so called 'uncontrollable' behaviour had been motivated by my need to be with my siblings, especially Michael, my brother and my best mate.

In the senior side life was much harder. I was only thirteen or so, younger than most of the other kids on this side. The official eldest was sixteen but occasionally seventeen or eighteen year olds stayed. Some of them had beards and needed to shave. I had not even reached puberty yet.

I felt like an older brother being sent to live with criminal men. These were kids who'd been locked up before and some were set on a path that would take them to Mt Penang to prison. Those kids were institutionalized and career criminals. Once you were sixteen you were too old for Yasmar so the remand system sent you to Minda. Just like they had in Warrami, kids in Yasmar spoke about Daruk, Reiby and Mt Penang as being terrible places to serve time.

You had to do physical work instead of school work on the seniors side. One job was polishing the floors with a machine that I often joked should have been locked up itself for being uncontrollable. The machine and I were about the same size but I didn't have the strength behind me to manoeuvre it properly. It would throw me all over the hall way as I tried to control it and get the floor polished.

There was often lewd sexual talk and vicious assaults and beatings in this section that had been pretty well absent in the juniors.

We cleaned the ablutions and a whole lot of other stuff. It was punishment keeping us working all day, scrubbing the piss troughs and toilet bowls all day. We were treated harshly and reminded each day, 'You're not in for being good. Your parents don't want you. Society doesn't want you. You belong to the Queen and you stay here at her pleasure.'

One morning they got us up early.

'Transfer list boys. Listen carefully. Thornley, Nelson, Morella, Fisher ...'

As the officer read names, we were told where we would be transferred to to serve our time.

Chapter 6.
Daruk

We went into the dining room for breakfast. We ate with nervously twitching hands and anxious faces. We'd all heard the horror stories, now we were on our way to the venues where they occurred. Some of the kids broke down as they were taken to the bus. I showed no emotion. I was very afraid inside as they whisked us away to get ready for the bus. I was determined not to show my fear.

I am not sure if Michael was on this bus or not. One part of my memory is of him and others being there. I was so traumatized that day and my fear of the unknown stopped my memory of the bus ride being anything but blank, except that we drove through Rookwood Cemetery. We went on escort that day. One kid cried all the way there and for the rest of that day. They called the boy's parents to come and take him. How I wished I had someone to come and take me! But I mustn't cry.

I felt angry about that kid going home. It seemed so unfair that because he was so upset, he got to go free. I was angry because he had someone who cared for him. (As an adult I am pleased that he was sent home. He would never have survived.) He had a good family and I didn't. My Mother or father never gave a shit whether I was scared to tears or not.

I thought Michael and I were going to Reiby Juvenile Justice Centre. I'd heard there were girls there, older girls from sixteen to eighteen. I was looking forward to at least there being girls with us.

We drove through some gates and an officer announced, 'Here we are at Daruk gentlemen.'

We drove through the visiting area and the place looked like a nice little picnic spot with trees aligned around it. It was just a façade presented for visitors that hid the true horrors of Daruk boys home. We came closer to the business end of the place and there stood the Rec Hall on the right. The neat, well maintained flower beds suggested order and calm but they didn't fool me. I was just scared.

A large tarmac (the Deck) was bare but there were two big boys sitting outside the main office. The bus stopped and a man walked out of the office armed with a clip board. He called out the names of boys who were to get out here.

'Fisher, Glen.'

I looked at him but didn't dare ask, *Me? No, aren't I going to Reiby with my brother? I thought I was going to Reiby?*

I knew other kids on the bus were going to Reiby. Why can't I remember Michael being on this bus? I am sure we would have spoken to each other. My fear grew. I'm not going to Reiby. It's straight to Daruk for me.

I got off the bus then watched as it drove off. Totally alone. That's how I felt. Alone and terrified. I tried to take a look at the surroundings. Main Deck behind me, Office, huge grassed area. To my left were four houses in a row, with covered footpaths beside them. To my right was the Dining Hall and the sports hall.

All the stories I'd heard about Daruk ran through my head. I could hardly breathe. Kids get raped here at night by officers and inmates. Kids get beaten all the time. Were these stories true, half true, exaggerations? All I could do was wait to see. One of the kids on this escort was sobbing. He must have heard the stories too. *Toughen up soldier,* I thought. *Don't let them see you're terrified, lonely, unwanted.*

An older boy told us to sit on the Deck. We sat facing the sprawling grounds. The tearful boy was taken into the Office first.

A boy sitting beside me said casually, 'You can see which kid they'll be fucking tonight.'

My guts tied themselves in a knot. I didn't reply. I was too terrified.

I had flashbacks of Uncle Paul. Now I was old enough to know what had happened but not brave enough to speak about it. It would probably make me a target here if they knew. Being small and looking almost girlish was bad enough.

I considered running. I talked to one of the kids I was sitting with about it.

He said, 'Mate you won't get ten steps away.' I listened while he told me about the 'couriers.'

'Some of them older kids here, they work for the screws. Kids from Bunda house mostly. If you bolt they hafta chase ya. They let ya get away to the bush. Then they really chase you an' when they catch ya mate, they hurt you. They let ya get that far so no-one can see them beat ya and rape ya. No mate, not worth it. If the officers reckon ya need to be taught a lesson they get them Dingos to beat you up too.'

I looked over at the 'Dingos' or 'Couriers' sitting watching us. They wore brown jumpers and, to a skinny runt like me, they looked very big and probably much bigger than they were. They looked like young men, not boys.

'You been here before?' I asked the kid.

'Nah, but me brother has, hey. He told me lots. Said it's like the army.' He seemed relaxed compared to others who seemed agitated, like me. Kids off the bus were talking with each other. I'd had enough talking. I was now watching and wishing I could be anywhere but here.

There was movement from within the houses around the place. Boys poured out of them. All the boys from the first house, Bunda, wore brown clothes. They looked like men. As time went on I learnt that bigger and tougher kids were Bunda boys. They were more likely to get into fights and Bunda was the worst house to be in. Crabs (kids that play up all the time) were sent to Bunda to get beaten up or otherwise abused. The threat of being sent there was a good deterrent to bad behaviour at Daruk.

Kids came out of the house with military precision, marching out in single file to form a line of about five kids. Then another five to line up beside them and that continued until all forty or so had left the house. They stood in formation.

It was clever to send the Bunda boys out first because they were truly intimidating, somewhere between the army, prison and a movie. It felt surreal. I kept thinking of the boy who couldn't stop crying and what they reckoned would happen to him. I didn't know at this stage that he would get to go home. I could hardly breathe. I tried not to think of the rapist Uncle Paul and the pain and fear as his repulsive hand was held across my mouth, stopping me from screaming and almost suffocating me. I snapped back to the present day as boys came out of the next house.

These were Woollahra boys. They wore green and were called 'Chucks.' They were a little slow mentally or they were dangerous. Today we'd probably say kids with ADHD or mental health issues. There were a few kids in Woollahra who were sentenced for murder. One boy there had killed his parents and spoke about it graphically but as if he was just talking about making a sandwich.

All the houses gradually emptied in the same way. Kuma boys were next, dressed in pink. They were the runaways and general crime doers. Bradley was one I still remember. He had a stutter.

'What are you in for mate?' I asked him one time.

'C c c catching the train w w w w with with without a ticket, 'n runnin' away.' People often made fun of him. He was a little slow but I thought he had more smarts than kids gave him credit for.

Daru boys in blue came out next. These were the troublesome, rich kids who had no real reason to get a sentence.

At last all the boys were told to 'stand at ease' and we waited for roll call.

'Attention!' Everyone stood to attention.

'Hill?'

'Sir!' Hill replies loudly.

'Russell?'

'Sir.' And so on and on.

An officer shouted, 'Quick march. Left left left right left …'

As he shouted the boom of his voice went right through my body. It reminded me of American movies I'd seen where an officer would roar into the face of one of his men.

The boys marched with their arms swinging beside them, looking directly ahead and looking for all the world like an army platoon. They approach the Deck.

'Left wheel!' the officer roared.

Every boy put his left hand beside him, fist clenched and kept marching in a precise left turn. If it wasn't so frightening it would have been fascinating to watch. I thought they must do this a lot to do this so well.

'Company halt!'

Boom. Boom. The last two steps were like thunder.

'Right face.'

Everyone turned to his right stomping his left foot down hard. Some do it harder than others to be smart. Some are wearing boots and work clothes: grey shirts and their house jumpers. They all have crew cuts and are clean shaven.

It was an intimidating sight to see so many young men all facing me as I sat nervously on the deck.

Mr Webster, the Superintendent, came out of the office holding some papers.

'Company at ease!' he orders. The irony!

I didn't feel at ease at all. I didn't look up but I stole sideways glances at these young men. I couldn't believe there were so many bad kids in one place! It looked like a thousand to me. *Keep a low profile*, I told myself. There were a lot of kids here who were probably indigenous and there were a couple of European looking kids.

Us, the new arrivals, were told to sit on the veranda with the Couriers. Mr Webster addressed the crowd. Or should I say battalion?

Someone had tried to abscond the previous day and this was addressed by the Superintendent. He spoke about the loss of privileges the culprit would suffer. Mr Webster spoke about all sorts of things and he seemed very aggressive and angry. When he'd finished ranting an officer named Mr Holt took over. He was the officer in charge at Kuma house and he was, I would soon see, an arsehole. He was the Deputy Superintendent too and an abuser of children.

The boys marched from the Deck to the Dining Hall for breakfast. Each house had its own dining area in the vast room. Each area had six tables and ten places set at each. Breakfast was porridge and fried toast. I watch as groups marched to the dining hall.

For me, the first hour at Daruk was overwhelming. I kept looking at the long driveway we had driven in on and thinking about running away. I kept thinking, *I can't stay here. I can't do this.* All my senses were heightened. I could hear every sound, smell the freshly cut grass, see the whole place and hear everything that happened. Hyper vigilance. Fear of the unknown and of the known possibilities.

Suddenly Mr Webster's office door opens and the kid who still can't stop crying is taken into another room by a woman who must have been one of the house matrons. Each house had a matron.

The house I'd be going to was Kuma. The Matron was Matron Hayes who was the nastiest piece of slime on the planet. She loved the sound of her own voice, loved her power and made it her mission to make our transition from Yasmar to Daruk even scarier than it needed to be.

All morning I listened for a kind voice, some comfort from any one, to assure me that I'd be all right. The best I got was from the boy who told me not to run. The urge to run was almost overwhelming. If you run they beat or rape you in the bush. I never wanted to experience that pain again.

Each new kid had a talk with Mr Webster. I was taken in for my talk and Mr Webster began by reading my sentence.

'So, you have been sent to us because you are unable to live in society like normal people,' he says threateningly. 'You're a scumbag, worthless piece of shit. My job is to turn you from a piece of shit into someone able to live in society without stealing people's cars or breaking into people's houses.' That's the gist of what he was saying.

'Ever stolen a car Mr Fisher?' he asks.

'No Sir,' I reply sheepishly.

'I had some maggots steal my car once. They burnt it!' He glanced over my file. 'Hmm. Warrami, Yasmar. So you've already been a guest of Her Majesty?'

'Yes sir.'

He went on to explain the rules in Daruk. 'This is my home and we have no problems here. You can do easy time here or you can do hard time. The choice is yours.'

I could see his mouth moving, knew what he was saying but my head was still trying to come to grips with the size of the dingos and the horror stories kids had told me about this place.

Mr Webster concludes with, 'Just remember this Fisher. I can keep you here until you are eighteen years of age.' He pauses then roars, 'That depends on you boy!' I could see he enjoyed his power.

His speech seemed rehearsed and I could imagine him standing in front of his mirror practicing looking big and scary. It is easy to put fear into children. I was petrified. I wonder if he carried that much power when he was with adults.

'That's all for now,' Mr Webster says. 'If you have any problems you speak to the officer in charge of your house. That is Mr Holt.'

Mr Holt was another officer who loved to make children afraid. He had a nasty habit of being hands on with the kids and a rumour that he and other officers touched the kids surfaced often.

I left Webster's office and waited on the veranda until Matron Hayes came for me.

'Follow me,' she says coldly.

She took me and two other boys to Kuma with a Courier escorting us.

You can't have a matron alone with criminals like us.

When we reached 'our house' Matron Hayes spoke non-stop about how our beds had to be made, how our clothes had to be folded and so on and on and on. So many rules! We were taken into a storeroom and given sports, work and school clothes with shoes for each outfit, a belt, socks and underwear. Fantastic. I was in pink! I hated pink.

We were deloused, covered in scabies cream, nit cream and then we showered. There was no privacy.

Another kid in pink came in and taught us how to make our beds, hospital corners and all. If you didn't have the sheet folded over exactly the right distance and your bed rock hard, they'd strip it and you'd have to make it again and again until you got it perfect. Sometimes they flipped a coin onto the bed and if it bounced off, you'd got it right.

We were shown how to fold our clothes 'three boards square,' a measurement achieved by matching folds with three floor boards. Socks had to be individually folded, belts rolled a certain way. More and more rules for more and more things.

At last we put on our school clothes and were sent to lunch. We had been going since about five in the morning and there had been a lot to take in over the seven hours since. By lunchtime I was emotionally and physically exhausted.

Now the real hard part began, meeting the kids who were already living here. They just stared at us and said nothing. They interacted with each other but us new kids stayed invisible. You were not allowed to speak at the table other than to ask for someone to pass you stuff.

We were automatically put in 'Six Section.' One Section was for best behaved and Six Section was for the new kids and the bad kids. You could progress through Sections but I never got past Five Section. Six Section kids didn't get a little bed side radio, more food, better quality things or more privileges. At lunchtime extra food was handed out, starting at the officers' table and moving through Sections. Everyone could salivate and hope. Us kids in Six Section usually saw the plates empty before they got to us. The only days I got extras were Sundays when most kids had visitors and I didn't.

After lunch we were sent to school, a u shaped arrangement of demountable buildings. This was where we met the boys from other houses. I was put in the metal shop class. About half an hour in, everyone ran to the window. A car was coming in and suddenly a few kids ran out of the metalwork shop to the car, jumped in and the car took off out of Daruk.

I heard later that a guy named Brett was the driver and the car was probably stolen to get the kids out.

All of us were called out of school and lined up outside the ablutions area. As we stood there, kids told us new ones about Grogan. I didn't know if Grogan was just a story used to scare us or a true story. It seemed real enough to me, a boy susceptible to such possibilities, like the time Maureen had seen spirits and I thought I did too. Much later I found out that the story was true.

Grogan was a child who was in the home earlier. He decided to play a prank in the ablutions block. He stood on an upside down bin and put his head through the towel roll, the single circle of linen that rotates when you pull it. The bin slipped and his neck was broken. They reckoned that his ghost runs up and down the roofs at night. Some kids swear they've seen him when they're in the Boob (Isolation cell) or up going to the ablutions. I never saw him but thought about him the two times I went to the Boob.

Meanwhile the boys' escape was big talk for inmates. The officers were not happy.

At night time if you needed to go to the toilet you had to get out of bed, stand beside your bed then stamp your foot. The officer on duty would be sitting inside a glass room where he was safe from the kids but he could see what was going on in the dormitory.

One night I woke up badly needing to pee. I was so afraid I might wet the bed even though I was doing that a lot less now. I made sure I got up and stood beside my bed with enough time to get there. I'd seen other kids do this before. I stamped my foot and stood at attention waiting for the officer. He must have heard me but he wouldn't look up from the book he was reading. I stamped my foot again.

'Don't stamp again,' another kid whispered. At first I thought he was threatening me but he whispered, 'If you stamp more than once they make you wait. Or worse, they'll make you clean the ablutions for an hour.'

I stood there for about twenty minutes and this arsehole didn't look up at me once. After forever he decided to eyeball me and wave me to go.

I walked really fast to the toilet and as I walked I heard someone else stamp their foot. I thought he might be in for a long wait or that the officer might think it was me again and I'd be in trouble.

The relief of peeing at last! I turned around and standing right behind me was a really tall aboriginal boy. He would easily have been six feet tall. He was a gangly, odd looking kid. He had his penis out and he looked at me and said something along the lines of he wanted me to suck on his dick. What I wanted to do was run.

I tried but he grabbed me hard and threatened me. I was shocked at how strong he was, he was as big as an adult and equally as strong.

'Do what I tell you Maggot or I'll smash your head in.'

I stood there petrified. He looked so weird I thought he could easily smash my whole body in. I didn't want to do what he said. I was too afraid to even move. I tried to talk him around but he grabbed my hair, still long, and forced me to the ground. He tried to put his penis in my mouth but I wouldn't do it.

'Let go of me or I'll scream to the officer,' I said through clenched teeth.

He slapped me hard across the face and said, 'Yell and I'll bash you every single day you're here.'

I was stunned for a second. He grabbed my hair and tried again.

'I'll scream if you don't stop,' I said. 'I'm telling you, let go of me or I'll scream.' My voice was much louder now. He grabbed my head and held his hand over my mouth. Memories! I hoped I was capable of screaming this time.

'Shh! Be quiet,' he said. 'Okay, okay, okay. Just go back to bed. But if you tell anyone I'll fuck you up.' Meaning he would bash me.

I got past him as fast as I could and as I walked back to the dormitory I noticed the officer, Mr Bulliens, standing near the ablutions block. He must have seen the whole thing. I thought he'd ask me if I was okay or if something had happened. He could not possibly have missed seeing what had happened. He didn't utter a word.

Mr Bulliens walked over to the kid in the ablutions and I heard them talking quietly but I couldn't make out what they said. I got back to my bed, so scared. There was no way I was ever going to go to the toilet at night again.

I started to drift off to sleep when I heard a sound like a tussle and muffled moans. In the bed next to me was a boy who looked similar to me. The boy who had followed me to the toilet was raping him. There was a part of me that wanted to jump up and push him off but the rapist wasn't a boy. He was big enough to be a man. I couldn't take him on. I could hear his threats about not making a sound.

As I write this I wish I could say I was tough and got out and that I had helped that boy or had at least gone for help. I didn't do anything. I was a frightened little boy.

I had not even masturbated yet though I could hear most kids masturbating at night. They called it 'friggin it.' Kids use to yell, 'Bingo!' when they ejaculated. I hadn't reached that age where I was even wanting or thinking about sex. Had Uncle Paul stunted my development, I wondered? Or was I just developing slower than most?

After the rape finished the attacker got off, pulled up his pants and threw the blanket back up over the boy. He leaned over his victim and whispered fiercely, 'You say one word and I'll bash your fucking skull in.'

I lay there in terror while the kid sobbed. He sobbed so violently that the kid on the other side of him hissed, 'Shut the fuck up!'

I wanted and needed him to stop too because his sobbing was disturbing me, especially with all the other stuff grinding around in my head.

Eventually I fell asleep. I could never look at that kid again. I knew I'd let him down. Maybe if I'd stood up and brought it to the attention of the officers, I could have prevented it. I would have become a target, but it'd feel better to have behaved honourably. The guilt I felt contributes to my always defending people now.

Threats like those made to me and the victim could be carried out because other thugs like the rapist stuck together. It made each member of a clique more dangerous as each one was backed by the others.

The boy who was raped was moved to another bed in Section Five not long after this, probably to make way for a new kid. He was now closer to the kid who had raped him. I would often see them together and I know that he crossed into his bed many times.

The morning after that assault everyone knew what had happened in the dormitory. They kept teasing the kid but he didn't speak. I can't recall ever seeing him speak. He was now a target for anyone who wanted to rape him. He didn't fight them off. He was completely disempowered and vulnerable.

As I was making my bed that morning the victim came back into the dormitory carrying clean sheets. All of a sudden an awful hissing sound started. It was called 'Blowing sucks.' It was what boys did to a kid who was in trouble. There were many gestures and slang words we used in Daruk. Peeko Cat (don't stare), spastic, chuck, sucko, dag, slingo (someone was lying).

That hissing upset me. I didn't let anyone see but I felt so bad I hadn't defended that boy. There was no way the officer didn't know what had happened. I believe he knew and that he was complicit in it. I reckon that he told the rapist which bed I was in but he got it wrong. I can't be sure of that but I wonder.

I think if he had got me that night I might well have stabbed him in the Dining Hall. I'd decided that if anyone pushed me far enough that's what I'd do. I was always thinking about ways to hurt people who hurt me. I never did it but in my mind I was hurting everyone. I think that the most dangerous person is the one who is most afraid. Fear can make people do crazy things.

The only positive that I could see in that assault was that he didn't get me. Perhaps another is that it taught me, later in my life, to stand up to bullies. I never started fights but as soon as a bully picked on someone I'd bash into him. I didn't make a conscious decision to do that and someone helped me see that that was what I was doing, standing up for people. There would be many years though between this incident and that person who would defend the underdog.

I'd seen a kid in a fight very early on in my term who was beaten really badly and the officers didn't intervene. They just let the fight go on. That was their standard practice. They'd punish kids after a fight but, as many fights were instigated by officers, no-one broke them up. It was a savage culture. It was a frightening reality seeing how savage that fight was, and that no one came to the smaller kid's aid. I saw a few savage beatings in Daruk.

What annoys and hurts me now is that I was very capable of defending myself and others but I didn't recognize that yet. I was more afraid of the officers than the other kids most of the time. A couple of officers gave me a really hard time. Mr Bulliens was one and another was Mr Bush. I was regularly in trouble and would be made to march beside Mr Bush instead of in the line with the other kids.

How you were treated by other inmates and officers depended on your status. Your sentence, your fighting ability and who you knew. Officers thought they had the right to hit you or man handle you but they didn't seem to target high status kids. Runaways like me had no status and the officer I was most terrified of was Mr Holt. I won't go into ugly detail but he was as far as it's possible to be from a good officer bent on kindness and reform.

I hadn't proved myself yet and I had no confidence that I would if violence was needed. I hated violence. Kids boasted about the crimes they'd done either with others in Daruk or alone. I listened to them and I could walk up to anyone and have a conversation that would convince them that I was a car thief: get the car open, rip off the column, pull out the pin and bend it for the steering lock. I'd talk about the push rod or the slide hammer and whatever they needed to hear.

Yep, Daruk was a Criminal Training College where they taught you how to be a criminal.

Daruk taught me how to hate and resent authority. It instilled in me the idea that it's all about us versus them. The hatred for authority grew in me to the extent that I only had to see a copper and I was furious. This hatred and resentment grew. It applied to authorities and all adults.

Waking up at Daruk, I'd wonder where I was and then I'd remember and instantly feel sad. The lights would come on and the rituals began. Officers had their choice of wake up lines. There was the snakey one as well as a simple, 'Lights on' or 'Out of bed' or 'Rise and shine, Maggots.' If you didn't get out of bed fast enough you would be dragged out. This happened to me twice. I was always in trouble. It didn't take much for me to do something, anything or nothing wrong. I was in trouble for it.

Some kids in One and Two Sections were already up and gone. They worked in the kitchen and got up early to make breakfast. I was school age so I had to go to school. Apparently the year before I went to Daruk, the kids who were on work crews did 'Crow Shooting' all day, breaking rocks. I'm glad I wasn't there for that. The kid who I saw raped was young looking but he must have been older because he was in a work crew. I saw him putting work boots on and wondered how he'd go breaking rocks.

Most of the officers were bullies and if you were a target for inmates, you became a target for officers too and vice versa. If an officer took a disliking to you he would turn the kids against you by punishing them for things you did. If a fight broke out, there were a few officers who might break it up but there were those who walked away and others who would egg it on.

One morning I was making my bed. I was still a learner. Mr Bulliens yanked my sheet off and said, 'Make it again.' Mr Bulliens hated me and targeted me. He was the officer on duty the night of the rape. I had stared at him every time I saw him as if to say, I know what you did.

I remade my bed. Again it didn't pass inspection.

'Right,' Mr Bulliens bellows. 'All you maggots strip your beds! I can do this all day guys.' Everyone does as he's told.

Mr Bulliens says, 'Thank Fisher for this.'

Kids start in on me. 'Fuck you Fisher.' I became a target no matter how much I tried to stay under that radar.

There was a cook who they called Chef Nick but kids called him Gazoo too. The stories I heard about him made me glad I didn't work in the kitchen. His anger was legendary. If he knew you'd called him Gazoo, he threw knives at you. There were stories of him, Mr Holt and other officers raping kids. I had seen Mr Holt physically abuse kids many times. Officers would grab you by the ears or slap you up the side of the head and there seemed to be no limits on their behaviour. We were powerless.

'This isn't a holiday camp! You maggots are here because you don't know how to behave in normal society, so society has tasked us with the job of punishing you!'

As if we needed daily reminders!

One officer, Mr Bush, seemed to take a liking to me and he gave me and a few others special attention without there being a hint of his taking advantage of us. I think there was a lot of sexual activity at Daruk but I managed to avoid it.

During my first week at Daruk I got into a fight. A kid named

Andrew kept treading on my heels as we were marching to breakfast. I almost fell over every time he did it.

'Haircuts are good,' he kept saying as he marched. I still had long hair, though I'd soon get the dreaded crew cut. I was teased a lot about my hair that first week.

The more Andrew trod on me, the angrier I got. I turned around. 'Stop kicking my fucking feet,' I demanded.

He took a swing at me. Soon we were both throwing punches but Mr Bush broke it up pretty quickly. He grabbed me by the ear, bawled me out and made me march beside him. I was no fighter and I suppose it was a relief that he took action. Andrew and I both got UP (unprivileged). We had to stand under the TV and lost some privileges. Well, Andrew did but I hadn't accumulated any, except watching TV, so it was no big deal.

I didn't think much of TV in the seventies. It sucked. Hey Hey Hey It's Saturday or music shows were all that was ever on. I spent a lot of time under the TV.

I was ribbed about my long hair for a while but I liked my hair. It showed who I was. One day, early in my stay, kids who needed haircuts were lined up and I had no choice about it. I lined up too and got the compulsory crew cut. I hated it. It felt as if my identity had been stolen. I guess that was the point, to dehumanize and disempower us as individuals.

Kids used to get things from their parents on visits. They were usually bags of chips, lollies and other goodies. If you had parcels, being on UP meant you didn't get your parcels and you didn't advance in Sections. The rapist was in Five Section so I was quite happy staying in Six Section. I didn't get visits so that meant I also didn't get parcels. I just about took up permanent residency under that TV and my ear was constantly being grabbed by officers. They must have felt brave pushing the smallest kids around.

Visiting Day was the most important day of the week for most kids. Not having visitors had its upside. We got a great roast lunch! Most meals were dreadful so one good meal on Visiting

Day was some comfort for the unique loneliness I felt on Sundays. Each of those days was a painful reminder of how little my mum or dad cared. There was a small group of us and we played Chess or cards all day. My mum still lived in Mt Druitt which was only about twenty minutes drive from Daruk.

Every Sunday we all sat in our home waiting for a Courier to come and get us for a visitor. I always hoped that just once I would be called out. Yep, I waited and hoped every Sunday. It never happened.

After visits some of the kids came back very emotional and some would be all pumped up from their day with friends, family or girlfriends. I felt so envious. Those kids were allowed to bring back parcels that their parents had given them. One kid was Greek and he got bags of stuff every weekend. So many people came to see him and I wondered how a kid like that ever got into trouble and sent to Daruk. I knew it was wrong but I was extremely jealous.

The Greek boy would take other kids out on visits. He'd share his parcels with the cool or tough kids. He was a really nice boy who didn't have a mean bone in his body. He got on well with everyone. He might have shared with me except that I was always under the fucking TV, so the opportunity didn't arise.

Standing at ease under the TV and watching the other kids all sitting around eating lollies and chips, sharing with each other, was torture.

Anger was still building in me. I felt it every day but I kept it bottled up. I had a lot before Daruk but Daruk was pressing buttons to make it expand.

One day a miracle happened. I was in school and a call came that Fisher was to report to the Deck. As I got near I saw Henry, my mother's boyfriend, and my mother talking to Mr Webster. They turned up on a day that wasn't even a visiting day.

It blew my mind that I was allowed to go on day leave with them. As soon as I got near my mother I could smell alcohol. Henry drove us to a pub in Windsor where we stayed for couple of hours. Mum and Henry drank constantly. Mum played a song on the duke box. Some Days are Diamonds by John Denver. The words resonated with me.

'Some days are diamonds.
Some days are stone,
Some days the hard times
Won't leave you alone.'

That's how life felt to me. Though it should have said,

'Some days are diamonds.
Most days are stone
Why won't the hard times
Leave us kids alone.'

I'm not sure how long the visit lasted with Mum and Dick, drinking, listening to music, having fun, spilling beer all over the place, including on me. They were oblivious to the pain around them. Oblivious to the pain they caused others. Oblivious to the fact that others have hearts that hurt.

When other kids had come back to Daruk after visits they might be upset but I'd had no empathy. Now I understood. The impact is rough. I felt physically sick as we drove back into the grounds. As I moved from music in a pub to incarceration life felt very heavy.

For the whole day I'd been thinking, 'Run. Run rabbit. Run.' I could have taken off at any time that day but where would I go, unwanted as I was?

I had promised Mr Webster that I wouldn't run away so when the drunks dropped me off in the hell of Daruk, I had to resign myself to being there until I'd done my time.

After sitting on The Deck for some time Mr Holt arrived.

'Come with me,' he said.

Standard procedure when you came back was that they strip searched you to make sure you don't have a weapon, drugs or other contraband. Mr Holt smelt alcohol on me.

'You've been drinking!' he said accusingly.

'No sir. I don't drink.' I was angry. I couldn't stand even the smell of alcohol let alone drink it.

'No?' he asked aggressively. He took great pleasure at screaming in my face and roughing me up as he accused me of drinking.

'No sir. My parents took me to the pub and they drank but I didn't.'

Apparently that was a breach of the Daruk rules. My parents were fucking alcoholics so how could I have said I didn't want to go to the pub. For my crime I was escorted to the Boob (Isolation cell) by a Courier and an officer.

The Boob was at the back of Daruk near the ablutions area and it was usually occupied by the worst offenders. Most kids were terrified of it and I was no exception. It was a small room, very cold and at night it was terrifying.

There were rules about being in the boob. The duty officer gave me one blanket. He would come around every hour to check on me. I had to stand up as soon as I heard the door open and be standing at attention when he came in. Not being awake quickly could result in a beating or removal of your blanket or of your thin grey mattress.

The Boob was particularly hard for me. I was terrified of being alone in this small, cold place. My mind began to play tricks on me especially as I became more tired but not able to sleep. In the pitch black night I kept hearing noises and thinking it was Grogan's ghost. My mother had taunted me with a ghost story. She reckoned that a ghost touched us both on the shoulder once. My fear of the night had been fuelled by Mum, Maureen, the undead of movies I'd seen and by the Grogan story.

By the time they let me out twenty four hours later, I was jumping at shadows. I had to sit down with Mr Bush to see if I was all right. Every time he spoke I jumped out of my skin. He spoke gently to me which was so unlike Mr Bush who was always very loud and bullying. I think he could see that locking me up in the

Boob had a terrible effect on me. It took me days to get my shit together after that. I wondered whether officers on night duty did things to deliberately scare us or they told the Couriers to do it.

I had a second visit in the picnic area with my two youngest siblings. That day I looked at Samuel who I hated and thought how unfair it was to hate him. He didn't do much wrong really. Was it his fault that Mum loved him but she did not love the other three of us. He was treated like a king. The rest of us moved insignificantly in Samuel's world, only coming into focus when Mum needed a scapegoat or a punching bag.

I hadn't found that I had any particular skill yet. My chances to try out or train for anything were very limited. I was all right at singing, ballroom dancing, long distance running, squash, swimming and hurdles but I'd never excelled at anything.

In Daruk I surprised myself by picking up the game of Chess quickly and moving toward being the best chess player in our house. No-one could beat me. I was able to look at a Chess board and see five moves ahead. I was able to remember where every piece was and I knew what my opponent was going to do and what I needed to do. I worked out that people played in one of two ways: attackers or defenders.

I often think how my skills in Chess show intelligence and, had I been given a chance, I would have excelled at something. I played often when there was nothing else to do, on Sundays when other kids were on their visits and at night when we returned to our house.

Robert fancied himself a pretty good Chess player. He was able to beat everyone he played but he couldn't beat me. One day the kids were betting on us and I won.

Someone, begrudging a loss probably, goaded Robert. 'Bet you couldn't even beat Fisher in an arm wrestle!'

Next thing you know Robert and I were arm wrestling. I beat him! I won. Long arms came in useful for something. There was no time to celebrate though. As soon as I put his arm down he king hit me. It shocked me and gave me a flashback to my father hitting me without warning.

Something inside me snapped and I was having my second fight at Daruk. This one was different from the first one. I lost my shit and started swinging as hard and fast as I could in his direction. The anger of thirteen years of abuse and humiliation lunged through my fists. I wanted to hurt this gutless thug and badly.

I probably hit Robert ten times and he fell back onto the ground. An officer pulled me off him. If he hadn't I might not have stopped hitting him. I was still raging and I broke free from the officer. I picked up a chair and smashed it over Robert's head. *What! I've gone from silent to violent in seconds.*

I was going absolutely crazy. The officer wrestled me to the ground. The kids started chanting, 'Chuck, chuck, chuck.' Yes, I was in a temper tantrum and I couldn't control my anger. I'd never done this before and I hadn't recognized that I had all that bottled up inside.

It was back to the Boob for me. It was early in the day and I found it less scary this time. It took me two hours to calm down though. As night crept along I started to panic.

At dinner time my meal was brought. As soon as they opened the door I took off, trying to side step the officer and the Courier. I think the sudden burst of anger and the fear I was carrying made me much stronger than I really was. The Courier was twice my size and he and the officer had trouble holding me down.

I was flat on the floor with the Courier on top of me, whaling into me. I was screaming, 'Don't close the door! Don't close the door!' They eventually calmed me down and rather than putting me back into the Boob I was taken to The Deck.

The Courier waited with me and I was sure he'd make threats as soon as the officer had gone. He didn't! He was really nice to me. I think he respected that I had some fight in me.

'Where are you from mate?' he asked.

'Mt Druitt,' I said.

'It's scary in the Boob eh!' he said gently.

I didn't respond. I just sat there terrified of being sent back there. After a time I nodded in agreement.

We went on to have a conversation there on the Deck. I don't recall exactly what it was about but I appreciated his kindness.

He escorted me into the office where I was spoken to and told I'd be on seven days UP. Under the TV yet again. I would stay in Six Section. Nothing changed for me really. The one threat that was made that had an impact was, 'You'll never get out of Daruk if you chose to use violence as your language, son.'

This was in stark contrast to what we were being taught and shown at Daruk. Fight. That was the only way people respected you: meet violence with more aggressive violence.

I went back to the house and the other kids started chanting again. 'Chuck. Chuck. Chuck.'

Finally the officer pipes up, 'All right, that's enough.'

I took up residence under the TV again. I had to face them all as they watched the TV.

'Robert's gunna bash you tonight,' someone said.

'Huh! Let 'im try!' I said boldly. My 'chuck' had given me courage and a voice. I was answering them back. One of the bigger kids kept going on and on and I started to lose it again.

Suddenly Fred, a bigger kid, said loudly, 'Shut the fuck up! How tough are all of you? Fisher's younger than most of ya, smaller than most of ya but he's got more balls than the lot of ya put together. So just shut the fuck up.'

When Fred spoke, people listened. I didn't know why he stood up for me. Maybe he hated bullies too.

The bullying soon stopped and I was accepted by the other kids. I went from the kid everyone bullied to just another one of the boys. Although my fear of being hurt by other kids subsided I still lived in fear of the officers. I seemed to be in trouble all the time and the way they replied to my supposed bad behaviour was always by grabbing me by the ear or screaming into my face. Back under that TV.

On sports day we played cricket or footy with Mr Hiley. Mr Hiley bowled a full speed cricket ball at me once and it hit me right in the knee. He bowled me over in fact and I saw him laughing at me as I hit the ground hard. He thought it was hilarious. Soon my knee swelled up almost as big as a cricket ball and Mr Hiley thought that was amusing too.

One day when we were playing football with Mr Holt a kid got the ball and he kept on running and running into the bush. Two other kids seized the moment and took off too.

Two dingoes were called upon to chase them. They went one way after two kids and Mr Holt went the other way after the other kid. Mr Holt could run fast. I remember him sprinting past me and before the first boy got to the bush he crash tackled him.

'You boys sit together there and don't move,' Mr Holt said as he marched past us with this kid held by the ear. He didn't want anyone else taking off.

We sat there and saw Mr Holt beat the hell out of the kid he caught. He flung him about as if he was a dirty rag. He then frog marched the rag boy up to the Boob. Today I still get angry about that. What right did he have to hurt that kid? What right did any of them have?

One of the others who ran got away but the other was caught. The dingoes beat the hell out of him. He had two black eyes, his nose was bleeding and he had bruises all over his body. I saw the two boys after they got out of the boob. Seeing them reinforced the fact that these people could do anything they liked to us and there was nothing we could do. Surely they should have been accountable to someone for their actions.

Mr Holt used to say, 'You'll be here until you're eighteen Fisher. You can't even get past Six Section. You're a fucking crab!' I did get to Five Section once but only because new kids came in. Mr Holt often told me that by running away from home I proved myself to be a bad kid, a piece of shit who no-one wanted.

I still had the problem of jumping out of my skin at loud noises. If an officer yelled I'd jump and put my hands up around my head to protect myself. It made Daruk kids laugh, just like the kids at school had done. I had a habit of drifting off into long periods of thought which left me more susceptible to being startled.

At least the fight with Robert showed me that if someone attacked me, I'd be hurt less if I hit back. It sends out a warning too: I might be small and you may be able to beat me but I'm not backing down.

I started to turn being bullied around. I won't go as far as to say that it stopped but it happened less often as I came to understand that I could stand up for myself. I had discovered my resilience. I could choose to be a target or I could stand up to bullies. Or I could become a bully but it isn't in my nature.

Mr Bulliens, bully and smoker, would have a cigarette in the Rec Room then stub it out, leaving a bit of unburnt tobacco in the ashtray. Kids would snatch the bumpers and either finish smoking them or save the tobacco to roll into pages of the Bible to make their own cigarette.

One time I managed to collect a few bumpers although I didn't even smoke. I managed to get some bible paper and roll a smoke, thinking it would boost my popularity. Some kids were interested in my produce. They had a system for getting rid of cigarette smoke: blowing it directly into the loo. One kid had a way to light the cigarette so he went to the toilet first, smoked a few draws then left the cigarette on the floor for the next kid. I had my hand up to go, so I was next. I smoked about five draws then put the cigarette very carefully on the toilet roll bracket. The last guy went in for his turn. We didn't have the education that kids have today around smoking. I started young. Thought it was cool.

Suddenly Mr Bulliens got up, walked over to the ablutions and caught the kid with the smoke. He grabbed him and dragged him by his hair to where the rest of us were.

He yelled at us, 'I want all other boys involved with smoking to come to the front. Right now!' He paused and I wondered what I should do. 'Now!' He roared.

I came forward and another kid did too. UP again! I hated

Mr Bulliens. (And Mr Bush. And Mr Holt. And Mr Bran. And standing under that bloody TV).

A deterrent to bad behaviour worse than UP was the threat of being sent to Bunda. I think it was on the same day I got caught smoking, I was taken to see Mr Bran. The Bunda boys watched as I walked nervously over to him. Mr Bran was an older, gruff looking man. He was big and spoke rather loudly. Even Bunda boys were afraid of him so I wasn't looking forward to meeting him.

He started yelling at me in front of the Bunda boys. I did my best to stand tall as he whaled into me using his unique punishment that didn't look as if it hurt. It does. He flicked me in the middle of the forehead. It hurts and so does being humiliated in front of the Bunda kids.

'Mr Fisher, would you like to join us here in Bunda?'

Fuck no. Not that! I thought.

'Boys, how do you think he'll go here?'

The boys responded repulsively, mostly with sexual comments. Some said, 'We'll get him into line Mr Bran.'

I was sent back to my house Kuma and never went to Bunda.

I am not sure how long I was in Daruk but release day was usually a big day for most kids. Many knew the exact date they were going home but us runaways never knew when our time would be up.

I was called to Mr Webster's office one day out of the blue. I went into the foyer and my dad was standing there. I thought he must have come for a visit. I was taken into the office where Mr Holt and Mr Webster looked me up and down.

'You're going home today Fisher,' Mr Webster said dispassionately.

No goodbyes. Not that I had any real friends to say goodbye to. No lavish send off Just it's your time to leave so away you go.

Thank fuck that is over, was all I thought.

Mr Webster and Mr Holt made a speech about not coming back because next time it will be Bunda. That will be twice as hard, blah, blah blah. To the outsider looking in it might give the impression they were human and cared. They were deviants, abusers who relished their power.

Kids being released were given a property bag with their possessions in it and their name and a number on the outside. My bag had jeans and a t shirt and a pair of shoes and socks. It felt so good to put civilian clothes on again and leave the pink clothes of Kuma behind.

I was so grateful that my time was done. The only down side to being released was that I was going back to my father's place, a place I did not want to be.

It took some time to adjust to being free.

Chapter 7.
Dumped

Was I excited to be free and returning to live with my father Barry? Free? No, I wasn't excited. It was out of the pot and into the same old fire. I wondered how long I'd last before I ran away again.

It took some time for me to readjust to being out of Daruk. I would awaken early, make my bed the way we are shown in Daruk. I thought often about the kids in that place.

Dad had a new girlfriend, Dee, who didn't take a shine to me. One day we had an argument and she chased me with a broom. I don't think she caught me. There was an old water tank on our block but it was no longer used for water. It just sat empty on a timber stand. Dee told me to jump in and give the inside a clean out. I did as I was told and climbed in. Suddenly Dee came up and sat near the opening at the top of the tank, holding a piece of wood.

'Think you're gettin' out, do ya? Well, yer not,' she said. 'Nuh, you can stay there 'til yer father gets home.'

It was so hot in there! Dee obviously didn't have the brains to realise that although it was probably thirty degrees outside, inside the tank it must have got up into the forties. Not to mention it was dark and full of spiders. It was so hot that I had trouble breathing.

Lucky for me Barry came home and she let me out. If he hadn't come when he did this could have turned out far worse for me.

Dad's relationship with Dee didn't work out and she left. Soon he started seeing Judy from Wyong who had two sons that I got on well with. We all went to a disco one night and got blind drunk.

Pretty soon I found I couldn't handle being around my father so I decided to run away again.

I went to Kings Cross for a couple of days and stayed in squats with some other streets kids. Then one day I went by train to Campbelltown to see my brother Michael at Reiby, the juvenile detention place. When I turned up there they said Michael had been moved that day to another place in Campbelltown. I think it was a kind of halfway house where kids were helped to prepare for the outside world. So I ventured out to this other place to find him.

It was so good to see Michael again! He told me that some kid there had been bothering him. I was over bullies so I fronted up to this kid but I got kicked out before anything much happened. I believe that as a result of my behaviour, Michael was sent back to Reiby. I heard that a few years later and felt really bad. I hadn't gone there to cause trouble. I missed Michael and I wanted to know he was okay. I wanted him to know that I was waiting for him.

I didn't think it was smart to keep hanging at the Cross. It would only be a matter of time before I was arrested, charged with running away and again sent to Daruk. So, where to next?

I went to the Mt Druitt Youth and Community Services office and saw the welfare officer, Mr Hubble. I wanted to convince them that I was tired of being bashed and abused by my parents and I didn't want to keep running away and be sent to boys' homes. I had to make sure they understood that I was not going to either my mother's or my father's place to live. I'd ask them, beg if I needed to, to please help me.

Mr Hubble seemed to be genuinely concerned. I spent the rest of the day in his office as he tried to figure out where I could go.

'There's a family in Mt Druitt that takes kids in but they told me they won't take any more,' he said after a while. 'Pity, I think they might be perfect for you. I'll have to do some sweet talking to see if I can get them to take you.' Then he added a disturbing piece of news. 'They've just had one of the kids in their care die. They are pretty devastated and we're all still grieving.'

Well, if they are going to send me there it must be all right. It couldn't be worse than my drunkard mother or my abusive fathers.

'It's Mr Hubble from YACS here Mrs. Chambers,' he said over the phone. 'I have a young lad here who needs a placement. How would you feel about it?' By the end of the conversation Mrs. Chambers had agreed to meet with me, although she stated that I'd have to meet Mr Chambers and find out what he thought before the final decision could be made.

I knew I was a bit rough around the edges and I wore an ear-ring, smoked and acted like a street kid. What would I do if the Chambers didn't like the look of me?

We got a nice warm welcome from Mrs. Chambers at her house in Blackett. She was loud but nice. There seemed to be people everywhere in her house. She had her own three kids, two elderly men and her daughters' boyfriends. It was only a three bedroom house! The back room had two bunks where the old guys slept and one of the boyfriends slept there too.

Mr Chambers was a big man with a big voice and I was instantly scared of him. The first thing he said to me was, 'You have a choice, lose the fucking ear-ring or stop smoking? Which will it be?'

I took the ear-ring out and then he said, 'You look like girl with that ear ring.'

I was in! I was introduced to everyone, unfortunately as Fisher, not Glen. I hated the name Fisher and I hated being called by it. The Chambers became my foster parents. I soon learnt that here, barks were worse than bites. Mrs. Chambers seemed to really care about me.

'Call us Mum and Dad,' she said on my first day there. She made me feel welcome but she was the only person who did. I called her Mum and she was as close to a mother as I would ever get.

Mr Chambers was a good honest man who worked hard and took good care of his kids. I think he and the kids just didn't have the same passion for street kids as Mrs. Chambers did. I felt like a nuisance and I suspect that the kids resented me calling their parents Mum and Dad. Soon I found myself trying to win Mr Chambers' approval and respect. He was rather intimidating.

My bed was in the back bedroom. Mine was the bottom bunk and Daz had the top one. He talked a lot about liking sex with young girls. Larry told me he'd had sex with one of the girls who lived with the Chambers. Larry was in the other bottom bunk next to me.

I got an uncomfortable feeling with Larry. He was extra nice to me. I was asleep one night and I woke to Larry, the old creep, giving me oral sex. I jumped out of bed and went off my head at him. Mum Chambers got up after hearing all the commotion.

'Shh. Settle down Fisher! You'll wake Dad up and he's got to go to work at four.'

I screamed about what Larry had done. Mum moved me from that room for the night and to their youngest son's room where there were two beds.

I heard Mum and Dad talking later and I think Mum might have told Dad what Larry did because later I heard Dad and Larry having a very heated argument. Later I had to go back to the bunk room because new people had to be accommodated.

Larry worked at a factory driving a forklift and had a bad gambling problem. He spent the whole time I was there propositioning me for sex, offering me money and cigarettes. He was grooming me and my blood still boils when I think of it. I was an attractive young boy who looked a bit like a girl. Larry was a repulsive paedophile who I have since learnt had a prior conviction for raping a two year old child.

Mr Hubble never came to check on me. They did however arrange for me to have visits with my siblings. The Chambers family didn't do anything about the paedophile in their house. He was Mum's driver and helper in everything and it felt to me that he was more important to her than I was. I was a new kid and if I made too much of a commotion I may have to be moved on.

Apart from Larry pestering me, this was a really good home. There was so much food! I could go to the kitchen any time and eat whatever I wanted. I had never been allowed such luxury. We got really good meals too. I was fed so well that I ate more in that time than I'd eaten in the previous three years with either of my parents or in a home. I ate more for dinner each night than I'd eat in a week with my parents.

It took me ages to get used to being allowed to eat when I was hungry. If I was making a snack and someone came in, I'd stand still and wait to get into trouble. I was in trouble sometimes but not ever for eating.

Soon after I moved in it was Christmas. The youngest kid got so many presents from the family. The six year old was beside himself with happiness as he ripped paper off present after present. I hadn't expected any gifts and I remembered being a little envious watching him. The best present was a Pee Wee 50 from his eldest sister. He was loved by everyone, the right way, the way a family should be. I couldn't help thinking how nice it would be if our family was like this instead of Christmas being about drinking or my father's constant, spiteful mind games.

The Chambers' were a family who loved and cared about each other. I loved being there with my foster mum. I started to think that the others weren't that bad either. I hated Larry being there, always forcing me to be defensive but he was the only stain in that place. I had to make sure I was never alone with him.

I was really missing my siblings though, especially Michael. One afternoon Margaret and Dick turned up out the back, drunk. Mum was screaming at Mrs. Chambers, 'He is my son! Mine! He should be with me.' She raved on and on. I was so embarrassed and afraid.

The elder daughter jumped to my defense. 'Go home Margaret. He is staying here with us. Just leave him alone.' It felt good to have someone defend me.

That day they all got a better understanding of what I'd come from. My defender that day, Christine, slowly warmed to me and became nicer to me. She told me that she thought Margaret was crazy. There were other times when Margaret and Dick would arrive drunk and get out of the car screaming at us. Then they'd hop in the car and drive off as if nothing had happened.

Dad Chambers started taking me places like motor bike riding and we did things as a family too: playing footy, outings, picnics. I didn't go to school. I was fourteen years old and close enough to the legal leaving age. Two of the Chambers kids worked in the abattoir at Homebush and they helped me get a job there. I was proud to have a job and be responsible for earning my own living. I paid board to Mum and still had some of my wage left to spend how I liked.

After a while another boy came to live with us and Dad Chambers instantly connected with him. He didn't need to work for respect or approval. It just happened. That made me feel heavy, like a misfit. This kid was more into cars and motor bikes than I was.

All the same I felt that these people were my family. They let my brothers and my sister come over one night and we played poker for money as we did every Friday night. I cheated to try to win money for Michael.

'Uh Fisher, were you just cheating?' Dad Chambers asked.

'No Dad,' I lied.

Next thing I know I was hit and I fell on the floor! Just like Barry! Now I had a tangible reason to be frightened of Mr Chambers. He was trying to toughen me up I think or make me more honest. I hold no animosity towards him. He didn't know about Barry. At least with Dad Chambers I knew he had a reason to hit me. It wasn't a random rage attack or something he'd been brewing on for months.

I went to visit my siblings at Margaret's house in Bidwell one day. She was actually sober and she seemed to be acting nice. Maybe I saw what I wanted to see if I am being honest.

'Me and Henry are moving away,' she told me.

'Where to?' I asked, surprised and slightly uneasy.

'Whyalla, South Australia. Henry's got a job in BHP. He'll be earning big money and they've got us a place to move into when we get there,' she said.

I found it hard to get a grip on this. We live in Mt Druitt. We don't go off to live in other states!

'We really want you to come too,' Mum said.

Me? What do I say? Do? Think?

'We've both stopped drinking,' she announced. 'Come with us. We really want the family back, all together.'

Hadn't she dumped me on Barry, and gone on with her life without giving a dam how or where I was? Hadn't she ignored me for all the time I'd been away from Mt Druitt? Hadn't she despised and hurt me when I lived with her? Hadn't held the threat over me every day that she would have me sent back to a home?

I was happy now and I was getting my act together more than I ever had before. The people I lived with accepted me and liked me and taught me good things. I was safe, apart from Larry. My foster parents were not insane, not drinkers, not cruel. Dad Chambers had accepted me. Maybe not connected with me as he had with the other kid, but I was stable and without any violence. No-one ever got drunk, well, except Dad Chamber's on Christmas day when he made his own Tia Maria and had a couple too many. Yes, they yelled a lot but it was piss and wind and after a while I leant this was just their way of communicating.

It took me two days to work up the courage to tell Mum Chambers that Margaret had asked me to come home.

'Fuck Fisher. Come on. You're not seriously thinking of going to live with a pair of drunks! What's the matter with you? Don't you know when you're well off!' She teased and berated me all day. 'Fisher wants to go back to his mother.'

Today when I speak to my foster parents they still call me Fisher. Not Glen . I hate being called Fisher. It's my father's name.

She told Dad and the whole family went off their heads at me. I was sitting in the lounge room and they just tore shreds off me. 'Fisher wants to go back to live with the drunks. Not happy here with a nice family. Off to the drunks he goes.'

The more they gave me a hard time, the more determined I was now to dig my heels in and refuse to deny the possibility that I would go.

If they had said what they thought in a loving way and spoken to me civilly it would have made a huge difference to my thinking about it. If they had sat with me and discussed why it was stupid to go back, I would have listened. Instead they made me feel like a fool. I knew my parents were a violent bunch of drunks. But my siblings were not and I loved them and missed them. No matter what I said to the Chambers, they didn't get it. They behaved as if I wasn't grateful to them, or that I preferred drunks. To be with my siblings was still my most urgent wish, as strong as it had been all my life. No one seemed to get that. Why?

I felt torn. I really loved my foster family, especially Mum Chambers. I wanted to stay. Although I had only been there a short time I grew to really care about them. I loved my brothers and sister too and I really wanted to be with them. Had I known what awaited me in Whyalla, I would have concreted my feet to Mum Chamber's floor. Who knows what my life might have been if I'd stayed. The fear that my siblings would move to South Australia, hundreds of miles away, without me, was more than I could bear.

For two days straight the Chambers family went off at me telling me how stupid it would be to go. There was that word again. Stupid.

'I've decided to go home,' I told them. I was being stubborn about my choice and the more they teased and insulted me the more stubborn I was.

Yes, I've made the right choice, I kept telling myself.

Mum Chambers got really upset and that hurt me terribly. I never wanted to hurt her. She'd been so good to me treating me almost like her own son.

Then came the ultimatum that defined my future. Dad

Chambers said, 'If you go home to your mother Fisher, you can never come back here.'

Never! They will never know how much that hurt and confused me. It was a fucked up thing to say to a very frightened and confused kid. It set me up for fear and insecurity. I had no way back if things went wrong. Why not say, 'Look we don't think it'll work because … But you give it a go and when or if it fails, come back to us. We'll still love you.' That's what I would say to a frightened child.

For the next couple of days Dad Chambers spent all his time with the other kid working on a motor cycle and all sorts of things. He ignored me. He'd walk past me without even speaking. I needed his comfort. I needed to hear him say things would work out. I felt so hurt by his extra attention to Ben. They all kept pointing out to me how upset Dad was by my choice.

It was time to pack my bags. This time I had two of them. I had clothes and things of my own.

Rather than hug me and say, 'Well, good luck mate and if all else fails come home,' I was sent away with what seemed like a 'Fuck off then' attitude. It hurt.

I said goodbye to each person individually. Every one of them ignored me except Larry and Mum Chambers who were driving me.

Mum Chambers tried one more time to talk me out of going. Larry did too and then he drove me with Mum Chambers to my mother's place in Bidwell.

I was fourteen then and aching to be with my siblings. I didn't have an adult's perspective on anything and I didn't know how to process the love they'd given me with the love I had for Michael, Tina and Sam. I was so susceptible to my mother's lies. What had I done for the rest of the Chambers family to turn on me and for Dad to say I could never come back? If they had been separated from their own siblings I challenge them to see what choice they would have made. They'd kept talking about my mother but I kept thinking about three other kids who I loved.

The drive to Bidwell took about five minutes and I was very nervous and scared remembering the floggings, the insults and the cutting of my fingers. It got harder the closer we got to Margaret's. Ringing loudly in my ears was Dad Chambers' ultimatum. 'If you go home to your mother Fisher, you can never come back here.' I couldn't have turned back even if I wanted too.

I cried again as I said goodbye to Mum Chambers. 'I'm sorry,' I said and she cried about the parting too. I wish I could have brought my three siblings to stay at her place.

What mood would Margaret be in today? I dared to hope she really had stopped drinking. What if we could be a happy family in South Australia?

Mum Chambers and Larry watched me walk gingerly towards the door. I turned to take one more look at Mum Chambers. My heart ached but I had to keep going. I knocked on the door, gave one last wave to Mum Chambers then Tina opened the door.

We went inside together. There was no welcome home. My mother, well guess what? My mother was drunk. My hope faded away and I recognized the stupidity, the futility of trusting her. She'd be whacking me, hurting me and calling me names again in no time flat.

'Aah the prodigal son returns,' she slurred, staggering to her feet. 'Little Lord fucking Font Roy. Come in your majesty,' she sneered and gave a little bow that nearly toppled her over except that the flourish of her unsteady hand seemed to save her.

I wanted to run, to chase the car down the road, to beg and plead with them to take me back. Mum Chambers and Paedo Larry might still be outside. It's not too late. Run. Run fast.

'If you go home to your mother Fisher, you can never come back here.'

I was trapped. How could I have conned myself into believing things would be different? By wanting it so badly. That's how. I wanted a day like that day at court where Mum and Dad had both been nice for a whole day. I wanted my mother to run to me, hug me and say, 'You're home. Thank goodness.' She might even say, 'I love you.'

Sorry. Wrong movie. No happy ending here.

I walked out the door and I could see Mum Chambers and Larry still sitting in the car watching. I wanted to run back, say, 'Please forgive me. I've made a terrible mistake.' Pride, fear and that sentence from Dad Chambers fixed my feet to the ground.

My real mother must have got worried because she screamed, 'Get the fuck in the door now. Now!'

I was trembling as I closed the door. I hoped Mum Chambers and Larry could hear and come and rescue me. The initial joy of seeing Michael, Tina and even Samuel was suffocated by fear.

Later in my life Mum Chambers told me she'd heard what went down. Why not get the police then or DOCS or Dad Chambers to rescue me. Get anyone to come and help me. I guess I made my bed and now I had to lie in it.

Margaret kept yelling at me so much that I didn't even know what she was saying anymore. A ranting drunk who beats children should be in prison. (She was sick and didn't know it. Later she was diagnosed with mental health issues: schizophrenia and personality disorder.) She grabbed my bags from me as I stood silent and very still. I was stuck on the spot, unable to speak or move. Trying to come to grips with the fact that I'd made a horrendous mistake. A hideous, destructive error of judgment.

Mum ripped my stuff out of the bags. She found my money and mumbled, 'Need that for petrol,' and shoved it in her pocket.

The next day when she'd sobered up Mum told me, 'That money you had, we need it for petrol to Whyalla but we'll pay you back.'

Yeah right! Course you will. You can't afford to feed us properly. You piss every cent up a wall.

The two weeks prior to leaving was bloody hard work. Mum and Henry got drunk at the Bidwell Clock every day and most days we sat outside from opening time to closing. Sometimes they'd give us twenty cents each to get into Emerton pools or other times we sat outside the pub all day with a dollars' worth of chips to share between us for a meal.

I had been eating properly at my foster parents' place. At Bidwell there was nothing in the fridge or cupboards. Until I'd lived with the Chambers, I'd thought an empty fridge was normal. I was so hungry now and I found myself wishing I could just run in front of a bus. I could run away again and end at Daruk in Bunda House. A terrifying thought.

Poor Tina was now Mum and Dick's slave. Any food that was cooked was cooked by Tina. Any rooms that were clean had been scrubbed by Tina. Any washing that was drying or ironing … and so on. That poor kid did everything a parent was supposed to do. Cook, wash clothes, ironing, cleaning. What's more she had also become Mum's new target for insults and abuse. All three of us were in her sights now. Only the Golden Child escaped insult or abuse. I cannot recall seeing our mother say one bad word to him, ever. I could handle it when the two so called adults treated me like shit but it was so hard to see her treating Tina and Michael badly. I thought it was my job, as big brother, to protect them. But, to be honest, I was still very afraid of Margaret and Dick too now. Their potential to send me to Daruk was the main weapon in her arsenal and so I dared not challenge her.

Some nights we kids would be home alone and late at night I'd hear the car drive into the driveway. I'd lie in bed scared to death listening for whatever noise they made. Sometimes they would get out of the car screaming at each other and at other times they'd be laughing with other people they'd brought home from the pub in party mode. Most times they were fighting and many of those times my mother would come up stairs and drag me out of bed. I'd have to stand in front of them all including Rowena, Dick's cousin who lived around the corner.

'See this bloody cunt,' Margaret would shriek. 'Thought he was fuckin' better than us and buggered off to live with a foster family!'

I am better than both of them but I couldn't see it then. As a child the only right I had was to shut the fuck up and cop the abuse.

My mother would keep screaming, 'Are you better than me, little cunt? Are you? Who do you think you are? You're nothing but a little cunt, a pissy, little skinny little wet the bed fucking grub.'

Writing this brings up some horrible dark feelings in me. What did I do to make her hate me? I thought everyone hated me as a child.

I started wetting the bed again regularly at Margaret's. At the Chambers place it only happened once or twice and they didn't make a fuss. They would say, 'Don't worry Fisher. Just put your sheets in the washing machine and hang them out later.' I didn't wet the bed after a month of living there. Even at Daruk I think it was only once. At mum's I was so scared of wetting the bed, I'd dream I was going to the toilet and then wet the bed.

Tina did too. Mum never called her by her name. She called her 'Fanny Adams.' Barry called her Floss. Mum called Tina all sorts of other nasty names and, of course, she had some for Michael too.

She often said to Michael, 'You're not my kid. They gave me the wrong bloody kid at the hospital.' Her words could be as hurtful as her fists.

Michael seemed to handle things differently from me. I felt rejected and smothered but Mike seemed to let it wash over him.

Before we went to South Australia Margaret and Henry took us to Glenbrook for a picnic with Uncle Paul Paedophile and his family. I stayed as far away from Paul as I could. Henry and Mum got drunk. I went off bush walking for a while and then walked back to where they were picnicking. No-one was there. Could they have gone without me? Am I in the right place?

I stood there in the mountains alone, distraught. It was about eight at night when a ranger came through and saw me.

'What are you doing here mate? Is everything all right?' He

drove me all the way back to Bidwell. They claimed that they thought I was in the other car.

Pretty soon Michael and I were helping Henry pack the trailer then Mum, Henry, us four kids and the sausage dog piled into the old HR Holden heading to Whyalla.

Henry drove and I'm sure we stopped at every pub from Sydney to South Australia. We stopped at caravan parks in Wilcannia and Nyngan. While they did the pubs us kids sat in the hot car with the dog. How we didn't end up dead from dehydration, starvation or a drunk driver accident is anybody's guess. Eventually we arrived at Whyalla and stopped at a caravan park. I was excited to finally be there, to see our new house and somewhere deep down I hoped life might improve. The place looked beautiful. Grapes seem to be growing at the front of every house and it was a very pretty looking town.

'We have to stay here in the caravan for a while,' Mum said. 'Just 'til we get the house sorted out.'

Lie number one: Henry had a job to go to. He didn't have a job at BHP or anywhere else. Lie number 2: there is a house waiting for us. There wasn't even a Housing Commission home ready for us.

All we had was a place at the caravan park but when Mum realised how much it would cost to stay there, she decided it was too much. There was no room in the caravan for me so my bed was the back seat of the car. Margaret set about making life hard for Michael and me, her scapegoats. The cost of keeping us was more than the extra she got on her Child Endowment benefit.

On our very first night Mum and Henry had a fight. Henry hit Mum. Michael and I stood up to him. He was about our height but much heavier and older. We gave him a run for his money. Mum called the police about us boys but they didn't do anything. Henry could hit mum but we were not allowed to defend her! When the police arrived Margaret kept screaming and raving at them. The officers looked stunned and confused and they looked at us with some sympathy. They seemed disgusted at our mother's behaviour and Henry's too. I think they recognized that both her sons were sober little boys and she was a drunken, raving fruit cake.

Next day Mum took me to the hospital and demanded that I be seen by a psychiatrist. When that was over the doctor said, 'This child is quite normal lady. I wonder whether you have considered that your alcohol abuse might be the problem.'

He went on and what he meant was, *You are the problem lady. Stop getting pissed and being violent in front of your kids. Glen's response to your partner's abuse was absolutely normal. He's fourteen years old and if he wants to defend his mother, his mother should be grateful. Although I must point out that it is obviously not his responsibility to keep you safe.*

She didn't like that. She told me to get out. Not sure where she thought I should go in a new town, in a state we had never been to.

She took the other three kids to the local school to register them. I went to the school and got Michael and we ran away together. Well, is it running away when you're not wanted and you have nowhere to go? I think Mum kicked Michael out too. Only three weeks before, I was living with the Chambers and now I'm homeless again.

We began hanging around the streets of Whyalla and there was a group of Skinheads we got to know pretty well. They recruited young kids like us. We went to a Skinhead called Boogie and he helped us that night.

The next day we went to Social Security. We told the lady at the counter, 'Our mother kicked us out and we haven't got anywhere to go.' She took down our names and ages. She looked surprised by the ages we told her, probably because we were so small.

'Where's your father,' she asked. We told her and she said, 'Well, let's see if we can get your fares back to Sydney somehow. You could see the social worker who's familiar with your case back at Mt Druitt.'

She shuffled through papers but she couldn't find a way to help. 'Hmm. You don't know anyone in South Australia?'

She thought for a while then decided that the best she could do for now was to take us home with her. I'm sure she wasn't supposed to do this but she saw a need that she could fill, so she did it. That night I filled her in on the last couple of months. She wasn't used to this kind of story.

She talked to Mum but Mum wanted nothing to do with us. She rang Barry next.

'He's agreed to pay your fare back to Sydney. You leave tomorrow morning. Isn't that good?'

Going back to live with Barry? No, it's not good, but we didn't say so.

Michael and I were put on the bus to Sydney the next day and we got off at Oxford Street late in the afternoon. It had been a long trip and although they stopped numerous times for meals and snacks, we had no money so we were starving hungry when we reached Sydney. It was almost torture watching everyone get off the bus, have a huge feed while we stayed on the bus with our hollow guts.

Barry was waiting for us and as we got closer, I got more nervous. How will he receive me?

I found myself remembering all times I'd been abandoned. That feeling started a relentless journey to the front of my consciousness again. Dad went straight to Michael and greeted him warmly. He didn't seem to see me.

'I'm so hungry,' Michael said.

'Well, let's get something to eat,' Dad said and they began to walk off. I followed. Dad turned to me and said, 'Where are you going?'

I was confused! I just stared at him. He said, 'You're not coming with me. You're on your own.'

My gut twisted. I looked at Michael as if to say, *You coming with me mate? Or are you going with him?* Michael went with Dad. I can't blame him. He was so young, vulnerable and starving. I sat there with no bags, clothes or money. A few weeks ago I'd had a safe place to stay but now, at the bus terminal at Oxford Street, Sydney, I have nothing.

Stunned and confused. What the fuck I am supposed to do? Where do I go? I was really angry with them both but it wasn't Mike's fault that our father was a complete bastard. It hurt that my brother had left but in hindsight I'm glad he didn't stay.

I was really hungry, really tired and mentally exhausted. I sat for about an hour with my head in my hands no doubt looking dejected. A man came and sat down beside me.

'You all right mate?' he asked.

A little naïve, I tell him what has happened. I tell him about Daruk, the foster parents, the ultimatum, going home, the last few months.

'Let me buy you something to eat,' he said.

He seemed friendly so I began to trust him. His name was Terry and he told me he was a butcher. He took me for a walk down Oxford Street and he bought me some food. He laughed as he said, 'Look, I have a place not far from here. You can come and stay with me if you need somewhere until you figure out what you want to do. Can't have young people on the streets now, can we!'

At first I trusted him and I was relieved to have a kind man with a good listening ear who offered to give me a safe place to stay. As we walked to his place I got an odd feeling and I started to wonder why this man would offer to help me. Warning bells were going off inside me and it must have shown.

He tried to reassure me. 'You'll be fine. I've helped other kids just like you. Don't worry.'

The bad feeling intensified. Terry the butcher was much bigger than me, well over six feet tall, and he must have weighed about a hundred and fifteen kilos. We started going up a stair case in Taylor Square.

I suddenly said, 'I'm going to go to my foster parents place.' He got annoyed and tried to talk me around. He had opened the door to his apartment and as I tried to leave he grabbed me hard by my arm. I broke free almost stumbling as I ran down Oxford Street towards Central Station. He was yelling after me and he was really angry.

What's scariest about this is that if I had gone with him, no-one would have looked for me or reported me missing. My foster family thought I was with Margaret. Margaret thought I was with Barry and Barry didn't give a fuck where I was.

I caught the late train back to Mt Druitt and walked for an hour to my foster parents' house. As I walked I was going over different things I should say. I thought I'd be greeted with humiliation and I was afraid. I was so afraid that I considered walking back to Mt Druitt station.

Rusty the dog would be in the backyard and I was afraid he would bark and alert them that I was back before I could explain.

I sat on the front verandah for what felt like hours. It was very early in the morning. I was freezing, my stomach ached with hunger and I was trying to muster the courage to knock. I sat there quietly knowing that Mr Chambers always left early in the morning by the back door and out to his car.

'If you go home to your mother Fisher, you can never come back here.' I needed to wait for him to go to work.

At around seven Rachael's boyfriend came out the front and saw me. He said loudly, 'Guess who the fuck is standing at the door! Master Fisher has graced us with his presence.' He seemed to be welcoming but was he worried about how I'd be received? I think he was. 'Come in mate. Don't just fucking stand there shivering.'

I walked inside nervously. Rachael was the next to see me. 'What the fuck are you doing here?' she asked, surprised to see me.

Mum Chambers came out from the kitchen and she was more receptive than the others. I sat on the lounge and I told her what had happened, I was very emotional.

'What's that bruise on your arm? Did your mother do that?' she asked.

'No, that's where a man tried to grab me,' I said, not wanting to go into details that might stop me being accepted back here.

No-one else said anything. Mum prepared food for me while she listened to me. That was so like her. I scoffed the food down gratefully. I was really afraid. I didn't want to be here. Well, I did but I knew I couldn't stay.

'Can I come and stay again?' I asked Mum sheepishly without much hope of a yes.

'I think you can but you know I'll have to talk to Dad.'

It was a nervous wait that day. The others all had their bit to say. Larry, of course, was happy to see me and was the only one who talked with me besides Mum. As much as I hated Larry, I was accepting of any care shown to me by anyone, especially that day. I felt defeated. So much so that even the attention of Larry was welcoming.

When Dad Chambers finally got home after work he saw me and walked straight past me. I guessed someone had told him before he got to the house. He didn't even look at me. Ben had been working in the shed and I felt extremely jealous. It was like my jealousy of Samuel. Why was Ben more the kind of kid Dad Chambers liked? He knew a bit about cars, bikes and sports. It hurt me deeply that he was accepted so readily. The other people there liked him too and part of me felt that they deliberately showed that preference just to hurt me. That might not have been true but that was how I thought. It seemed as if the only people on the planet who showed me attention were disgusting paedophiles. Well, there was Mum Chambers, the only decent person who cared.

Dad Chambers walked straight into his bedroom and Mum followed him. I heard loud voices as they argued and I heard Mum say, 'He is my son and I am not letting him go again.' I think Mum even said she loved me. I know she cared for me a lot. She understood me. She and Larry probably remembered the hostile reception I got when I went back to Margaret.

No-one spoke to me that night and Mum slept on the lounge. My foster parents argued all the time but never to the point where they couldn't sleep together. Their arguments were usually funny but this one was far from funny. Especially knowing I was the cause of it.

Dad Chambers went to work the next day and all day Mum said to anyone and no-one was, 'He can just fuck off that husband of mine. Fisher is staying here and that is that.'

Christine came to me and I thought she would really give me a hard time, but she said, 'Why don't you come and stay with Nathan and I?'

They had got engaged recently and had their own place. Christine had never been particularly fond of me but she was not intentionally mean either. She just had an abrupt manner and I was so sensitive that I took even minor criticism as rejection or an attack. I felt I was always defending myself, even to Mum. I never did anything right. If I washed up, I did it wrong. If I hung out clothes I was too slow, or too lazy.

I felt uncomfortable with Christine's offer so I asked her, 'Can you help me look for a place like a refuge or something?'

She did help me. We saw one refuge that was located in Kings Cross. We rang them and they agreed to take me. Christine took me to Mt Druitt station and gave me five dollars. She drove off as soon as she had dropped me at the station with barely a word.

I was now officially on my own and from then on there would be no real mum, real dad, foster parents or any one to care for me. I would care for myself.

Chapter 8.
Kings Cross

No one wanted me. It's a horrible feeling. I felt afraid knowing I was completely on my own but I also felt a sense of liberation. I would no longer be controlled by my drunkard mother or my self-centred, abusive father. I knew that F.A.C.S. (Dept. Family and Community Services) could send me back to Daruk if they found out I was away from foster care.

Could I make my own way? Tread my own path in a world of my choosing? I was fifteen, way too young to be on the streets alone and way too naive about the potential dangers of Kings Cross. It was exactly the wrong place for a vulnerable, homeless kid like me. All I saw were bright lights and the many different and amazing looking people. I imagined I'd be part of the bustle and fun. I pressed down my sense of rejection and set off to explore my place to belong.

I walked past the neon Coca-Cola sign, over the bridge and I found the refuge that Christine had phoned. It was called the Opposition Youth Refuge and it was directly opposite the old Kings Cross Fire Station. The front door looked a hundred years old. So old was the building that at first glance it could be mistaken for a squat. A few street kids sat outside.

The Opposition took in people from fourteen to twenty one years old. It was run by the Sydney City Mission. I wasn't afraid to walk in. I knew if I didn't like the place I could just leave. I was my own boss. No one was going to tell me what to do any more.

I passed a group of girls in the doorway. Interesting! A lady counsellor greeted me at the door and took me in and as we went through the main room I thought how run down and basic things were. Kids were just hanging out all over the place. In the back room I was asked to give my details. I'm not sure what name or age I gave but I pretended I was someone else. Nearly every kid who arrived at the refuge gave a false name and age because they had run away from home. No-one actually tried to find out if you were a run away or on the run from police. After the paperwork was done the lady showed me around.

There were kids everywhere. Blankets were used as doors and each room housed four or five people. You could see the Hyatt Hotel and the Coca-Cola sign and the main street from the doorway. Close by were the Waxworks, El Alamein Fountain, Sweethearts, Alice's Restaurant and Les Girls. Some of these landmarks and other well known venues are still there today.

Many different types of people of different ages stayed at the refuge. There were addicts, runaways, Punks, Skin Heads, street workers, kids covered in tattoos, often 'boob' tats – done in institutions, and some had professional ones.

Although I was fifteen, I looked about eleven. So, many of the girls adopted me straight away. Indigenous Yvonne and Ada tried to mother me, as did an older Aboriginal girl whose boyfriend was called Slime. They were streetwise and particularly wanted to take me under their wings. Some of the older boys tried to educate me too. I remember one kid named Phil, a street wise kid who had long hair and did martial arts as well as working as a male prostitute.

Staff in the refuge warned me of the dangers of the Cross but I was not listening. I was sick of being told what to do. No-one would tell me what to do or hurt me anymore. I was angry and I thought I knew everything I needed to know.

I was shown where my bed was and then left to wander the halls. I was taken into a room by a group of girls aged in their late teens. They talked about sex and drugs, asked me if I was a virgin and even offered to have sex with me. They seemed to think it would be funny to be the first one to have sex with this little boy. They didn't know that I had my own sex history and none of it was good. It was more a joke to them, corrupting this kid who seemed willing to do anything to fit in. They asked me questions like, You ever smoked pot? Ever got drunk? Hoping for acceptance I pretended I had done it all.

Some of the older boys saw me as someone they could train to help them do crimes. Lots of people see young kids in dollar signs or as someone to corrupt. You're a commodity. However, many people were sincere in trying to educate me and protect me. The hard part was determining who was who. I wasn't listening to anyone and, in hindsight, this might have been a good thing. Had I been dumb I could have been educated by anyone to do anything as many new arrivals to the streets were. I so wanted to impress, to be accepted, to belong.

I didn't bother to take the time to get to know any of the kids in The Opposition refuge. I met a few but a little voice inside me said, 'Go to the streets.' The streets drew me out like a magnet. I wanted to walk around and see this place for myself and by myself. Michael and I had come here once as kids to the Snooker Room to play the Kiss machine. I'd been here a few times but never for more than twenty four hours. Now I lived here.

At the first opportunity I was off outside. It didn't take me long to venture down the main street with lights in my eyes and no clue of the filthy underbelly that lurked beneath the brightly lit facade. I had to be back at the refuge by eight thirty at night. The rules were that if you had booked a bed and didn't get back by then, you'd be locked out for the night, left you in the street. That was said to me by staff and by other kids repeatedly on my first day. It didn't really frighten me. I felt fearless and I was clueless.

I was full of excitement about the many wonderful and odd looking people in the streets. My eyes darted left and right as I saw things I had never seen before. Red lights shone outside some places, street workers on every corner, some jokingly propositioning me.

'Up for a bit of fun tonight honey?' they'd ask.

I'd say, 'No thanks.' And they would laugh at the obvious.

I passed strip clubs, night spots, pinball parlours, sex shops, tattoo parlours, street workers, homeless men, alcoholics, street kids. Motor bikes littered the street. My eyes just couldn't absorb all the many wonders there were to see.

I did a slow lap of the main street and as I passed the entrance to the station I noticed a man selling watches from a suitcase. Sam. He and I get to know each other later on. I kept walking, past a pinball parlour called Slots, the Snooker Room, Pink Panther Club opposite the Pink Pussycat. So much colour, light and noise.

There were lots of kids in the pinball parlour and a little further along I came to the Snooker Room. I went up the stairs and inside there was a mixture of dodgy looking men and a lot of young people all playing snooker. A few of the young people glanced at me but I quickly took off back down the stairs, not ready yet to try and make friends or engage with anyone. There was still so much more exploring to do. I passed the arcade opposite Roslyn Street where Alice's Restaurant and Les Girls were. On my left I saw the famous Wax Works and yet another pinball parlour.

I crossed over to the Bourbon and Beef restaurant, a fountain and a seedy looking park where very young boys hung out. The place was only dimly lit. I walked innocently through the park unaware that men watched me furtively. The kids sat idly, some alone, others in small groups.

I left the park and made my way back down the other side of the street. It seemed that every second place was a strip club or pinball parlour. In between were shops like Woolworths or small businesses that seemed to only be open during the day.

I kept walking and as I got close to the Chicken Spot opposite the Goldfish Bowl, two boys of about seventeen, weird looking and possibly twins, approached me. With them was a very dark, stocky African man holding a brown paper bag with a bottle in it. He was obviously drunk. I recognized a drunk easily. He had a very rich accent and could hardly speak English.

'Hey there mate,' one of the twins said. After a short conversation I sensed something sinister in the looks they were giving each other and in the over the top kindness they were showing me. Something was wrong.

'Do you smoke pot?' one of them asked while the other one whispered with the African man who they said was Nigerian. He kept looking at me and it felt menacing.

'Come home and have a cone with us,' they said aggressively.

I had tried pot but never really took to drugs or grog. I smoked cigarettes but not enough for it to matter if I had any. I smoked O.P.'s, Other People's, cigarettes. I hardly ever had money to buy them and didn't have the street smarts to accumulate funds yet.

The twins kept trying to get me to go with them. They wanted to know where I was from, where I lived, and so on. I imagine they were desperately trying to get me more comfortable with them. It seemed as if the Nigerian man was demanding that they get me to go home with them for cones and drinks. His demeanour scared me and I wasn't going anywhere with him. Eventually I walked away from them.

Something about the Snooker Room drew me back. I walked in again and this time I took a longer look at the many faces staring back at me.

As I walked back down the stairs two men were walking up and they called me over. I ignored them but one grabbed my shoulder and spun me around. I was shocked and ready to give him a piece of my mind when one of them said, 'Mate, we're from the police. Come here.'

They didn't show a badge but, from my past experience of police, I could sense they were the real deal. They were Kings Cross detectives. I already hated police. I didn't trust them. They were all bullies. I learnt later that Kings Cross Police were classic bullies. They were part of the fabric of corruption in Kings Cross.

I looked into one man's eyes and ask, nervously, 'Yeah, what?

'What's your name son?'

'Glen.'

'And where are you from Glen?'

They didn't write anything down in a little book like most coppers did.

'What are you doing in the Cross?' he asked arrogantly.

'Just stayin' in the Op,' I replied with a hint of cheek.

'You're at the refuge? Then fuck off back to the refuge.' I looked at him as if to challenge him telling me I had to leave. I had made a decision no one was telling me what to do any more. Then he roared, 'Now!' I complied with his orders.

I would see one of these two coppers many times over the next few years but tonight I listened to them. I gave them a smart ass look as I walked away making a bee line for the refuge. I wasn't sure if F.A.C.S. or other police were looking for me as I was now a runaway.

As I got near the Coke sign I was grabbed from behind and it was one of the twins I'd met only fifteen minutes earlier. The Nigerian man was still with them.

The one who had grabbed me said, 'We're heading off now to have a smoke and we got some alcohol too. We're going to have a party. What do you drink? What do you smoke?'

I still felt there was something very creepy about them.

'Come over to our place and party with us,' they demanded.

The Nigerian man called out for a taxi and when it pulls up beside us, they try to muscle me in.

'Come on mate. Let's go,' they insist.

'Look, I have to go back to the refuge.'

They still wouldn't take no for an answer and despite alarm bells going off in me, I came so close to going with them that night. I was trying to fit in here at the Cross.

Lost in space, Danger Will Robinson! Danger!

My wits were the only way out of this.

'Ok, look. I'll come but I have to go back to the refuge, tell them I won't be back or they'll keep all my stuff.' Of course I had no stuff. I owned nothing. I was getting less clueless by the minute as I paid attention to my gut feelings. The more aggressive and demanding they got the more I sensed these were not people I wanted to go with. One of the twins told the Nigerian, 'He's coming with us. He's just going to the refuge first.'

Fortunately he thought that was all right and waved the taxi away.

I dashed to the refuge and they followed me a short distance behind. If I had gone with them anything could have happened. I could have been raped or murdered. I don't know what their intentions were but later I heard from a man who knew them that the three of them were gay, that the twins were having sex with the man. He liked to get young boys, tie them up and rape them.

I met him on and off a couple of times over the years in all sorts of situations which I will talk about later. Something about him always reeked of extreme danger. The twins disappeared not long after I met them that night. I don't know if they left the Cross or went to prison. The man disappeared for some time too but resurfaced many years later, a heroin addict.

Some years later I was told a really dreadful story from another street kid about something he did. He told me the Nigerian man took a kid to a hotel room, tied him up and bound his hands behind his back. He tied the boy's legs to a bed and raped him repeatedly for over five days as he got more and more drunk. He did other horrible and demeaning things too. I told the kid to report him to the police but the kid laughed. 'The cops here are worse than him,' he said. Another lesson I had yet to learn.

I got to the refuge and the three of them stood on the corner watching me go inside. Once I was safe inside I didn't think too much about what had happened. I let it go, determined to see what other adventures would be waiting tomorrow.

I feel now that I had dodged another bullet. That was twice in a few days. Terry the butcher then the twins and their mate.

The room I had at the refuge was shared by four other kids. Next morning I got up before the others, didn't wait for breakfast and I dashed out to explore again. Many of the refuge kids hung about in little cliques at the refuge all day but I was drawn to the streets and had no interest in sitting around inside. It was as if the streets were calling out to me. I felt that if I didn't get out there, I'd miss out on something. Talk about curiosity killed the cat!

Once again I headed down the main street to see what or who was about. I wasn't afraid to talk to anyone or to go into any building. I must have looked so out of place, being young but looking even younger, curious as hell, just walking in and out of everywhere.

The Cross was so different in the day time, especially in the morning from eight o'clock to around ten. There were people walking to work, kids walking to school and a remnant from the night before, people who had been in clubs all night. And, of course, the usual addicts, local street people and the like who seemed to be there day and night.

Drunks who were sleeping in shop fronts or on benches were moved on as shops started to open. Still one or two ladies would be working but the red lights had gone out. Street cleaners were clearing away the rubbish of the night before.

It looked more like a normal town in the day time except for the strip clubs, sex shops and the occasional bad looking person. They looked at me as I darted here and there trying to take the whole place in. I honestly had never felt as free as I did in those first few weeks. I spoke to everyone who would talk to me and that was pretty much everyone. I was so young, no threat to anyone so people were only too happy to have a chat.

As I walked beside the Pink Pussycat I saw pictures of the strippers who danced inside. I was astounded to see a male stripper I recognized. It was Carl, a friend of my father's who had lived in Wiseman's Ferry with his wife Ruby when I was younger. They lived near the water in a caravan and they had a huge shed nearby. Carl had a pet snake. He would take us on bushwalks down a majestic pathway that led to the river where we swam. There'd be Barry, Maureen and all us kids and Carl and Ruby. We'd stay for a night at their place. All the adults slept in the caravan and the kids slept outside. Given what I know about my dad now and about Carl, I have to wonder what the relationship was between the four of them.

When I saw Carl's photo I asked the doorman, 'Is Carl in there now?'

As we spoke at the door a man and woman who were mud wrestlers walked inside.

Then I saw Carl walking in behind them.

'Carl? It's me. Glen.'

As soon as I told him who I was he was he said, 'Little Glen? Barry's son?'

'Yeah, that's me,' I replied, excited that I knew someone.

'Well! If you ever need anything just you let me know.'

Carl introduced me to Peter, the manager of the Pink Pussy Cat. Later in my time at the Cross, Peter spent ages trying to get me to go with him. He liked little boys and I seemed to fit the bill.

I kept moving around the streets meeting everyone who was local when one day I met Tommy who was a tough Fijian kid from the inner city. We instantly became good friends. Tommy was street wise. He was bigger than me but still fairly small compared with most Fijians.

Tommy was about fifteen years old. We talked for a while and then we decided to head up the main street to the Snooker Room and the pinball parlours where most other kids hung out. Tommy introduced me to a lot of street kids and addicts, pretty much every local we came across.

I also met two Aboriginal girls, Jayjay and Kelly. Jayjay was a tough, no shit person who could fight like a man. She wasn't like Margaret my mother though. Jayjay was like a mother to us younger kids even though she was a heroin addict. Many of the older girls mothered me or saw me as a little brother, someone to protect. Some people saw me as someone to exploit but in Tommy I had a strong ally. I looked up to him.

Kelly, Jayjay's friend, was very attractive. Hot actually. I developed a huge crush on her but to her I was just a little kid. She was interested in men, not a little boy.

Tommy, Kelly and Jayjay would be my first real friends in the Cross. Every day was like an adventure. I met so many people that I can't actually remember how early on I met these three but it was pretty soon after I arrived.

It didn't take me long to be accepted by them. Faces came and went in the Cross but there was always the core group. Some kids came, acted tough and tried to push their way in but they weren't accepted. I was a timid kid at first rather than a raging bull and I think that was a big advantage.

Some of the older kids started lecturing me.

'Why are you on the streets?'

'Kings Cross is no place for little children. Go home.'

'Go where?' I'd ask. 'I can take care of myself.'

It wasn't so much the locals who questioned me. People who visited the Cross did. Every weekend when I was out late at night people used to walk past me and say, 'Go home little man. Where is your Mummy?'

I knew where my mother was but she didn't want me there.

Many people who lived in the Cross were unusual. Despite them being addicts, dealers and the like, they took me under their wings. Many times they would help me in different ways. They would give me food, make sure I had a place to sleep and protect me from people who were a threat. To this day I have not met more genuine people than the good ones I knew there. They were outcasts, rejected by family and society but in the Cross your weirdness made you unique but not a pariah.

Another guy I met was Scar Faced Ray. I think his real name was Paul but that didn't matter. Scar Faced Ray was older than me and he was known to be a street fighter, a rough guy who took no shit from anyone.

'Anyone ever hurts you kid, just tell me and I'll sort it out,' he told me.

He told everyone on the streets I was his brother and today there are still people who think he was my older brother. He died from a brain aneurism a few years down the track, but he comes up many times in my story. He was someone that most people knew not to mess with and a friendly bloke to those who knew him.

Very early after my arriving at the Cross I was sitting up near the park on a little wall next to Slots Amusements. I needed to go to the toilet so I asked the other kids where to go. Ray said, 'There is a toilet right there in the main park.' I walked into the toilets and outside men stood around watching me. I went into the cubicle sat down as I needed to take a crap. As I sat there through a hole in the wall a man's penis came through the wall.

I stood up and screamed out, 'You dirty prick!'

I had no idea that this was where men met to have sex. I took off like a bat out of hell and was rather animated as I returned to the group. Someone asked me what had happened and I started to explain.

Ray said, 'Show me who it was, kiddo.'

I obediently followed Ray back to the toilets and pointed out the sicko who had done it. Ray grabbed the bloke and beat the absolute hell out of him. I remember the sound of each thump, how ferocious Ray was. I thought he was never going to stop beating him. The man fell down as Ray boots into him, blow after blow. Screaming, 'That was my little brother you sick fuck!' I remember feeling very afraid as Ray beat the man. I thought he was going to kill him.

Sometime later I saw an ambulance arrive and the man was upright, walking and covered in blood. It was a terrible reminder of just how violent this place was. It showed me another side of the man I admired. If I had known Ray was going to do what he did I would have never pointed the sicko out.

Big Al and Chad were doormen at the Love Machine, a strip club. I met and became friends with them too, especially Chad. They were possibly two of the most violent men I would meet but both were loved and respected by the street kids. They looked after the younger people of the Cross. Chad and I shared a love for dance. Barry had forced me to go to ballroom and disco dance classes when I was at Yattalunga. I didn't like ballroom. When I came across break dancing and funk I loved them. Chad had also done disco and we were both pretty good at it.

It was common for me to bust out in a little dance wherever I went. I could barely hold a conversation without practicing moves of either martial arts or dance. Break dancing was hitting the streets and I was teaching myself.

When we first met, Tommy asked, 'Where do you live?'

'At the Op.' I replied. Although I had been staying at all sorts of places most often I was at the refuge.

'Fuck that mate,' Tommy said and he took me to an old abandoned hotel that was being pulled down. A lot of kids were staying there. Most street people lived here or in another squat called Manning Street. There were so many squats back then and I would go from one to another. Some were in The Rocks and others were in the city, Darlinghurst, Woolloomooloo and Kings Cross.

Manning Street was a rundown old convent and you had to climb under a fence to get into it. It was a haven for drug users and alcoholics and a dangerous place to go alone if you were not from the streets. It was so spooky and big and there had been many deaths from overdoses there. I didn't like going to Manning Street alone even after I became known as a Cross kid. A young girl called Ada died there soon after I arrived in the Cross from an overdose.

People died all the time as heroin was abundant and cheap. I had trouble understanding drug use. Jayjay used every day. Why? She was a top chick when she had her gear but don't get in her way when she didn't. Although I'd grown up with alcoholism I didn't understand how addiction worked.

When Tommy and I got to the squat we went into a room that my three friends shared. There were a couple of single shabby old mattresses on the floor, crates made up as tables and a couple of candles. A bong sat in the middle of the room. Graffiti decorated the walls as it was customary to tag whatever room you stayed in. It didn't take long for Tommy and I to mark our names up on the wall. I liked to draw so I was always drawing on the walls too. It added to the character.

I really looked up to Tommy. He was street wise and he had an infectious laugh and a really good sense of humour. I felt safe with him and he was my best friend. He saw I was small and vulnerable and he acted like a big brother. I was grateful. I'd seen a lot with my mother and in the homes but when it came to the streets of Kings Cross I didn't have a clue. Being friends with Tommy made me friends with everyone in a short time.

When I'd lived with the Chambers in Mt Druitt, predator Larry called me Cockroach.

'You got a nickname?' Tommy asked one day.

'Aah. I used to get called Cockroach,' I told him. I never mentioned how I hated the bastard who called me that and I hated the name.

'Righto. Let's call ya Roach then. That all right?'

From then on I was either Glen or Roach. No more 'Fisher' as I'd been called in homes or foster care. Certainly not any of the names my mother called me. I made a conscious effort to never reveal my surname to anyone.

'How come yer called that?' kids would ask.

'I used to break into places. I was so small I could get into anything.' There was an element of truth to that, just not the breaking in part.

I didn't want to tell them it was a pet name given to me by a pervert. Remembering him still creeps me out. One of many predators I'd meet over the next five years.

Sleep had been a problem for me for a long time. I was afraid of what might happen if I gave in to it. I had wet the bed every night and I'd had night terrors. Now I was scared that if I wet the bed in the squat I'd be ridiculed. I needn't have worried because I never wet the bed. Not once. No trauma to fuel anxiety here and no Margaret or Barry. No-one ever said I talked in my sleep and I never woke up terrified in the squats.

This was my time to try new things and it was about this time I began smoking pot and getting drunk sometimes. I'd tried pot before but now it became almost a routine. If someone had a bit I'd share a cone. Then all I wanted to do was eat.

As Tommy and I sat in the squat one day, Kelly and Jayjay

came in. Jayjay got out a spoon and a syringe and started heating up some pink powder. She squeezed lemon into it. I watched her tie a rope around her arm to get the veins up. Then I watched as she drew blood back like a doctor and injected the drugs into her arm. She dropped the rope and sat there nodding off. She looked so peaceful! I was absolutely fascinated with the process. It should have been a warning for me but I just wasn't aware of the insidious spell Jayjay's using cast on me.

I kept asking her questions.

'Why do you use? What does it do to you?'

'HEY ! this is stuff for grownups kiddo. You ever use, I'll beat ya senseless. Got it?' she replied angrily. Then returned to her stupor.

Tommy hated drugs, especially heroin, so that was my stance too. What my hero believed in, I believed in.

I slept in the bed next to Kelly some nights, cuddling up to her but not knowing how to make the next move. I had not even reached puberty yet and I was overwhelmed by her being much older and more developed than I was. I think she loved the attention from me anyway. Everywhere we went she had men propositioning her. She let me cuddle up to her and she knew about the crush I had. I doubt she ever intended getting with me, the child. I think she just liked that I was attracted to her. She led me on a little but I was like a little brother to both the girls.

A down side to looking young was that the police would often spot me. Each time they approached me and asked for me my details, they'd write it all down in their black books. Some would warn me or even threaten me to leave the Cross. No, I was staying and that was that. Once they knew who I was they left me alone but that took a while.

Tommy and I were walking back to Kings Cross from Central Station one day. We passed a petrol station and a kid about my age, in light blue overalls, was working on something in the engine bay. He looked up and our eyes made contact.

'What the fuck are you looking at?' he challenged.

Tommy said to me, 'Don't take that shit from him bro!'

I wanted Tommy's approval and I wanted him to know I wasn't weak. I'd never stood up for myself as a kid but I'd learned a thing or two in the homes. I was not really a fighter. Well, there seemed to be a fight brewing now and I was in the middle of it. I gave Blue Overalls a bit of lip. He didn't like it so he came over to me and we did a bit of push and shove.

'Smash 'im Roach,' said Tommy. He seemed to believe I could!

Blue Overalls kept coming at me, trying to hit me. I stood with my arms in front of me like I was a prize fighter but inside my heart was beating about a thousand times faster than it should. What had I got myself into? As Blue Overalls advanced I threw my arm out and back, out and back. On the third stroke I landed a punch on his nose, more due to my arms being longer than his than my being able to fight. Blue Overalls backed off.

Instead of admitting defeat, he ran off to his brother who was working under the bonnet of another other car. We hadn't noticed him. The brother was much older and bigger than Tommy. As soon as he got wind of what had happened he was gunning for us.

'Come here you little pricks!' he yelled.

Laughing, we run off. They decide to chase us so we took off giving cheek as we left.

We ran through the back streets of Central, through Oxford Street and ended up down near St Vincent's Hospital. It felt like we ran for fifteen minutes and we probably did. Blue Overalls and his brother weren't gaining on us but they weren't giving up either. So we got past the hospital and ran through a laneway beside a butcher shop. We turned left on Liverpool Street then right on to Darlinghurst Road. Surely we'd lost them by now. No, they were still after us! We kept running to the Cross where we became much more brave and bold.

'Come on then mate? You're on our turf now! Have a go!' We taunted.

The big brother looked around, taking in his surroundings. Tommy and I kept taunting while we tried to catch our breath. I was thinking about what I'd done too. *I hit someone! See that Uncle Aaron, Barry, Margaret, all of you!*

It wasn't really intentional but I made his nose bleed. I'd been concentrating on protecting myself but I landed a punch! A lucky punch but I did it. I, Glen, Roach, stood up and defended myself. The longer I was at the Cross the more courage I would get.

If those two had dared to take up Tommy's challenge, an army of street kids would have come from everywhere. Our loyalty to each other was strong and reliable. Anyone who came to the Cross and messed with any local, took on every local or they made sure the fight was fair.

Retreat was the best option for the brothers and they took it. Blue Overalls seemed very disappointed. We didn't venture down near the petrol station for at least a few weeks.

Another change in me was that I became increasingly desensitized to violence. I had always been afraid of it and I loathed it but as I saw so much in the Cross, it almost felt normal to me. I had grown up with violence so it was always normal but only when I was the victim. I still wasn't a violent or aggressive person and I still didn't like violence. If fights happened on the streets with other kids I was always the one trying to break it up. But every night there were vicious fights, especially with doormen and sailors or groups of men who came to get drunk and start savage fights on the main street. They always ended badly.

Kings Cross kids looked after each other. *I belong here,* I told myself. Kings Cross was my home. Like an addict, I couldn't go too long without my fix of being on the streets. If I was off the street for even a few hours I would have to drift back down just to see who was around, sit with the locals and listen to all the crazy shit that people did.

I woke up one morning and walked down Main Street as I did most mornings. Tommy wasn't there so I went off to look for him and to scab some coins from someone for breakfast. I ran into a prostitute who we called Sammy and she gave me five dollars. That wasn't all though. She taught me a way to use five dollars to eat well and feel full for quite a while.

On Sammy's advice I bought two bananas, a carton of custard, a buttered roll and a small carton of milk. I put one banana on the roll, broke the other up and stuck it in the custard. I drank the carton of milk. Sammy was right. I had a few bob left so I was even able to play my favourite pinball machine, the Kiss one.

Street kids liked to sit on the wall just outside a pinball parlour called Slots on Maclay Street. It was about eleven in the morning when I decided to go inside and play a pinball machine. I was sometimes able to win free games on this one.

A bloke walked in and came straight over to me, the only kid there at the time. He put a couple of coins on my machine. This usually let you know that that person wanted to play the machine when you finished

As I played the guy said, 'Are you winning mate?'

I replied proudly, 'Of course I am.'

He laughed and started up a conversation with me. His name was Derrick. He asked if we could play doubles. I was popping free games and had credits in the machine so as he went to put his coins in, I took them from him and stuck them in my pocket. We didn't need them. I pressed Two Players when I'd finished my game.

I was about fifteen and he was older than me, maybe twenty five, but seemed pretty cool. He seemed to talk the talk and he bragged that he sold pot and was well known in Kings Cross. He told me he ran a shop in an arcade on Main Street called The Erotic Boutique. It was a sex shop but I had not connected the dots at this point. I was more interested in my game. I listened to him when he said he knew lots of people, that he sold pot for Gentleman Bob who was some big wig at the Cross.

Pot was a currency and although I wasn't a regular user, getting my hands on a supply would make me more popular with other kids especially with Kelly who I still had this big crush on.

152

'You win,' Derrick said when we finished. 'Are you hungry?' he asked. 'How about we get something to eat. My shout.'

He took to me to the Astoria Cafe, a cheap restaurant at top end of the main street. Derrick paid for us both.

After that we went to his place and he gave me a few cones. I fell asleep and when I woke up, the next day, I was on the lounge with a blanket over me. He hadn't touched me or led me to believe he was anything but a cool guy. I didn't have an inbuilt alarm system about the kind of men who hung around pinball parlour's trawling for kids for specific purposes.

I saw twenty dollars on the table and a few cones for me to smoke.

He'd left a note that said, 'Glen I am at work,' and he'd written the name and address of his shop on it. 'Get yourself some food.'

I took the money and the cones and went looking for Tommy. When I found him I told him about what had happened. We went to the squat and we smoked the cones with Kelly, Jayjay and others. Tommy and I went out for munchies then and played pinball for ages using Derrick's money.

Later that day I talked Tommy into coming with me to the shop where Derrick worked. We worked out that Gentleman Bob's shop was a sex shop that also sold pot.

Derrick was busy with customers buying pot as well as kiddy porn when we arrived. Kiddy porn was a big industry in Kings Cross. Still a child myself, it didn't register with me that this was wrong. I didn't see the harm in it. It would be many years later I would come to see how repulsive and criminal it is. What should have been a red flag was that the porn was kept under a table and that most of the men who came in, middle aged or elderly men, all asked for it specifically.

No-one had ever treated me like a grown up before but Derrick did. I was allowed to sit behind the counter, even serve people. This made me feel special and important. In hindsight I see it as a very clever way of procuring me. He was predatory and he was grooming me.

I wanted so much to be treated as an adult, to have somewhere safe to go, to be protected, respected and to have close friends. Derrick offered three of these. At first I thought he was going to give me all of those things. I wasn't conscious of my needs then but looking back I see it clearly.

Tommy wasn't impressed with Derrick or the sex shop so he left pretty much straight away. Derrick spent the day telling me about things in the shop. He sold pot from home and the shop.

He started showing me sex movies that began with guys and girls, then guys having sex, which I told him was gross, then he even showed me some porn with young people having sex. He told me I could be a movie star too. I took it all as a bit of a laugh. I didn't realise that I was firmly in the sights of a predator.

After work he took me for a meal again then we went back to his place where we drank piss and smoked pot. I fell asleep again and this time when I awoke he was giving me oral sex. I went off my head and I hit him. I slapped him across the head and yelled at him. I was so angry. I was dreaming about sex and awoke to this dirty maggot having his way! It felt like every time I fell asleep there'd be some bastard man trying to have sex with me. Why did men keep hunting me?

Derrick kept saying, 'Look, I'm sorry mate. All right. I'm sorry. Sorry.' Then he said, 'But you were enjoying it.'

I had an erection. I was so embarrassed. Back then I'd get an erection if the wind changed! It confused me all that day as I thought about what had happened.

As I was getting dressed ready to storm out of there, Derrick said, 'I'm gay Glen. I like little boys.' I kept dressing, didn't want to know. But he tried to draw me in. 'I can look after you. I care for you. I'll give you money, food, a place to live. I can protect you.'

I stormed out and headed for the squat. I was too embarrassed to tell anyone what had happened. I tried to block it out but for days it stayed roamed and around in my mind. Should I tell Tommy? Or Jayjay? Maybe go see Scar Face Ray? What should I do?

There was another voice in my head. 'I can look after you? Give you a place to live? Care for you.' Care for me. I suppose it sounds pathetic but those words were all I ever wanted to hear from anyone as a child.

Not too long after this incident with Derrick the police Juvenile Squad started to hassle me. I was in their sights. 'Where do you live?' 'Why aren't you at school?' 'Get off the streets or we'll lock you up.'

They'd seen me every day and hadn't even looked at me but now they saw me, stopped me, warned me and told me several times to leave the Cross.

Should I have heeded the advice and left? Where would I go?

There was so much police corruption in the Cross back then that I very much doubt that they were trying to save me, as you might think. They were probably keeping track of me. Corrupt police were able to blackmail predators. Most of the drug trade in Kings Cross was police controlled. They didn't deal directly but they ran protection rackets and sometimes had stakes in these dealers' businesses and took a cut in the profits. They called it 'a drink.' Criminals paid huge amounts of money to the police to either turn a blind eye or to shut down their opposition. Was I about to be recruited into the opposition?

After I stormed out of Derrick's I stayed in the Cross but there was an incident that led me back to Derrick's for the safety he offered.

It was late in the evening and I was wandering about enjoying the sights when a fight broke out on the corner of Roslyn Street outside Alison's Restaurant between bikers and doormen. The minute I heard someone yell, 'Fight!' I was drawn to it, front and centre. I saw two big bikers bash into one big islander doorman.

The fight started off with two bikers and one big islander but it soon escalated into an all in brawl. Doormen and bikers came from everywhere. Kings Cross was usually neutral turf for the many biker groups that hung out there. How all these people got to the fight so quickly amazed me. Doormen had buzzers that alerted other doormen if there was trouble. This time though men came from everywhere and there seemed to be a woman amongst it all.

The fight got very vicious. No-one was talking. They were all just swinging their fists and hitting each other.

When a man fell, someone would come and stomp on his head. One man had a huge chain that he whirled around smashing other guys with it. It was bedlam. The crowd around me grew quickly and I got stuck at the business end of the fight.

A young girl who was a street worker or a stripper jumped on the back of a huge man, grabbing him around the neck trying to gouge his eyes. She was screaming wildly at him. The man turned around and punched her hard straight in the face. It knocked her to the ground. She was out cold then another girl jumped in and sat on her and kept smashing her face. Another man in the crowd threw the attacker off and picked the unconscious girl up but the damage was probably done. Men lay on the ground bleeding and moaning and I saw and heard a man screaming as two others stomped on him. He went from screaming to motionless in seconds.

The whole terrifying ordeal continued and more and more people arrived. I was stuck dead smack in the middle of it. I wanted to get far away from it but I was pressed in by the crowd of onlookers. When I'd taken my place to watch, I thought it was a simple fight between three men. Now it looked like an ugly, ferocious war, only with an audience.

I'd gone to the fight as a curious kid but now I was almost in tears, paralysed with fear. I needed to get away. This was a level of violence that you might see in a movie but not real life. I tried to get through the crowd but I was knocked over each time I tried. There were people everywhere throwing punches and I just wanted to get away from it all.

I kept struggling to get free then out of nowhere a guardian angel in a suit grabbed me hard, dragged me out of the crowd and said, 'Get the fuck out of here kid! Go home to your mother. Get away from here!'

A girl yelled at me too. 'What's a little boy like you doing in Kings Cross this time of night?' I was very frightened. I just ran.

No-one I knew was about. I thought I knew everyone! I was free but I was so fucking scared that I ran all the way to Derrick's door with his offer to keep me safe and protected pounding in my head. If ever the devil was at work, he was here.

Chapter 9.
Guardian

That terrifying fight really rattled me. It was the first time I had felt afraid of anything in the Cross. I'd witnessed a lot of violence since being here but never had I felt so vulnerable as I did as I stood witness to the violence I saw that night. Even the squat didn't seem safe. I hadn't liked going alone into either of the squats at night but if Tommy and the girls were with me I felt okay. But they weren't at the fight.

I must have been as white as ghost when I banged on Derrick's door. I didn't even think about why I had run away from there a few hours ago.

'Open the fucking door, please!' I yelled.

Derrick welcomed me in, sat with me and calmed me down. He packed me a cone and I took it eagerly. Anything to get myself calm. I'm sure I spoke at a million miles an hour as I tried to tell Derrick what happened and how I felt.

'No-one survives up here on their own, mate,' he said gently. 'You need someone to take care of you. I can do that.'

As he said this he packed more cones for me and gave me alcohol too. I was willing to take anything that would settle me down. It didn't take long for me to feel safe. I had been thinking I'd leave the Cross but I literally had nowhere to go.

Job one of grooming - make a child feel safe and special. Mission accomplished, Derrick.

He spent a lot of time and energy telling me about his connections in the Cross, assuring me that he knew the right people and that he was protected. He knew the police and the man he sold the drugs for who owned the sex shop. Derrick reckoned that this person was one of the big movers and shakers in the Cross.

I wasn't absorbing what he said. I kept breaking down as I got flashbacks of the fight. I had been a victim of and witness to violence all my life but that fight and all those people involved in it was on another level.

'Is it always this violent on the streets? There'd be people dead from that fight,' I remarked. Derrick reassured me that I'd be safe with him.

As I started to focus on what he was saying, I was impressed. I didn't know any better. He was a mine of information. He told me a lot of violent things he had seen and he warned me that people did die, almost every weekend. Was he trying to scare me? If so, it worked. His stories made me feel dependent on him, that I was only safe under his watch. I loved the Cross generally and I wanted to stay. I was hooked. I had friends but I didn't want to see that shit again. What I really loved was the other street kids. They had accepted me. I was one of them. It satisfied the yearning I had, much like the yearning I had for my siblings.

I told Derrick about the police hassling me and he said, 'If you stay here with me, they can't hassle you. Once you have an address you're safe.' Drawing me closer in, he added, 'Look, I'll speak to them and you'll be left alone.'

I don't know if he did speak to them or if it was a coincidence but the cops didn't bother me again for some time.

Derrick kept giving me alcohol and cones, 'To calm you down,' he said. Even so I was cautious. I wasn't going to let him get too close to me. As I relaxed I became acutely aware of why I had run away from him recently. The trouble was that I was more afraid of going back to the street that night than I was of staying with Derrick. I felt sort of safe at his place. Safe from being beaten up. Not safe enough to fall asleep though.

He didn't seem like a threat physically and I felt able to control any situation involving sex by just telling him I wasn't into that. He didn't try anything that night. He didn't again for a while. Grooming takes time.

Derrick offered me a room in the back of his flat. I moved

in and a posse of other kids came with me. Tommy, Jayjay and Kelly came and stayed too. Derrick was only there at night and I was there all day. The others came in the daytime while Derrick was at work.

As time went on, I saw doormen beat up a lot of people. People would come to the Cross, get drunk and then be a little too hands on with the girls. They were beaten to within an inch of their lives or worse. Doormen jumped on them landing their body weight on the backs or torsos of the gropers. Police and ambulances were called. While ambulances ferried the victims away doormen would stand around chatting with the police as if they were long lost buddies.

With beatings, over doses and suicides, someone would die nearly every week in the Cross. On Friday and Saturday nights there'd be huge fights in most of the nightclubs. I have a very clear memory of seeing Big Al and Chad, doorman from the one of the strip clubs, beating up five men and one of them stomped on the head of a man who was already unconscious. That's the violent side of those two men but I also knew the good side of them. Chad danced and was a good friend to me. Gino, the club owner, looked after street kids. If anyone hassled them they answered to Big Al and Chad.

On the streets kids talked about the big names operating in the Cross. A nightclub owner and a major player in organised crime were mentioned a lot. I took it all in. Kids talked once about a woman who had gone missing (Juanita Neilson, anti-development campaigner). They reckoned she was buried underneath the Hyatt Hotel. Others said it was another hotel. They talked about a rogue cop who shot people or had them warned off. A lot of the talk had to be taken with a grain of salt because a kid might hear a snippet and he'd add a bit to try to make out he knew more than he did to impress or scare you.

The next time I saw the police was when they raided Derrick's home looking for evidence of dealing. They hardly ever raided people to bust them. It's most often a shake down, a ploy to warn the person off someone else's patch or to check for blackmail potential. They probably used me and other kids to lead them to Derrick's and assess his possibilities.

I'd been at his place for a couple of weeks when Derrick asked me to sell pot from the flat we lived in. He would leave me a heap of sticks to sell each day. After a bit I would buy them from him for fifteen dollars and sell them for twenty. I sold between twenty and two hundred a day. That was a lot of money and pot, so even more friends started hanging around and I was more popular.

Each day person after person came and that made me feel important. Tommy and I would sell to them then share the profits. We didn't really need money. Most people who sold drugs had habits or needed money for other reasons. I didn't need it so I made mixes up and shared them with the other kids. We spent most days listening to records of Elton John or other albums Derrick owned. He had a big record collection. The house was always a mess and that really pissed Derrick off.

When I was fifteen I really wanted to get some tattoos so Derrick took me to The Red Light tattoo parlour next door to sex shop. A lot of bikers hung out there. Two brothers did the tats and they decided to put three on my legs. I got a woman on the inside of my right calf and a panther on the same leg. On my other leg they put a dragon. I don't remember any pain so I might have been a bit stoned. These were my first professional tattoos.

Other kids gave me tattoos while I was at Derrick's. My left hand said 'Mum,' thanks to Jayjay. (Later I had that removed.) I can't recall who did my others but they included 'JJ' and 'Tina' (my sister) on one arm and 'Bunny' on the other. Later I got blue birds on my top right arm done at the Red Light tattoo shop.

All day we sold pot from Derrick's place. He propositioned every kid who came in. Some would get with him and some refused.

I told him I wasn't interested in having sex with him but he was so wrapped in me that he often bought me gifts and gave me money. He got me a Davy Crocket hat made of fur with a tail on the back that I really liked and then he bought a set of Tom Tom drums. I busked on the street with them and people would say, 'Oh look at that cute little boy with his drums.' They usually put money in the cute little fifteen year old's hat.

Derrick took me to a car park that was owned by Bob, his drug supplier, and I watched as he gave Derrick a garbage bag filled with pot. There were all types of shady people there and Derrick seemed to command a lot of respect. He made the pot up into one ounce bags that he sold at the shop and he sold in bigger amounts to other dealers. Most of them would pick it up at the shop. He'd bought an out of service ambulance that we drove in to drop off supplies to other dealers. I only sold sticks from the flat.

Derrick would sit for hours weighing the pot and making up sticks then putting them into bags of twenty. I knew where he stored them but no-one else was supposed to know. I kept my supply in a hole in the lounge and I kept about five in bags down my pants. All the kids knew where they were but no one ever raided the stash. I was now a drug dealer and this made me even more known on the streets. Older kids treated me with some respect and I liked that a lot.

One time Derrick took me to Bondi to do business. As we drove down the hill toward the beach, one of the wheels came off the car! He'd been working on it and didn't tighten up the nuts. Too stoned I guess. Luckily we just avoided a disaster.

The police raided Derrick's place several times. He was never there when they came. One time they took us all away because we had pot in the house. Within about two hours Derrick had us all out of there, no charges. I don't know how he did it but it made me believe his stories of dealing for big wigs and that the police were all a part of it. Derrick told us someone called Bob got us out.

On one of their raids the police asked me quite a few times, 'Is Derrick a paedophile? He is, isn't he?'

They kept trying to get us to talk but no-one did. I think it was a test to see who would dob and who wouldn't. The cops of this era were interested in one thing only. Money. If some dirty sick predator had a house filled with kids and was having sex with them all, the police didn't care as long as he paid them to turn a blind eye. I have no doubt Derrick paid for police protection.

It wasn't long before Derrick started giving me less and demanding more. I don't want to elaborate other than to say Derrick and his friend, Taxi Michael, abused me while I was staying with him. Derrick's demands got more and more insistent. Lots of kids depended on me to eat, smoke and hang out now. Derrick had the power to make all of that stop in a puff of smoke. He held that threat over me every time I said, 'No,' to his advances.

My friend Kelly was picked up by the police and sent back to Wellington where she was put in a girls' home. I still had a crush on her and I really missed her. So I made a plan to go to Wellington and break her out. I told Tommy and the others but no-one would come with me. Well, I was going no matter what. I hitch hiked to Wellington and within two hours of arriving there I'd found the home. It wasn't like any home I had been in. It was more like a refuge. You could come and go as you pleased.

I went to the door. 'G'day Kelly. How's it going?'

She wasn't glad to be there.

'Well, I'm comin' back tonight to get you and take you home.'

I'd met some guys in Wellington that day who'd stolen a car and they gave me the keys. I couldn't drive but I thought I'd be able to wing it. After a few serious kangaroo hops along the road, one of the boys said he'd better drive.

We picked Kelly up.

'Where'd you get the wheels?' she asked.

'Stolen.'

'Great. We can't use that. The cops'll be watching for it.'

She knew heaps of people. We went to her aunty's place on the highway and then to a friend of aunty's who lived in a caravan.

We all got drunk and I fell asleep. I awoke early in the morning to the sounds of moaning and groaning right beside me. Kelly was having sex with a man she knew and I could see and hear everything. The caravan was bouncing up, down they were going at it so hard. I was broken hearted.

I jumped up and walked out. How could she do that to me when she knew I liked her! Fuck, I'd come all this way to get her out then she sleeps with some other bloke, right in front of me! I knew I was just a little kid to her and she was grown up but that didn't help. The guy she was with was about twenty five.

I took off hitchhiking and I got a lift from a bloke who let me tell him how I came to be here. He agreed to take me back to where Kelly was and see if she wanted to come back to Kings Cross with me. She did.

The trip back was very quiet because I was annoyed and didn't want to talk to her. Back in the Cross I went to Derrick's and never had anything more to do with Kelly. She was a top chick and, looking back, I understand why she didn't want to get with me. I hadn't slept with a girl yet.

Derrick threatened to take the pot dealing and other perks off me if I didn't do what he wanted. He threatened to kick everyone else out of his flat too. He did it but just for while because I eventually gave in. I just couldn't see any other way to keep what I had: money, a roof over my head, my friends around me, drugs and freedom from police harassment.

At first he only wanted to give me oral sex. I hated it. As time went on his demands got even more distasteful to me. As if all that wasn't enough, I went the toilet one morning and as I pissed I felt extreme burning. I told Derrick.

'You've probably got a urinary infection,' he said knowingly. I didn't think much more about it 'til later that night when I noticed that I didn't just have burning urine but I had pus too. It was like pissing razor blades. I'd caught an STD from him. The Clap. Gonorrhea. Derrick took me and another kid to a clinic in Albion Street for treatment.

I think us kids got an antibiotic but Derrick had to have a needle up his penis. I recall him explaining it all to us. The women at the clinic told us there were other diseases out there too and we had to be aware of them. Other Sexually Transmitted Diseases. After a few days my case was cleared up. I remember this well because it had been excruciating going to the toilet but now it wasn't.

Derrick had a few paedophile friends who'd come around with their young boys too. The men seemed to target me. I was the prize kid because I seemed to be so young. They all kept trying.

I hated the sexual stuff with Derrick and as much as I could avoid it, I did. He was a dirty rock spider who took advantage of kids by giving them drugs, grog, money, gifts, food and a place to crash. He took advantage mostly of young boys like me who hadn't reached puberty and couldn't even ejaculate. He liked young girls too but he'd rather watch me having sex with them than doing that himself. Not all the kids staying there were abused but many were.

Chapter 10.
Send Me an Angel

You wouldn't usually find us kids hanging around Kings Cross train station but on this day Tommy and I thought we'd hang there. Tommy and I had been inseparable. He was my closest friend and we'd had a few girls hanging around. I have no idea why we went to the station that day. Sometimes you can be at just the right place at the right time. We knew we were at the right place when two beautiful girls came through the turnstiles. One had beautiful jet black hair and amazing blue eyes. I was instantly drawn to her. Her friend was just as beautiful.

I wasn't known for chatting up chicks but something about the black haired girl gave me courage.

'G'day! Haven't seen you around here before. What's your name? I'm Glen by the way 'n this is Tommy.'

I'm Linda,' said the most beautiful girl I'd ever seen. 'This is me friend Gemma.' She almost sang it.

'Gemma,' she said very clearly with a laugh and a twinkle in her eye.

'Hey Gemma. Where are you from?'

'Macquarie Fields,' they said together.

The conversation went on and they told us they were fourteen years old. I was just a year older. Linda and I fell head over heels for each other that day. Linda had a presence about her that made being around her exciting. She would turn boys' heads wherever she went. She was fun, outgoing and had an infectious laugh.

'So where are you off to now?' I asked, hoping she wasn't going far.

'Just to buy some lighter fluid.'

'What d'you want that for?' I asked.

166

'To sniff, of course! What do you think?'

I had never done that before and I don't think Tommy had either so we agreed to get some and try it out with them. I think I would have followed Linda anywhere to do almost anything that day.

Was it fate that brought us together that day? I often wonder how her life would have turned out if we hadn't met. Would she have ended up with predators or would she be just another street kid? She would soon be the most important person in my world.

The four of us went to the tobacco shop and bought three bottles of lighter fluid. We took them to Derrick's place and Linda showed us how to pour the liquid onto a rag and then sniff the Fumes. We all got off our faces, hallucinating. I was in another world and it was more frightening than enjoyable.

We only did it twice and then we stopped. I didn't like taking drugs that made me lose my ability to control myself. Of all the drugs there are this is one of the most dangerous. It can cause serious brain damage. People have sniffed lighter fluid then walked out in front of cars or trains. Others have jumped off tall buildings believing they could fly. Many die. It kills cells in your brain.

Linda and Gemma stayed at Derrick's for about two weeks and Linda became my girlfriend. At about the two week point I went with the girls to Linda's home in Minto to get a few things. Later other girls from that area followed Linda to the Cross: Sherie, Jenny and Nerida are a few that come to mind. But for now it was just Linda and Gemma. We were just kids but I was in love with Linda and she seemed to be in love with me. In a few weeks I asked her to marry me and we even went as far as organising an engagement party. It shows how young and naive we were but for us it was real. It felt right. We had no understanding of love and all its complexities. I had seen someone get engaged and that was an expression of their love so I mimicked what I had seen.

Derrick helped throw a party for us and I even invited Mrs Chambers, my foster mother. Larry the paedophile came too because he was her driver. Mrs Chambers never went anywhere without being driven by Larry. I hated him with a passion. Mrs Chambers was warm and it was so nice to see her. I think she might have been shocked about my living conditions. Our engagement party was a bunch of kids with a few lollies and chips, getting drunk and smoking pot. We didn't think much about the future because we lived in the present. But to us this engagement was a real commitment to each of us to be true to each other. The only love I had ever seen growing up was with my parents and foster parents. So I didn't have a lot to model from.

When Mrs Chambers left I felt sad but I knew I didn't want to leave the Cross any more, even if I could have.

We kids on the streets hardly ever spoke to each other about our home lives before the Cross. We just existed and carried on like every day was a new adventure. One of the beauties of the Cross was that our past was behind us. Who we were, where we had been or what we had been through just didn't matter. All that mattered to us was the day we were in. I do recall some conversations with kids around their home lives and it appeared that many came from situations similar to my own. We spoke more about what homes we had been in as most of the kids of the Cross had been in and out of institutions.

Derrick paid for Linda and I to have a night in a hotel a few doors away. We spent the night having sex and enjoying time alone after the party. I was enjoying my first relationship and an innocent, normal sexual experience. It was untainted by any feeling of repulsion or violation. We couldn't keep our hands off each other. I remember the night so well.

We spent most of each day at Derrick's place or we'd hang around Slots or the Snooker Room. Tommy and I were still close and now our group had grown. There were three boys: Joey, Tommy and me. There were three girls: Linda, Jenny and Gemma. I seemed to be popular for the first time in my life! I'd gone from being a bullied pariah to a kid who people liked to be around.

There was an old guy who played the harmonica outside the

Snooker Room who held a saucepan for donations. On the saucepan he wrote, 'Roach, king of the street kids.'

'Every time I see you Roach, there's a posse of kids follerin' on behind ya,' he told me.

We didn't have leaders so I wouldn't say they were following. Each of us had a voice and we listened to each other. I loved those kids like we were siblings.

If we wanted a change from the Cross we'd jump the turnstiles and have a day out. Bondi was a favourite. One hot summer night a group of us spent ages dawdling up and down Bondi Beach and we thought we might as well spend the night there. We woke up at about two o'clock, shivering with cold. Sleeping next to the water hadn't been a good idea. We walked back to Bondi station in the middle of the night and as we passed a shop we found that crates full of flavoured milk and newspapers had been delivered, left on the path outside the shop.

We helped ourselves to a flavoured milk each but one of the kids thought it would be fun to throw the papers everywhere.

'Stop it mate,' I told him. 'You're being a goose.'

Tommy backed me up. 'Yeah mate. Stop. We don't want the cops coming after us. That's the last thing we need.'

Being under sixteen meant that the police could pick you up any time if you were on the streets and they could charge you with Uncontrollable or Exposed to Moral danger. We stood out for all the wrong reasons, we looked like street kids and at the Cross we blended in with the many other street kids. Outside of the Cross if Police saw us they gravitated towards us every time.

Sometimes newcomers were picked up by the police and taken home but they'd be back in a few weeks. There were also kids who disappeared and never came back. Our core group could always find each other somewhere in the Cross.

Now that I was engaged to Linda, I refused to have sex with Derrick. I wouldn't let him touch Linda either. He wasn't happy.

'You don't give me sex, I don't give you money to look after everyone. Got that Roach,' he said.

One time he watched as Linda and I had sex. As an adult looking back it just infuriates me that this maggot was able to manipulate all of us so much. It's complicated to explain to an out sider how these men manipulate kids, make you reliant on them. I just wanted to be with the other kids and Linda.

Dealing pot for Derrick had been something I did when he wasn't home. I wasn't worried about money. But now there was a whole heap of us that needed to eat, smoke pot, play pinball machines, so selling pot became a need and not just a thing to do. I began to take dealing more seriously and it wasn't unusual for me to be carrying hundreds of dollars. As I knew so many street kids I had my own market. Derrick already had about thirty regular people who bought from him at the flat and he sold at the sex shop all day long, usually in larger amounts.

Most of my days were spent sitting at the flat selling sticks, listening to music, getting stoned and having fun with the other kids. At night I'd hang out at the Snooker Room or Slots and sell pot to other street kids. Now that I had to take selling seriously we started sleeping during the day and hanging on the streets pretty much all night.

We sold enough to support all six of us. I was always the one carrying the pot but we all sold it from time to time.

One morning there was a really loud knock on the door.

'Detective Jones from Kings Cross Police. Open the door!'

Must be a joke, I thought. Lots of kids did that all the time. But the volume of the knock and the depth of the voice made us stand at attention. There were probably about twenty kids in the house. Most bailed out the windows when we realised it really was the cops. The flat was on the ground floor. Had I had more time to think, I'd have followed the others. It was funny watching the kids bailing. I grabbed the pot from my pants and stuffed it under the lounge. I stood up to answer the door.

Only a couple of kids were left by the time the police came in. There were about four detectives and a couple of men in uniform.

'We have a warrant to search this property,' one said.

The atmosphere went from party mode to pretty serious in a matter of minutes.

'We've been informed that someone's selling drugs from these premises.'

'Really?'

'Yeah. Really. So do you want to tell us where it is or do we have to play hide and seek?'

'I'm not telling you shit,' I replied. I was still young, raw and naïve. I was very cheeky.

If I'd known then what I'd learn ten years later I'd have been more polite and said,

'Yes sir.' 'No sir,' and let them go through the process. Instead I back chatted them the whole time and then we were all arrested.

When we got to the police station I saw a list that read 'Kings Cross street kids,' on the wall. There were about twenty photos of kids and mine was at the top.

'We keep lists of you lot,' I was told. 'Kids are always going missing, disappearing, that sort of thing.'

The rumour on the streets about kids going missing was that a man known as Rolls Royce Roy was responsible. He was a well known paedophile who drove a Rolls Royce. He would drive past the park, scanning it for vulnerable kids. He was very secretive and very selective. He trawled alone. He pointed for me to come over and talk to him once and I told him to fuck off.

There was a boy at the Cross who went with Roy and he was never seen again. Two stories spread about it. One was that he was being very well taken care of and was living with Roy. The other possibility was more sinister and he might never be seen again. Kids were always disappearing. Some went back home, some were put in homes and some were living with predators. Others literally vanished.

I sat in the police station for ages. One of the detectives hit me at one stage. This initiated a running battle between us for years to come.

The police kept saying, 'Derrick's a kiddy fucker isn't he. You one of his boys now?'

They said a lot about Derrick's history with children. When I finally walked out of the police station about twenty kids were waiting outside for me. Once again I wasn't charged with anything. Derrick had come along and got us out. The police clearly knew I was going to a paedophile.

We all went back to Derrick's place which had been turned upside down in the raid. We weren't house proud and it was often a mess but this was far, far worse.

I was sitting in the park on the little wall near Slots thinking of ways to get away from Derrick when I noticed an O'Brien's Glass truck driver scoping the park. He came over and started talking to me. He asked if I wanted to go with him. I told him I didn't but somehow he convinced me to go. To this day I don't know why I did. He, Ken, took me to his place in Tempe raped me and that's all I want to say except that I became really upset and left. Ken has recently been convicted of raping me and others. I put my self into a vulnerable position. I was still so young and naive.

When I got back to the Cross I was still shaken and upset and I went to Kings Cross Police. The guy at the counter knew me. I started telling him what had happened and he laughed at me. He told me it was my fault. Deep down I wondered if maybe that was true. If I had not gone with him it would not have happened.

'Fuck off,' he said. 'No one cares.' He found a heap of nasty names to call me as I walked out. His attitude added to my reluctance to speak with police about anything.

It wasn't much longer after this that Derrick started saying, 'Glen you're going to have to find another place to live.' He was filthy at me having so many kids staying at the place all the time and that I refused to have sex with him.

He didn't just throw me into the street though. He had an old Ford panel van that had been cut in half. The back half made a trailer of sorts for sleeping in. It was kept near the car park of the place Bob owned. Six of us kids went to live in the trailer designed for two. Being kids we were able to sleep in it comfortably. We owned nothing so we only had to fit blankets, a bong and ourselves inside.

The first night there we sniffed lighter fluid and I decided it would definitely be the last time I did. My problem was that I had a terrible hallucination. Linda was holding a serving tray and on it were all our friends who were shrunken and were being served up to people. I think that the fumes inside that small space hung around for ages. It was too freaky to risk repeating.

We stayed for about a week then early one morning we heard knocking. The others were still asleep and Linda and I had just had sex and were giggling like kids and enjoying each other's bodies. The knocking outside was loud and insistent. I opened the back doors dressed only in underpants.

'What the fuck man … ?' Expecting to see other streets kids hanging around or someone chasing after Pot.

It was two uniformed officers! They asked, 'Who else is in there? What are you doing here?' One of them recognized me and said, 'You can't live in there!' I was starting to be well known to Kings Cross Police. They knew me by name.

The other kids started waking up. Linda had time to put knickers on and a t shirt. Jenny and Nerida were lying in knickers and Tommy was mostly covered with the blanket.

One of the coppers was staring at Jenny. Linda noticed. 'Having a good geek there mate?' she asks. She put a blanket over both girls. Linda's confronting words really angered the cop.

'Get out of the van, all of you!' he ordered.

Linda swore at him and said, 'Yeah right! You'd like that wouldn't you? We're all just about naked. Shut the doors and let us get dressed.'

'Get out now!' He demands.

The other copper slammed the door shut. 'You have five minutes to get up and get out of there,' he said, a little more calmly than his mate.

We slowly got dressed and I opened the doors when we felt we were covered up enough. The cops had gone! Tommy, still waking up, said, 'Turn off the light!' He could always make us laugh. The light was the sun shining in. We had a giggle and then there was another knock. This time it's Michael! My brother, Michael. It was great to see him.

He'd been living at North Sydney in a refuge called Lemon Grove Lodge. I wasn't sure why but Michael got upset with me about something and walked off not long after we said hello.

We headed down the main street and got some breakfast then we started to walk back to the trailer.

Suddenly Tommy said, 'Shit man! There's smoke coming out of the van!'

We ran over and sure enough the van was burning. 'Who left a smoke in there? You? You?' The night before we had used lighter fluid so that could have set something off. But when we thought about it we knew this could not have been an accident.

'I reckon the bloody pigs did it. To get us out.'

Jenny was the most upset because she'd left her jeans in there. She was wearing shorts and a T shirt and now they were all the clothes she had.

Later that day I went to see Derrick to try to get him to let us stay at his place again. I walked in and saw another little boy behind the counter. Blond haired and about thirteen years old, sitting behind the counter just like I had when I first went there. Seeing him made me angry, though I didn't understand why. To be honest, I was a little jealous that he would now get all the perks I wanted, though I never wanted the sex that went with them. If I'd been replaced it was okay with me. I think it upset me to see that he had exploited another child, I was onto his game now.

We spent a few days at Derrick's place then we had a night at the Snooker Room, sleeping up the back under the tables. The guy who owned the place, Max, was pretty cool. He looked out for street kids. They had a little room at the back where we could crash when we needed to.

One day I was just hanging out near the Snooker Room when Craig from Mt Druitt and two other kids I knew walked past. Then three more came behind them. They all wore western shirts. I knew Craig from childhood from a time when I came down to stay at Margaret's place. Michael had told me that Craig and some other kids had been bullying him at school.

Being the big brother I said, 'Where does he live?'

We went around there to confront him. He was inside with a group of mates including his sister Leanne who I was keen on. I called him out to fight me.

'I'm not goin' up against your mates Craig. I'm here for you,' I told him but the whole group of them came out ready to fight me. Michael and I had to run off but that day had stayed in my mind. Suddenly there he was, walking past me years later! We had unfinished business that I needed to deal with.

At that time there was rivalry between Westies and City kids. It was kind of odd because I was both and so was Linda.

I saw Tommy just after I spotted Craig and in minutes we gathered a little posse of kids. I confronted Craig.

'Remember me, mother fucker!' Trying to act tough.

I threw a punch at him and it landed on the target. Craig and his lot panicked and all took off for the station. If he'd known us he'd know that we were more noise than action. About four of us chased them then a heap of girls joined in. There was still more of them than us but we had the home ground advantage. We jumped onto the escalators and rode down them like they were a long slippery dip.

As I slid down I overtook one of Craig's lot who was still running down the stairs. I grabbed him as he got to the bottom. He was shitting himself when I went to hit him. He put up his hands to defend himself. He looked so frightened.

That action pulled me up. How many times had I raised my hands to defend myself like that? I hated bullies then and I still do. I got flashbacks of my mother attacking me and putting my hands up to stop the blows.

One of our crew got ready to hit the kid I was holding but I said, 'No! He isn't the one. I want Craig.' I went from attacker to defender.

We left that kid behind and bolted down to the station. They jumped on the Bondi train that only went a few stops then it terminated. There is no way back to Mt Druitt from Bondi by train without going through the Cross. So we decided to wait at the Cross station as each train came through from Bondi heading to the city to catch Craig. We raced up and down the platform looking for him and his lot, doing our best warriors impersonations.

'Warriors! Come out to play. Warriors come out to play!'

Unlike many groups in the Cross we never really got into fights. There were a few incidents like the time walking back from Central with Tommy when the service station man chased us. There were a few times when men had tried to touch our girlfriends. It was usually us kids versus adults.

We waited as train after train came in and we hadn't caught Craig. I said, 'Let's go to Bondi, catch them there.'

About seven of us went. When we got off the train at Bondi we stalked up and down the station looking for them. We eventually jumped the turnstiles and, as usual, said, 'Street kids!' and the guard let us through.

When we got to Bondi station and couldn't find the boys from the West we decided to walk to the beach as we didn't have enough money to catch the bus. I was relieved when we couldn't find the gang at Bondi. Our lot was getting pretty fired up and I felt that if we ran into the others, something bad might have happened. Pack mentality can be dangerous. We weren't into violence or crimes. We just wanted to be kids who stuck together.

We walked along the beach. Linda and I were hand in hand. We decided it was time to go back where we belonged. Unfinished business didn't seem to matter so much.

An older man, Max, worked at the Snooker Room and we told him that we'd been kicked out of Derrick's. Max asked if we wanted to come and meet Terry, a friend of his. He had a street kid called Brett with him so we trusted him.

Six of us went to a place in Surry Hills where we met Terry, a big drug dealer. Brett was about seventeen. He was a heroin addict who sold the drug for Terry.

The night started off with Max inviting us into his spa. He had a smorgasbord of drugs: heroin, cocaine, pot, pretty much everything and in huge amounts. Terry apparently supplied all the dealers in town.

We didn't analyse the situation. All we saw was free everything and a place to stay. Later that day Linda and I used heroin. We were really off our faces. Terry offered us money to let him video us having sex. We were having sex anyway and if some sicko wanted to pay us, so be it.

The heroin made me get an erection but I wasn't able to ejaculate, so I had sex for hours with three girls. I was off my face. Another boy we knew was involved too. As time went on I found that paedophiles liked filming me having sex with girls of the same age. They gave us money and drugs and we didn't think much of it. As an adult it infuriates me that there were so many sickos ready to take advantage of whatever was happening. As a kid I remember thinking we are having sex any way and I think being around Derrick had desensitised me to sickos.

We all got up and left later on. The next day once the drugs wore off I started to think about the night before. I was starting to get pissed off with every adult we met wanting sex with us kids. None of us was even sixteen yet. We were homeless street kids who had no-one but each other to guide us. I knew no other way to survive. Selling pot was the only other way I knew of to get money.

Not long after that night Brett (the heroin user) ripped a huge amount of money and heroin off Terry. When Max saw us at the Snooker Room he said, 'Terry's put a contract out on that Brett. Wants him taken care of.'

Clearly I needed to find another way to get money. Sam was

the man who was at the entrance to Kings Cross station every Friday and Saturday night selling watches from a brown wooden suitcase. Sam said they were all brand names but that he got cheap because they were hot (stolen). He offered me a job helping to sell watches. He told me I would get a commission of each watch I sold, the more I got for the watch the more I would earn.

In selling those watches I found I had the gift of the gab. Men would come along with their girls often they were really drunk after being in night clubs for hours. Then they would come and look at the watches. Drunk men with really hot ladies would try to impress them by buying a flash watch.

If we caught a rabbit, (A person likely to buy) Sam would walk away, pretending he needed to leave for a second. Then I would say confidentially, 'Mate look at this one instead! You couldn't afford that one.'

The men with huge egos took it as a challenge to prove they could afford the dearer watch. 'Can't afford it! Mate, I could buy all the watches in that box and you too.' They would explain.

'You probably could buy all the watches and me, but this watch, you definitely couldn't afford,' was usually my next line.

Depending on the person and the money we thought they had, we could charge up to five grand. On this night I had a man looking at a watch that I told him would cost fifteen hundred dollars. He said, 'Mate come down a bit and you might have me.'

'Mate, I've already come down. That's a three thousand dollar watch. You buy that anywhere else you're looking at about eight thousand,' I told him.

Sam walked away and that was my cue. 'Listen, the boss has just walked away and I really want to make a dollar. Like you, I have a little lady I want to take out for the night.' Reeling him in. 'If you can get eleven hundred, I'll give it to you now. But you have to take off straight away 'cause if he sees I've sold it for that price, he'll go ape shit.'

The customer disappeared but he was back within minutes. 'I can get only nine hundred.'

'Mate I can't. The boss is back. Just wait.'

Sam saw that the customer was back and pretended to be talking to someone else. The buyer thought he was getting the better of the fifteen year old kid so he hands me the money. He tried to short change me fifty bucks. I'd seen exactly how much he'd counted out.

'Go before the boss sees!' I told him and I slip the cash into my pocket.

Sam said certain watches like our middle range ones weren't worth a hundred dollars. They were probably worth about twenty if the truth be told.

I hand the cash to Sam. I wanted his approval.

'Did I do well Sam? How's that eh?' I was more concerned about pleasing my boss than adding up how much I'd actually get for the deal.

I sold about three more watches that night, mostly for around the three hundred mark for ones Sam said were our one hundred dollar ones. I would rope customers in then Sam would close my deals.

By four in the morning I was almost asleep on my feet. Linda had checked on me but she was with the crew so I knew she was okay. When it came time to split the cash Sam pulled out a big wad of cash and gave me four fifty dollar notes.

'I keep a certain amount from each of your takings,' he said. 'You'll get it at the end of every month. It's a protection thing for you, to make sure you have money.' I must have looked dissatisfied because he went on. 'If I give it all to you now, you'll just go and spend it on your girl. Then you'll have nothing.'

Fifty was a lot of money for me so for now I wasn't arguing.

Sam had taken home a lot of money that night and he did the following night too. About half way through that night a man who looked upset came up to Sam and said, 'I bought this watch from you for five hundred dollars last week. I was really drunk. I spent the family money. I thought the watch was real! It's not only fake but the numbers are actually falling off!'

Sam exploded on this poor guy. 'Where the fuck do you think you are? This is Kings Cross. Mate You either fuck or get fucked here on the streets,' Sam replies rather loud an animated. Obviously designed in a way to intimidate the man. Sam then told the bloke to fuck off.

The guy got a bit more lippy and before you knew it a fight was on. Sam just flipped out on this guy and started punching into him. Like all fights a crowd gathers and I was standing there again in the middle of mayhem.

I thought, *Fuck this. I'm fifteen. I hate violence. If I keep doing this for Sam, it'll only be a matter of time before I get beaten up or into some kind of situation.*

It wasn't in me to hurt people or rip people off. When I said that to Sam, he said, 'Fuck off kid. You'll never make it here. You need to toughen up.' He gave me fifty bucks and said, 'Best you go your own way.'

I knew he owed me lots more than fifty but I wasn't about to argue with a man willing to get violent over money.

We were staying in the Manning Street squat again and I didn't feel safe there. Anyone could walk in at any time and they usually did. At all hours of the night drug users would come and have a shot. Some would then leave but others would get really loud and even aggressive.

One night four or five Skinheads who were about twenty had a shot of heroin and then they went from room to room rolling drunks. They got to the room where four of us boys and about six girls were staying. All of us were under sixteen and probably looked like little children to them. They were big aggressive looking guys and they were off their heads.

'Fuck off you lot,' Tommy told them.

The Skinheads got more aggressive, talking about the girls.

'Fresh meat!' one said, sniffing around like he was on heat or something. 'Smell that bro? Young pussy.'

Tommy stood up. He was a good fighter and he didn't back down from anyone. But he was way too young to take on these men. I started to feel frightened but I stood beside Tommy. If they went ape on us I don't think we could have won. There were four of us boys and the girls would probably have jumped in too. Before anything else happened we saw torches shining up through the windows. I looked out.

'It's the cops,' I said. 'They come by every hour to check on the kids here.'

They didn't even come in usually. They just stood out the front and caught any addicts coming or going. Once they came to another squat when Jayjay and Kelly were there. They just broke their bong and told them to go.

My warning was enough the scare the Skinheads off pretty quickly. They left me feeling very vulnerable. I'm sure we all felt unsafe. We moved from squat to squat but all of them had groups of older kids staying in them.

I didn't have an answer for the questions about a safe place for us to live but the kids I was with were my family now, the family I had always craved so desperately for.

Sometimes I worried so much about the kids and our life that I thought about suicide. If Linda had not been with me I might have chosen that option as other people around us did. I think it was a common thought for all of us on the streets back then though I knew it was not a normal way to think for a kid of my age. One thing that I thought about was that if I did end it, it would show all the people who took advantage of me how much they had hurt me. The police would have to tell my mother and my father that I had killed myself and they would ask my parents why I'd taken such drastic action and why I wasn't living with either of them.

Realistically, my mother would have said, 'The weak cunt!' My father would be upset that I had interrupted his day. My foster parents may have been upset.

Chad and Big Al were still at the club. Big Al is written up as a murderous thug in a book I read but the Al in that book is nothing like the man we knew. The man we knew protected children in the Cross. He didn't tolerate anyone who got too hands on with the girls either. His punishment for them was to administer some of the worst violence I ever saw.

Chad was a slim and fit Asian Australian whose specialty was martial arts. He was an expert. He loved to dance too, especially disco, and he was very skilful. I was good at disco but I'd been learning Break Dancing, the new craze. I could mix Disco, Funk and Rap.

'Why don't you and me go in that comp,' Chad asked me one day. You seen the posters? At the Talofa club.'

I agreed to give it a go and we practiced our dance for about two weeks to the song Born to Be Alive. Barry had sent me off to dance classes when I'd preferred footy but now I was grateful to the dance teacher for all I learnt from her.

The Talofa Club let me in although I was too young to be there. Chad and I were second up on stage. A man and woman team danced before us and they were pretty good.

When Chad and I came on, in the words we would have used then, 'We tore that shit up.' The audience seemed amazed by our blend of old and new routines and our timing was spot on. Neither of us put a foot wrong and our unique moves bought the house down.

We won! Easily. Chad was a good person to be around. Later I danced with other break dancers at the train station and Chad who was usually working on the door opposite the train station would come over and join in. A lot of the young rappers use to watch and you could almost see them thinking, *That's old school mate, not what we're into now.* None of them had the courage to tell Chad any different.

Two new boys, a bit older than us, started hanging around the Snooker Room, trying really hard to come on to the girls. At first we didn't get on too well but that gradually changed. I don't recall exactly how it all came about but those boys told us they were from Kingston in Queensland.

'Wanna come up there with us?' they asked the girls. 'We stay at this really big joint owned by a couple of record producers and singers.'

'Where are we going to get the money to get to Queensland?' I said.

The man who was in Kingston was paying our way there!' Matt said.

Matt and his mate paid for Linda, Michelle, Mouse, Mel and me to go to Brisbane. We didn't know what we were getting ourselves into but we knew we'd be meeting a producer and I hopes I could talk to him about dancing. The girls were the ones invited, I really went to make sure they were ok.

When we finally arrived we were met by an older balding man, Bobby, and a younger guy, Jason, who was twenty five or so and had long hair and a long beard. They were very welcoming. They gave us free food and we stayed at their home right near the shops in Kingston. At night lots of kids would hang around the shops, a little bit like at the Cross.

They told us they wanted to make some movies of the younger of the two men having sex with some young girls. Matt, his friend and another young guy with an abnormally large penis made a movie with Mel. Then they made one of me and Linda having sex. It didn't seem like a big deal back then. Sex was currency. We made a film that was supposed to be for fun, of me and one of the other girls. I refused to let any one touch Linda. One of the other girls with us made the movie with these guys.

Bobby himself was a Paedophile and his interest was in me.

We were taken to a party where we seemed to be a novelty of some kind. There were about forty rich people, all off their faces and all ogling us and introducing us to everyone else. They gave us pot, alcohol and offered us pretty much any drug we wanted. Drugs were not our thing but we accepted the pot and alcohol.

We were surprised to see them showing the videos of us at the party. They'd been professionally edited and we were the stars. They were not the kind of movies I had dreamt of as a boy. These are the types of movies I saw often in the sex shop Derrick worked at. Why adults wanted to watch kids having sex was beyond me. Everyone was commenting on how Mel was able to manage to have sex with the man with the big penis. Mel was only fifteen. If you read this book Mel, I am sorry I didn't protect you. We thought these people were people treating us like rock stars when really they were treating us like objects. Although this lot of paedophiles preferred girls, Bobby himself liked boys.

Back in Sydney most of the abuse had involved us boys. This was one of the few times that someone exploited the girls. I regret that I didn't protect them. Mel wanted to be involved. She loved the idea of being the star in a porn movie. We didn't know that Bobby and Jason were part of a porn industry that served a widespread paedophile ring in Brisbane.

Suddenly I understood what was going on. We had been brought up here by Matt who was paid to find young girls to star in porn movies.

I got really angry about that and the videos being shown. I demanded that we go back to the Cross. They wouldn't buy our tickets despite the fact that they would probably make a bundle selling the movies. We had to hitchhike back. Hitching from Brisbane to Sydney was not as easy as hitching from Yattalunga to anywhere like when I was younger. There are so many towns between the two capital cities.

Two of the girls went off first and then the other three of us got a lift together. It took several days to get back. The only things going for us were that we were so young so it made it easier to get lifts.

In nearly every ride we got someone propositioning us for sex. I worried seriously about the other two girls but they got back with no drama.

Back at the Cross, none of us spoke about the trip to Brisbane. Once again we had been abused and used as sex objects for someone else's sick and twisted pleasure. Those scars stay with you for life.

I was starting to tire of the whole sex thing. Even sex with my girlfriend didn't seem the same. I wanted to just live without the fear of someone wanting something from us.

It was after this trip to Queensland that I said to myself and the others, I am fucking sick to death of these fucking Predators and no one, is ever touching any of us again.

A Poem: She was Only Fifteen

I first laid eyes on her
Kings Cross station 1983
I stood there in admiration.
You walked straight up to me.

Both of us street kids
We moved into a refuge together
I loved you so much
You were my forever.

Carefree and young
We got up to all sorts of strife
Then in 1984
Predators took your life.

Kings X police put them in prison
Twenty years is what the judge said
I could not believe
My dream girl was dead.

Then they set them free
Released on an appeal
I felt angry and broken
This cannot be real.

She was only 15!
Not even yet of age
Judge Yeldham set them free
I read on a newspaper page.

He himself with dark secrets
He keeps hidden inside
Then when he's exposed
He commits suicide.

I miss you my darling
Each day brings new pain.
Stay gold my Linda
Until I am with you again.

Glen Fisher
14/9/2018

Chapter 11.
Good Guys are Bad Guys, Bad Guys are Worse

As I sat outside Slots with other kids who were part of that scene, I noticed two girls in school uniforms walking into the park nearby. I think they were from a catholic school, perhaps the one in Woolloomooloo, judging by their uniforms. School uniforms in the middle of the day? The girls were out of place. Alarm bells went off in me. Danger Will Robinson. Danger! I wanted to protect them.

Although I wasn't so good at spotting danger for myself, I could spot it for others. The El Alamein Fountain was a haunt for so many predators. They preyed on young kids, boys most often, who would sell themselves for money. Street kids called it 'cracking it'. I didn't particularly understand it at first but I'd been told by other kids not to go into the park alone. My only experience there was with Ken, the O'Brien's Glass man and that went south fast.

'Look at these kids walking around in the park!' I said to an older girl sitting next to me. New kids had usually heard rumours that you could make big, easy money there and I assumed these two had heard it. They seemed to be scanning the park. They looked younger than us. We ranged from thirteen to seventeen.

Predators were already circling them like sharks, ready to grab at prey. A large, bald headed man came into view and he walked up to them boldly and started a conversation.

My protective instinct compelled me to get involved in the conversation. As I walked over to them I factored in that the man was much bigger than me and that was intimidating. When some other kids followed me they gave me courage. My shoulders grew broader and I grew ten feet tall in seconds. Now I had enough courage to blurt out, 'What the fuck are you doing talking to these girls mate? Bit of young meat hey? Sick fuck.'

The kids with me started to circle the predator. One in, all in. Every kid there had my back. Fear was irrelevant. If I hit him they would have attacked him as if in a feeding frenzy. I didn't like violence and I generally avoided it but if I had to protect the girls, I would. I behaved like a tough guy, circling and taunting. 'You like little girls mister? Is that your go?' Grandstanding for my audience. 'Like them nice and young mister?' Other kids were shooting off their own remarks.

The man stood his ground although he was outnumbered twenty to one. That was worthy of some kudos I suppose but I had to achieve my goal. We had to. I was a tenacious and determined leader just then, even if I was just an undernourished boy.

'My name is Richard,' said the big bloke. 'I work for the Homeless Children's Association.' He points to a name tag on his shirt.

When he said he was a youth worker and spoke with such authority, I was taken aback a little, slightly intimidated. But I resented authority and it spurred me on to stop him taking those girls anywhere.

'So fucking what?' I said, shrugging my shoulders. A park bench became my soap box. I jump onto it for the next part of my act. 'I don't care who you are. Get away from those kids!'

It wasn't really just about the girls any more. It was about me saving face. I still needed to be liked and respected. If I'd just let him walk off with the girls I'd look weak. I felt like I represented all of us kids and I wasn't going to let them down.

Richard was becoming agitated. He'd identified himself and thought that I should let it go. He tried to stay composed. 'I work at the refuge just down on Liverpool Street.' He paused, looked around at the kids as if he might find an ally there. 'I intend taking these girls to that refuge to find out where their families are and get them home to their parents.'

'And I'm here to stop you taking them anywhere!' I said.

I pondered over what to do next, realizing I'd backed myself into a corner. On the one hand maybe he could help them but on the other hand maybe he was just another creep like every other predator in the park.

Another kid, Mark, a heroin addict, said, 'Ah yeah. I know this bloke. Seen 'im at the refuge a few times when I been there.'

I didn't know Mark that well. He was a loner. I'd seen him standing at the fringes of our group. I thought I should at least listen to him because for him to speak at all, he must have something worth hearing.

'There. I told you I'm trying to help,' Richard said. He turns to the girls and says, 'My car is over here. Come with me and I'll take you to the refuge. Let's see if we can help.'

The girls now looked awkward. They probably wondered who all the people fighting over them were. I almost backed away but what Richard said next set me off again.

'It's better that you come with me than have the police pick you up and put you in prison.' He pointed to the police station as he said it.

I perceived Richard's words as a threat and I became more aggressive. He was using fear to control the girls just like my mother had with me. I was almost yelling when I said to Richard, 'Listen cunt! You're not taking these fucking girls anywhere!'

Richard and I argued for ages. No matter what he said, I was not going to let the girls leave Kings Cross with any adult, especially a seedy looking bloke in a car. At last he seemed to realise I was tougher than I looked. He compromised.

Speaking softly and gently he suggested, 'Look, what about you come with us to the refuge?'

I thought about that for a while. I looked at the other kids hoping someone else would come up with a better solution. They had my back but they seemed to be yielding to Richard's authority. Some kids were dawdling away. Some were paying less attention. He'd managed to make them wonder if he was a good guy after all. It took years for some kids to understand that even the good guys are bad and the bad guys are just worse. Sometimes the better they seemed, the more likely they were to be bad.

Richard was resigned to the fact that I wasn't going anywhere while he had the girls. As brave as I was pretending to be, I wasn't prepared to go anywhere with Richard without other kids with me. My sense of being ten feet tall and bullet proof didn't cover getting into a car with him.

'I can't fit you all in the car,' he complained when kids started walking back to me.

I had the solution to this one. 'It's on Liverpool Street you said? Right next to the hospital?'

'Yes, near St Vincent's hospital,' he replied.

'That's just up the road. Ten minutes away. Let's all walk there. Come on. We'll all come. Make sure no cops get involved and no one hurts them.'

We started off, hoping Richard would follow on foot. We finally marched down Darlinghurst Road. Twenty kids, the schoolgirls and Richard who left his car and joined the parade to the refuge.

People in the street asked, 'What's going on?' Some people even joined in without knowing what was happening. If something happened in the Cross, crowds drew in automatically. Fights, arguments, buskers, anything at all, onlookers would come to gawk and get involved.

The girls looked as if they came from good families. They were well dressed, clean cut and very polite. Someone loved them, I was sure. Richard walked beside me and he spent the time talking himself up, telling me what an important youth worker he was and so on. He relied on his identity tag a lot but I thought it looked bogus. He looked like one of those butch looking men you see on Oxford Street in their leather outfits with the bums cut out. He was minus the outfit but he had the same aura. He wore a leather vest and blue denim jeans.

I got clear of Richard as we walked and met up with the girls. I explained to them how I'd spent time in boys' homes for running away from home. I hoped I could make them see that the punishment the law hands out to kids who run away was no picnic.

When we were opposite the refuge, Richard said, 'That's the place.'

He pointed to a derelict looking terrace with the number 429 on the front. It looked like a squat. Next door was the equally dodgy looking Richardson Centre, a soup kitchen.

The Richardson Centre had nothing to do with the refuge. It was possibly the seediest looking soup kitchen on the planet, worse than any squat I had ever been in. It was used by drunks, addicts and other homeless people, mostly elderly men, who sat around drinking soup and eating sandwiches. It was hardly a safe environment for children.

I was so sceptical about Richard's place being a refuge.

'Are you fucking kidding me?' I asked him. 'That place!'

Mark said, 'Yeah that's the place bro.'

Richard had told me about the man who ran the thing, Simon Davies. As other kids caught up with us they said they knew the place too but didn't know much about it or who ran it. Some of them knew Simon Davies but they didn't elaborate on that. I wish they had. The refuge was founded by the children's magistrate Blackmore together with Simon Davies and others.

'Well, go and get Simon then,' I told Richard. 'None of us are going in there.'

Agitated, Richard crossed the road and the girls stayed with us. Some kids had bought drinks for the girls and they talked while we waited. I saw a lot of kids walking in and out of the refuge and most of them were young heroin addicts who I recognized from the streets: Steven and Anne, Sean and his sister.

Five minutes passed and nothing happened so the girls and I walked across the road to look inside. Seeing so many locals in there made me more comfortable and more curious.

A lounge room with a beat up old lounge and kids scattered everywhere, all off their faces. On the ceiling a fishnet hung down with all sorts of things hanging in it. The place resembled more of a drop in centre or a drug den than a refuge. Other refuges I'd seen were very much regimented and their aim was to protect kids. This place had the same kids who hung around Slots and the Snooker Room every day but they were more relaxed.

Richard walked down the stairs and noticed that we'd come in.

'Yes, come on in,' he said cheerily now that he was back in control.

At the top of the stairs there was a dormitory of sorts and there was an office with a small bedroom off it, above the lounge room.

A man sitting in the office turned and his appearance was very off-putting. He had a Wok eye. One eye looked at the wall while the other looked at us. He was wearing a beret.

'Hi. I'm Simon. Simon Davies, the C.E.O. of the Homeless Children's Association. I also do freelance journalism,' he added. 'Mostly for the Sydney Morning Herald. And I'm an author.' *And you like to blow your own trumpet*, I thought.

The Homeless Children's Association? I'd never heard of it and I wished later that I never had.

'Of course,' the trumpet went on, 'there's a lot I do in fund raising too. We want to have multiple properties where we can assist homeless children. We are creating a place called Forest Farm just now.'

There was no visible off switch. He rambled on forever as Richard tried to phone the girl's parents.

Richard told Simon about my refusal to let the girls go with him, adding that half the kids of the Cross had followed me down the street to the refuge. Many of them had gone by now but a few of my closer friends were hanging out downstairs talking to the other kids. Richard's report seemed to ignite Simon's interest in me. Any kid who had a posse of kids with him was a kid these men wanted to know.

Simon said all the right things to get me in. He asked me where I came from, where I'd been living and so on. Half way through telling him about my life, he gently interrupted and said, 'Glen, I know your story oh too well.'

He showed compassion and that hooked me. He talked to me as if I mattered, as if I was important, clever, strong and everything I wanted to be. He knew that I had been sexually abused, that I came from a broken home and had spent much of my life inside institutions. He said he knew my story because it was the story of most kids who walked through the doors of the refuge.

'Glen, we've created this refuge for kids like you. Kids at high risk, to keep you off the streets and safe.' He was on a roll and went on to say, 'We work closely with the Children's Court, Rob Blackmore for example. Rob's a good mate of mine.' He told me about the high profile people who founded the refuge to help kids like me, to keep us safe. He liked to name drop: the Prime Minister, politicians, businessmen and entertainers. He knew them all. In time I'd see that he did have connections with many of the so-called elite.

'Think about joining us Glen,' he said. Then the news any street kid like me wants to hear. 'We have no rules except that we don't tolerate violence among our guests. We don't have a curfew like other refuges. You're free to come and go as you please.' We were allowed to drink and use drugs, just not on the premises. I'd smelt pot as soon as I walked into the refuge but I let that go. To street kids, being told we could drink, do drugs and come and go as we pleased seemed too good to be true. Predators know what it takes to manipulate young, impressionable kids and I was no exception.

Simon, who saw himself as a revolutionary, told me that they had an agreement with the police that kids who stayed there didn't get grabbed by the police and sent to homes.

As I said, I was no good at spotting danger for myself. All I saw was a safe place to live, no police to harass us or lock us up and I could have my friends, who were now my family, with me. Safety and freedom. Sign me up. On the downside, there was no kitchen, no food or clothes. At least there was the soup kitchen next door and the safety and freedom seemed far more important.

I found Simon easy to talk to and I soon told him about my time with Derrick, Uncle Paul and other sexual abuse I had been subjected to.

'This is the very reason the refuge is here, why I started it.' He looks at me very deliberately and adds, 'To protect kids like you, Glen.'

Grant was another person I met through the refuge. He stood out because he was a big man with a beard and he always wore a suit. He wasn't paid to work there but he seemed to be there every day. He worked for an insurance company.

Simon sometimes stayed at the refuge in his own little room and at other times he went home.

Harry, another worker about sixty five years old, lived full time at the refuge and had his own little room right near the office. He was a social worker who sold pot. Richard was a social worker too. Then there was Annette with her side kick, Ian. They hung around on the streets and were a first point of contact for some street kids. They met and introduced them to the refuge.

The last man who we were introduced to, Paul Chetwyn-Jones, was yet another social worker. He wasn't officially at the refuge but visited often. Paul lived at Petersham in a house that was always filled with young kids, mostly boys but they could bring their girlfriends along too.

I thought I was so lucky to be meeting all these wonderful people who had our best interests at heart. I saw Simon Davies as this great saviour of street kids so I was sold on the idea of living under his roof. To my everlasting pain and regret, I sold the idea to other kids too. (I've carried huge guilt with me through my life about that. I can only say that I thought I was helping.)

My girlfriend Linda came with me to the refuge. I loved being there with all my friends in one place. If any of us got arrested, Simon just walked up and demanded that we be set free and we were. That was awesome! This was a dream come true. We tattooed each other's names on ourselves using a sewing needle and ink. I got just about everyone's name on me. I've still got a few of them today. We got the needle, dipped it in ink and just kept stabbing the needle into our skin. It confirmed our belonging together.

I saw Simon as a great leader and role model. I was in awe of him. I spoke highly of him to every kid I came into contact with to convince them to come and stay.

Over the next few weeks it seemed like us kids had taken over the refuge. The older kids, mostly heroin addicts bent on chasing the dragon's tail, spent most of their time in the lounge room using heroin then sitting around stoned. As more of us younger kids came, the first group moved into different buildings provided by the HCA. I was fifteen and our youngest kid was twelve or so. I am still friends with her today.

At the start our younger crew hung out upstairs in the back bedroom smoking pot, occasionally using acid and a variety of other drugs. It was a big deal to have a safe place to experiment with all that stuff. We weren't addicts. We were only recreational users at this point. We didn't look for drugs or money but if we came across them, we'd experiment. One of us boys was always being given something to use. It was easy to get drugs then, around 1982.

There was a third group of kids who just came to the refuge for a few nights or lived there but were not a part of the other two groups. Two girls who worked at a strip club, Veronica and Kathy, slept at the refuge. Each night they'd shower, dress up in lingerie and high heels then put big black jackets over themselves and head off to work, looking like ordinary young girls in big black jackets. Veronica looked so hot in her work outfit.

We soon noticed that the people employed at the refuge were always drinking. Simon loved his Scotch. Grant loved a beer. Harry was a pot head. Annie and Ian were always drunk at the Rex hotel. Paul was a poly drug user who loved pills like Mandies and Reds but he smoked and sold pot as well. He looked like Mick Jagger and he was very effeminate.

Simon took a special interest in me and that seemed to upset the older boys who had lived there before us. I didn't understand why. I knew Paul was bad but the fact that the staff members were drunk all the time made them feel like one of us. The refuge felt like a big continuous party. Would my safety bubble burst?

We would tell the staff when we were about to use drugs and they'd laugh and egg us on. They never ever tried to stop us or suggest it wasn't a good idea.

It was night time and I was sitting in the office with Simon. He was drinking scotch, playing the guitar then he poured me a drink. Wow! An adult is letting me drink with him! No authority had done that before. Not even my mother let me drink. Drinking in the office with the boss. I felt special!

We played guitar all night. He played two songs: Teddy Bears Picnic and I Hate Wogs. Simon was fiercely racist. He plied me with alcohol and I got quite drunk. Sometime through the night Paul arrived and Simon got some tablets, Mandies I think, from him and gave them to me. I took one and drank some more grog. The night passed by somehow.

When I woke up next morning, I was lying in bed next to Simon. Simon was half naked. I felt so many emotions. I was very confused, embarrassed, angry, gutted but most of all I felt betrayed. I was fucking livid. Betrayed! Simon knew that I'd been abused and that I hated it. He'd painted himself as the protector of kids, from this exact thing!

I asked myself, *Why does this keep happening to me?*

The impact Simon's betrayal had on me was profound. I had admired him absolutely. He'd been my new Zorro, my knight in shining armour. Now he was just another stinking paedophile.

Snippets of the night filtered through my addled brain. I felt disgust. I felt afraid. Imprisoned by this thing that had taken away my sense of safety. As I got dressed details of the night kept creeping back. That sick fuck Simon had exploited my vulnerabilities, in particular my longing to be loved.

The other kids were just outside the door in the back

bedroom and I was afraid of them seeing me come out of the room where Simon slept. They would all see me. It was nothing they hadn't seen at Derricks' before but we all knew what Derrick was. This was such a huge deceit. I went down the stairs, blind to other kids. I headed to the street. It was early in the morning and most kids slept during the day.

Grant was walking towards the refuge. He spotted me and as soon as I saw him I broke down and said, 'I've been raped.'

His face showed concern and he said in his very gentle voice, 'By whom Glen? Who did this to you?'

'Simon. Simon, fucking Simon.'

Grant's face changed from concerned for me to panic. I was crying. Grant thought about what I had said to him for some time before he responded, He said, 'Right. Here's what we'll do. You meet me at the Colonial Coffee Lounge later tonight, say six? And we'll discuss what happened.'

I agreed and left. I walked the streets in a kind of depressed daze. Sometime through the day I told Annie what had happened too. She looked equally concerned but her concern wasn't for me. Then I sat quietly outside Slots, not wanting to talk. My mind was torn and confused. The disgusting betrayal, the fear of the consequences, the refuge that had been the best thing to ever happen to me, was a ruse. I felt so angry!

Linda came along and sat on my lap. 'You okay?' she asked.

I said nothing. My head was too full of the night before. The more I straightened out, the more I remembered. The more I remembered, the more upset and angry I got. The tablets I had been given coupled with the alcohol had sent my mind somewhere else so Simon Davies could have his way. To rape me!

'Are you okay?' Linda asked more insistently but I still couldn't talk. I started to cry. 'Glen, what's wrong?' She really wanted to know but I couldn't tell her. I was so angry. I had left Derrick's place to get away from that shit. I'd walked straight into it again. I was fucking livid, broken. I was unable to tell my girl or my friends about my pain.

Scar Face Ray came along and he kept asking me what was wrong too. I wanted to tell him but I knew what he would do. Ray was a tough, no nonsense kid who looked after younger kids. He told everyone I was his younger brother and if anyone ever hassled me, he'd beat them to pulp. I thought he'd just about kill Simon. I didn't want Ray in prison for me. I had flashbacks of the day I told him about the man in the toilet.

I sat there all day with Linda on my lap. I hardly said a word. I couldn't believe what had happened. What did it mean for us and the refuge?

Why did abuse keep happening to me? I dressed like most boys: jeans and a black t shirt. My body was slight and effeminate and I was mistaken for a girl almost every day. It probably didn't help that Linda and the other girls had dyed my hair blond. The attitude those creeps had to me made me angry. I couldn't help how I looked. I never ever wanted to look like a target for sicko men.

One time, just for fun, the girls dared me and another boy to dress as girls and roller skate through the main street of the Cross. They dressed us up with makeup and all, then we put on roller skates and completed the dare.

On the way back down the main street we were standing outside the Chicken Spot when a man approached us. He tried to chat me up.

'Uh, mate I'm actually not a girl. I'm a boy, just dressed up.'

The girls joined in, laughing and enjoying their success. 'Yeah, he is. He's a boy!'

No matter what we said to this guy he was convinced I was a girl. I had to take the top of my dress down to show him I had no breasts. I was pre-pubescent and my voice hadn't broken. That day had been a bit of fun but now I felt as if fun was a different continent to the one I was on.

The Colonial was a café near the park where I was to meet with Grant and Annie. As I got closer to it I noticed Simon had come too. Another betrayal! I needed to meet Grant alone to talk about the rape, not be ambushed by the most deceitful, disgusting person I could possibly think of. I was whirling with anger.

'What the fuck is he doing here?' I asked Grant belligerently.

He took the gentle approach. 'Just sit down Glen and we'll talk.'

When I try to recall the conversation, I find a lot of it is buried in a dark place but parts of it I still remember as if they happened yesterday.

I told them that I was angry and deeply hurt, that I felt betrayed and humiliated.

Annette said almost accusingly, 'This is Kings Cross Glen. This is how the Cross works.'

Grant chipped in, 'Every kid here has a man who looks after him. Simon loves you.'

As pathetic as it may sound, I was taken aback by that. Simon loves me?

Grant told me, 'I have a boy myself who I look after. Every adult man about the place has a boy they take care of.' He told me that Mark was his boy. Mark! The very kid who told us about the refuge! (Not his fault.)

It did seem that nearly every boy I met had a man in his life who looked after him. Sex was the price they paid for 'care'. Many of the girls did too. Not the girls at the refuge. We took care of them ourselves. I still thought of myself as the ten feet tall and bullet proof provider and protector even though I was possibly the most vulnerable kid in the refuge.

I came away from that meeting believing that the town I had chosen to live in worked the way those people said it did. More importantly I believed Simon Davies loved me. For any adult to love me, Glen Fisher, it had to be a miracle. So now I was a confused kid who had a girlfriend Linda and a man who loved me. I lived in a safe place where I should expect to have to do things I loathed while I learnt more and more about how things operate.

That meeting made it obvious to me that all the men working at the refuge were gay. (Later I learned about the vast difference between gay and paedophile men but back then they all seemed the same to me.)

I often went to the Colonial and saw Simon and Grant talking with Annette. I overheard some of their conversations: discussions about who had slept with which kids, which kids had reached puberty, who had a big penis or a smaller one, who could ejaculate and which kids did what. Annette was always a part of the conversation. As a kid I didn't understand how sick and criminal this was. I knew that I myself found it repulsive but I was probably desensitised to it as criminal abuse. It seems normal if everyone around you does it and expects it. This is one of the things Predators do well, they have you believe that what is happening is normal, when it is anything but normal.

I was at the refuge one day when Grant came in, sat down and said, 'How much money does Simon give you?'

I thought about it for a second trying to understand the question.

'Nothing,' I replied. 'I don't crack it.' Why would he pay me if he does it because he loves me? I didn't see what was happening between Simon and I as a soliciting thing.

It's hard for me to admit but I was confused about my sexuality too. I was into girls and always had been. I clearly had a girlfriend. But with all the male attention I got and the feelings I had around Simon loving me, I was getting very mixed up. All I ever wanted was to be safe and for someone to love me. That's why I loved my friends at the refuge so much. It was like the family that I kept getting taken away from. I don't believe that I was really questioning my sexuality so much as to trying to understand what it all meant.

When I told Grant that Simon didn't pay me he looked surprised. 'What? Nothing at all?'

What was I supposed to say?

Grant said, 'I give my boy fifty or a hundred dollars every time!'

I was speechless.

'All the kids who get looked after, well, the men look after them financially too. If my boy needs anything, I get it for him.' He then suggested that I go with him and he'll pay me!

Something did happen with Grant and me that day and he gave me money. I'm extremely embarrassed, filled with guilt, shame and remorse for criminal acts that followed, even though I was not a criminal but a victim. I was so vulnerable to manipulation. I don't want to elaborate and the details really don't matter. Suffice it to say these things groomed us to adopt a lifestyle that included prostitution and drugs. It is only when I started to become an adult that I realised the gravity of what had happened.

Grant taught me to think of my body as a commodity. If I wanted to survive in the Cross, I had to accept men's approaches and expect big money. The younger and the less desperate for money you looked, the more money you commanded and the less you had to do for it. Less attractive kids and those with drug habits and desperation for the money were not popular. Men liked kids like me: uncorrupted, not addicted to drugs or money. They seemed to get an extra kick out of corrupting young minds.

Paul, Grant and Simon saw kids as conquests, as minds to corrupt and bodies to exploit that they could then brag to each other about. But Simon loved me and that was different. I wasn't a commodity to him.

The longer I stayed at the refuge the more it became a brothel specializing in young boys. The kids who didn't use drugs and hadn't reached puberty were hot property. I got to know every sick creep in Sydney. Most were high profile men who seemed to feel entitled to come to Kings Cross and buy children to abuse.

Us kids never had any spare cash. When we did get some it would usually be from one of us boys getting it from an abuser. It went fast. We lived day to day. If someone got a hundred dollars, that was spent on that same day. Some weeks we would be lucky to have twenty dollars between us but we managed to get by.

Richard held a party at his home and another kid invited me and most kids of my crew to come. Richard was staying in a very expensive looking two storey home with a pool out the back. When we got there, heaps of kids in their swimming costumes were playing about in the pool. Other kids sat around the lounge room smoking pot and drinking. There were about thirty or forty altogether. Richard seemed to be the only adult there.

He invited me inside and I smoked a couple of cones and changed for the pool. A kid I knew invited me upstairs. Richard was waiting in his bedroom and tried to get me on to harder drugs.

'You're going to love the sensation this one gives you mate. Just try it.'

I had a snort of something and the sensation at the back of my throat made me want to sit down. I sat on the end of the bed for a while talking to this kid Greg who offered me a drink. I had some to wash away the taste and I started to feel my senses fading.

Greg was talking Richard up but I was struggling to understand anything he said. I thought he was trying to talk me into having sex with Richard and him in a threesome.

'Nah, don't wanna do that,' I slurred. Even in my current state I was intimidated by Richard. He was a big, athletic man and I felt afraid I might get into a situation I couldn't get myself out of.

Greg kept talking about how nice Richard was.

'No. Don't wanna,' I slurred again then I passed out.

I woke up some time later, half naked. Richard was raping me. I jumped up and started to scream at him. 'You bastard! You fucking piece of shit.' I was fucking furious.

Richard and Greg panicked. I really went off my head at them and started walking down the stairs. Apparently everyone had heard me going off my brain. Someone helped me out but I can't remember who it was. I was furious and everyone knew it.

I was put into a taxi and another kid came with me. When we got to the refuge Grant was waiting for me. I told Grant or Simon what had happened. I was disorientated and raging.

After that night I never saw Richard again. I assume that he was sacked for his behaviour at the party. I don't know for certain that that was the reason. I just know I never saw him at the refuge or anywhere again.

Was this all my life was? People hurting me? Getting me off my face and then hurting me. I was over being abused. I mistrusted anyone who gave us drugs, especially adults. It became a theme in my life: people give me drugs so they can abuse me or they befriend me so they can abuse me. I felt gullible and ashamed and I thought about suicide constantly.

Linda had been my girl for some time but lately we seemed to be drifting apart. We'd been on again, off again and it wasn't uncommon for different people in the refuge to hook up with each at such times. Different girls at different times had jumped into my bed but it was, more often than not, just hugging and affection rather than sex. There had probably been about six girls I had slept with either for the pleasure of others, or just nights where they hopped into my bed and we got on.

One day Mouse invited me to her family home. She went into the bedroom and came out in lingerie.

'Do you like this type of stuff?' she asked seductively.

'Not much,' I told her. I think she was stunned.

'Come on, get dressed. Let's go home,' I suggested. We went back to the Cross.

We were like a little dysfunctional family in the refuge. Looking after each other, changing allegiances within our group and getting money however we could.

Simon Davies called me into his office and said, 'I have a job for you.' I was surprised but I listened. 'You could help us with a new project for the refuge.' He told me that they were creating a new refuge called Forest Farm and they'd be building the place in Kariong on the Central Coast. It would house lots of street kids. Simon wanted me to collect donations for it. He had bought me a BMX bike for my birthday and thought I could use that in my job.

I didn't know at the time but the other property owned by the refuge had been donated by the government. The refuge we lived in was owned by St Vincent's hospital and was used by the refuge people rent free. Apart from electricity there would have been no expenses because no food or anything else was provided for residents. I wouldn't be surprised if they'd found a way to get free electricity as well. Simon was very skilled at making people believe in him and the so-called 'Cause'. If only donors had known what was really going on: the exploitation of kids and staff who used donated money for themselves, to go on trips and get pissed.

The only way their clients, we kids, could get money was by having sex. Simon never paid. He would abuse kids a few times then move on to the next one. Grant and Paul paid, but always made out that they were doing you a favour. I was in such a fucked up place that I believed they were helping us when they gave us money. They would abuse you, give you money, however much they felt like and you would be saying, 'Thank you.' We were thanking them for raping us! I was the kid they wanted, me or one other favourite boy. I learnt later that Simon had a hole in his wall that enabled him to watch the girls having showers. Sometimes if we had no money and were really hungry, I'd ask Grant for five dollars and he would give it to me.

After Simon bought me the silver BMX for my birthday, I rode it everywhere, through the Cross and even down the Chapman steps. Simon would tell me where to go to pick up envelopes that I had to deliver to him. He told me all the money I collected was going towards building Forest Farm.

'We're having a big meeting with the Prime Minister soon,' Simon told me one day. 'There'll be a lot of influential people there: state and local politicians, judges, police, social workers and the like.

All the wealthy and powerful people of New South Wales would attend.' I was easily impressed by all the big names Simon knew. He told me this would be the second meeting they had.

The meeting was to be held at the Hilton Hotel's Marble Bar. It was a chance for Simon to explain the wonderful new concept of Forest Farm that the HCA (Homeless Children's Association) was promoting.

Simon said, 'I need you to come with me to the Hilton Hotel, Glen.' That made me feel really important. 'I want you to be the kid who all these people can question about the refuge and what we do here.' He had often told me that he noticed how other kids warmed to me and he thought I could charm the influential set at the Hilton too. I agreed to help out. He was always telling me I was articulate and that others listened when I spoke.

For the big meeting, I dressed in the clothes I wore every day. Old jeans, a t shirt and shoes with holes all over them. Sometimes I got new gear from paedophiles but my current outfit had come from the Salvation Army or St Vincent De Paul and it was all I had. I looked like a street kid and probably smelled like one too. I didn't own many clothes, especially not nice ones. Simon just grabbed me on the day and said, 'Come on. It's time to go to the Hilton.' I would have showered if I'd known this was the day.

Walking into the Hilton Hotel with Simon, I felt important. I was the epitome of what kind of person Simon reckoned he was helping. I was at Simon's side everywhere he went at the meeting - in his nice dress jacket with blue jeans, joggers and a t shirt. He usually dressed daggy but on days when he did important things, he had the gear. Most of the people at this event were men, all in suits.

I wondered why Simon hadn't got me to dress nicely too. I didn't understand that I was being paraded around like an exhibit while Simon told everyone about my poor pathetic life and about him being my rescuer.

His spiel went something like this. 'This is Glen, one of the many kids on the streets that we house at the refuge, the HCA. Glen's mother is a violent drunk. His dad is very violent too and he's an abuser. Glen, like most of our kids, grew up in the system, being moved from home to home or foster care. Like thousands of these poor kids, he's ended up on the streets of the Cross with nowhere else to go. Glen is what we consider a high risk child.'

Simon kept telling me to show people my hand, to let them see what my mother had done to my fingers. That made me start to wonder about this whole thing. I started to feel like an exhibit, not a person. But I kept on because I believed in Simon.

I didn't know what he was talking about when he said 'high risk.'

He went on to say, 'We at the HCA take these kids off the streets, find them suitable accommodation and try to reconnect them with their parents. We want to set up a place near Mangrove Mountain, at Kariong, to create a safe place for kids to go, to get them away from the abuses that can happen in the Cross.'

The man begging for money was the King of abuse! Simon Davies, CEO of the Homeless Children's Association. The audience ate up his words and couldn't wait to help. There was a lot of hand shaking and congratulating him on his great work and vision. They are all desperate to clean up the homelessness that plagued the streets of New South Wales. I think Bob Hawke was there but I am absolutely certain that he played no part in the abuse. I believe he was a good man trying to make a difference and he saw Simon as a person who could achieve it.

'We have learnt that if a child is exposed to street culture, after seven days it's pretty much hard, if not impossible, to get them out. They get hooked into prostitution, heroin, strip clubs or, heartbreakingly, they end up dead.'

Simon and his cronies had groomed me so well that I didn't speak about rapes or prostitution. I believed in Simon and his cause.

The refuge was great for me as long as I told myself the abuse was not abuse but love in mine and Simon's case, and just what we had do to survive in other cases. I valued having all my friends under one roof and I valued the absence of rules and structure. We could do whatever we wanted to and, if we did fuck up and get arrested, someone took care of it for us. Simon usually. He'd turn up at the police station and use his gift of the gab to get us out.

Just as I had, many people at the meeting saw Simon as the saviour of the kids of the Cross. The trouble was that I had seen many in this crowd at the Cross themselves, doing business with kids. Kings Cross was the Devil's playground, a Predators' Paradise where it was hard for kids to know who were the good guys and who were the bad. Rich and powerful people came to buy children so they could act out their vile fantasies. Children desperate for love, homeless and in need of money could easily be persuaded that what they had to do was not perverted but just normal. As I heard my story repeated so many times I realised that Simon was the sort of person he claimed to be protecting me from. I felt exploited and humiliated each time I had to show my fingers and I was offended by being put in this position. I now recognized what a spiel was and how Simon Davies manipulated people with it. All this was just to get money to piss up the wall with his mates.

Simon told my story over and over again that night but it seemed more like a piss up than a real charity event to me. There was so much alcohol between the handshaking, backslapping and promises of funding and help. I was the main exhibit, a lost puppy that needed to be found a home. Simon was there to get money, politicians to get votes, journalists to cover the story and me to please Simon, my hero.

The HCA had a stand in the Hordern Pavilion at the Easter Show too, manned by Simon. It displayed photos and pamphlets to show the fabulous work the staff did at the refuge and the pathetic kids they helped. One of my friends was in a photo, drugged off his face, sitting on a step and looking very unwell. The photo was staged. There was a one of me too and some other kids who were full on addicts and are now dead. Photos of the refuge and of the property where they wanted to build Forest Farm were shown too along with the model. People walked around looking at it all and there was more backslapping, handshaking more promises of funding. I was exhibited again only this time with a girl too. We had to talk to people who looked interested and Simon would try to secure donations.

All sorts of people spoke to us and I think it made them feel better if they listened to your stories and asked how they could help. Did they go back to their lives and forget about the kids of the Cross? What was really happening to the money? People like Simon and Annette built careers of this refuge.

I liked going to the Cross library to read the Asterix and Obelix series. I was reading one day when I noticed a man staring at me. A kid I knew called Darren came in and he walked straight up to the man who was staring. They left together and I knew what that was about.

A few days later I was at the library again when I looked out the window and saw Darren meet Peter (the same man as before) in the park. Darren came into the library and I asked him, 'Hey mate, can you give me a couple of dollars for food?' I was broke and starving.

'All right,' Darren said. He introduced me to Peter.

Peter offered to give me fifty dollars to masturbate with him and he said he wouldn't touch me. I agreed and went with him to a hotel. The relationship with Peter would last for years. I met him around 1982 and I last saw him about 2008. Although he liked young boys he didn't look for lots of different kids. He wanted to have just one kid and he really liked me. He would often meet me at the pub just up from the refuge. Unlike the many predators who dropped into the refuge to pick up kids, Peter refused to go there or interact with other abusers. He disliked paedophile's intensely and never saw himself as one but the truth is he was. He told me to call him Peter which I later would find out wasn't his name. Peter would go on to be as close to a father figure to me as I would ever have in my life. Unlike the many predators on the streets he genuinely cared for me and would even save my life multiple times.

There was an incident or two involving sex at the beginning of our relationship but the more father-like he became, the less sexual stuff happened. He was a loner who lived with his mother. He hated women and wanted a friend more than anything. He was an incredibly private man and never wanted any one to see him out and about. He used to fill his pockets with change so when he walked in the park he could give silver coins to any kid who asked. He had a caring heart and although I'm sure he liked kids flocking around him he did it that because he cared about them and he never asked for anything from them in return. He was a devout Catholic and he was in the Army Reserve.

I had a love hate relationship with Peter. I hated that part of him that brought us together in the first place and I loved and appreciated that he cared about me and would do anything within his power to help me.

There were groups of paedophiles' hanging out at the Cross. People like Grant, Simon, Richard, Maurice, Paul and so on who would meet and compare notes about their conquests. They used the guise of social workers and, as such, they had an unlimited supply of children. They actively recruited boys who were young, good looking and came from broken homes. Those boys were the easiest to manipulate.

I often saw and overheard them when they were drunk at that coffee shop. Annette was always present and listened as they spoke graphically about what kids did what. It makes me sick thinking about it now. It was like a twisted competition to be first to get a child and corrupt them. They'd talk as if they'd found gold. A virgin was a prize. Annette had what she would call a legitimate reason to stay close to these men and the refuge. She disgusts me as much as the men do. She claimed she was researching a revolutionary new way of working with abused kids. In her twisted theory it was valuable to know both the abusers and the abused in detail. She even recruited her own subjects, street kids she picked up, who'd stay at the refuge and be drawn into the deception. She was on the HCA board and she certainly seemed to enjoy her research and the good times that went with it. She made a video to raise funds for the refuge and then went off to do research, laughing along with her paedophile friends. Annette knew full well what was really going on in the refuge and she chose to ignore her obligations to protect children and report crimes to the police.

At the refuge we usually bought pot from Harry, there on the spot. One day he didn't have any so Tommy, Linda, Jarrod and I set out to buy some from another source. We caught the train to Petersham to go to Pauls' place in Corunna Road. He lived there with a group of kids and we knew pot was readily available there.

We knocked on the door and as it slowly opened. A wall of smoke and the smell of pot hit us. There were about twenty kids scattered throughout the lounge room. We knew most of the kids but there were some we didn't know at all. We started talking. A girl called Nadine took an interest in me straight away, asking heaps of questions as Linda chatted with someone else.

Linda was my girlfriend but that didn't worry Nadine one bit. She had eyes for me and to be honest I had eyes for her too. Linda was always the most beautiful girl in any room and I still don't know what it was that attracted me to Nadine. She was very good looking but Linda turned heads everywhere she went. I think Linda and I were so comfortable together that we might have interacted more like brother and sister than partners. Although we were very sexual we were doing our own thing more and more.

Paul Jones, the owner of the place, was a masseuse and chiropractor who would help kids out if they had a physical problem. I had a problem with my tailbone, undoubtedly from a childhood injury and I mentioned it to Paul.

'Come up and let's see if I can help you with that,' he suggested.

I went upstairs, believing that Paul would help. But I was assaulted instead, then given pot and money. I went back downstairs like nothing had happened. I sat down dazed and Greg packed me a cone.

All the kids, including our girlfriends, knew what was going on but we knew that this was what we had to do to survive. Being tricked into being assaulted was as normal as eating or drinking. I was very protective of the girls and kept an eye on anyone going anywhere near them. I'd use the money I was paid to look after us all. Now I wish I had protected myself as well as I protected everyone else.

Nadine and I talked exclusively for most of the time we were at Paul's. It was obvious that she liked me. It could be that I was more of a challenge to Nadine because I had a girlfriend. Nadine had a boyfriend who was staying at Paul's place too. He was a pretty boy who'd only just arrived on the scene. There was a leader kid, let's call him Mal, who lived with Paul and he had been at Richard's the night I got abused.

Mal would act as a go between for paedophile's and kids he met on the streets while he was selling pot. He introduced me to other men including another Paul, manager of a Hungry Jacks place in Town Hall. I don't blame Mal. He had to find his way of surviving. He was a dealer and a user, not quite an addict. Kids relied more and more on being off their faces to survive. This was slowly happening to me but I didn't see it. I just knew that I had to be off my face for a paedophile to get me.

As we all sat in Paul's lounge room Mal was packing cones and the bong was passed to me. Nadine lit for me and Linda, who kept giving Nadine death stares, was not pleased. I was always faithful to Linda and she was to me. I would never have cheated on my girl but I did like the extra attention from Nadine.

If anyone had tried to get with me, street etiquette would kick in. The other kids would do something about it. The same would happen if a guy tried to get with Linda. The kids would say, 'Hey, she's with Glen. Don't go near her.'

Nadine and her boyfriend were new to the streets and so they might not have known the rules.

'Come on. Let's kick on back up the Cross,' Tommy said after some time.

About five of us left, all stoned, but we'd kept a stick to take back to the refuge. At Petersham Station the police spotted us. We looked like street kids and we were probably loud too. We were loud everywhere we went. Especially Linda and I. We were probably the two most attention seeking of the kids and we were always doing silly things.

I had a bag of pot on me and some money, probably fifty dollars. That was the usual amount kids got for sex because it was how much they needed to buy heroin.

Jarrod said, 'Grunt. Grunt. Copper cunt.' Street talk for, 'Cops are coming.'

As the two officers walked toward us, we weighed up our choices. We could run, which we'd done many times before and discovered that the police hardly ever bothered chasing us unless we'd actually done a crime. Or we could stand our ground. There was only one way leading in and out of the station and there was nowhere really to run to so we stood our ground.

The coppers asked for our names and addresses.

'We live at a refuge in the Cross,' we told them.

Their ears pricked up.

'We're going to search you,' they told us.

They found the pot and the money I had. The cop held the money in one hand and the pot in the other.

'Where does a kid your age get this much money?' he asked.

'I get the dole and today's pay day,' I tell him. I wasn't really on the dole because they always found reasons not to give it to me.

The train was due in about five minutes so I said, 'We are waiting for the train that's about to come. We're not causing any one any trouble.' I said it a bit cheekily, disrespectfully, as had become my habit. I didn't like police.

The copper looked at me coldly, handed back my money, dumped the pot in the bin then left after giving us a bit of a talking to. We continued waiting for the train. Just as it pulled in Tommy grabbed the pot out of the bin and jumped on the train.

We travelled on a train nearly every day but not once did we buy a ticket. Sometimes we had the money but we just never did pay. We knew a few ways to get out of the station. For example as the Bondi train left, you could run up the tunnel, jump over a wall into Woolloomooloo then walk back up to the Cross. We only did this when there were police or ticket inspectors about. Official ones.

Our most common method was to say, 'Local,' to the ticket collector and keep walking. Or we would say, 'Street kids.' They never bothered trying to hassle us. We were known to most of the station attendants and most of them were friendly. They knew me as Roach. The other option if an unknown collector was there we would run out jumping the turnstiles at the same time then keep on running. No one was going to chase us for fifty cents or whatever price it costs to catch a train.

On rare occasions someone would try and grab one of us but all of us would get together then and make a scene. That made the over vigilant collector let go. It wasn't worth the hassle. Sometimes I'd jump the turnstiles and keep walking. I didn't even look back. Or I'd pick up old ticket off the ground and hand it to them. They never checked the date on the tickets anyway.

About two weeks after the night I met Nadine, Linda and I got into an argument. We often had silly fights like most young couples and one of us would say, 'You're dropped!'

Arguments between us were rarely serious and I don't recall what this one was about. Linda was never jealous of any one and I wasn't either. That was one good thing about the kids at the refuge. No one ever tried to sleaze onto another person's partner. Anyway, for some reason this argument was a big deal to everyone. Other relationships went on and off around us but ours was a constant. Linda and Glen, always together. Linda was unique. She was honest, true to herself and she was loved by everyone. Recently our relationship had become more like two best mates though, rather than lovers.

Linda was drawn to the Cross the same as I was and she'd

go up there every night later and later with other girls. I was scared about her doing that but no one controlled Linda. If you had to pick two kids who were the least able to be controlled, you'd have to pick Linda and me. We'd had enough of people trying to control us growing up. My life before the Cross had been abuse or taking orders. I wasn't having any more of that. No-one tells me what to do now. I thought as a boy I was in control but the sad truth is, I was a gullible child being manipulated daily.

Grant bumped into me that day. 'What happened with you and Linda this morning?' he asked.

'Just had a fight,' I told him.

He said, 'You guys are so beautiful together. You're meant for each other.'

That's what I'd thought but things had changed.

Grant went on. 'Can the two of you meet us tonight and I'll shout you both dinner?'

'Yeah, all right,' I said.

At around the time I was supposed to meet Grant and Linda, I was walking towards Slots and a group of kids were sitting on the wall. I saw Nadine amongst them. She was excited to see me. We started talking and I told Nadine that Linda and I had had a fight. Nadine's eyes lit up straight away. She and her friend Julie started whispering and giggling.

'Do you want to come over to my place with Nadine for a while?' Julie asked.

I had no intention of breaking up with Linda but I was attracted to Nadine and wanted to know more about her. Linda and I sometimes had fights but we always got back together. I agreed to go to Julie's place. I felt as if I was kind of cheating on Linda.

Three of us got into a taxi heading for Julie's place. I spent the night there. We all slept in the same bed because they only had one and nothing happened except a lot of talking until we fell asleep. Nadine said she liked watching me dance so I'd spent a lot of the night showing her my moves. The things young people do to impress each other! I still couldn't stand still and have a conversation without busting out different moves.

I went back to the Cross the next day with Nadine. Everywhere we went people spoke about Linda being pissed off. I thought it was inevitable that there was going to be some kind of big argument or even a fight between Nadine and Linda though I had done nothing with Nadine. I don't know what it was about her. Maybe it was just that she really liked me. We seemed to connect on a different level than what Linda and I did perhaps?

Later that night I ran into Linda alone at the Snooker Room, so we sat down and talked. I told her that I liked Nadine and I didn't want to fight. I said, 'I'm confused because I love you but I'm really attracted to Nadine.'

Surprisingly, Linda was really cool. We were like best friends. She said, 'If you like Nadine and she likes you, I'm okay with that. But what I didn't appreciate was hearing it from other people.'

I respected that. I would have felt the same had other people told me Linda had done the same thing. I hated betrayal, loyalty to me meant so much.

Other kids were more upset with me than Linda was. What I hadn't known was that Tommy and some other kids had seen me get in the taxi with Nadine. They knew Linda was my girlfriend and they knew Nadine was interested in me. I'd gone about this the wrong way. It was now official, I was going out with Nadine and Linda was my best mate.

I took Nadine to the refuge and all the kids were out the front hanging out and talking. It was good because the attention wasn't on Nadine and me. We were holding hands and everyone started looking at Nadine.

A kid named Mitch, whose special skill was stealing cars, had got his hands on a Statesman. He was standing outside the car.

'Want a ride?' he asked us.

We never went for joyrides. This would be a first. Tommy jumped in the front passenger seat and Nadine and I got in the back. Mitch started screeching all around town. Car stealing was so common and easy back in this era, so many kids got into stolen cars and often would get into serious accidents.

Tommy hadn't spoken to me or Nadine yet so I said to him, 'This is Nadine bro.'

Tommy said, 'Who?'

'Nadine, mate,' I told him.

'Who?'

I was getting agitated, so I said loudly, 'Nar-fucking-Dene mate.'

Tommy looked at Nadine and said, 'Oh, Nar-fucking-Dene. Hi Nar-fucking-Dene.'

That was it. She was accepted and would be my partner now for the next two years. Tommy insisted on calling her Nar-fucking-Dene all that day.

'How are you going, Nar-fucking-Dene?'

Mitch parked the car in the lane at one point.

'Can I have a go at driving?' I asked him.

It was a manual and I didn't know how to drive anyway. I kept stalling and kangaroo hopping but eventually I got it to go forward! I bumped right into the car in front of us. So much for my first drive of a stolen car. We all got out and walked away.

The second time we got into a stolen car Tommy was driving and there were four of us there. We drove through the main street of the Cross and we were spotted by the police. They chased us. We came to a corner at Woolloomooloo and we lost control. We took the back end off a parked car and careened head on into another one.

I instinctively jumped straight out and ran up an embankment. Within about thirty seconds the cops arrived and arrested the other three kids. I lay on the embankment watching. Not one of the others dobbed on me. They were charged with Car Theft and Conveyance, the official name for being in a stolen car.

Not long after that we told Mitch to stop stealing cars or if he did steal them, not to bring them to the refuge. We didn't want the heat.

A bit later we got news that Mitch had died. That was distressing. Mitch was the second kid from the refuge to die recently. Jacob, the boy who Simon abused regularly before I came, got into trouble with the police and was extradited to New Zealand. Not long after he was involved in a motorbike accident and died. It felt like members of our family dying.

It gradually became known to paedophiles that the refuge was a brothel, similar to Brett's Boys down the road. The refuge was a gathering of children where abusers could walk in and pick a child for sex. All sorts of men would come who were either directly connected with the refuge or connected to one of the kids. Many of the kids, not all, had a man who 'looked after them or had been abused by someone.'

It shows how confused and messed up we had become. These men made us that. They made us dependent on them.

As an adult and father now, it makes my guts churn thinking how those adults preyed on kids and how the men who ran the refuge used us to get huge grants from the government in the name of helping at risk kids. The worst thing of course is the affect they had on our lives. More of that as my story goes on.

There was one night when we had no money but were all so hungry that we made a hole in the wall between the Richardson Centre soup kitchen and the refuge. I think it was as much for fun as for food. We broke in and got something to eat. I didn't actually go but some of the kids did.

The following day the police turned up and we were all questioned about it. No-one was charged. You might want to argue that it was pretty shitty of us to break into a soup kitchen to steal from them. Or you could ask where the huge amounts of money that had been donated to the refuge actually went if not to feed their starving kids. No food or any help was provided other than a place to sleep. There was a burnt out kitchen at the back of the refuge so there was no way to get anything to eat. The refuge was about ten minutes walk to the Cross if you had money to buy something.

I arrived back at the refuge one morning with a few of the kids. Grant and a man named David who ran another refuge were awaiting us. They looked grim.

'The refuge is closed,' one of them told us as we walked in trying to prevent us from entering.

'What? What the fuck are you talking about?' I said. It seemed like a joke. Or a lie.

'Sorry, but the building's been condemned,' Grant said. 'We've been told we have to get out.'

It was like I'd been shot! I said, 'No! There's no fucking way we're going.'

'Well, that's how it is Glen. It's closed. Condemned.'

Was my world falling apart? They could go if they wanted to but I wasn't going anywhere. Ten of us stayed put. We refused to go. This was our home and we'd hold out for as long as we could and do whatever we could to stop this unfair thing happening.

Later I was told there had been an accusation of misappropriation of funds as well as the building being unsafe to live in. I spoke to Grant many years later in prison and he said there was a directive issued to close the refuge and it referred to kids being abused there.

I decided I was not leaving without a fight and the others agreed. If they wanted us out they would have to forcibly remove us. Grant or David told us that we needed to speak to the CEO of the St Vincent's Hospital as they were the owners of the building. We never saw Simon or Annette at the building again. They didn't come to see if we were okay or let us know what was going on. We did know the HCA owned other properties and Harry and some other kids went to stay in one at the Rocks.

John Ireland, CEO of the hospital, was our target when we marched into the hospital emotional and angry. I demanded to know where he was. I found his office and walked straight in. I think he was shocked to see a skinny little blond boy barge in like that and start screaming at him. I was our self-appointed leader of this rebellion.

'Why? Why are you kicking all us refuge kids onto the street? That doesn't make any fucking sense. We have nowhere to go!'

'The building isn't suitable young man. They don't even have a kitchen to feed you!' he said with disdain. 'There are no workers there to watch over you anymore.' There had never been any food the entire time I had been there, why did it suddenly matter now?

I thought for a second and said, 'Well this is a hospital, right? You guys serve food to all the people here every day. How hard could it be for you to provide meals for us at the refuge? There's only ten of us left there. We have nowhere to go. Don't you get it! We have nowhere to live!'

The thought of all of us being separated again was too much for me to bear. We'd all put up with so much to keep our little family together. No fucking way I was leaving easily.

I think Mr Ireland was a little overwhelmed by my passion and desperation. I think he felt compassion for us. He said we could stay for short term. 'I'll provide meals for you. They'll be delivered and we'll try to find another place for you kids to go.'

'We want to stay together,' I snapped back, relieved. 'We don't want to be torn apart. Please! If we've got nowhere to live the police will lock us all up in homes. We're a family. All of us. Family.'

Mr Ireland said, 'Okay, calm down.'

I kept on pleading our case. Maybe he didn't want a commotion. If we made too much noise, the plan to shut the refuge down quietly and turn us away would be exposed. Moving us back onto the streets wasn't going to be as easy as they'd hope. I was headstrong and ready to fight for our home. Sure, we had not been safe at the refuge where we were constantly preyed upon, not fed or cared for. No-one spoke about the predators but I think the authorities must have known. Maybe there was a lot more being said behind closed doors without us knowing. Simon and the others all disappeared without a word and we ten kids had to use the back door to get inside our boarded up home.

For the next week the hospital delivered food for us. All sorts of workers from other places came to see us, trying to explain that we had to go. As our spokesman I stood up to them and said, 'We are not fucking going? We have nowhere to go!' Why couldn't they see that?

I rang the Daily Telegraph to see if they could help us. I figured if we go public they wouldn't be able to remove us. They sent out a camera-man and a journalist, Stuart McLean. A photo of us kids sitting on the lounge appeared in the paper with an article about the house for runaways. We learnt from the story in the paper that our refuge had once been a butcher shop. Although I had told the journalist about some of the abuse that went down in the refuge, not a word of that was reported.

The story said that although our building didn't look much, it was home to us runaways. It said that I was our spokesman and had implemented rules that we lived by and so forth. I thought it was pretty good because it showed we were homeless but as civilized as we could be in our situation. The public was now aware that we existed and no doubt heads came together and asked, 'How do we fix this?'

I kept going to John Ireland for updates. I was afraid. I knew once they closed the refuge completely they would tear us apart. As I think about this time now, I feel the same deep, deep sadness as I felt back then.

Few refuges offered to take the girls but no-one would take all of us together. Although the HCA had other buildings that might have been available, none was offered to us. Were we trouble? Too hot to handle? I reiterate that I am told years later that a message came through that It has gotten out of hand. Grant was referring to us being abused.

One of the key men who got the refuge closed was a priest named David. He ran a refuge but he refused to take any of us. He must have seen us as drug addicted prostitutes. He said he couldn't take us in because he would have to keep other kids safe from us. He commented about track marks on my arms. What track marks? I didn't have any.

I hope you read this and know that kids started to die after that refuge closed. This David though was a part of the cases later against the abusers of the refuge.

About two weeks of waiting passed and then loud unusual noises woke me one morning. The police were yelling and doors and windows were smashed. Most of the other kids were asleep upstairs. Police were everywhere. Detectives and uniformed cops were rampaging about as if we were a huge criminal gang. I ran through Simon's office and escaped down a pole but, being loyal to my family, I came back to be with the other kids.

We were manhandled, roughed up, yelled at, handcuffed, arrested and thrown into the back of a police wagon. I fought, screamed and yelled as they threw us in the wagon. We were taken to Bidura Children's Court in Glebe. We were treated like criminals. The real criminals had fled. I cannot even put into words the fear I felt that day. Not the fear of Police, or the fear of being locked up. The fear was of my family being torn apart. I had endured so much to be able to keep us all together.

Bidura had once been a nasty home for girls but a thirty million dollar facility replaced it. It was a co-ed home and in comparison to places like Yasmar, Daruk and other homes, it was so much nicer.

Ironically the judge who worked at Bidura was one of the founders of the refuge, Senior Magistrate Rob Blackmore. The HCA closed in 1995 but was renamed Mangrove Mountain Trust. Rob Blackmore was the chairman.

I was let out of Bidura the following morning. I would have preferred to stay there with the other kids but I was now sixteen years old. It was in the interests of the authorities to let me out and away from the other kids because I was our leader and they needed to shut me up. The rest of the kids, my brother included, were held in Yasmar. Tommy and two of the girls were wanted over that car stealing incident that I had run away from. Tommy was convicted of car theft and sent to the dreaded Mt Penang.

So I headed back to the streets. Within days, I'd got a few kids together and we broke into Bidura to get the girls out. Some of the kids got caught breaking in but I got free. It was in the paper. *Kids break into Bidura.* Derrick had a place on a nearby street in Glebe so we had thought we could go there. We didn't get the girls out but Bidura was a holiday camp compared to other homes.

This was the beginning of the end of my little family. I was heartbroken. What was worse? Simon Davies was nowhere to be seen. He disappeared but my saying too much would get him to reappear soon enough.

My refuge family the day 429 was condemned. I'm the blond boy in the front row. *(Source: State Library of New South Wales)*

Chapter 12.
Mr Ombudsman

I was out of Bidura and I had no charges outstanding. At sixteen I could no longer be picked up as a runaway so I was out on my own while the other nine were in custody, some wanted on charges and others held as runaways.

I felt empty. I was free but I missed the other kids. I was hurting. I'd been the one who'd stood up and spoken out for us all. By separating us the authorities were able to silence us.

There was a girl named Tammy who lived in the Cross and she liked me. She was heavily addicted to heroin. I stayed with her for a few nights. I had nowhere to go and the offer to stay with her was too good to pass up. I had made the choice that I was not staying again with any adult men. It masked the emptiness I felt. We met some locals in the park and a guy we knew came along with a sheet of acid that someone had given him. He offered to share it with us and we accepted. He cut us each a trip and we used it there in the park. Usually when you buy acid on the streets it comes in little squares of cardboard. This was still in one sheet as it is when it's apparently made. It was my second trip and I remember hanging out all night on the street with Spin and other kids. Acid was commonly used in the sixties but would occasionally surface on the streets of the Cross. I didn't usually like taking this type of drug as I often felt afraid from the effects. After the trip Tammy and I went to her place to sleep.

She had a little flat and worked in a few brothels. She had become like a big sister to me. We slept in the same bed but I never considered having sex with her although she asked me several times. I'm certain that, like me, she hated sex. She had to tolerate it to support her habit. I think she really just needed someone to love who would love her in return. That person couldn't be me because I loved Nadine. I couldn't get to sleep because of the trip so we walked up the street.

At the end of November that year (1983) Tammy, some local kids and I were sitting at our usual spot on the wall next door to Slots. I saw two familiar detectives walking towards us.

'He'll do. Mr Ombudsman,' said Officer Smith.

As the police were walking towards me I heard one of the officers say to the other one, 'He'll do.'

Then they put me under arrest with another young boy I didn't know and my friend Spin.

They claimed that some one had done an assault and robbery nearby and that the person who had been hurt had described me as having committed this crime.

I was way too small to beat up a grown man but they claimed I had five other kids with me. They knew that we hadn't done anything wrong, I'm sure. We were just easy targets when arrests needed to be made. One of the detectives reckoned he'd shown the victim a photo of me and that he'd identified me as the attacker. I had recently made a complaint to the Ombudsman and here was their chance to lock me away where they could control me.

They took me to Darlinghurst Police Station. I sat with the detectives who I'd known for years. When they interviewed me about the crime Tammy came as my support person to see if she could help. She had been with me for the previous twenty four hours and she knew I hadn't bashed or robbed anyone. They wrote in their report that she was my sister because she pretended she was.

One of the arresting officers worked with the detective I had complained about to the Ombudsman. They all kept calling me 'Mr Ombudsman'. It became my nickname to the police of the Cross. When I was sitting there they asked me to make a statement. I refused. I said I am not making a statement on something I didn't do. Then suddenly one of them threw a typewriter at me when I refused to sign a statement saying I had committed the crime. That's the kind of freedom police had back then. Being innocent in Kings Cross meant shit if the cops had it in for you.

My complaint to the ombudsman was about a time Michael and I were arrested by Kings Cross Police. At the station they spat in Mike's face.

Mike said, 'You do that again, I'll spit back at ya.'

They spat again so Michael spat back. They both turned on us as I stood up to defend my brother. My brother didn't ever back down, especially from Police. I had trouble with a certain detective many times. He was corrupt and an arsehole and I gave information about him and other detectives to the Royal Commission into the NSW Police Service that focused on corruption many years later.

One thing that the police didn't know was that it wasn't actually me who had written the letter to the Ombudsman. It was a kid on the street who I had told about the thing they did to Michael. He penned the letter for me. I didn't even know who the Ombudsman was or what they did but I wasn't going to tell the cops that.

This time I was charged with 'Assault and Robbery in Company'. Bail was refused because the crime was violent. I was held at Minda Remand Centre. In a home again for no reason except that the Kings Cross Police wanted me out of the way. The people who'd run the refuge no doubt did too. I was a liability. I can't be sure if the two points are connected but I know Grant had a very good relationship with the Kings Cross detectives.

I was put on the junior side called Lawson at Minda. The senior side was called Pattison. I was really angry at being unfairly locked up once again. Minda held kids aged from sixteen to eighteen and I knew most of the kids who had some clout among the inmates. Many boys were held for serious offences and built their reputations on the crimes they'd done. It was a very rough place but I was lucky I knew so many other people there. I'd only been in homes for running away but now I was in for something serious. The others didn't know I was innocent and I thought they didn't need to know. I met a guy called Andrew who was tall and blond and was there because he was accused of killing the Greek consul and a school teacher. His co-offender had lived at the refuge. I was well known in homes and on the streets so this time my stay in a home was easier.

I had recently broken up with Nadine over finding her in bed one night with Chad the doormen. He was starting a new disco in Kellet Street Kings Cross. I walked up to look inside early one morning and caught her with him. It really hurt me that she had done this. I hooked up with another girl who was stunning Leslie.

Leslie, my stunning girlfriend, came to visit me quite a few times in Minda. When she walked in in her mini skirt, guys would stare at her probably wondering how I landed such a hot girlfriend. I sat cuddling and kissing my girl as other inmates stared at her beauty. Another friend, Bunny a stripper in the Pink Pussycat who was equally as stunning but a little older, came one time and she told everyone I was her brother. As hot as Leslie was, I still missed Nadine and it hurt to remember her and Chad together. The relationship with Leslie only lasted a few months.

The case against me was brought before Rob Blackmore. A few people spoke up for me including Grant and, to my surprise, Simon. When I got to court I saw police looking at me with such hatred in their eyes. The man who I was accused of assaulting had come out of his alleged coma but he refused to come to court. My guess is he didn't want to be pressured into identifying me as the perpetrator when he knew I wasn't the one.

Without a witness and without the police proving I'd had anything to do with the robbery, the case had to be dismissed. The judge though didn't just agree to let me go on my own.

Magistrate Rob Blackmore released me into the care of Simon! King Predator himself. Maybe Simon was worried that I might say the wrong thing in court. It was definitely in Simon's interests to get me out and keep me quiet. Simon, the hero, to the rescue again. Apparently I could have told him to get fucked and gone my own way as I was over sixteen. However, I thought the law forced me to stay with him, so once again I was in his so-called care. Under his power, under his spell and believing I was indebted to him. The man I believed loved me had rescued me from the police yet again.

Other people I loved and cared for were still locked up. Linda was in the home at the front of the property in Bidura with other kids I knew from the streets and institutions and I'd I seen her as I'd walked free from Minda just before Xmas.

As I stood outside Bidura Court one of the detectives asked to speak to me. He looked angry. We went to a quiet place at back of the courthouse. Suddenly he grabbed me by the throat, pushed me hard up against the wall. With his face just a breath away from mine he snarled through his teeth, 'I don't want to hear one fucking word about this.'

He was referring to my report to the Ombudsman. Kings Cross and Darlinghurst police were being investigated at the time so they were having a rough time and were probably frenetically working to hide their involvement in all the illegal schemes they were involved in. They would kill to protect their criminal empire. The last thing they needed was a smart ass street kid making waves. They were probably scared I'd make another complaint.

Simon took me by train to his parents' place at Summer Hill.

'You have to stay with me as instructed by the judge,' he said and I believed him and stayed.

We shared the front room and his sisters had the next two rooms. His parents lived there too. Simon was writing a book about the Islands of Sydney Harbour at this time. He had finished writing Shooting Up which he based on what he saw of the kids at the refuge. Simon loved titles. Freelance Journalist was one he often dropped into conversations when he wanted to impress. He always talked himself up to be far more important than he actually was. He had powerful friends but at the end of the day he was broke, a drunk and a paedophile, sponging off his parents.

Simon told me that I wasn't allowed to go to the Cross so I was pretty much forced to be with him all the time. I went with him when he did research for articles he said he was writing for the Sydney Morning Herald. He said he had been asked to write for Home and Away, the television series, too. He was always telling people about his achievements, real or imagined.

Despite all that had happened I still believed in Simon. I hate writing about this. I was so confused, because of this man. One of the hardest things for me to write in this book and make people understand is the relationship between an abuser and the abused. The abusers are usually very skilled at making you reliant on them, look up to them and even care for them. Simon did this really well. My confusion was the two feelings I held for Simon. One was a deep rooted anger, even the thoughts of retribution, the other was the admiration I had for him.

Whilst staying at Simons home one time we went to a place opposite Central station to a sex shop where we watched short videos. As we watched there was a girl no older me, maybe younger, having sex with a pig, another young girl was being screwed by a horse! Bestiality. Simon was enraged by this and he wrote an article and bragged to me that he'd fought to get this place shut down.

He also wrote an article disclaiming the benefits of light beer. I could have added that this journalist was always drinking scotch while he conducted his tests. I think now that he was rightfully enraged by what he saw that day, yet the morality of him being in charge of a refuge for vulnerable street kids and exploiting them sexually didn't seem to matter.

I am not sure how long I'd been staying with Simon when one of his sisters first approached me. She took me into her room and said she was very concerned about me because she knew that I was sleeping in the same single bed as Simon.

She said, 'It is just wrong.'

'I've got nowhere else to go,' I told her. 'The refuge I was in has closed. The judge said I have to stay with him so I won't go back on the streets.' I remember her showing a real genuine concern for my welfare and for some reasons that made me really like her. Someone took the time to actually care about me.

She must have spoken to their parents about her concerns. Each night I had dinner with the family and soon it became clear that they were all concerned about the sleeping arrangements in the front room.

One morning Simon sat me down on the bed in his room and said, 'My parents want us to move out of the house. I think we'll be able to move into a flat I've found in Annandale, right next to the Uni.'

Simon introduced me to the landlord as his son. Blind Freddy could see we looked nothing alike. I had had a bit of a growth spurt and I was nearly six feet tall by then. Simon was a short little fat man with a wonky eye. The very first night we moved in Simon said, 'I can't stay here tonight. I have a story to write. I'll get back to you in a couple of days.'

As he left I got a sinking feeling that he would not come back but I thought Judge Blackmore said I was obligated to stay with Simon so I waited. I got those feelings inside I did the day my father dumped me at the bus terminal at Oxford street a few years ago. Instinctively I just knew Simon wasn't returning but I kept repeating to myself, the Judge said he has to care for me and he will.

He didn't come back when he said he would so I didn't leave the place for the two weeks, waiting for him to return. The landlord asked me every day, more and more sceptically, 'Where is your dad?'

I always replied, 'I honestly don't know. He is writing a story for the Sydney Morning Herald.' Then I'd add, 'He'll be back.'

Before long the landlord announced, 'Your rent was due yesterday. If your father isn't back by tomorrow, you'll have to leave.'

I slept in the flat alone. I hated being alone. I preferred to be surrounded by kids as I had been for the last couple of years.

The following morning I waited nervously for a knock on the door. Even then I held on to the hope that Simon would appear with the rent. Maybe he was just running late? *He'll be here soon,* I told myself.

The landlord knocked and I knew it was him. I waited a few moments. He knocked again. 'I know you're in there! Open the door or I'll open it myself.'

It was time for me to face the fact that I had been dumped, again. That Simon needed to get rid of me. He'd paid two weeks rent for a seedy flat and left me there with no money, food or care. There is none so blind than he who will not see. Now I saw.

How Judge Blackmore had failed to have someone check on me, to see where I was sleeping and what care I was getting, boggles my mind. None of them gave a shit. I suppose that in his mind Simon the saviour was taking care of me. How do you be the founder of a children refuge in Kings Cross and never go inside to see. If he had no one would of allowed what went on there to commence let alone to continue on as it did.

If I'd gone to the Cross at this point I'm sure I would have found Simon with Grant preying on the streets, as they always did, for new talent. Trade. Little boys.

I felt as lonely as I had the day Barry dumped me at the bus terminal in Oxford Street. Would being dumped keep being a theme in my life? Simon had hurt me so much recently. The day the refuge was closed down he wasn't even there to explain what was going on. His unexplained disappearance hurt. His abuse certainly hurt a lot and ate away at me. How could I have been so Naive. This anger would stir in me for many years. Sure he turned up, out of the blue, at Bidura but that was for his own protection and now he'd dumped me again. I was a liability. I spoke out too much. I had found a voice. Had I reached my use by date? I was sixteen, street wise and I could speak for myself. I had become everything a controlling paedophile doesn't want.

I wish the day I was at court before magistrate Rob Blackmore I had had the courage to tell him right there he had abused me. His jaw would have hit the ground. Not I believe at the revelation, more so at my saying it in the court room.

Fear threatened to take control of me! *What am I going to do?* I was upset and afraid. I went slowly to the door, defeated, and opened it.

'Time to go kiddo.' He looked at me half with empathy, the other with determination that I was leaving.

No property to gather, nothing. I left. Just me and what I was wearing. I wandered down the stairs to Parramatta Road.

I walked along beside a big sandstone wall probably built hundreds of years ago, heading towards the city. It's the only direction I knew. I went to the Cross. I ran into Grant and he asked me where I was living. He asked me did I want to come home with him to Parramatta. He offered to give me money. I didn't want to do that anymore but I had no money and I needed a place to live so agreed to go with him. Grant was one of the nicer adults I knew, aside from being an abuser. He had this way of abusing you but making you feel like he was doing you a favour. Like I said they are very skilled at making you believe they are doing you a favour, like they are your saviours when the truth is they are evil paedophiles.

We went to Parramatta where Grant had a flat that he shared with Simon, a fact he didn't tell me until we were on our way there.

'What! That bastard dumped me in a flat in Annandale!' I said. I got angry then repeated, 'He fucking dumped me.'

Grant became awkward. 'He wouldn't do that to you, Glen,' he said. 'Simon loves you' he told me. Obviously Simon hadn't broken the news to Grant yet.

Their flat in Parramatta was in a nice high rise block that looked out to the Parramatta River. Simon arrived home with a little blond haired boy. This made me angry. Just seeing Simon made me angry, but that he had replaced me with another child infuriated me even more. He did that to Stewart, replacing him with me and now I was replaced with this child, a fresh kid who wasn't corrupted yet.

I was shocked and I was angry. I went off at Simon, 'You fucking dumped me! Now you go and get a new fucking kid to abuse?'

Grant's jaw dropped and he didn't know what to say. Simon turned to him and asked, 'What's he doing here?'

All the pieces started to fit together and I knew that Simon had freed me from Minda to shut me up and then deliberately dumped me. He clearly thought he had freed himself of a problem but there I was right in his face.

I felt so angry, so betrayed. I walked out. I recall catching the train from Parramatta back to Central then a bus to Glebe. Derrick lived at Glebe and I thought maybe I could borrow a few dollars from him. I thought about the last two years of my life. I became more and more angry as I thought about what they had done to me and my friends.

Now I could admit that Simon was the king of bullshit. He had told me once that 'words make the man.' He said you can get through any situation in life with the right words. To prove his point he taught me two big words. Antidisestablishmentarianism and levatorlabiisuperiorisalaequenasi or some stupid thing like that. (Since then I've found out that the second one is actually five Latin words that he strung together, to impress me I suppose.)

'They are the two longest words in the English language,' he'd said. He liked knowing big words. He bragged a lot. He did a good job of making people believe in his lies. At least now I was wised up to him. My bullshit radar was improving rapidly.

Soon after as I walked along Parramatta Road I reached the traffic lights at Glebe Point Road and saw a huge hotel on the corner. It had probably been a luxury hotel a hundred years ago but now it was really tired and run down. There was a blackboard outside that said, 'Rooms for rent. Inquire within.'

Inside, the place smelled of stale alcohol and old people. There was a staircase so I started to walk up when I saw an old man coming down.

'Hi there,' I said, trying to sound positive. 'There's a sign out the front that says rooms to rent.'

The old man told me where to find Mrs Jones, the lady who looked after the place.

Mrs. Jones lived in a cluttered little room with her son who looked quite familiar to me. We talked business and she wanted to know about me. I told her I was from the Cross. The connection was made. I knew her son Zack and his brother Ray from the Cross.

She rented me one of the hundreds of rooms that all consisted of four walls and a bed. The other tenants were mostly elderly people who were heavy drinkers. There were shared bathrooms along with shared noise and smells. The room was small and inside I felt sadness at the loneliness that room seemed to posses.

Social security was where I needed to go next. I explained some of my stuff and they gave me a cheque.

The following day I headed back to the room I had found at Glebe. I scouted about the hotel and I found an old ballroom at the back and it had a little room and a kitchen connected. To a break dancer like me that was exciting.

Wow! I could rent this. I could teach dancing. I could bring all my friends. I'll open a dance school. My imagination almost got me to the level of producer of magnificent shows in Hollywood! As a kid I'd loved watching Fred Astaire dance, especially to the song Singing in the Rain. He was so graceful and elegant. And then there were Prince and Michael Jackson.

Mrs. Jones was drinking with her son Ray when I got to talking to her. That's when I worked out that Zack, one of my good friends from the streets, was her other son. I told Mrs. Jones that I was a break dancer and that I knew lots of kids on the streets. She agreed to rent the hall to me. The back room could fit at least fifteen kids and it took no time for me to round up a posse of street kids and break dancers.

To get a dance group together I needed more kids. I put ads in the paper asking for good dancers to contact me. I hoped we would be good enough to enter in competitions. I met two girls Na and Kitty from New Zealand. They were interested and Na suggested that we call this thing Megazoids Dance Studio. Mega meant 'many' and Zoid meant 'street kids she explained.' So the old white chalk board out the front no longer just showed the faded notice, 'Rooms to Rent.' I had a graffiti style sign made up advertising Megazoids Dance School. I had no permit or professional training but many people, including parents, walked in off the street with kids who wanted to learn to break dance. Slowly we transformed the hall into our dance studio. Dwayne, Nick and I did a lot of paid dancing work too to buy stuff we needed. People came when they read the ads in the paper too, all wanting to help. We held auditions and chose the best dancers to join the Megazoids.

One day, out of the blue, Nadine walked back into my life. She moved in with me. Nadine got a job in the florist across the road from the dance hall. We were both determined to make this our own place and one we couldn't be kicked out of.

The back room became our little place to live. There was a working kitchen with no fridge but we never used the kitchen anyway. Other kids from the Cross were living at the studio too but they couldn't dance.

After a while I got a job at the Glebe Fare performing in the street. At other times I busked on the streets and in cafes and other places for small change. Money was never the sole objective for me with my dancing. It was a lifestyle. I was creating a new life for myself and my dancing was usually just me expressing myself. It helped me escape from the memories of the Cross. I was getting a dole cheque so that helped me to pay the rent, along with the money I earn busking or doing shows.

A couple of the predators I knew from the Cross came to see me. Peter and Grant came to visit but I had made a firm decision that no one was going to abuse me or any of us kids again. I took the street kids in so they didn't have to deal with paedophile predators and we never welcomed anyone who was suspicious. Grant and Peter would just turn up occasionally. I was not interested in sex or their money.

Nadine and I were like rabbits. My sex drive had kicked back in. Nadine laughed one day and said, 'I reckon we've had sex over a hundred times!' She was guessing but I think it was most likely true. We were young and we believed in love. We were creating our own life and that was intoxicating. The only adult we had to answer to was Mrs. Jones. We gave her rent money when we could but she would never hassle us for it. Not once. She saw us for what we were. Street kids. She was very compassionate. The back hall had never been used anyway and we were not using rooms she could rent. The hall rent put money in her pocket. Mrs. Jones was not the owner of the hotel but she collected the rents and managed it.

I needed to get our group known so I approached all sorts of people and businesses in Glebe to ask them to let us perform. To my surprise Bidura staff thought it might be a good idea for the kids inside to learn dancing and I was given the job of teaching them. Then a kid I was in Daruk with pointed out one day that I was friends with all the kids in Bidura and had been an inmate there myself not long ago. That spelt the end of the job. It was sad because I'd enjoyed seeing Linda and the others at dancing.

In that hall we danced all day and night. During the day, if I wasn't teaching we'd go all over the city busking or entering competitions. The dancers were getting very good. We had two groups: those who danced well and those who didn't but wanted to dance anyway. So we developed Megazoids Seniors and Juniors. Nick, Na, Kitty, Dwayne and I were the seniors.

The Megazoids use to dance with a group of Maori kids from Bondi called the East Side Rockers. Easily the best two groups in Sydney we were. But lots of kids had rich parents who could get them better set up than I could. Every time anyone danced and did something I couldn't do, I'd meet them and spend ages learning their moves. I made up my own moves too. There was a move where you spin on one hand then go into the Crab and walk in a circle on your hands. I could jump as I did it. My specialty was dance itself, thanks to the fact that I'd had rhythm drilled into me as a child at dancing classes.

A man called Martin approached me one day. He had seen us performing and was impressed. He offered to be our manager and made all kinds of promises that included real gigs and real cash.

We decided to accept the offer and we started doing really well. Martin had us dancing at a few clubs for a couple of weeks and one was a nightclub in North Sydney opposite a refuge called Talumundi Youth Refuge.

With Martin managing us we were professionals and he got us bookings in all sorts of places that we wouldn't have approached. He made videos of us dancing to show to club owners and he filmed crowd responses to us. He told them we had groupies that followed us from club to club. That was true but most of them were our own friends, too young to get into clubs but Martin could pull strings.

One night at a club Eric, the man who usually paid Martin, paid me instead. The five of us had been getting fifty dollars each to dance at three separate clubs.

Eric handed me well above the amount I thought we'd get.

'You've given me too much mate,' I told him.

'No. That's what we've always paid you guys,' Eric replied.

'Oh. Okay.'

When I told Martin about it he said, 'That's what I get paid.'

We argued. Martin was pocketing about two hundred dollars at each event and giving each of us fifty dollars for all three.

We spent hours each week learning routines, practicing them and then getting to the clubs and performing. All Martin had to do was ring the clubs and take us to the events yet he was taking four times as much as us. I didn't see that as fair. Maybe if he had explained this at the start, I'd have accepted it but it seemed that he was cheating us. So I told him to fuck off.

With hindsight I saw that as a bad decision. Before Martin came along we danced on the streets and earned maybe a hundred dollars on our very best days. We had to dance all day for that. We found people on their way to work were very generous. I didn't really understand the manager's role. All I thought was this is another adult betraying my trust. I was over being reliant on adults.

When I told Martin to leave I decided I'd manage us myself. But soon I found that I didn't have the knowledge or the skills or even a car to get to gigs or interviews. Well, I thought I'd rather go in competitions and busk than be ripped off by the likes of Martin. We could make good money when we danced.

Nadine and I were taking care of kids again, buying food and seeing that they were okay. Nadine got a wage from her job at the florist and I danced. Most of the street kids didn't dance. We had three crews now: streets kids from Cross, homeless dancers and kids who had responded to the ads in the paper but who were not interested in just busking. The third lot was interested in dancing at a high level and I was too. I just didn't know how to make that happen.

One day I sat down with some pencils and paper. Thinking about our dancing, I created an outfit that I felt would be perfect for street dancers. I had previously designed an outfit for us to perform in and Martin called it a rap suit. It had padding in certain areas and it had sleeves that you pulled out of the main sleeves to spin on. Martin had said he would get the uniforms made up for us.

Martin knew where we lived and now I had sacked him it occurred to me that we knew very little about him. Where did he live? What did he do when he wasn't working for us? Did he have a wife and kids? Was the car his? I was uncomfortable knowing so little about him.

A few weeks after splitting with Martin and slowly losing dancers like Nick, Na and Kitty, I was in Grace Brother's store with Nadine and Peter. I had won a dance competition there only days before. My prize was a tape recorder. It was the perfect prize for me. It ran off batteries or mains power and it had two large speakers that clipped on the sides of the player. As we went through the shop I saw an outfit for sale that was identical to the rap suit I had designed. Was it a coincidence? It hadn't been hard for me to come up with the design. Every dancer would have wanted the features I had put into my creation. But the display outfit was identical to mine, even down to the silver and red parts I'd drawn. Had my design been stolen from me and sold by Martin? Who knows? Another thing I hated adults for. My brother Michael turned up on the scene around this time.

One night there were about twenty kids at the studio. Another kid had hired lights and stuff from a place called Disco City for an event and then we could use it all for one night at the studio for a party. I'd built a DJ Box and with the rented lights and other stuff from DJ City, plus turn tables, strobe lights, a smoke machine and mirror balls and we were all set to go. We'd been tagging the walls but now we put mirrors up as well as decorating walls with Throw Ups (street art) too and the place was starting to look like a dance studio. We looked more professional with all the gear we had. Even though it was only rented supposedly for that one night.

The kid who rented the stuff disappeared or was arrested and never came back to get the equipment and return it and we never took it back either. No one ever came looking for it.

To rent a studio like that in the city would have cost a fortune. Apart from the first weeks rent I gave Mrs. Jones I don't recall giving her much money. I might have done because I was an honest kid. I do remember whenever I gave her money, she wrote out a receipt. Generally she just left us alone to do our thing.

When party night came around heaps of kids came. We partied on and some of the kids got hold of alcohol. As the night went on a couple of kids got some rocks and stood on top of the hotel roof overlooking Parramatta Road. They started throwing the rocks at passing cars. We'd worked so hard to create this safe happy place and if I had known what those kids were up to, I'd have put an end to it.

The police knew we were living there but they left us alone, knowing that we weren't causing any trouble. Now we had other kids visiting who were now causing trouble.

The morning after the party about fifteen of us were arrested for throwing rocks and being in possession of stolen goods. We were paraded before the judge at Bidura. My record shows an appearance at court in January, 1984 for receiving stolen goods. That might refer to the DJ equipment. No conviction was recorded against me for the throwing of rocks.

When we walked away from the court we were yahooing and enjoying our freedom. As I walked down Glebe Point Road towards the dance studio I noticed smoke coming from our building. Fire engines were everywhere.

I tried to get into our home, our life.

'Are you mad! You can't go in there,' a fireman said. 'Too dangerous.' I remember standing there with the other kids of the Cross sad by what I was seeing. It felt like every time I got some where we could all be together something would destroy it. Fire,. Paedophiles, Police.

We were homeless again! Megazoids was over. Another dream crushed. Another home lost. I was shattered.

What bastard got us arrested just so they could burn our place down? Most of the kids took the loss less heavily than I did. Nadine was upset but I don't think the loss had nearly as big an impact on her as it did on me. The place was my creation. My dream. I'd built it from the wreck of Simon's dumping me. I'd formed an abuse free, creative welcoming refuge and now it was ashes.

Back to the streets. I felt like I was surrounded by strangers and I missed the warmth of the familiar faces: Linda, Tommy and everyone. I knew so many dancers so I immersed myself into dance. It was an escape that gave me a sense of belonging. I belonged to something much bigger than me. Rap grew from the streets and the streets were my home.

I had Nadine at my side, but that didn't seem enough.

One night we were asleep in a doorway of the Cross. It was about four in the morning when a street worker, a Maori lady, approached us.

'Where do you kids live?' she asked.

We told her we were homeless.

'Come and have breakfast with me,' she said. Her name is Roseanne. We followed her to a restaurant called Alice's. She bought us breakfast then took us home to her place. She lived in a flat in the Cross with a group of street workers. They all mothered us and looked after us and that felt nice and comforting.

We stayed there for a few days.

'Let's make some tea,' Nadine said one morning.

We pulled out a sugar bag and just as we were putting sugar in our cups, Roslyn and Sammy came in. They looked as if they were going to have heart attacks.

'Bloody hell! What are you kids doing!' Ros said snatching the bag away. She went mental.

'How dare you leave that shit around for the kids to find!' Roseanne challenged.

Everyone seemed to go into meltdown then and it became clear that the sugar was in fact heroin, a lot of heroin, and we had just put about a gram of it in our tea.

Roseanne found us a hotel room where we could stay for a few days. Each day she would go to work at the brothels, then she'd come home to us with food and to make sure we were all right. She cared for us like we were her own children. She worked in one of the clubs on the main street.

Soon after we met her Roseanne got a Housing Commission place in the Captain Cook Towers at Waterloo. She let us go with her but after a few days we got itchy feet. She was becoming too controlling. We felt very grown up and able to take care of ourselves whereas Roseanne treated us like kids and set up all kinds of rules we had to follow. As much as I am forever indebted to her for her kind, generous heart, rules were something a street kid like me couldn't stand.

I said, 'I want to go to Whyalla and see my mother and my brother and sister.'

So we left one day when Roseanne was at work. We left her

a nice thank you note. Before we left we went to the streets and I saw Linda, my ex-girlfriend. She was my best friend and like a sister to me. She was now hanging with older guys who had come from Town Hall and she was using heroin. I noticed a few other girls from the refuge using there too. I was devastated that they were doing heroin. I talked to Linda about it and she assured me that it was only a one off thing and she wasn't using regularly. If I had known maybe how things would play out in the coming months we would never have left for South Australia.

We headed off to Lumea station so we could get to the highway and hitch hike to South Australia. I had the address of my mother and two younger siblings. I thought Dick would be there too. Murphy Crescent, Whyalla. That was our destination. I had no idea whether we'd be welcomed or rejected.

Chapter 13.
The Dancer

At the refuge we rarely talked about our families. I knew some of Nadine's story and I met her dad and brother once. I'd spoken a little about my mother being a drinker but I never said anything about my life before the Cross. Nadine had no idea why we were going to Whyalla. To be honest I didn't have much of an idea either. Years had passed and I was almost seventeen. Nadine was sixteen. We had nowhere to go but my sister Tina was somewhere down south and I longed to see her.

The train took us to Leumeah then we walked out to the highway. Nadine sat down and I stuck out my thumb to hitch a ride. A lot of back packers hitched hiked all over the country to see as much of Australia as they could on a very small budget. It didn't take us long to get a ride.

Drivers took us as far as they were going then we'd get out and wait for another to take us further. Everyone who picked us up was nice and each one took us closer to my mother. Eventually we got a lift with a truck driver who was going all the way to Adelaide. We chatted a bit as we went along. We told him we were from the streets and we said a little bit about our story. We said we were on our way home to see my mum and brother and sister. The driver was very concerned about our welfare. He kept saying there were bad people out there on the roads.

'Any one could pick you two kids up and do anything to you.'

He told us stories of bad things happening to hitch hikers as we travelled with him, no doubt intended to scare us.

Being from the streets and believing I was streetwise I said, 'Yeah right. They try anything, I'll break their noses.'

I can only imagine that big tough truck driver looking at us skinny kids and realizing just how vulnerable we were. Our ignorance made us a danger to ourselves. The driver had to make a couple of stops on the way and when he stopped for a feed he took us both in and got food for us as well. We climbed into the sleeping compartment of the truck and went off to sleep.

It was really early in the morning when we got to the Adelaide hills. The trucker woke us up and said, 'All right kids. Here's where I leave you. You'll get a ride to Whyalla from here. Be careful won't you.'

It must have been about four o'clock in the morning. It was still very dark. He intended to drop us off then go on his way but I think he was concerned about leaving us.

'I'll get on the CB and see if we can get someone going your way,' he said.

He got back in the cabin and asked via his radio, 'CQ. CQ. Anybody got a copy of the Big Red Fox? Come on? Yeah listen mate. I got a couple of kids going to Whyalla.'

Straight away he got a response. 'Can do Red Fox. Can they wait twenty minutes for me?'

We waited in the cold, shivering and cuddled up to each other and then a big Kenworth truck pulled up and the driver beckoned us over.

'Are you the two kids going to Whyalla?'

I replied eagerly, 'Yes sir. That's us.'

'Jump in,' he said.

The warmth inside the truck was bliss. The driver was friendly and he asked us what two kids were doing hitch hiking. We explained that we were from the Cross and that we're going to see my mother.

'Street kids, eh?' he says. 'You look so young!'

'I'm seventeen,' I tell him, as if that matters. I thought I was pretty grown up because of the life I'd lived. I still looked younger and I think it must have been obvious we were homeless kids by the way we were dressed and the fact that we had no possessions.

In his cabin he had a big photo of him and his family. One of his kids looked about my age.

'He's real good at sport that one,' he said proudly. He seemed so proud of all of them. Does that explain why he was so concerned about us? He gave us some tips for staying safe while we hitch hiked.

'You make sure you look after your girl Glen. When you get a ride, make sure you get in first and Nadine gets in last. Same idea when you get out. You be the last to leave. You leave your girl in a vehicle without you, they can just take off with her. Just don't trust everybody.'

We both really felt grateful for his concern and it felt a bit like a father advising his kids I think.

The sun gradually came up and in a few hours we arrived in Whyalla. The driver pulled out a road map and asked, 'Where exactly are you going?

'Murphy Crescent, Whyalla Stuart,' I told him.

'Yeah. Here it is. So, you hitch a ride to here,' he says pointing to a spot on the map, 'then you'll be able to walk there.'

We were about to climb down when he said, 'Na Fuck it. It'll only take me twenty minutes to get there. Lets go.' For him to make the extra effort to drive us to the door was a huge and generous act of kindness.

'Thank you,' I say sincerely. 'Thank you so much.'

As we got closer to my mother's place I started feeling nervous. Will she be drunk? Will she even let me in the door? Or has she stopped drinking. She might be her nicer self. I was excited and I was afraid. I didn't want to be humiliated or embarrassed in front of Nadine. My mother was good at making me feel worthless but at least by now I was better at standing up for myself. I was equally worried about her partner Dick who was always drunk like Mum. We'd spent two days travelling to get there and I didn't want to be told we were not welcome.

We pulled up at the house that was clearly a Housing Commission home like others in the street. There was a caravan out the back but no car in the drive. It looked like no-one was home. Then it dawned on me: What if they don't live here anymore?

The truck driver gave us a toot as he left and I thought what a lovely gesture that was along with bringing us right to the door.

Nadine and I stood there. I found the courage to knock tentatively. So many emotions ran through me. Excitement, fear, anticipation, uncertainty.

'Someone's at the front door,' I heard a voice say. Tina? Samuel? I don't remember. I was so strung out.

'Who the fuck would be at the door at this hour!' That was definitely mum.

I didn't imagine she got visitors except perhaps welfare people or people from churches. I couldn't imagine she had friends.

The door opened and standing before me was Tina.

'Glen!' she squealed excitedly.

Samuel walked by and mumbled something like, 'What the fuck's he doing here?' He'd grown a bit and I guessed he might be twelve by now.

My mother sauntered out to the door.

'What do you want?' was her greeting.

My heart dropped. Fear rose up.

'I came to visit. Introduce you to my girlfriend,' I tell her turning toward Nadine.

'I hope you brought money with you.' What a welcome for Nadine! 'I can't afford to take care of you.'

'We have money,' I lied. Nadine was busy wondering what to say. 'And we'll go to the dole office and get help. We can look after ourselves.'

'Well good then. Come in,' Tina said, smiling at each of us.

Samuel paced back and forth in the background, trying to assert his authority as man of this house. I paid no attention to him. I was already thinking what a bad idea this had been and what a long way it was back up to the Cross.

I was glad to find that Dick wasn't there. He and mum had split up. Mum was enough to deal with without having that nasty little monster about.

'They can stay out the back in the caravan,' Mum told Tina.

Nadine and I went to Whyalla Stuart shopping centre some time through the day to look around. I think we went to the dole office to see if we could get money to get back to Sydney. Of the three people I knew in Whyalla, only one was pleased to see me.

I don't recall whether we stayed in the caravan that night but I remember Mum kept heaping shit on me: that I looked like a poofter and other really mean and horrible stuff. Samuel was being lippy too and I really felt like decking him.

Why was I here? I didn't need this. Nadine looked sad at seeing the way our mother behaved. She kept reassuring me that we could leave any anytime I wanted to. I felt hurt and embarrassed. I don't know what I'd been expecting. My mother was the mother she had always been. She still despised me.

Tina was a changed person. She didn't take shit from anyone. She told Samuel off about something then got into a fight with Margaret, our mother. I think this was about the start of a new adventure for Tina who was about thirteen by then. Sis wouldn't put up with the way Mum treated me. Nadine was just shocked. The saddest thing was that Margaret seemed to be sober and this was who she had become. Nadine and I had made the decision to leave.

'Fuck this,' I told Margaret. 'We're leaving.'

Tina said, 'I'm coming with you.'

Was that the best thing I could do for my sister? Take her away? I've wished many times that I could go back to this day and do things differently.

Tina had looked up to me and I guess she saw this as her chance to escape the cruel drudgery of being the slave of nasty, vicious mother and her golden child.

Before you could say Jack Robinson, Tina, Nadine and I were standing on the highway out of Whyalla Stuart, heading to Adelaide. It was harder to get a lift with three people but we did get some. By night time all three of us were pretty tired. We stood on the road across from a petrol station or truck stop. There was a field of corn behind us. We were too tired to keep hitching so we decided we'd sleep among the corn. We made ourselves comfortable and in no time I was asleep. Nadine and I were accustomed to sleeping anywhere and even Tina accepted this because she was as happy as Larry being free with her big brother.

The next morning I woke up at about eight. I sat upright. I looked to my left then to my right. No one. What the …? I didn't panic. I knew Nadine was street smart and she'd look after Tina. They were together.

I yelled out for the girls but no one answered. I walked out onto the highway and that was when I noticed the little truck stop for the first time. I started to wander over to see if the girls were there using the toilets. We had no money so I knew they wouldn't be buying anything. I saw a police car pull up. I was already feeling nervous about not seeing the girls but the minute I saw the police my mind went into over drive. What's going on?

I went inside. 'Hey mate,' I say to the man at the counter, 'Have you seen two young girls come in here?'

'Yeah mate. They're in the back room.'

Talk about reliving a horrible memory! The time Michael and I were arrested at the Kincumber pub. Would it be Tina, Nadine and I now?

'Why are the police here?' I asked.

In walked the two policemen. The girls had been arrested for stealing. I didn't know who had done what but I knew Nadine had a habit of stealing stuff anywhere, anytime. All three of us were taken to a home called Zarach. It was much like Bidura. Males and females were held there and there were the usual facilities. I didn't know why I was arrested but there I was.

In the middle of the night someone woke me up. Two big men handcuffed me and shackled my legs.

'We've pulled up your criminal history,' they tell me. 'We can't hold you in a minimum security place like this.'

If they had looked at my record properly they'd have seen I had no actual convictions for crimes. Running away was all I'd done. These two men thought they'd caught a hardcore criminal and they weren't going to listen to his pleading for them to read his record properly. I was put in the back of a car with a big man on each side of me and I was escorted, handcuffed and shackled, to a prison, in the middle of the night.

This was a prison with cells in a circle and tables in the centre of the circle.

Finally I went to court. It wasn't like Bidura. In this one judges wore wigs, the building was old and cases ran like they did on television. After our cases were heard I was set free and I met up with Nadine. Tina was sent to a refuge.

Nadine went to see Tina but I wasn't allowed to see her except under supervision. That was a court directive. Nadine and I stayed with a couple in Adelaide. The guy had long hair and Nadine was attracted to him despite the presence of his girlfriend. Nadine, who couldn't help herself, stole something from them and they asked us to leave.

I only got to see Tina once before the courts said Nadine had to leave South Australia. Her dad paid for her return trip to Muswellbrook where he lived. I saw Tina out the front of the refuge with a worker supervising my visit. I presume they thought I might encourage her to leave with us. I never intended to take her to the streets of the Cross. I just wasn't letting her stay any more with that psycho we called Mum. I didn't think the thing through thoroughly.

I hitch hiked back to Sydney and then out to Muswellbrook to get Nadine. I didn't know where she lived but I thought she probably wasn't still with her father. I walked around the town asking people whether they knew Nadine and at last I found someone who did. He took me to the place she was sharing with another girl. I'd had a feeling that our relationship was coming to it's end but I wanted to see how we'd go.

'We need to go back to South Australia to find Tina,' I told her.

'Oh I don't really want to go back there,' she said, clearly reluctant to leave. I think the thought of hitching all the way was just to daunting.

Next morning I went back to her house and this time Nadine agreed to go with me.

As we were standing on the highway to Adelaide, a yellow Holden Torana pulled up. The driver was Taxi Michael, a known paedophile who I'd met in Kings Cross. He drove us all the way to Adelaide and he didn't do any propositioning.

On the streets we ran into a kid we knew at the Cross, Dennis. He took us to the place of a man who kept trying to get me to drink beer. Something about him gave me the creeps. Dennis was the kid who stole from two paedophiles in the Cross. They had put a contract out on his life. He was the same kid who took the refuge kids to a house where we were plied with drugs all night. That was many years ago.

This man in the house in Adelaide seemed desperate for me to get drunk. I didn't drink very often and that might have been a blessing on this particular day.

'We need to go,' I told Nadine and we left before more pressure could be put on me.

Much later I saw a story on TV about a man who gave boys laced alcohol then he raped and beat them for days before murdering them. When I saw his picture on the screen I went cold. I can't be certain but I think it was the same man.

There were as many paedophiles in Adelaide as there were in the Cross. They met at night in toilets at the Torrens River and they preyed on street kids. I recognized a lot of people from the Cross. Street kids and abusers alike. I no longer wanted anything to do with them. I did run into Taxi Michael again in Adelaide and got away from him quickly. I noticed a lot of the Predators from the streets of the Cross in all the pinball parlours in Adelaide.

Rundle Mall was popular as people would come and go in all directions and on Hindley Street there were pinball places to attract kids. Needless to say these places were haunts for predators looking for runaways and vulnerable kids. There seemed to be more kids on the streets of Adelaide than there were in the Cross. They were concentrated on a long street full of clubs, pubs and pinball parlours. There were kids everywhere, runaways and the rich kids, all searching for something.

Nadine wanted to leave South Australia but I didn't want to leave Tina on the streets or in a refuge in Adelaide. I wasn't allowed to visit her or go near her but I needed to make sure she was safe.

'You go home and I'll stay for a while and catch up with you in Sydney then,' I suggested. When she left a few days later I missed her but I guessed our time together was over.

I started to busk in Rundle Mall, rap dancing. This was the only means I had of making money and I found other dancers on the streets who I quickly connected with. It was easy for me to get a dance group together and soon I'd created the Electrical Connection. The kids had a tape deck and a good collection of music that was handy. I had nothing.

I very rarely saw Tina. She had her own life now and her own group of friends. She didn't want me around but I found it hard to leave in case she needed me. She was hanging out with a boy who appeared to be older than her.

I put all my energy into dancing, hoping to make a name for myself. The best thing about my busking in Adelaide was that my style was more advanced than the dancers in Adelaide at the time. This town had taken to the craze about four years after us in Sydney so they were still learning and doing lame old moves like the worm, mime, the window and stuff while we moved on. I'd had much more experience as well as a background in ballroom and disco dancing.

The Electrical Connection had outfits and a stereo and we started busking on the streets. We were able to make much more money in Rundle Mall than we had in the Cross. Many more people, people with money, loved to watch us perform.

One time we were employed by a person who had a shop in Rundle Mall. We had to wear outfits that were sold in that shop.

There were dance competitions all over Adelaide and I kept entering them and winning. However, when the competitions were held in night clubs, we had a bit of a problem. You needed to be eighteen to get in. That was frustrating because we were all too young. There was another group whose picture was plastered up everywhere and who entered and won so many competitions held in clubs. I managed to see them dance once and I couldn't stop laughing, knowing our group was much better.

I was lounge surfing at that time and my emotional health was all over the place. Dancing was about the only thing I excelled at and my passion and strong belief in myself as a dancer meant I just had to find a way to challenge the other group in a competition. Everywhere we went we saw posters of them - the best dancers in Adelaide. In Sydney I had danced with the best. Groups would come to Martin Place and we'd have pop up dance comps. In Adelaide it was all done in clubs and not so much in the street. Most of the kids in Adelaide's groups came from good homes whereas our group came from the streets.

'That should be us up there,' I'd tell the kids. 'We're better. Not just a little bit better. We are leaps and bounds ahead of what they're doing.'

I found a martial arts studio on Hindley Street and I managed to convince the owner to let me teach dance in his studio. Break dancing was a new fad everywhere. The kids who came saw me and our group dance and were amazed at the new moves we were doing. They wanted to learn too. So the class filled up quickly with adults as well as children. I never felt comfortable teaching the adults. I felt like it was a kids' thing but lots of people in their twenties wanted lessons. I only managed to do this for 3 weeks as fete was about to step in.

To earn money I taught two classes a week. I charged a flat rate. I was also doing martial arts lessons there, learning Nunchakus. I wanted to incorporate Kung Fu into my dance moves. I didn't have a place to live at the time so I stayed in a house with a lot of other kids in a flat behind Hindley Street.

If I'd had someone to manage or help, I really could have made it big in Adelaide I think. I was the only person there doing what we'd been doing in Sydney for years. Our group was ready to compete but we were blocked by the age limit in clubs. I choreographed routines that we took busking in Rundle Mall. One time the group that was always winning stopped to watch us and I challenged them to a competition there on the street. They declined.

'If you want to compete with us you'll have to go through the properly sanctioned channels,' one of them said. I felt inside like they looked down on us, we were from the street and that alone had them thinking they were better than us.

'I want to challenge you right here on the street and let's see what the people think,' I told him. They refused once again.

I spotted a competition sign outside a night club on Hindley Street one time. A stairway led up to the entrance where two burley doormen stopped under-aged people getting in. Near them was that picture! The one of our rivals. I got agitated. I went in to speak to the manager to try to get him to accept us in the competition.

'Sorry but you're not old enough,' he said.

I argued with him, claiming that we were the best group in Adelaide. I honestly believed this when I said it.

'How can you claim they are the best group when you don't give anyone a chance to challenge them?' I asked him. Was it my passion that managed to convince him to let us dance? Or it could have been the moves I showed him. He put conditions on our entry.

'All right. Here's what we'll do,' he said. 'I'll let you dance but the minute you finish, you'll all leave the club. No hanging around for drinks or chat. Just dance and go. I won't put my license at risk.'

I agreed with whatever conditions he specified as long as he let us dance. We had our group name put onto our shirts: Electrical Connection on the front and the name of the martial arts studio on the back. Our pants were baggy so we could move freely. We practiced every day for the two weeks leading up to the comp. Our song was Rocket by Herby Hancock. We also were practicing a second dance in case we had to dance twice. This was to one of Michael Jacksons songs beat it.

The big night came and there were scores of entrants in the competition. Of course the poster group, touted number one, was there and their leader said, 'I've seen you dancing in Rundle Mall. You are very good. Where did you learn to dance?'

'In Sydney. On the streets,' I say. 'That's where Rap Dancing originates. It's from the streets. It's raw.'

I could tell they were worried about us as they kept staring over at us and pointing. I knew we were the best but I wasn't confident that the judging would be fair. It struck me as odd that in Sydney I never cared about winning yet I often did win. Here my reputation counted on winning.

I was talking to the leader again when he said, 'Got to go! 'We're up next.'

I watched them perform. Shit they were good! They were much better than the one time I'd seen them and they had a new dancer who did break dancing. Their routine went for the whole two minutes.

Our outfits that were nowhere near as professional looking as the others. *Well,* I reminded myself, *this is from the streets and we look like we are from the streets.* I enjoyed watching the other dancers and we clapped along with everyone else. I was getting excited. We were about to unleash our energy.

I kept reminding the boys, 'Stay in time, smile and heaps of energy. Keep it clean.' Every time we trained I kept saying, it has to be clean. Every one of us must be in time

with each other or it wont make sense.

At last the M.C. called, 'And now let's see The Electrical Connection!'

Rocket started playing and Brett and I were ready on stage. We opened with my signature move – Electricity — jerking our bodies as if we were being electrocuted. As the song progressed the other four join us. The routine involved people dancing in twos at different stages and then we all came together in a harmony of energies. At the finish I popped my pigeon chest.

The crowd was going off. Even the headline act could see that we had something special - raw, real, street dancing.

'Well ladies and gentlemen,' the M. C. says, 'it seems that we have three groups in the top position in this contest.'

The crowd cheered and we did too. We were one of the top three!

'The judges have asked that we hold a dance—off to determine which team is the winner. So remember to cheer heartily for your favourite as they do their final routines.'

We performed again to deafening cheers and to finish our act I did a moved called The Rock: I landed in The Crab and jumped as I bounced around on my hands before spinning on my head to finish. The South Australians hadn't taken head spins on yet.

The leader of the headline act came on stage, took my hand and lifted it in the air in a victory gesture. The crowd roared.

Vindication!

We were awarded the trophy and the prize money. I didn't care too much for the trophy and one of our members took that. The cash was good but this had been about establishing us as the number one group. We were now recognized. If I ever felt better in my life I don't know when.

Other dancers came and grabbed us. 'You guys are sick man! You beat the top team.'

'No-one's beaten them before.'

I thought, *If only my dad could see me now. Always telling me how shit I was. Or Linda, Nadine or the kids of the refuge. I'd love all my refuge family to be here with me in this one time of feeling like a winner.*

The manager didn't insist that we leave straight away. There was time for a couple of conversations. One was with a man who said he worked for an advertising company and that he wanted to use street dancers some ads. The other was with the club owner who asked if I'd come back to perform some time. I agreed to both but nothing ever came of them.

We had just experienced the best moment of our life coupled with possibly the worst in a very short space of time. My world was about to collapse.

We left the night club full of triumph and bragging and back slapping. I was on a natural high. I had been validated and that meant so much. I knew if judges fairly we would win and we did.

I saw a familiar face waiting for us. It was Jarrod, one of my best mates from the refuge in Kings Cross. He didn't look good. There was an air of sadness about him. Had he seen me dance I wondered as I move towards him excited at his presence.

'Jarrod,' I said excitedly. 'Great to see you bro. How's it going? What are you doing down here?'

I will never forget his reply.

'Glen, Linda is dead.' He just blurted it out. You could see he was hurting. I knew instinctively that his words were true, but I was not ready to accept them.

My beautiful Linda! My street sister. My one time girlfriend and first love. My best mate. I grabbed Jarrod by the jumper and pushed him up against the wall, trying to fight away what he said. Jarrod could have fought back against me pushing him but he knew I was hurting so badly. He offered no resistance just reiterated what he had just said. Glen Linda is dead.

'Don't even say shit like that, Jarrod,' I demanded even though I could see in his eyes he was telling the truth. But some small part of me hoped he would take it back and it wouldn't be true.

He said, 'Glen, she's dead. It's true mate.'

I'd lost a few friends before this but none had the impact that Linda's death had. She was only fifteen when she was murdered. No death has been harder to bear than Linda's. The news cut through me like a knife and left me speechless. I had never been a quiet kid but this was the worst news I could possibly hear and there was nothing to be said. Linda. We all loved her so much.

Ten minutes ago I'd been euphoric. We were winners. Champions. We had money and a trophy. We were on our way.

Now? Well, now there wasn't any meaning to any of it. My old life had called me home.

My memory is hazy about the rest of that night. I'd love to find Jarrod and talk over our memories together. Later I heard the story of how Linda's death came about.

Two men had sent a known street worker to find a young girl they could have sex with. She found Linda and took her to party with the men. They gave Linda heroin and she overdosed on it. The men didn't get help for Linda for fear of being caught with heroin and an underaged girl. They tried to escape from the room when they should have been getting help for Linda. They were charged with murder and were sentenced to twenty years in prison. They appealed the sentence before Judge Yeldham, the same judge caught having sex with young boys at Wynyard and Museum stations. He set the killers free.

Jarrod and I bought alcohol that night after the competition. We sat in a school to drink and talk about Linda. We drank to our sister, my ex girlfriend, one of the kids of the Cross. A refuge kid. I blamed myself. What if I hadn't met her at the station that day? What if she had not followed me to Derrick's place? What if she hadn't followed me to the refuge? What if I hadn't moved to Adelaide when I knew that she was starting to use heroin?

All those 'what ifs' didn't eliminate the pain? I still carry it.

Jarrod and I got very drunk and I decided to go back to the Cross. I wanted to go to Linda's funeral. I needed to be there. I felt gutted.

An Adelaide kid called Jim decided to come with me. We got a few lifts and then someone drove us all the way to the outskirts of Goulburn, leaving us on a corner beside a paddock. I had a bag of things this time: a stereo that I used to busk with, some clothes, my Kung Fu stuff for dancing including a pair of nunchakus. I didn't care about anything but getting to Linda's funeral then.

'Let's just sleep in the grass,' I said.

It was very cold that night but we managed to get to sleep. I was so distraught it felt like my world was ending. This was different to losing people through being removed from them. I was never going to see Linda again. Never. So final.

It was early in the morning when we woke up. I stuck my head up and at exactly the same time a police wagon passed by. It pulled over and the cops got out to see what we were up to.

'We're hitch hiking back to Sydney to go to a funeral,' I told the officer.

'Where from?'

'From Adelaide.'

'We're going to search your bags,' one of them said.

He rummaged around in my stuff.

'What's this?' the cops asked, pulling out my stuff.

'Nunchakus,' I tell him. 'I perform with 'em.'

We were both arrested.

The charge was a Section 9, the same as for carrying a knife. Then the charge was upgraded to a Section 13 as for carrying a gun.

Next stop, the cells of Goulburn Police Station. We were held there for about two weeks. What made that worse was that Jim had picked up the flu and I caught it too. We were refused bail because carrying performance style nunchakus is as bad as carrying a gun.

I missed Linda's funeral.

Eventually we went to court and I was given a bond and a fine. Jim was ordered to go back to Adelaide. YACS paid for my ticket to the Cross. As soon as they let me go I took off to the highway and hitched again. I made it as far as Campbelltown and I rang the Snooker Room. I asked about Linda and the guy I spoke to told me to get a taxi from Campbelltown they'd pay for it. I didn't take him up on his offer. I hitched another ride that got me to Newtown and then from there I caught a train back to the Cross.

I was angry. I was hurting badly. I needed to find the truth of what had happened to Linda. It felt like the whole of the Cross was grieving for her. I didn't go to the police to ask what was being done because I was afraid of them and I didn't trust them. That is sad because they knew what had happened.

My view of the world had changed by the time I got back. Not that I'd had a great view of it prior to this. The refuge kids were like my brothers and sisters and we had just lost one of our immediate family. Two others, Stewart and Michael, had died as well.

Should I go back to Adelaide and pick up where I left off? I was home now. Angry but home and the streets were hurting.

When I first arrived the streets seemed alive, bright and exciting. It didn't have that appeal to me now as I returned. As I walked down the street the predators stood out. Paedophiles in every place I looked, drug dealers, addicts, thugs and corrupt police.

I was hurting, really hurting, unlike any pain I had ever experienced in my life. I had felt many highs and lows. Fear, alone, abandoned but everything seemed to dim after learning of the death of Linda.

Chapter 14.
The Needle and the Danger Done

Walking about in a daze of sorrow I ran into Simon and Grant. Grant told me that he had been to Linda's funeral. He said how sorry he was about her death.

I looked straight at Simon and said, 'One day I'm going to write a book about that fucking refuge and all about Linda. I'll hold all of you accountable for what you did to us kids.'

Simon laughed at me and sneered, 'You won't even live to twenty one!'

I said, 'If you guys had done your bloody job instead of having sex with us all, Stewart, Mitchell and Linda would still be alive.'

I blamed myself for Linda's recent life and for her death. If only I had not met her that day at the station. Maybe if I'd taken her to Adelaide? If I'd seen the signs when she started hanging with older kids who were using heroin? I couldn't shake the guilt and it was around this time that I started to see drug use differently. Until then I'd been repulsed by it. Although we used sometimes at the refuge, we were not addicts. I saw addiction daily at the Cross and could never understand how beautiful people could do that to themselves every day. I was ignorant about addiction. I often said to addicts I knew, 'Just stop doing it!'

Those days at the refuge were the worst and the best days of my life. It might sound weird but the best days were when I shared time with some of the most amazing kids on the planet. It's still hard for me to articulate what my heart feels for them. Before the refuge I'd never had really close friends. I never lived at one place long enough or I was bullied because I stood out for all the wrong reasons. The kids of the Cross, particularly those at the refuge, accepted me for who I was. I didn't have to pretend to be tough, smart or talented. I could just be me.

Simon Davies had created a culture without limits that was attractive to kids like us and ultimately it made us more accepting of abuse. He and his colleagues had an opportunity to save kids lives, to give us direction and purpose. Instead they chose to abuse us. I hold them responsible for the loss of Linda's life. They were given generous resources to help us yet they chose to use that money to take overseas trips, to stay drunk or high and to purchase children for their own sexual gratification.

Linda's death and the demons of dealing with the loss, brought all the exploitation into focus for me and I was very angry. I still am. I couldn't stop crying. All the tears that had been dammed up inside me for years now came flooding out. They were not just for Linda. They were for my wretched childhood and what could have been. Before Linda's death I never thought about how painful my life had been before I came to the Cross. Bad memories popped into my head occasionally but I would change my thoughts so I wouldn't feel anything. I hated feeling or thinking about my parents or other events. It was like all the abuse that had happened was magnified. I saw it as the abuse it was and I was deeply wounded and angry.

I made a promise to myself that one day I would hold them all accountable for their actions. A lot of time would pass before I could make that happen. I couldn't just walk into Kings Cross Police Station in the 1980s or 90s and report crimes that the police had sanctioned or been involved in. The likely result would have been me found dead with a needle in my arm or me thrown overboard somewhere with a washing machine attached to my legs. This decade came to be known as The Green Light Period. Anything goes and police corruption was rife.

I didn't make a conscious decision to become a drug addict. It was just that drugs gave me an escape. They stopped me feeling. I had no idea that they would take me on a life long journey of addiction. When the journey began I felt really torn apart inside and I literally couldn't stand feeling the way I did. I not sure that I made the connection in my head back then between the pain I felt and the journey to addiction.

In the past I'd smoke a couple of cones and I'd be happy. In Adelaide I may have smoked pot on rare occasions but my passion for dance meant I needed to be fit, not spaced out, so I generally left them alone. As my journey to full on addiction went on, I lost the will to dance and the energy for it as well.

My only experience of intravenous drugs was one time when Jayjay injected me with a shot of heroin. It caused me to spend the day throwing up everywhere I went. I hated drugs. I'd seen so many people get in trouble, die or be imprisoned because of them. Those people had been my guides but now I was such a mess. I needed a proper, solid role model to show me how to deal with my circumstances. I turned to the only thing I knew would ease the pain.

A huge group of users lived on the streets and I knew them all. I was like their little brother. I saw them differently now. I saw them as people hiding from pain. I started hanging out on the streets every day, using whatever I could get. I didn't care what.

By the time I was eighteen the face of the Cross had changed for me. When I first arrived everyone was weird and wonderful but I fitted straight in. Now I was remembering past events every day, not just Linda but further back too.

Christmas time was the most upsetting time. One Christmas day I sat with a busker outside Woolworths. I was hanging out on drugs and he played the song Needle and The Damage Done by Neil Young. Did he play that song to me as a warning? I often wonder.

On my eighteenth birthday I decided to get drunk. I didn't usually drink. I hated alcohol. My mother had done enough drinking for all of us. The only abuser I still had contact with was Peter from Hornsby. He would meet me often in the city and shout me dinner and give me money. He never asked ever for anything in return. I had lunch with Peter on this birthday and he bought me some new shoes and gave me some money. I started drinking early in the afternoon. I was usually a peaceful guy but by night time I felt restless and agitated. With each drink I could feel anger building up inside.

I don't know how I ended up in Oxford Street but when I was walking past a club called Patches, I saw a group of pretty girls go in, so I followed. Jack, the doorman, seemed to take a liking to me. He was a gay man with dyed blond hair. Like most men I had met he liked little boys and I still looked much younger than my years. I could still hop on a bus and pay the child's fare.

Throughout the night in Patches I made friends with one of the barmen, Nifty. He was about the same age as me and he was straight, like me. The club catered for gay and straight people. Across the road was the Exchange Hotel that closed at two in the morning. Their patrons would come across the street to watch the drag show at Patches. I had met the famous Carlotta from a club on Roslyn Street and often had a chat with her as she walked down the street to Les Girls.

The people in Patches early in the night were mostly young couples but as the night wore on and the hotel clients came in, the ambience changed. Somehow I got into an argument with a bloke who came in with a group of men. They were being assholes and I was carrying a massive chip on my shoulders. Full of alcohol and bad memories of birthdays past, I was itching for a fight.

The guy said something that upset me. I said my own shit back at him and before I knew it, I was punching on with him, some guy I didn't even know! His friends quickly came to his aid and the doorman rushed in to break it up. Jack, Nifty and a few others separated us and we were ejected from the club.

I sat down outside but the guy decided he wanted a second go at me. He was feeling pretty tough with his mates beside him. I wasn't put off by the friends and I kept screaming.

'Come on then! One on one, fuck ya. One on one.' Full of rage and alcohol I pointed to the man who'd upset me. 'Come on fuckhead. You and me. One on one.'

For the first time in my life I wanted to fight. Eighteen years of holding back my anger, being the person that everyone took their anger out on had built up inside. I wanted to fight. 'Come on!' I screamed.

Nifty came out from the club.

'One on one boys,' he said. 'You want to fight?' he asked the guy. 'Then fight one on one.'

They were willing to fight three against one but now the numbers were evening up, they decided to leave. Nifty and I sat and talked for about fifteen minutes.

'It's me fuckin' birthday,' I mumbled to Nifty. 'Eighteen today.'

'Eighteen and never been kissed,' he replied, trying to be funny. If only he knew!

Nifty and I really connected despite my angry, drunken state. He was a knock about guy who could fight. His brother was in prison for armed robbery.

Nifty was able to get me back into the club where he introduced me to Johnny, the boss. Johnny was gay and he really liked Nifty who he knew was straight. Nifty loved his job as the Bar Useful at Patches. The money was good and there were lots of hot women who he could easily hook up with.

I waited for Nifty to finish work at four in the morning. He had to do the clean up so I helped him. We had it done in half an hour and then we headed to the next place everyone went to. The Taxi Club on Flinders Street, Darlinghurst.

We met two girls there. One was Allita, a sexy blonde about my age who was a very good rap dancer. We danced together and had an amazing time drinking, talking and, best of all, dancing. I was amazed by her talent. Very few people could break dance like Allita.

Nifty and I became firm friends. We had a similar sense of humour and we thought like each other too. The following night Nifty took me to Patches with him and asked Johnny if he could use another Bar Useful. One had quit not to long before this.

Johnny thought about it for a while and then agreed to take me on. My first real job in the Cross!

'What's your address?' Johnny asked.

'Uh. I'm homeless at the moment,' I replied. I thought it better to be honest than try to pretend to be someone I wasn't.

Jack was there at the time so he said, 'I have spare rooms at my place if you want to stay. It's in Surry Hills.'

'Well then. That's settled,' Nifty interjected before I could reply. 'You work here now mate and you live with Jack.'

Jack had an ulterior motive in his offer I guessed, but I felt much more able to handle it than I had been in the past. Jack would just have to give up.

He was the main drug dealer of Patches. He sold pot and caps of speed for twenty dollars. There were three main groups who sold drugs between Patches and the Exchange Hotel. Two drag queens, one who sold speed and the other sold cocaine at Patches and they had two boys selling for them at the Exchange.

I took to my job with great gusto. At the start of the night I'd get a cap of speed from Jack and we'd inject it in the bathroom. I could run around like a crazy man all night on speed picking up glasses, stocking ice and doing pretty much whatever needed doing. It didn't take me to long to learn how to inject myself. I had used speed a couple of times but only by snorting it.

We were the grunts of the club. We had to keep the bars stocked, keep everything clean and be extra pairs of eyes to spot any trouble makers. We often had to become doormen when fights broke out. They were bound to happen with the mix of young people and lots of alcohol. Most of the patrons were not violent or aggressive but if a fight broke out it would usually involve men who'd come in off the street. All night long people would ask me or Nifty to score for them so we'd take them to Jack.

I stayed at Jack's place for about three months before he started trying to have sex with me. He thought he was a tough man but I felt I could easily have cleaned him up. He was probably around forty and I was young and fairly fit from all the dancing though I hadn't filled out much yet. Jack tried to come on to me when I was asleep and drunk. I'd wake up and go mental. I feared

I would hurt him. No man was putting his hands on me ever again, especially when I was asleep. There would be no more Uncle Paul or Larry, Simon or Derrick or any of them. No! Those days were absolutely over.

Jack triggered my hatred for men who abused children. He went after every kid who came to the club, first trying to hook them in with drugs so he could later abuse them. Although you had to be eighteen to get into Patches it wasn't uncommon for clubs to let underage kids hang about, especially attractive little boys. People were always asking how old I was so I had to carry ID on me all the time. Kids much younger than eighteen would come to Patches and Jack would let them in, but usually only boys. He had to be careful because if the police found an underage kid in the club they would get a huge fine. Patches had a restaurant license too so they had to serve food. The cook would do basic food like chips and steak sandwiches all night to keep the license.

After an angry tussle with Jack when I awoke to him trying to have sex with me, I went to Nifty at work and told him what had happened. I had a steady income now and I was able to find a bed sit in Surry Hills on the same street as the Taxi club.

That same night Sky, one of the drag queen dealers, and her boyfriend Shane approached Nifty and I offering us a taste of their speed. Speed is also known as Gas, fast, quick, the poor man's coke. They gave us ready made up shots in syringes. Sky used to make it all up in needles and carry it around in a toothbrush box for her or her partner to use. The rest she had made up into twenty dollar deals. She wanted to recruit Nifty and I to sell for her. She saw people coming to us, that they trusted us and that we were sending them to Jack. She knew that we, as younger, more trusted people, could work up a bigger clientele. She quickly learnt that I was angry with Jack and wanted no part of him.

After work that night we went to Sky's place. She had an eye on Nifty but he was straight and not at all interested in a drag queen.

Johnny, our boss, had an eye for Nifty too but they were respectful of people's orientations. They might joke around but they never harassed anyone who wasn't interested. It took me a long time to understand the difference between gay men and paedophile's and at this stage I was always uncomfortable around gay men. I put them all in the same box and that was a mistake that I learned about later.

So, at Sky's place we had a shot and chatted for hours. In the end Nifty and I agreed we would buy bulk from Sky and make up our own deals. A big change was coming at Patches because five dollar cuts from Jack were over. Jack wasn't going to be happy when we took the majority of customers. He'd had two puppets in Nifty and I but when we saw the value in selling for ourselves, we grew up fast. It wasn't any one person's market and other dealers used to sell there too.

The problem was that Nifty and I had become addicted without even knowing it. We needed speed to keep running all night and get the work done and sell drugs all night too. We made a decent profit operating our own action.

I had unconsciously replaced food and emotions with drugs. I was skinny anyway but using speed made an already skinny kid even thinner. The new job, the lifestyle and the drugs kept the demons at bay. It all distracted me from what I was really feeling deep down: hurt, broken and angry.

There were times when I came down from the speed and I became overly emotional. Then I'd shoot up more to keep me going. I'd be awake for four or five days at a time. Eventually, no matter how much I used, my body would just say *Enough* and I'd collapse. Coming down like that was dangerous for me because every time I did, I thought about suicide. I was reckless and I didn't care about my health. I would lay down on my bed when alone and think of violent ways to suicide. Jumping in front of a train, or off the Harbour Bridge. I wanted to make a statement with my death as if by doing this people would finally understand just how deeply I was hurting.

My bedsit next to the Taxi Club was just a room really. A bed and little cupboard that came with the place were the only furniture I had. Each night Nifty and I got the speed from Sky then we'd make up envelopes out of Playboy magazines at my place. When we had about fifty deals each set up we were nearly ready for work. We'd take a huge shot each and have three more to ready to get us through the work night. We kept our twenty five hundred dollars worth of merchandise in a tooth brush boxes. We dipped into our profits a lot by shooting up ourselves or shouting girls shots.

My body couldn't manage all the needles I was putting in it and my veins started to collapse. The scar on my left arm, still there today, was enormous and I had to start finding veins on my body every day. I was covered in trackmarks and made no attempt to hide them. I didn't care what others saw or what people thought of me. The biggest scars I carried were deep inside and no-one saw them.

Speed took away the peaceful person I had always been and turned me into someone else. One time while I was picking up the glasses at work, I hooked up with a really hot looking blonde girl who'd been hanging about that night. I had met her a few times in the past and she wanted to go with me but I'd had nowhere to take her. Now I had my own flat but I had to keep saying, 'I can't go until I've finished work. Nifty needs my help.' She was absolutely stunning. Every time I stopped to sit down she would sit on my lap. She was all over me. She'd got speed from us earlier and she was drinking all night. The drink tickets I got from work every night weren't any use to me because I hardly ever drank so I gave them to her. I usually sold the four of them for ten dollars and people used them to buy cocktails: Orgasms or Black Russians.

The night went on and Ricky, one of my mates from the streets, turned up at the club.

'Keep an eye on my girl for me while I'm working will you mate?' I asked him. 'Dance with her and have some fun and just make sure no other guys try to get onto her.'

At the back of the club there was a room where the Drags used to go to prepare for their shows. I noticed Ricky and my girl near the door and she was sitting on Ricky's lap, dry humping and kissing him. I snapped. I hadn't slept for days and I felt pretty psycho. I strode up to Ricky, grabbed his head from behind and bit his nose. He screamed and the girl jumped off him. I had never, ever done anything like that before!

It really embarrasses me to write this but I need to tell the truth about how fucked up my behaviour was. Drugs changed me from a peaceful guy who hated violence, to a raging thug who could get so out there that he'd bite someone's nose. I didn't like the person I was when I used speed.

Fights would break out at Patches and I'd usually just grab people, stop them fighting then ask them to leave. If we looked them straight in the eye and just said, 'Go' or 'Fuck off.' they would. Now I'd be so off my face some nights that it would take very little provocation and I'd be fighting. I started to enjoy being angry and violent. Lucky for me and those I fought with, Jack or Nifty would stop me. Nifty and I got into a few fights with patrons in the club and as soon as we got the upper hand, we ejected them.

Patches was a great place for meeting girls. I met twins there who were both hot and both liked speed. They hung off whoever was dealing the shit - Nifty and I. I particularly liked one of the girls Hazel. One morning I was walking along Oxford Street with the twins when we found an envelope similar to the ones Nifty and I made up except that the packet was bulkier. It was about four inches compared to our one inch ones. I picked it up and found about three grams of white powder inside.

We didn't know what it was but we assumed it was cocaine or heroin. I really only knew speed. We decided to go to my place. I tasted it. It was quite a distinct taste. Three grams was a lot of whatever it was. I decided to try it out. I put some on a spoon. I had no idea what I was injecting and I didn't care. I'd had friends die on the streets from Hot Shots (battery acid). It didn't stop me from trying whatever this stuff was. As soon as I got it half way into my arm, lights out. The gear was so potent or my tolerance was so low at that stage that I overdosed before I finished injecting.

I woke up to find an ambulance man leaning over me.

'All right mate. You're all right. We've given you Narcane. It'll reverse the heroin,' he explained. I was confused and I took a few minutes to recall what had happened.

One of the twins was still there. Lucky for me she didn't just go when I passed out. Some people did back then. When someone dropped, their buddies would panic and leave the victim for dead. People were afraid to call for help because the police would come along with the ambulance. The laws have changed now so that people are not afraid to ring for help.

The other twin had disappeared with the heroin because she thought the police would come and there would be trouble for her. Her sister said it was because they thought I was dead. She probably sold the shit we found. We sold speed for twenty dollars but the equal quantity of heroin would bring in a hundred dollars so that girl must have made a bundle.

One thing was clear to me after the overdose: my drug use had become an issue. Even my easy going boss Johnny said, 'Glen, you've got to cut back on using or you're going to lose your job. You're getting high on your own stuff mate. You've just got to cut way back.'

People could use drugs for a night and not have any more for months or years. Not me. Not any more. I was putting five or more shots in my needle at once then every hour I'd go to the toilets and spend ages trying to get high. I was covered in track marks and blood, I wasn't eating and I was probably suffering with psychosis. I couldn't do this thing recreationally. I'd become an addict. I didn't know that yet. I didn't understand addiction. In my head I used speed but I wasn't a junky. *Junkies can't stop. I could if I wanted to but I don't want to.*

Nifty was the only person who didn't change how he was around me. He kept saying, 'Bro, you're using too much.' But I wasn't listening. Inside me a tornado whirled and drugs distracted me from the turmoil. I was my own worst enemy.

One night at work I was picking up the glasses when someone introduced me to a man called Mitchell who lived off Crown Street near Darlinghurst. Lola was a drag queen who had a girlfriend called Sharon. Usually when shows were on we delivered drinks or speed to the change rooms. Lola and Sharon were into the occult and so was Mitchell who they claimed was some kind of leader. Everything was distorted for me.

Mitchell told me he was The Arch Angel Michael.

'Feel the back of my head,' he said.

Sure enough he had two lumps on the back of his head that he said were horns. To a drug user, easily manipulated, that was very creepy. I had no idea who the Archangel Michael was but this was creepy.

Mitchell saw how much speed we were selling at Patches and asked me if I wanted to sell Cocaine.

'Speed is just poor man's cocaine,' he told me. 'You'll make a lot more money with cocaine.'

He gave me a small sample and I went to try it out in the bathroom. I'd get nice rushes when I first started using a drug but that stopped after a while. I was always looking for another rush. When I injected the cocaine, I got the weirdest rush I'd ever had. That night I went with Mitchell to his place. We made a deal. He supplied five grams of cocaine for me to sell at a certain price and I had to give him a cut of the money. I was in.

After I sold about five hundred dollars worth, a friend and I used the rest of the cocaine within days. I didn't bother turning up to work. It was what I called a 'morsky drug'. I just wanted more and morsky straight after I'd had some. Shooting it up gave me a huge rush that I wanted to repeat with every injection.

My decline from here was rapid. Johnny sacked me. I was too preoccupied with drug use and selling.

Mitchell met me at Patches sometime after I'd lost my job. He wasn't angry with me. He told me he was a chef and was opening a nightclub on William Street. He asked me if I wanted to help him build the club. He needed a DJ. He was gay and he was seriously attracted to me. I was heavily attracted to cocaine. Mitchell was connected with corrupt Kings Cross police. I had no idea at the time. I had to put my life in danger before I discovered the truth about him.

I hardly danced any more but early in my time at Patches, my mate Screbsie and I had danced in a competition where performances were judged by the crowd applause. The winner that night was a drag queen and Screbsie and I came second. Mitchell had seen the competition and that's when his thing for me had started. He had a lot of money and a lot of it came from selling drugs for corrupt police. I didn't know that yet.

So, my next job was to DJ at Mitchell's club. He wanted me to help build a music area in his club. I'd done this once before with Chad, the doorman I'd been friends with earlier. Chad had been given a club to manage too but after the police learnt of my involvement they told him to piss me off. It was after my letter to the Ombudsman. The cops didn't like Mr Ombudsman being around any of their businesses.

Mitchell was a very strange man. He hardly ever spoke and seemed focused on building his club and selling cocaine for the police. He was always trying to get me and others to believe he was a warlock. He owned a lot of strange artifacts of the occult.

He lived with a young man who was an actor. I moved in to Mitchell's place too, unaware of how deeply he was involved with organised crime. His flat was in a lane in Darlinghurst and the area was well-known as a place to buy heroin. Mitchell accepted that I wasn't going to be in a relationship with him and I wasn't going to turn down a place to live rent free. Mitchell said he enjoyed having me around anyway. Drug use had overtaken me and he helped me cut down my usage a bit. I still used cocaine when he gave it to me but I wasn't doing shot after shot now. He tried to teach me that you could use drugs without having to punish yourself.

When I was off my face one time Mitchell showed me the back of his place. It overlooked neighbours' back yards and beyond.

'These are all my people,' he announced, letting his hand drift across the scene. On the wall he had two weird looking masks. Either he was mad or a genius. Whichever it was, he was easily able to manipulate my young, drug-fucked mind. His place was just a terrace flat with a back yard that overlooked his neighbours' yards. Even Lola and Sharon looked up to him as a high ranking occult leader. He spoke all the time with such authority and apparent knowledge. He had an explanation for everything and all his crazy talk seemed to make sense.

One morning he said, 'We have to go to Coogee. I have to meet a few people.' I loved the beach at Coogee so I was keen to go with him.

We went to a night club in the middle of the day. There were no patrons there but the people we came to meet were in an office that overlooked the ocean. Mitchell and I sat down and I stared out to sea while Mitchell spoke to the big man who kept looking at me.

He asked Mitchell, 'Who's the kid?'

I was now eighteen years old but I looked about sixteen. I still had dyed blond hair and still could be mistaken for a girl sitting there watching something in the middle of the ocean. I was so fucked up by cocaine I probably saw something that wasn't even there.

There was a loud and almost familiar knock on the door. It opened and three big men walked in. Kings Cross detectives! Shit! I recognized them immediately. The cops were as worried about me as I was about them.

'What the fuck is he doing here?' one of them asked Mitchell.

'He is with me,' Mitchell said forcefully. 'He's okay.'

Mitchell was a skinny, timid looking man who you could

knock over with a feather but he was so well connected that he had some kind of power with these heavy weights.

'All right, whatever,' the copper groaned. 'Got something for us?'

Mitchell brought out the brief case he had with him and put it on the table. When he opened it I was stunned! There was so much cash, more than I had ever seen in all my life. Stacks of fifty dollar bills!

One of the other detectives gave me a death stare and I started to feel afraid. Given what I know now, I see they could have just as easily pulled out a gun and shot me right there on the spot. They'd done it to others for less.

Once the money was on the table the cop stopped staring at me and stared at the cash. They threw a brick of cocaine on the table. I'd never seen it like that before. Mitchell put the brick into his bag.

'Nice talking to you,' he said and got up to leave. I stood up and sheepishly followed him.

As we left one of the detectives said to Mitchell, 'Next time leave the kid at home eh.'

Mitchell didn't look back. He wasn't intimidated but I felt quite fearful. The fear lasted for some time, even in my bombed out state. What I'd just witnessed wasn't lost on me. The danger was real. Mitchell had no idea of my history with these people. He didn't know that they really hated me or that I was in more danger than he understood. I wanted to tell him but I just kept quiet.

With the brick he'd bought Mitchell told me that, like heroin, cocaine was graded. Grade four was pure and he had just got a stash of pure cocaine.

'If we sell this on the streets, people would be dead from just the smallest amount,' he explained. 'They would all have fucking heart attacks.' He chuckled, as if the thought of people everywhere having heart attacks was amusing.

He put the cocaine on a big mirror and broke it into four parts. I couldn't believe how easily the brick broke down when he cut it with the razor. Then he mixed it with some powder to get it to fifty percent purity. Later I discovered that if I shot up gear cut with Epsom Salts, I got a rush that tasted odd and also a rush from my backside.

Mitchell said, as he kept cutting his product, 'I'll sell it to the next guy and he'll cut it again and so on. By the time it gets to the streets it will have been cut that many times, there'll only be a very small bit of coke left in it.'

I nodded, dozily waiting for my cut.

'Even on the streets it can still be very strong. Depends what they cut it with.'

'Uhuh.'

'Could be icing sugar, baking soda, Epsom Salts.'

As he spoke it didn't bother me that I would shoot up any of the other stuff. I just wanted the coke, however it came. I watched as a small amount on the mirror grew. After a while I used some and it blew my mind away. I was on it for about five days and going with Mitchell to the restaurant. He had a big opening night and many known street roughs, crime syndicate members including police came to celebrate the business. I worked in the kitchen washing dishes, stuff like that.

Mitchell taught me how to do different cuts in meat or vegetables too. I could work as a kitchen hand with that. I got really good at knowing the different kinds of cuts I had to do. I also got really quick at chopping up the vegetables into the many shapes and sizes he requested.

I helped him build the dance floor downstairs. Different people were coming and going before the DJ box was installed. I knew that would be my spot but for some reason that changed. Mitchell desperately wanted to have his own nightclub. He got the off duty police moonlighting as doormen. The police didn't earn much money at their regular jobs. Mitchell reckoned that was why so many were so corrupt and often had to work two jobs.

'Money. Money equals power,' he used to say all the time.

I saw that the police were just bad men. I saw a lot of big, well known people from the Cross but the ones I remember the most were the detectives. One night after the club officially opened there was a group of police sitting down stairs in the dance area. That wasn't unusual as the place was filled with locals Police or well known crime figures. They had some young girls with them and I was bringing them drinks. One of the coppers kept staring at me.

All the people there were important underworld figures: policemen, detectives, rich people with reputations. Looking back now I must have stood out like a sore thumb. Here I was a former street kid, drug user, Mr Ombudsman, serving drinks to corrupt police and gangsters. I was in way over my head and I knew it. As that cop stared at me I kept looking at him. Fear probably showed in my face. I'd heard stories and I witnessed these corrupt men doing their corrupt things all over the Cross. At the club they were treating the young girls like animals, man handling them and sitting them on their laps. The way they laughed spelt evil to my mind. They were evidently drunk, had this attitude that the girls were just pieces of meat and that the world revolved around them. They saw themselves as important and everyone else was just in their world for their convenience. I saw them as abusers. Several times throughout the night I saw the detectives in deep conversation with Mitchell and they seemed to be looking at me. I wondered what they were telling Mitchell about me. Was it paranoia or was it real? Time would tell.

The following day at about ten in the morning I was asleep when I heard a loud knock on the door. The knock was familiar in that police always have this very loud and distinct knock. Mitchell was at the restaurant and his partner wasn't home so I got up and answered the door. Three detectives were there, one I knew well and there was one called Trevor who I didn't know very well.

One grabbed me by the throat and said, 'You are moving out today.' I tried to wake up a bit more. 'Get out of this place and don't come back. Don't show up at the club either.' It was impossible to miss the threat in his words. The detective speaking didn't have his jacket on and his gun was visible, hanging on his side. Deliberate I guess, to intimidate me.

I was intimidated in that lane with them when the main street was about a hundred metres away! I started to walk away, trying to look as if I wasn't afraid although I knew I was in real danger. Their guns were easy to access and that wasn't lost on me. I thought about another person shot dead in a back lane not too long ago by Detective Rogerson.

'Don't walk boy. Run!' I heard one of them say.

I was terrified. I sped up. I thought that he was actually going to shoot me. I still believe that was an option they had considered. I kept looking back. I saw them still standing at the door with very grim faces. The loud mouthed one had his hand on his hip close to his gun. I didn't look back again. I ran flat out and turned right towards the Cross.

With nowhere to go, I found Lola and Sharon's place behind The Opposition refuge. I asked them if I could stay a couple of days.

'Yeah. Course you can,' Sharon said. There was one bedroom, a lounge room, kitchen, bathroom and a small sunroom. I put a mattress that I got somewhere in the sunroom and slept in there.

After a few days Lola said, 'We're moving to Wollongong. There's a night club there that we're going to do shows in. Do you want to take over the lease here?'

I was still occasionally getting speed from Sky and dealing, mostly to drag queens and a few mates. I wasn't making much money but it was enough to pay rent on the flat so I agreed to take it on. We went to the real estate agent who, to my surprise, agreed that I could take over the lease. I had no identification, almost no income and no history of renting.

Sharon and Lola moved out soon after. I had this flat all to myself. It was pretty good having my own place in the beginning but after a while I was wishing the others kids were here. I kept selling for Sky at first but one day I wasn't able to get anything to sell.

The speed I'd got was shit and I ran into Pig at the Snooker Room. Pig was a mate I'd known for a few years from the streets.

'I'm trying to score a couple of grams mate,' I told him.

Pig took me to a place not too far from my place. It was a little cul-de-sac where a biker lived. Pig ducked inside then came back.

'You can come in,' Pig said.

He introduced me to a biker named Snake. He turned out to be a really nice bloke, for a biker.

Pig talks me up. 'Roach sells speed at the night clubs up on Oxford Street. Knows a lot of people at the Cross and they buy from him.'

Pig knew me also as Glen but I always said my name was Roach when I sold to people. Snake disappeared then came back and threw a five gram bag of gas on the table. I think I had a couple of hundred bucks on me.

'Three hundred,' Snake stated.

'I haven't got that much,' I told him.

'Pig says you live at the back of the Cross in the flats?'

'Yeah,' I said reluctantly. I knew better than to mess around with bikers.

Pig said, 'Mate we'll sell that easily today.'

I looked at Pig as if to say, *What are you talking about!* Pig said, 'I'll help you.'

We took the gas back to my place. We had a shot. I shouted Pig, to thank him for getting on for me. Then we made a heap of deals up. I gave a few to Pig and he went off to offload them. A few people bought from me too. Pig came back within an hour and he'd sold all he had and three more people were with him.

Before I knew it I was selling between five and ten grams a day. My flat needed a revolving door. I had people knocking all day and night. I suddenly had girls that worked in the clubs coming to me and just about every street worker in the Cross too.

I didn't ever cut it and I gave them good sized deals. Better than anyone else. I was making so much money I didn't know what to do with it. I always felt the best rules for selling were to never run out, always give good deals, never cut it and be available all the time.

Nifty was still working at Patches so he would bring me people from the clubs. Pig brought people from the street and it grew so fast. I started getting very paranoid. With the better quality speed and my habit of taking as much as I was able to, I was a mess in no time.

I was shooting up nearly every hour. I often stayed awake for days at a time. When I did eventually fall asleep, I had to get one of my friends to come and keep selling while I slept. I never voluntarily went to sleep. It would usually be after four or five days of straight using.

I got more paranoid every day. I started looking out the window every five minutes. Every car I saw I thought must be full of detectives and those people I saw talking down there must be talking about me. What were they planning to do to me? And who was that man standing at the corner?

One day Nadine came to visit. I had not seen her since we'd left Adelaide. I still very much loved her but she was living her own life now and there was no place for me in that life. Her visit was only to get a deal of gas. I didn't charge her and off she went as quickly as she had come. I felt sad that the days of her and I being side by side were gone. At that time Nadine came there was some girl who I think said she was my girlfriend now.

As a dealer I had a lot of people hanging out with me. Good dealers never used the shit they sold and they never had people come to their homes to buy. I wasn't selling to make money though. I sold to support my habit. I had friends who I knew would leave if the drug supply dried up but I had some like Pig and a few who lived with me who were very close and loyal to me.

I had all sorts of beautiful women throwing themselves at me but the speed left me not wanting sex that much. There were times when I did though and there was always some hot girl or other more than willing to oblige. I was the man with the drugs and cash. The twins from Oxford Street came sometimes. Hazel would stay with me for days at a time then disappear again. Her sister didn't stay.

I thought I was so lucky. I was very thin and fortunate that no-one ever came to try and rob me. Knowing who I sold for carried a threat I think. If you robbed me you were robbing the bikers. If I had any trouble all I had to do was yell and help would arrive. I never needed to. I had a few people who got credit that didn't pay but most people did. If people asked me for credit I would often just shout them, depending on who they were.

My behaviour was becoming very bizarre, especially when I was home alone. I went as far as putting stuff against the front and back doors to stop anyone or anything getting in. I'd lie down when taking my shot, looking under the front door for shadows. I'd have my shot quickly and be ready for … whatever. Whoever. I'd hide my speed then forget where I'd put it. There might be five or six people waiting to buy, sitting in my lounge room, while I searched all over the place trying to remember where the stuff was. I didn't know this was weird but a few people told me about it and if I wasn't high, I could see the weirdness, vaguely.

Someone pointed out to me that if the police ever did raid and I had a heap of deals made up, they'd charge me with 'Supply.' If it was in one bag I could say it was for personal use. Given the amounts of money I had and the number of people who came and went, it wouldn't be hard to know I was supplying but I stopped doing caps anyway.

It got to the point where I needed speed to stay awake. I hardly smoked pot but most of my friends did and I would get it for them. People would often ask if they could swap pot for speed. Most of the local working girls and strippers came to see me. The man they used to buy from had gone to prison for putting a pool cue through the eye of a man in the snooker room.

Sharon and Lola had used the flat for séances and stuff like that before I took over the lease. When they went to Wollongong they left two things behind. A Ouija Board and a big black cloak like a Warlock might wear. It was hung up on the wall in the far right corner of the ceiling.

What happened with the cloak sounds bizarre but in my mind at the time, it was real. Now I can see it was probably psychosis or a hallucination. I was sitting alone in the lounge room having been awake for several days and things were looking pretty out of whack. Suddenly the cloak on the wall filled up with a body. It floated to the middle of the room and then dropped to the floor. That completely freaked me out! It had to be a spirit and my experience with them had never been good.

Another time I found a letter with my name on it, left by Lola or Sharon. It had my name one it and it seemed to be a spell:

By all the powers of Three times Three
This spell bound around shall be
To do no harm or return on me
For as I do good so mote it be!

I suppose it was written to fuck with my mind but why would they want to do that? As a drug user it had me believing they had cast a nasty spell on me. It freaked me right out. There were other things that went on in that house too. Speed really messes with your mind. When my head is clean and well, I don't believe in demons or that kind of stuff. I believe there is good and evil. I actually have a belief in God, its men I don't believe in. Every man I ever met tried to abuse me or tells lies.

One day I ran out of speed! I'd been awake for many days and I desperately needed sleep. So many people had knocked at the door but I'd ignored them. I'd stayed awake waiting for the distinctive sound of the Harley delivering my gas. No good. Better take some Serapax or Rohypnol to get to sleep. They are both types of sleeping tablets that were common back then. Just after I took a tablet I heard the Harley outside. Snake delivered the stuff and left.

The pills had taken effect and I was fighting my own body to stay awake. I went into the front sunroom and started to mix up a shot of speed. I was still paranoid so I faced the door when I lay down, watching for shadows under the front door to my apartment. I knocked the spoon over. I was very emotional whenever I was coming down because I often thought about the kids who'd died from heroin or been murdered. It made me angry that I was now in this mess. I felt the kids would be ashamed of me. There was even a part of me that believed they were watching me.

As the speed spilt out of the spoon I punched the glass door to the sunroom. It cut my wrist open. Blood gushed out and I knew it was a bad cut but I just didn't care. Rather than try to get up and do something about it, I lay down and fell asleep. That is the last thing I remember.

I don't know who found me or how they got in. It might have been Nifty. He was there as I regained consciousness in hospital. There was no surgeon available when they brought me in so my wrist had to be wrapped up as it was. I woke at one point with charcoal coming out of me. That's a drug used to get rubbish out of your system. People thought I had attempted suicide and so they were concerned about my mental health. Different people kept coming to speak to me asking how I had cut my wrist, asking me what pills I hadn't taken and if I was trying to suicide.

At some point a micro surgeon came to stop the bleeding and stitch me up. I'd cut an artery and two tendons so they had to do surgery. I was not allowed to leave the hospital because I needed rest and there were concerns about my mental state. Apparently I told the ambulance staff that I didn't want to be around anymore and they should just leave me to bleed to death.

A psychologist came to talk to me but I don't recall much of the talk. Later that day Nifty came to visit me in my room at the hospital.

'Mate I need to get the fuck out of here,' I told him.

He replied, 'Mate you're in a gown. They've taken your clothes and you're attached to a drip on a big pole.'

I was determined to leave so I followed him out the door into the lift dressed only in a hospital gown, arm attached to the drip and bare bum on show to the world.

A few years before, Nadine had been in that hospital having tar baths for eczema. I'd got a flat nearby at the time because we wanted to be near each other whilst she stayed in hospital. She would leave with her drip still attached, come to the flat in her robe and later return to hospital. Walking down to Nifty's car reminded me of that time. I felt pathetic, half dressed with a drip attached to me. As soon as we got to the car I ripped out the thing in my arm and got into the car. I had to press my hand on the spot to stop the bleeding.

We went home first to get some gas for Nifty and then we'd go to Bondi to see some people who'd been wanting to score. When we went inside my sunroom, there was so much blood on the floor! I quickly got some clothes on. Time to go to Bondi. Clean up later.

A bit later that day I'd just had two people come to my door to score. They used what they bought straight away at my flat, before they left. That had been the last of my current supply. I let people use at the flat so that they didn't leave my place and get busted with drugs in their pockets. A few of the girls took their shots with them to use at work so they could get through the night.

Paranoid as usual I was watching out the window and saw a car drive past. Soon it was back driving past again. It kept driving up and down the street, straight past my window. Every four minutes, there it was again coming down slowly. I could see the men in it looking up at the flat.

In my mind this happened every day. Was this real though? I dismissed it and sat down trying to ignore my imagination running wild.

Bang. Bang. Bang on my door. That was real! I instinctively knew it was the police. I opened the door and there stood a group of detectives most of whom I knew. One was the detective whom

I knew very well over the Mr Ombudsman thing, Detective Jones, and he was still out to get me any way he could.

'I've got a warrant to search your home,' he sneered.

'I want to see it,' I told him.

He pulled out his gun, pointed it at my head and said, 'That's my fucking warrant, arsehole!'

Did they even have a warrant? I certainly wasn't shown it and I was too messed up to press the point. I was at the mercy of corrupt police. Four months before this, Snake the biker and his girlfriend had rented the flat above me. They didn't have to deliver my stuff by motorbike any more. I could just walk up the back stairs and knock. A lot of the time Snake's girlfriend was home alone but she gave me what I needed.

The Police spent ages looking through my place while I sat in the lounge room. I knew I had nothing because I'd sold the last of it to the couple who'd left not long ago. After an hour of searching a cop came out from the kitchen with a single cap worth twenty dollars. It was definitely in an envelope and it appeared to be one that I used to make using Playboy magazine. I thought for a moment it may be one I would have stashed but I never stashed away little envelopes. I had stopped making deals up. I kept it all in one bag and made deals up for people as they asked for them. Most times I put it straight into the spoon. I'd only put it into an envelope if the person wanted it to go straight away.

The cop with the envelope said, 'Got you asshole.'

I didn't know that at the same time they were raiding Snake's place too. I was arrested, thrown into the car and taken to Darlinghurst Police station to the detectives area upstairs. It was a room that oozed evil and corruption and very dangerous detectives who thought they were above the law worked there every day.

I was handcuffed and sat at a table. An officer kept asking me questions.

'We know you're dealing. Who do you deal for?'

I said, 'I don't know what you're talking about.' They kept baiting me and slapping me.

I refused to say shit. I wouldn't write a statement about where I bought my drugs. I knew you didn't ever dog on your mates, especially to corrupt cops.

Eventually they charged me. I was wearing a really nice watch and had a lot of cash on me at the time, around a thousand dollars. They took me down stairs to the charge room put me in the cells. No Simon to get me out this time. Or any of those refuge perverts. Hours later I was released. I recall I went to the desk sergeant at Darlinghurst police station to ask him for my money and my watch. He replied. "you didn't come in with any property mate. I actually put in a complaint to him and as we spoke the detective Jones came to the counter and told me to fuck off out of there or he would lock me up. Something about that man frightened me. I often saw him jogging in the back lanes of the Cross and he seemed to have his finger in everything I saw at the Cross. I just left, without my money or watch.

I went up to see Snake and he told me they'd raided him too. They'd found an ounce of speed.

'Man, that's a heap! Glad you got bail,' I said.

'It cost me ten k. Ten thousand fuckin' dollars to drop the charges!' he said.

They had to make some type of arrest so they charged his girlfriend with 'Possession' and said they'd found one gram. Snake obviously knew I hadn't dobbed. I'm sure the police would have told him if I had. I was surprised they hadn't said it anyway, just to get me beaten up. Those cops had a habit of saying your co-offender had dobbed on you. That would make you dog on them.

For a while Snake stopped selling so I had to rebuild my base of clients. I managed to get some gas a few times from the streets but for five months or so, my psychosis was so bad that I never left the house. I still had a few hundred dollars that I had stashed in the house which the detectives didn't find. That was unusual as they had a nose for finding money.

I had a friend staying hanging out with me for a few weeks. He was from Holland. He was a former heroin addict and not really into speed but sometimes he took it. We spent hours trying to find speed in the Cross. We came across a man who had pink rocks for sale. He sold me a hundred dollar deal of heroin that we took home and used.

After about six months of shooting up speed every day, not eating or leaving the place, ignoring the thousands of people coming to my place to score, and now using heroin, it's hard to describe how it made me feel. Unlike speed which sent me paranoid and going a million miles an hour, the heroin instantly relaxed me. I felt so calm. My head stopped chattering.

I had used heroin at Derrick's place once and I'd spent the day throwing up and I'd accidentally overdosed on stuff we found in Oxford Street. Well, this time I knew what I was using. Heroin. The saddest part is I liked it. My head had been manic before the shot with a million thoughts and demons wrestling for control.

Now hush. Complete stillness. No demons.

I got up and said, 'Let's go up the street.'

The guy from Holland was shocked. 'But you haven't wanted to go out since I've known you!'

He was right. I'd only go out the door to buy drugs or go down stairs to get a Sustagen drink. I lived on that stuff. Anyway, we walked up the main street of the Cross. I bought rice cream at the chicken shop and some other food. I ate ravenously. I walked up to the Snooker Room, my old haunt. I saw some my mates. This place was always a reminder of Linda and all the kids of the refuge. They were the reasons I hadn't been up there for a long time.

Many of the kids in the Snooker Room were shocked to see me. One kid, Des, who I'd met in the homes said, 'What the fuck are you doin' here? Like, what are you doing out of your cave?'

I liked heroin. People don't usually just become addicts with just one shot. That is pretty much how it was for me though. I'd found the one drug that calmed my head and took away the pain in my heart. Heroin distracted me from the fullness and emptiness I couldn't delete from my mind.

I wish I had paid more attention to the addicts I'd seen over the years. They were always either looking to score or sleeping on benches. They looked peaceful. In my mind everyone always seemed better off than I was. The truth was everyone was suffering their own demons, silencing their own voices, masking their own pain.

No one tells you the rest. The part where you're perfectly willing to sell your soul to get heroin, where you go through terrible, agonizing withdrawal if you can't get it, where you lose many of your most cherished friends along the way. I would have to learn all these things and more for myself. Heroin Misery and death were now very close allies.

Chapter 15.
Downward Spiral

After the raid Snake decided he was having a break. I understood his reluctance to sell. I wonder if I had served my purpose and he'd find someone new who wasn't so hot to the cops. Maybe the police had warned him off working with me. I assumed that the Police had said something to him as they really hated me. The complaint to the Ombudsman was bad enough but I was very cheeky as a kid. I really didn't comprehend just how dangerous the Police of this era where. As much as I thought I was street smart as a child I really didn't understand how dangerous Kings Cross was, or the people that lurked in its underbelly Preying on the vulnerable. I seemed to meet them all at varying points of my childhood. When I look back writing this I can see as an adult just how vulnerable I was, an easy target for Paedophiles, manipulation and corruption. Now I was a drug addict.

It didn't take me long to become a full on heroin addict. Where speed blew my mind, heroin would take my soul. I'd gone from crazy to desperate within weeks. Heroin was a different addiction from speed. I had used speed daily but if I couldn't get it, I didn't go through withdrawals. It just gave me a chance to come down and regather my mind. After using heroin for a few weeks, even the thought of a shot of speed made me feel sick and if I did use speed, it made me hang out worse for heroin.

My head had never been silent. I'd always been restless. Always thinking of death, institutions, my parents, cops or the sexual abuses. When I shot up heroin, there was silence. Instant calm. It was like my mind and heroin had some chemical connection that allowed the voices that never silenced to cease.

My body was covered in scars from trying to inject myself. My body already held scars from many different forms of abuse as a child, now I was self abusing. Every vein had collapsed. My left arm had scars so deep that you could see them from twenty feet away. They are still visible today although I've been clean for many years. I still maintain though that worse scars I carry like many survivors of abuse are the silent scars not visible. Yet this kind of scaring I seem to be able to identify in others today.

Heroin was comforting and distracting but with every shot I had, my tolerance to it increased and I needed more heroin each time to get the same effect. For that I needed more money. Heroin was much more expensive than gas. Fifty dollars would get me one point of street quality heroin. I got to the stage where I needed at least four shots a day and I needed better quality. One thing addicts do well is follow the trail. We are able to see where the drugs are, who had the best and cheapest. With that though you dive further into the corruption of the Cross. Heroin is a very lucrative business that people get rich from. They are the grubs that don't touch drugs, they just get rich by destroying other peoples lives. I was about to see so many people die from this hideous disease we call addiction.

When I was new to the heroin scene I bought street heroin. Sometimes the gear was good and other times I didn't feel any effect at all. I couldn't even be certain that what I was buying was actually heroin. I had to learn which dealers sold quality and who sold more for less. It's weird to call that garbage 'quality' stuff but that's how I saw it in those days.

For the first couple of months I was able to get money each day in all sorts of ways. It came from predators I'd known like Peter or Grant. Knowing now where to buy the gear, I would score for other people and take a bit out for myself. I sold speed when I could get it but I wasn't able to keep myself cashed up enough to deal because every cent I had went up my arm. I preferred to shoot up rather than eat, pay bills or do any self care.

After about three weeks I was using larger doses several times a day so my need for money became more desperate.

One morning at the flat I woke up feeling really unwell.

'Fuck mate. It feels like I've got a bad flu,' I said to my friend.

He said, 'No mate. You're hanging out.'

'Hanging out? What the fuck's that?'

He explained that my body was literally dependent on heroin. 'If you don't get some,' he warned, 'your body will be screaming in pain for your next fix.'

I always became very emotional when I was in withdrawal from heroin. The memories would come flooding back and so did thoughts of suicide. The reason I took heroin was to silence those voices I often heard. In withdrawal I thought a lot about Linda and the other kids, the abuses and every other dark thing I knew about. I couldn't close my eyes without seeing something that I didn't want to think about. The one thing heroin can promise you is, if you survive being a user, you will witness the loss of countless lives. Linda's was the first to have a big impact one me but I saw so many deaths of friends it's hard to count them all.

The friends I had now were different sorts of people to the kids of my earlier years in the Cross. Now they were users of heroin, criminals, street workers and drug dealers. Overdoses, suicides and even murder took so many of my friends away. Each one who died sat in another place inside my head waiting for my next withdrawal when I would think about them and get emotional. Grieve.

It seemed to me that the streets themselves had changed from the bright lights that little boy had followed, into a dark, grim place where children became drug addicts in filthy stinking streets.

Everyone sees you differently when you're an addict. Roach, that sweet kid, was a boy who everyone wanted to stop and chat with. Now he was a nineteen year old addict who only stopped to talk when it involved getting drugs. The main street felt like a war zone now. Everyone was hooked on heroin and it was dog eat dog world. All my senses had come to life. My eyes burned all the time. I was aware of things I hadn't noticed before. My whole body ached constantly. I was always tense and very aware that Kings Cross literally stank. I could smell the stench on the streets, especially in the early morning before the street sweepers came to clean up the filth of the night before.

I had lost myself. My life now was totally consumed by heroin. My need grew worse each day. I had seen other people like this before and I'd wondered, *Why do they do that to themselves?* I had become what I had never liked or understood.

I chased the calm I'd got when I first injected but I never fully got it again. Even if I got a shot that got me high, I knew it would only be four hours before I needed more. There wasn't time any more to sit back and enjoy the calm. I had to set off to try to get my next lot of cash to get my next shot in time.

After a day of bustling and using I got to the flat to get some rest. I hadn't paid rent and I was hardly ever home. I fell asleep only to be woken by the too familiar banging of police at my door.

Bang, bang, bang. 'This is the police. Open the door!' My addiction meant that I saw more of police in my life.

This time they were accompanied by the real estate agent who had been trying to get in touch with me. They evicted me on the spot. They threw all my stuff out onto the street and me with it.

I sat on top my things for a while. Nowhere to go. Again. Nothing I owned was of any value. The police had already helped themselves to things like jewellery and my good watch. I just walked away from my stuff as my body screamed for gear. That was all I could think about. I managed to get a shot that day somehow.

Without a place to use heroin I resorted to back lanes or toilets. The back streets of Kings Cross in the early eighties were littered with drug paraphernalia, such as needles, spoons and even the bodies of people using or overdosed.

This day I chose Kings Cross station toilets to have my shot. My mate was in a separate cubicle. I put the spoon on top of the toilet, pulled out my little kit and mixed up my deal. I pulled a filter from my cigarette, stuck it in the spoon and it sucked up the contents. I put the needle into my arm, jerked back the blood. As it filled my syringe, out of nowhere, a Railways Police officer leaned over the wall.

'Stop what you're doing,' he demanded.

Yeah right mate, fat chance of that. No addict would get so close to getting it then just give up his gear! I injected quickly then pulled the needle out of my arm as another railway copper kicked the cubicle door open.

'We're arresting you,' he said as he grabbed my arm and led me out.

Railways cops had as much power as street police in making an arrest. They took me into the Station Masters Office. To my surprise, he was very compassionate. He spoke to me kindly while I sat nodding off, not really caring what he had to say. I'd had my shot. That was all I cared about. The demons would stay quiet for another four hours.

'Mate, what are you doing to yourself?' the officer asked. 'Why would you do this?' He seemed sincere. He wanted me to know how stupid what I was doing was. I wanted to sleep. 'I've found so many bodies on my station. Drug users who we just didn't get to in time. I don't want to come across you one day. You are killing yourself mate.'

'I haven't been doing it for long,' I told him. 'Yeah, it's stupid.'

I think he felt good that he thought he was getting through to me. Up to that point I'd been an honest kid. I didn't do crime, apart from selling drugs and using them. I never intentionally hurt anyone or lied. But now I deliberately manipulated this man by saying all the things he wanted to hear. I talked myself out of his office by saying, 'Thank you. I will leave the Cross and get away from this garbage. I am better than this. Thank you.'

Who was this deceitful fiend? It wasn't me. An addict and a liar? I went straight back to using. I still had a long way to fall.

The court case from the time they arrested me for the cap of speed they found in the flat was coming up. Hazel, one of the twins, went with me. I was a mess. It was a simple possession charge but the thought of being sent to prison with a habit terrified me.

I wish the judge could have seen me for what I was though. I was lost and very much an addict. He may have sent me to a rehab place or even put me in prison right then had he known the extent of my drug use. It might have saved me from years of utter misery. Instead I was given a bond and a fine then released into the world I'd come from.

One day I had fifty dollars cash that I got somehow. Some days there were dealers everywhere so 'getting on' was easy but this was a day when addicts paced the streets for hours looking for a street dealer. The more you used the more dealers you got to know. I slowly learnt how to follow the trail. I'd find out who a person I scored off was scoring from. Then I'd find that dealer who probably sold bigger amounts and a better quality for less cash. I'd score there. I was scoring mostly from street dealers or low level dealers who had little flats near the Cross and were themselves dealing to support their own habits.

One dealer, George, only sold half weights, about a hundred and fifty dollars worth or three hundred dollars a gram. I paced about looking for other users who wanted to get on and that was easy. I found two guys.

'Let's chuck in fifty bucks each and get a half a weight and go three ways. Much better shot for all of us than buying single fifties that wouldn't do much for us.' Fifty dollars would buy one point if you were lucky but if you bought a half weight you got five points.

They didn't need much convincing. Off we went to Victoria Street to the chemist to buy needles at one of the few places that sold them. You could buy a kit with a spoon, a small vial of water and a syringe. We bought our kit and headed to Sweethearts Café where George was sitting. The other two handed me their cash reluctantly. Addicts were always being ripped off, so letting go of cash wasn't something people did easily. They watched me go and buy the gear from George.

At last we had what we needed so we headed down Roslyn Street and into the back of some flats behind the Pink Pussycat on Kellet Street. We walked up a few flights of stairs where the wind wouldn't blow our gear over like it had the day before. One of the guys was supposed to be a lookout for police while I made up our shots in the spoon. The lookout got distracted, watching me instead of checking for cops. I would have done the same thing. Some addicts would make a mix, pull up all the gear into the syringe then tip water in the spoon and say, 'There. That's yours. Pull it up.' I hadn't learnt that trick yet but he watched me anyway.

The half weight we had was plenty for all three of us. Just as I was opening the syringe packet three men came busting up the stairs. The heroin was still in the spoon waiting for me to add water. No time.

Kings Cross detectives, the Drug Squad, had arrived! 'All of you get up against the wall!' they shouted.

Fuck, fuck, fuck it. I thought, *Fuck.* I was desperate to get my shot in. We stood up against the wall. The spoon of gear lay on the floor.

'Who owns the drugs?' one of them asked aiming the question at me. They took our names, dates of birth and other so called relevant details. Two of them radioed through our names while the younger detective was left to keep his eyes on us. There was nowhere to run. This was a block of flats with only one way in an out and the two other cops stood on the stairs below.

As we stood facing the wall I kept looking at the spoon. *Fuck! It's so fucking close.* Then I notice the young cop was watching the other two downstairs. I reached down quickly, picked up the spoon and ate the gear. I threw the spoon back on the floor and faced the wall. It wasn't as if I had time to eat my share and pass it on.

'Where's the gear in the spoon?' a detective says when he comes back from talking on the radio.

He eyeballed the detective whose job it had been to watch

us. Then he looked at us, obviously confused. We stayed quiet. The other guys had seen what I'd done but they didn't dog. All I could think was, *I got my heroin. If they beat me, lock me up, at least I won't be hanging out.*

The lead detective was agitated. 'Oh fuck it. Just arrest them anyway.'

At Kings Cross police station we were told to sit down. Within a few minutes I was asleep. I haven't a clue how long I slept but eventually a copper kicked me in the shin to wake me up.

'Right you three. Out of here. We've got no evidence so it looks like you got away with it this time.' Then he quips, looking straight at me, 'Not hard to see which one of you got the gear.' I gave him a cheeky smile.

I didn't say anything as we walked out. Relieved at not being charged, free and not hanging out was a perfect result for me. Almost as soon as we got out the door one of the guys started demanding I return their money.

'You owe us fifty bucks each.'

'We're hanging out,' the other adds.

I reply rather angrily, 'Mate all three of us would be sitting in a fucking cell right now if not for my quick thinking.' Then, shifting the blame I said, 'It was your job to keep cocky, you fucking dickhead! There are three flights of stairs before they could've got to us and you couldn't even warn me they were coming! It would've been me charged with possession. I did you a fucking favour, you idiot.'

They wanted their money back badly. 'Want me to pull it out of my fucking arse?' I asked. 'I've done you both a solid. You would have sat all day, maybe even all night, in the cells hanging out. This way you got out and you can hunt again.' After some back and forth we realised that arguing was futile given that I had no money. We went our own ways.

In the early eighties clean needles were very hard to get. There were only two chemists in the Cross where you could buy them and both were only opened from nine until five. At night I often saw people walking around with the gear but no needles and they'd ask other users if they had one to share. Sometimes I could get a free shot by sharing a needle if I had one. There was a dead end lane called Junky Lane in the Cross and it had a little shed at the end where most of us went, day or night, to use. After having a shot, people would drop their needles on the floor and the pile of used needles probably reached thousands. The legal way to dispose of needles was to break off the tips then put the tip and needle into a bottle with the lid on it then throw them in the bin. Did anyone bother with that when their sole purpose was to get a fix and be ready for the next one?

Addicts like me would come down Junky Lane to find an old syringe and reuse it. It was definitely playing Russian Roulette because diseases like Hepatitis, many strains of it, and H.I.V started to spread. They could all be contracted by sharing contaminated needles. Did anyone care about the risk? Not much, as long as we got a hit.

Knowledge about using safely was mostly passed around by other users. Addicts taught each other. As time went on places like the Kirkton Road Centre sprang up where staff had to get to know and then educate locals users about health and needle exchanges. There were magazines called Street Wise and Users News too that had educational cartoons on safe sex and safe using. That place saved addicts' lives and saved others' too who might have trod on or been stabbed with infected needles.

I was reluctant to go to Kirkton Road when it opened because they made you sign in and I worried that if the police wanted to, they could look at the sign in book and find anyone they liked and grab them. I must have had an instinct for safety though because I was one of their first clients. I've heard that the police still use the sign in registers to find people they want so even today lives are lost because addicts fear meeting police in the shooting gallery or on the way in. In time there were about fifty of us locals living in the Cross who went to Kirkton Road Centre to get needles.

There was a time when I'd chuck my needles on the pile at Junkie Lane but when the black boxes were set up I'd use them. Slowly health issues were being addressed by the city community and addicts who spoke up for change.

In the early eighties addicts shot up wherever they could: blocks of flats, backs of houses, laneways or anywhere else where they could get a bit of shelter for a couple of minutes. Many of them died in the back street of Kings Cross or in local toilets. I used the Lane shed many times and I even found money or gear from people so off their faces they wouldn't know what they left where. I was so desperate at times I would go to the shed, pick up a needle from the pile, clean it out three times three, as taught by health workers, then use it. That caused trauma to already overly used veins. Water was easy to get from taps or bubblers until people who lived around the Cross started taking the handles off their taps to stop addicts stealing their water. I saw addicts get water out of toilets, they were so desperately hanging out. I would never do that because I was terrified of dirty shots. Some people got fresh water from toilet cisterns but that was still a health risk. Even tap water could be contaminated with bacteria like cryptosporidium.

Often the needles were so blunt that you would have to sharpen them using the striking side of a match box. They'd knock the needle too hard against the spoon when they pulled the gear up, making little burs on the needle tip. Those burs wreaked havoc with veins, especially with repeated use. Best to get those off too if you had time.

I saw people, especially women, shoot up in their groins, their feet or their necks. Addicts would rip the side mirrors off parked cars and use them to see where in their neck they put the needle. It all seems crazy to a non-user I suppose. It's very hard to understand how desperate you become to get heroin into yourself while you dodge police hunting for you in back streets, trying to arrest you. You also had to dodge other addicts looking for addicts with gear to rip off.

I kept my bent spoon and a needle that I'd use over and over hidden in an old yard in Victoria Street. I kept them stashed in a toothbrush box. If I was able to buy a pack of three or five needles, I'd use one and hide the others so that I always had one available. I didn't like carrying them on me because the arsehole police could charge you for having needles on you. Having clean needles at night meant I could sometimes get a shot from someone looking for a clean set up.

One time I pushed a needle into my arm so hard the needle broke. I was lucky that a little part poked out past my skin so I was able to pull it out. I had seen this happen once to someone else who had to go to hospital to get it removed. If things got desperate I used homemade needles. Making those took an inventive mind and a lot of talent. Such are the skills of people who can't think of anything but getting gear into a vein. There were glass syringes back then that you just changed the tips on. They were called Blue Ladies.

There were people, including politicians, outside the Cross who were opposed to the centre, arguing that giving people a safe place to inject would encourage more people to become junkies. Does my experience support that argument or give it any credence?

There was a place called Porkies where you could rent a room for five dollars then go in and use. Eventually someone might check on you. They might find it empty or not. People died there or got very close to it having overdosed. Some people got help in time. Many did not. The owner, in my opinion, cared more about the constant stream of five dollar payments pouring in all day and all night than about lives.

At the start of my using I was on the nod once sitting on a bench near Alices Restaurant when a biker who I'd known for years, came up to me and said, 'Why are you using heroin mate?'

He got really angry and emotional. He grabbed me by the ear and dragged me down to Porkies where a man had overdosed and died. He freaked out the ambulance drivers as he ripped the sheet from the body and showed me the corpse. He said, 'Any time you want a shot, I'll give you a hit that is guaranteed to put you on the nod.' He punched his hand as if to say he would hit me.

It seemed not that long before all this madness of heroin, needles and killing myself that I'd been break dancing on the streets. I no longer had the desire to dance but I often thought about it as I passed clubs and heard the music blasting out.

That was then but now I was well known as an addict. We were hard work for the ambulance personnel who worked in the Cross. I wonder now if they suffered from PTSD (Post Traumatic Stress Disorder). Every day they dealt with dead kids in the back lanes. If they got to addicts in time, they could give them Narcan that just might save the life. Narcan, because it reversed the effect of the drug enabling you to breath again, would give the patient an immediate, desperate hanging out for a hit again. Some would physically attack the ambulance men for reversing their shot. I didn't hit any of them but I often woke up and went off my head, screaming and shouting and complaining how they had killed my buzz.

Sometimes they'd try to explain, 'You were dead mate. We had to give you the Narcan to bring you back from death.'

'I was just on the nod, you fucking dickhead. I spent two hundred dollars to get like that and you fucked me up!' That was often all the thanks they'd get from me.

It didn't occur to me that my life had been saved. All I felt, vividly, that I was hanging out again. A shot of Narcan caused instant withdrawal. That wore off eventually and if the gear was strong enough you would return to being off your face.

Now that I was a street addict I rarely went into clubs. Every place in the Cross sold drugs at one point or another. I scored at take away shops, restaurants, pubs, clubs, pinball parlours, fruit shops, kebab shops, hock shops. The list was endless. Most addicts who hung out in pubs met with foul play or violence. Drug addicts and gambling addicts could all meet with the same end. I knew many of them to say hi to but I kept a safe distance from them. Unless they were selling and then I was their very best mate. The drug dealers seemed to be greeted like Rock stars in the Cross. The bigger the dealer and the better quality stuff they carried the higher in demand they were. There were some who would only come at a specific time. One would arrive at 7pm at night and leave by 8pm. She would have only $100 deals but her gear was very good and when she arrived each night she was met by a hoard of addicts. I would slowly learn who had what and when and how to get to know each of them personally.

I was homeless, addicted and owned only what I wore. I slept either at the back of the Snooker Room, in the park or in squats. The little park opposite the Police station was all right to sleep in and there was another one opposite the Gazebo Hotel. Just before the sun came up I'd go to the park, take off my shoes, tie the laces together and put them under my head then lie down to sleep. We kept an eye on each other but there were some bastards who'd steal the shoes off your feet as you slept if you forgot to take them off. I didn't have good shoes and if I lost the ones I had, it would be by rorting.

For example, someone might say, 'Score for me will ya mate. Leave yer shoes with me as collateral.' They'd give me a few hundred dollars thinking I was sure to come back with the gear if they were holding on to my two dollar shoes! There was times in the Cross I had left shoes for people and walked around literally bare foot. Peter would arrive on the scene and take me to buy me shoes.

Every waking minute was dedicated to finding money to buy drugs. Chasing the Dragons tail. If I had fifty dollars I'd spend it. If I had five hundred, I'd spend that. I'd use it all as fast as I could. No saving anything for later. You might be dead by the time later came. When I had a place to live I could keep a shot for the morning or money to score. Things were different now. That was speed. This is heroin.

There were times when I had kept money for the morning shot but during the night police would wake me up and confiscate it. They'd call it 'the proceeds of crime' if I couldn't explain to their satisfaction where it had come from. The Police robbed addicts and street workers daily. They gave you a choice, give up the money or be charged with goods in custody or whatever other charge they could dream up. I'd hang out with working girls on the streets and as we paced about trying to score, I'd see police demand money from the girls. They took a free service from the street workers too if they wanted to. There were stories of police taking girls off in police cars or bull wagons to rape them. They were rough and treated the girls really badly. They didn't pay but what could the girls do? Kings Cross Police, especially the detectives of Darlinghurst, were a law onto themselves. The boys who sold themselves on The Wall talked about a particular detective who used to force them into the toilets and rape them.

One morning I woke up content because I'd saved a shot to use. I'd kept it my down my pants. Before I could use I was pulled up by the police.

'We're going to search you,' they said.

I got really anxious, hanging out. Sure enough they found my gear and I watched, helpless, as they squirted it out onto the grass. After that I decided to be awake at night and sleep through the day. My best sleeping place was on the grass outside the Kings Cross Police Station in daylight. Nearly every night I was awoken by the police or someone going through my pockets or someone looking for drugs. Money and drugs were easier to get at night so I roamed by night and slept by day. I was more visible so less likely to be robbed or harassed by the police.

I could support my ever growing habit for a while with petty crimes. I knew where to score or who to fence stolen goods to, like an older man called Goldfinger who was a security guard. Everything he owned was either made of gold or painted gold. Even the pushbike he rode around on was gold. He was the man to see if I ever had gold to sell. And there was a well-known fence at one nightclub. He bought anything that was worth any money. Car stereos were big but anything electrical, as well as gold and jewellery, he'd buy. I'd wait outside the Snooker Room as people walked by and I'd say, 'Want to score mate? Uppers, downers, poppers, trippers, cars, watches, Visas or electrical goods.' I became quite skilled at promoting myself as the man to see, to get stuff done.

Often someone would have a lot of stuff stashed nearby in a car or somewhere. Brash guys would have car stereos in back packs. It only took a few seconds and a screw driver to get them from a car. Some you could rip straight out. It didn't matter if it damaged the car.

I scored drugs for people: pot, speed, cocaine, heroin or even pills. Whatever customers wanted I could find it. Most of the customers came from outside the Cross. I'd agree to 'shop' for people on the condition that I got a shot out of it. It meant I got very little each time so I needed to find other ways to get money faster. I hadn't been into crime up to this point, apart from scoring for other people or fencing stolen goods for them.

When my habit grew too big for small amounts of money I started to rort people, to rip them off. I had no conscience about it. I needed money and that was that. One of my friends showed me that for fifty cents you could go to the chemist and buy a quinine tablet. You then crushed it up and the pill coating became tiny shards in the powder that looked and tasted like heroin. To an experienced addict the taste proved that it was fake but the uninitiated were often easily fooled. They handed you the cash and got away as fast as they could to avoid police and have their shot.

Good heroin dissolved in water but quinine floated on it. I learned to taste whether the gear was heroin or not. Dealers would often sell stuff that didn't mix, like sugar or Epsom salts or whatever else the gear was cut with. The number one rule was, never rip off locals because you see them every day but there were plenty of visitors to the Cross.

Pink rock was new then and you needed lemon juice to mix it up. I started to go to the chemist in the morning and buy a tablet that I'd crush with a coin on the foil from the cigarette packet. Then I'd make up a few dodgy deals: two or three one hundred dollar ones and a couple of fifties.

Cigarette packets were useful back then although it was not because of the glamour people saw in smoking. You could mix up heroin on the side of the packet of a certain brand but I saw addicts try to use the wrong brand only to watch their gear soak straight into the cardboard. It happened to me once and I was so desperate I tried to eat the cardboard. I discovered for myself that there were quite a few ways to lose my shot if I wasn't careful. Once I mixed my gear in a spoon with water but the wind came up, blew the spoon over and my hit soaked into the concrete floor. I couldn't eat concrete. I was so desperate to get a shot and stop hanging out that I decided to rip off someone else.

There were dealers on the street who had agreements that let us earn money or drugs. Every time I sold three deals for them and brought one hundred and fifty dollars in cash, they'd give me a free deal. I got on for locals or people I knew.

Most days I looked like an addict. I wore the same clothes every day and rarely washed. I learnt a few tricks like pinching clothes off people's lines and also going to blocks of flats with shared bathrooms to use the showers to wash myself and shared laundries to wash my clothes.

I became quite skilled at rorting people, a skill I am not proud of but in my defense, if there is such a thing, I can only say it was a case of survival of a self-centred addict. I only ripped off out of towners. Probably the easiest rort relied on two people working together. It was high risk but brought high rewards. The risk was that the person helping with the rort could rort you or that your victim would catch up with you and beat the crap out of you. So, I had to learn to fight or to convince the victim that I'd been rorted too. I already had the gift of the gab, which was always my preferred option over fighting.

Fighting was par for the course though and I got more skilled as time went on. The desperation of hanging out helped fire me up. A lot of times I'd arc up first and my opponent would back down. I wasn't going to get beaten up if I could avoid it.

With two of us working together we'd arranged a place to meet after the rort to split the proceeds. My mate sat somewhere like a café with made up deals of quinine, a coffee to fill in the picture but looking like he was off his face. I walked up and down looking for a 'rabbit' who might want to get on.

'I know a guy at the café,' I'd tell the rabbit and steer them in.

'I just want ten bucks for the deal,' I'd say. More, if I thought we could get it.

After the rabbit got his 'gear' he'd take off quickly to have his shot. Sometimes they wanted me to go with them and I would go, trusting the other guy to meet me where we'd arranged later on. If I went with the rabbit to have the shot I'd have to act pissed off when they discovered that they have been conned.

'Wait 'til I get that bastard!' I'd say in my best outraged voice.

After ripping someone off there was a small window of time to find a real dealer, score for myself then disappear for an hour or so. Usually I moved from Kings Cross to Town Hall, Central then back to the Cross.

Most addicts didn't spend time hunting for you after a rort. They'd be out looking for money for their next hit. Most realised that finding the rorter was futile. They would already have spent your money and used themselves.

I didn't particularly like rorting and no-one had ripped me off. Yet.

Another technique was switching the deals. I'd have a dodgy deal of quinine on me and I'd score off the real dealer for some unsuspecting person. Then I'd switch the real deal for the dodgy one, give it to the buyer and take off to use the real stuff myself.

There were times when someone would score with me. We might only have fifty bucks each. I always made sure I was the one who did the deal and mixed the gear so no-one could rip me off. Eagle eyes watched everything I did so I had to create distractions for the split second it took me to put a few drops of water into the spoon. I'd ask them to make a filter.

'Hang on. I heard something out there,' I say suddenly. 'Go an' check it will you while I do this.'

I'd pull up all the heroin into the syringe then, in the blink of an eye, I'd put a bit more water in the spoon. Sometimes I managed this like a highly trained magician, even with someone keeping their eye on me. I'd put a few lines from the syringe back into the spoon. They got a shot but it wasn't nearly as potent as mine. If I'd been a total arsehole I would have taken the lot but I usually just took the lions share.

At times I even got someone to buy a hundred of gear and not put any money in because I could convince them we'd gone halves. Then I'd take the lions share for free.

I actually learnt this trick from others trying to do this to me. If I saw someone make themselves up the lion's share, I grabbed their syringe and put it straight into my arm.

I even followed dealers to where they secretly stashed deals, wait for them to go off selling and then I would steal their drugs.

I feel like an asshole writing these things down but it is important that people see how far my morals declined. I had been the kind of person who would give you my last five dollars if you told me you were hungry. Now I'd take your last five dollars and more, without asking and without any intention of repaying it, whether you were hungry or not. I excused my behaviour by only ripping off people who weren't full on addicts or out of towners. Of course is there is no way to justify it. I didn't want to go out and rob banks or break into houses. The idea of leaving the streets invoked fear in me. I just hung on the streets every day looking for any opportunity to get heroin. Most times I just sold gear for others and got shots off people. Those few times I ripped people off I felt bad about it but I could not stop.

I was so desperate for my next shot that after I'd score, rather than going to a back street or toilets to have my shot, I'd inject as I walked. I would walk about with water already in a syringe, get heroin then squirt the water into the bag, draw it out and inject in any context.

The friendships I had before my addiction were true friendships but the ones I was forging now were all based around drugs. I didn't pay attention to girls any more, to making friends, to eating or taking care of myself. I had become what I hated as a kid.

When I was straight I felt sick and my head wouldn't shut up with memories I didn't want to think about. One thing was certain; I would not survive doing this. I would either be arrested, beaten up or overdose.

How had I sunk so low?

Chapter 16.
A Disease

I had many friends on the streets and these relationships were based on our mutual use of drugs. I'd known some of them way before I started using and there were two were sisters who I got to know in a different way when I became an addict. One morning I woke up in the park and was told that one of them, Sandy, had died from battery acid. It was terrifying to hear that someone had deliberately given her a hot shot.

That news broke my heart because the sisters were always really good to me when I first came to the Cross as a child. A lot of the older kids were very caring of the younger kids on the streets. We were all part of a wider dysfunctional family, not like the refuge family, but we all knew each other and saw each other every day. The more I used drugs the more people I heard of who died. The sisters themselves had always warned me not to use when I was younger. I clearly remember telling them that I never would. I meant it when I said it but that was years ago.

The morning I got the news about Sandy I had kept a shot from the day before. It was mixed up in the syringe ready to use. I sat down and thought about Sandy. I injected myself to be free of the pain of her death. Usually I felt some kind of sensation but all I got that morning was a strange taste in my mouth.

Five minutes later my head felt like it was going to explode. I'd had a 'dirty shot'. Something had got into my stuff and I got really sick. My skin hurt, my head thumped and every part of me was aching. I walked up the main street screaming in pain. The only way to get rid of a dirty shot of heroin is to get another one that is good. Luckily I bumped into Maxine, a friend of around fifteen, who worked in the Pink Pussycat.

Maxine saw the state I was in and said, 'I'll get help for you.'

She had money because she was in high demand and she had just been given a decent bit of money from a punter. Maxine bought a deal of heroin and we went to her room and had a shot. Maxine was compassionate and helped me in the best and quickest way. I lay on the bed recovering from the dirty shot. I felt sad that we were using together now because we had met when neither of us used.

We lay on the bed chatting when Maxine said, 'You need to get off the streets and get clean Glen. Look how many of our friends have died already!'

She was an addict too yet she was telling me to go to a rehab centre. I'd never heard of detox or rehab. Well, I might have but I hadn't taken any notice.

Maxine said she was able to support her habit by working at the club but said to me, 'This isn't you Glen. You've changed so much.'

That struck a chord with me. I knew that something had to change or I would be dead before long. Before I was even twenty one.

Maxine took me to the Langton Clinic. She paid for the taxi and I was admitted. I had a shot before I went in so I was pretty relaxed. I wanted to get my self back, to be who I knew I really was. I despised who I had become.

It took a bit of adjusting to be in Langton. It was like a hospital except every patient was an alcoholic or an addict. Most were alcoholics but there were heroin addicts too. My perception of drinkers was that they were worse than users. I had always detested drinkers because they were unpredictable and violent. The alcoholics here seemed to look down on us heroin addicts.

I first heard of Narcotics Anonymous and Alcoholics Anonymous at Langton. On my third day there, we went to a meeting downstairs. Narcotics Anonymous taught me: *I am not a bad person who needs to be made good. Rather I am a sick person who needs to get well.*

At the meeting there were about sixty people. I listened to

the addicts who all seemed to have war stories to tell. They talked about how they hadn't used drugs for many years or about their time as users. I listened but I wasn't in a good frame of mind to receive information.

I was so ignorant. I kept thinking, *These people wouldn't even know what a habit is!* I focused on the differences between me and them. I didn't want to be there. I was in withdrawals and debating whether I even wanted to get clean. The addict in me kept telling me I could stop any time I wanted to.

The chairman of the group said, 'Red, do you want to share anything?' He was pointing to one of the girls.

Red stood up to share her story. I realised I knew her from the streets when Nadine and I had lived with a group of street workers just after the refuge closed. I'd seen her habit on the streets and in the street workers' place. She had used every day and she'd dealt for a well-known dealer. He use to have an apartment just up from the Hyatt hotel. He had 3 girls that would be at the window. You would walk up give them your money and out would pop your deal. Worked like a factory. I was there one day when it got raided.

Red was the real deal so I sat up and took notice. I hung off her every word. Maybe she had the answer!

'My name is Red and I have been clean for one year today,' she began.

Everyone clapped and cheered for her. I was sensitive to sudden eruptions of noise so the cheering alarmed me. I got emotional as I saw the love shown to her and how proud she was. Red got teary too as she told her story. I cried. I was so proud of her and I admired what she had achieved. I wanted that too. I wanted to get clean. I wanted to stand up there in one year's time and say, 'I am clean'.

Red gave me hope that day. I had not felt hope for a very long time. There had been no room for it when I was using. Red helped me believe I might find myself again and have a future, a life. She looked over and saw me crying. She recognized me.

She said, 'For you guys sitting there in detox, its fucking hard. You have a disease and it's trying to fuckin' kill you.'

I felt uneasy. She was looking right at me. We both knew so many who had already died. I found the word 'disease' very off putting. I was in my third day of withdrawals.

'You can fight tooth and nail to live or you can give in and fucking die,' Red went on, still looking straight at me.

I saw compassion in her eyes and also determination. Red boldly told the cold, hard facts. Soft pedalling around the thing wasn't going to save my life. Red told the brutal truth. I needed to hear it. I was so fucked up. I knew I needed help and the saddest part was, it could only come from one place. Myself. That is what Red said. I felt that the whole time she was speaking straight to me. How egotistical! She was aiming at all of us in Detox. I knew that she spoke the truth so I listened intently, as uncomfortable as that made me feel.

Red talked about being abused as a child and about living on the streets. The more she spoke the more I felt it could have been my story she was telling: abuse, institutions, streets, crime, rorting people, feeling sorry for herself, blaming everyone, pissed off at the world. Everything she said was true for me. Red spoke about never knowing love, never experiencing it and that resonated with me. I often thought about my parent, why they never liked or loved me. It may seem a small thing but to me inside it was something I thought about often. I watched shows like the Brady bunch and for some reason the show made me angry. That wasn't how life really was, and if it was that angered me more.

Next Red named the friends she had lost to heroin. I knew about some and she said some names whose deaths I hadn't heard about until then. Debbie had gone and so had Rob. Red listed about eight names, 'That was all in the last year.'

'There are only a few choices you can make. Get clean or die. Or end up in an institution. That's it. This disease wants to kill you and it will. It will lie to you. It'll tell you that you can get clean your own way. Well, you can't. It will tell you that you're not as bad as others. You are. It will wait for you to get a little bit clean and tell you, "you're okay now." And you'll say , "Yes I am okay. I have been good. I can have just one shot." You can't.' Again she looked at me and said, 'One is too many.'

Then the others in the crowd said with her, 'A thousand is not enough!'

There were signs around the room that I began to notice. *Let go. Let God.* There were others that are taught in Narcotics Anonymous.

I was a long way from where Red was. I was still very much in denial that I even had a disease. The concept seemed crazy. In my mind it was simple. *I like using drugs and if I wanted to stop, I could. I just don't want to.* But I didn't want to die either.

Was Red reading my thoughts? Next she spoke about denial!

When Red finished speaking she sat down and again applause erupted and people hugged her and they cried with her. They loved her. I felt love for her. Here was someone I knew who gave me hope. I felt uneasy but I had been given hope, energy and a goal.

Later that night Red introduced me to a man who looked like one of the Marx brothers. He was a shorter man with blond curly hair and his name was Brett. Brett was a famous artist but that didn't matter here. He was just another addict, no better or worse than me. Addiction doesn't discriminate.

Brett was a heroin addict and he was clean. Red wanted to help me but knew that during the first twelve months of getting clean it was better for men to support men and women to support women. We are vulnerable in the early years and we look for easy crutches. Sexual relationships are the last thing we need. Sick people entering into a relationship is not ideal.

I had no idea what a sponsor was but Red was handing me that gift. That saying is so true: *There is none so blind as he who will not see.* That epitomized me at this stage in my life. I didn't see the gift standing in front of me.

I spoke with Brett for a while. I felt a little uncomfortable with him at first. I was still sick and not thinking clearly. I didn't get what a sponsor was for but Brett took the time to explain to me more about addiction. I had no idea he was an artist or anything about him other than this kind man trying to explain that my thinking wasn't where it needed to be.

'All you need to do is reach out to others,' he told me. 'And listen, shut up, learn because you don't know shit. Whatever you think you know, it's wrong,' he said. 'Your thinking is stinking. Stinking thinking. You need to get to as many of these meetings as you can. Surround yourself with people from N.A.'

'Listen to these people.' That was the main thing and he said it repeatedly.

He spoke very differently from me. He was very quietly spoken. We drank tea, ate biscuits and talked for some time. People came up and said hello to him as we spoke but no-one treated him differently from the bloke in the next chair along.

Who Brett was wasn't important. I didn't find out until years later when I saw a story in the front page of a newspaper about a car falling off a building. That's when I learned he was an artist.

'Own your stuff,' he said quite often.

What the fuck does that even mean? I would think.

It felt like he was speaking a different language to mine.

I went upstairs after the meeting and sat for ages thinking about Red and the odd little man whose ideas I didn't really understand.

Other people had said useful things too like, 'If you put your head on the pillow at night and haven't used that day, mate you're a winner!'

'It works if you work it. Work the steps. Get a sponsor. Meet with other recovering addicts and, most of all, don't pick up. Your addict is doing pushups out the front waiting for you.'

That night was tough. I was in my seventy second hour without a shot. I couldn't sit still. I was so agitated. My head was the worst thing. It just wouldn't hush up. I kept thinking about my mother, her drinking, her drug use, her anger, her hatred. And my father, his sickness, his anger and hatred of me. I thought a lot about how easily they dismissed and rejected me. Discarded me like I was worthless. I didn't understand it then but this was how I saw myself.

Everyone always seemed to be happier than I ever was and better off too. Everyone had a family and love. Later I learnt that there are many people out there with stories like mine. Some are worse.

I went to bed but I couldn't sleep that night. It was the same for all us addicts in our first seven days. We spent hours trying to lie still. We'd go from the bathroom to the kitchen to make tea and back to sit on our beds. I thought about Red's talk. How well she looked with colour back in her face. Addicts have a death look as if all the blood has been sapped from their bodies, faces sucked in and they're hunched over. Red stood tall, proud and happy. It had been so long since I felt joy. When I first met Linda, that was joy. When I won dance competitions, that was joy. Red showed joy.

They gave us a medication called Clonidine to lower our blood pressure and we were given others medications too. Every hour a nurse came in and took our blood pressure and did Observations to make sure we were going okay.

My hands were shaking so hard I couldn't even make a cup of tea. While I was trying to, an alcoholic man who wanted hot water from the urn brushed up against me. It felt deliberate, like he was pushing me out of the way. I snapped. I started screaming all sorts of nasty stuff at him.

Other residents helped me calm down then staff took me to a chair. They gave me a warning. Any more outbursts and I'd be kicked out. The people I was withdrawing with seemed to care about me. If I got kicked out, I could blame that idiot alcoholic who provoked me.

I couldn't stop crying. All I thought about was Linda, the streets, my friends, siblings, everything was rushing through my head at a thousand miles an hour. My head that never hushed had returned but now it was louder and more vigorous. Part of withdrawals maybe? It was as if my life was flashing over and over in my head. If I did manage to fall asleep for short stints then I'd wake up from terrible nightmares. I'd be sobbing like a child and the girls would come and try to comfort me. I found that very embarrassing and I told them that and asked them not to do it but to leave me alone.

We were made go to a group session around lunchtime every day, then later that day we had to go for a walk. I hadn't slept apart from the first night when I was still high. I didn't want to go for that walk. I was angry but I didn't know what I was angry about. My situation? The system that created it? At myself, my parents, my stupidity, death, abusers, that people I loved kept dying? I had a whole lot to pick from. I went on the walk because we had to.

Later that day a new addict arrived. He was put in the dormitory with me and the other addicts. The dorms were not separated into male and female. The addicts were all in one room and the alcoholics somewhere else. We were near the nurses' station so they could monitor us.

There was a hot girl on each side of me in the dormitory. One was blonde and the other is a brunette. My hormones were running rampant in withdrawal but if I'd tried to have sex it would have been futile. Nothing seemed to work right in withdrawal. Everything, body and mind, were out of whack. It takes ages for a body to recover from the toxins you've put into it. Sex was the least of my concerns but it was still nice to get up in the morning and see the girls each side of me.

One morning we woke up and the radio was playing a song we all knew. 'We've got to get out of this place, if it's the last thing we ever do.' We all sing along with gusto and then when the song finished we debated which version it was. Was that The Angels or was that The Animals? That was a small moment when we were all distracted from our addictions.

The new guy had a seizure the day after he arrived. He'd been a really bad user of pills and seizures are one of the side effects of overuse. It was day four at Langton Clinic. We had compulsory groups every day and I was sitting in group while someone named Judy spoke to us. She spoke to me quite harshly and I wasn't ready to listen to her shit. She was the enemy to me, a dragon, and an angry bitter old lady. What the fuck would she know about being addicted to anything but her own voice!

I was so negative. So angry. We spoke about negative raving in groups. No talking about homes, prison, streets or drugs was allowed.

The only clothes I had were the ones I wore. Other addicts gave me bits and pieces. We were slowly building a brotherhood. I had only known these people a very short time yet we all seemed to be on this mission of recovery together. One moment I would want to leave then the group would sit around and convince me that it would be dumb to leave. I talked others out of leaving every day but I spent a huge portion of my time thinking of leaving, of ways to go without alerting the others. I wanted to run. Days three and four were hard. I couldn't sleep. I felt so bloody sick. I got the runs. My skin felt like it was crawling. It felt like every one of my senses was running rampant.

The new guy and I got talking. The police had bailed him to Langton. He didn't want to stay but if he left he'd be arrested. He had a car parked outside and he had a lot of cash. I'd noticed the cash. My addict mind noticed these things very quickly.

After about half an hour of talking about heroin, I had convinced him to give me a hundred dollars and his car keys. I was going to get us both a shot and bring it back here to use. I thought a little tickle wouldn't hurt. We just needed to take the edge off our withdrawals. I'd been so close to the edge and the new guy provided the nudge I needed to go over. He and the lying voices in my head helped me make a bad decision. I had already learnt that to do well at the clinic I needed to stay clean and to surround myself with people who were doing well, who wanted to succeed. Instead I went straight to the person who could help me fail.

I waited 'til after dinner. We had a compulsory meeting downstairs so Dragon Lady marched us down, told us to sit down and then she left the room. I did too. I was so cocky I believed I could beat the system. I'd spent the last two years being shifty and no-one had caught me. This place was just another small hurdle.

Luckily Nifty had taught me to drive and so now I drove the five minutes to the Cross and parked. In no time I'd scored two fifties. I used mine straight away but it had no effect at all. I injected the other one. My head didn't go silent but it calmed down a little.

Then I realised. *Oh shit! I've used the other guy's gear. I can't go back to Langton. No worries. I'll just get some cash, get on again and then I can go back. She'll be right.*

Still feeling like I needed more stuff I drove to see Peter. I convinced him to give me two hundred dollars then I went back to the Cross. I scored again had a shot then took more back to the clinic than I would have had with just a hundred bucks.

While I was driving back to the clinic the car broke down. I lifted the hood and managed to it going again. The N.A. meeting was long over when I got back so I sneaked upstairs to where my mate is waiting anxiously.

'Where the fuck have you been?'

He was beside himself. I handed him the fit. He quickly took it from me and hid it down his pants. I'd premixed the deal into shots so it was easier to use.

'They know you left,' he tells me.

I'm surprised. I believed I was in control, that I could manipulate the system.

'I'll just say I was asleep on the bed. I'll tell them they must have missed me.'

I lay on the bed then one of the girls in the bed next to me went to tell on me. What evil is this! How dare she tell on me!

She came back with two staff members.

'Glen, you have to leave the clinic. You've broken countless rules. You've stolen a car and brought drugs in. You've used.

You've put every other person's recovery at risk. We will not tolerate that behaviour here.' The other guy had lied about his car.

I didn't hear any of that. I focused on the person who dobbed me in.

'You fucking dobbed on me! You're a fucking dog,' I said to her viciously. 'You reckon you're from the streets!'

I refused to see that I had not only put my life and my recovery at risk, I had also jeopardized the other guy's chances and those of every other addict in the place. It was so selfish but I knew everything back then. The girl who dogged had really been trying to get clean and she was seven days cleaner than me.

The staff confronted the other guy and, with his hand outstretched said, 'Come on. Hand it over.' Reluctantly he did so, then it was back to me.

'Glen, you're not in prison. You're not on the streets. You're in a detox centre because of your addiction to heroin. We have to keep everyone safe.'

They gave that time to sink in then an offer was made. 'If you want to come back, you are allowed to after seventy two hours. Right? That's three days. It's up to you.'

All I could focus on was the betrayal by that girl who should have protected a fellow street kid. We always cared for each other out there. It should happen here too. I wouldn't see that she was doing exactly that, caring for me. Caring for me, herself and the others. I felt as if the group, my family in the clinic had turned on me.

As I walked out the girl called out, 'Glen!'

I looked back at her angrily. She was crying and through her tears she said, 'Please don't die. They said you can come back in three days. You should come back. Be here as soon as they open.' She was so distraught. 'I don't want you to die,' she wept.

I felt terrible. I had grown to care for these people in the four days I'd had with them. We'd had so many talks about our struggles and about our desire to be better people. That girl was fighting addiction because she wanted to get her child back. I put hers and everyones recovery at risk.

Feeling remorseful, I gave her a hug. I was stoned so it must have been hard for her to even be around me. She was rattling from withdrawals and shaking with distress. She had evidently wrestled with having to do what she did. She said as I hugged her, 'I'm sorry.'

All I could think for a moment was how selfish I had been.

'Glen, just go. Now,' said a staff member.

As we let go of each other I said quietly, 'No, no it's me that should be sorry.'

I turned to the others and said, 'I'll be back I promise. Three days. Mate, I'll be here. No worries. I promise I'll see you all in three days.'

Did they know it wasn't going to happen? They were addicts too and they knew how much an addict's promise meant. I'm sure that I meant it when I said it. I believed that I'd back. I knew I wanted to.

I can't even recall the third day. I didn't go back.

I could score not far from The Tropicana, the café next door to the Opposition Youth Refuge. I'd run to the toilets to inject then come back in for a chat. The Tropicana was where Narcotics Anonymous members met for coffee after meetings.

I saw Brett from time to time. I could tell some of the N.A. people didn't want me around but I never felt that with Brett. He recognized the battle I was fighting I think. Every time I ran past he'd nod hello to me. I couldn't stop for small talk. I just had to get a needle in my arm then I could chat. Sometimes Brett was alone and sometimes he had company though he was never surrounded by a lot of people.

He would say with a little smile, 'Here he is. The Runner.'

I presumed he referred to the fact that I was always running when he saw me. Chatting with this man with frizzy hair was calming somehow. Eventually I got to ask him pleadingly, 'How the fuck do you turn your head off?'

He laughed and said, 'That is a question we all wrestle with.'

Then after some thought he said, 'I promise you this much,

Glen, every day you are clean, it gets easier. Although, it will get much harder before it gets easier.' He said that part apologetically. There was empathy in his voice. I didn't see him for a long time after that. It was as if he disappeared.

One time I saw Brett he wasn't looking as well as usual. I'm not sure what year it was but Brett would keep fighting and falling backwards then fighting again until he passed away in 1992. I don't know the details. It hurt knowing such a wonderful man had died. He had been really kind to me and took the time to try to explain things to me. The best part about him was no matter what state I was in, he didn't judge me. I didn't know who he was and that may have been refreshing for him.

I was staying one night in a room that was right near the Wall. I was looking out the window when I noticed George. I watched him walk down a back lane and put something into a downpipe. Then he went to the park and put something in the garden at the corner. Was I about to get very lucky?

I retraced George's footsteps and waited where he couldn't see me, watching to see what would happen next. During my twenty minute wait a car pulled up and a bloke wanted me to go with him. I told him to fuck off. I watched a kid give George some money then George went into the lane. Five minutes passed and then he walked to the corner of the park, put something there and went to the Wall.

While he talked to some kids I fossicked in the garden. A heap of money! About a thousand dollars. I quickly stuck it down my pants and I ran to George's downpipe. I found a black canister. I stuck it in my pocket. George was always being searched by the police so he stashed his money and drugs where they wouldn't find them. I took off with George's stuff as fast as I could. I kept running until I reached the Cross. I got a room at the Lido Hotel. Safe inside the room I opened the canister. Deals! Already made up into fifty and hundred dollar deals. That would save me bustling for a few days.

I had a shot. I went up the street and ran into Pig who came back to my room and I shouted him a shot. It didn't take me long to go through the heroin and the cash. In the room next door was Eddie. He said he had been a champion boxer and now he was a drug dealing pimp. He had a few girls who worked for him and he always had heroin for sale.

I'm not sure how many days I stayed at the Lido but one night I was there with a group of street kids, including Dez from Woolloomooloo. We'd been in Yasmar at the same time.

Bang, bang, bang! Yes, the police were knocking. The door opened. The police came in and arrested us, though I think they had come looking for Dez. While they drove us to Darlinghurst Police Station Dez said, 'As soon as they open the door I'm gunna run.'

'Yeah, okay mate. Good luck with that,' I said. A lot of kids talked shit so I took his words with a grain of salt. I had no reason to run. I hadn't done anything.

When the police started to open the bull wagon, Dez kicked the door open, knocking one of the officers over. He ran flat out and one of the cops chased him. He got away! *Good on you,* I thought.

The rest of us went inside.

'Where'd he go?' the Coppers kept asking me. 'Whose idea was it? Were you supposed to run too?' The Darlinghurst police station, which is now closed, was notorious among locals, for taking people upstairs to the detectives office and beating them and also for bashing gay people in the cells.

Eventually I got out but not without a beating from the cops. I went back to the Lido Hotel but they told me to move on.

Pixie and Dixie were a girl couple at the Cross who dealt heroin. Pixie was a big woman who kept her heroin in her vagina. She usually sat with her partner Dixie at the end of the street in the early hours of the morning. Dixie was a skinny woman who you could easily mistake for a man. They'd been busted recently so they were very cautious. Instead of sitting at the end of the street they were playing snooker in the Snooker Room one night when I was there. Their gear was hidden in pockets of the table. I was playing with Pig on the table beside them. They were talking to two guys from the western suburbs who were probably punters.

Suddenly they grabbed the gear and bolted.

'Roach! Pig! They've nicked our stuff. Get 'em will ya.'

Pig and I chased them. They could run but so could we. We ran down all the back streets, through the arcades, up streets all the way through Woolloomooloo. We were gaining on them. I just about had one when he gave up.

He stopped and said, 'Wait. Wait.'

I was about to hit him when Pig said, 'Let's just split it four ways!'

'What about Pixie and Dixie?' I asked him.

Pig said, 'They have heaps of money bro and they don't give two shits about us. Selling us dodgy deals all the time.'

There was a lot of gear. I suggested that all four of us have a shot then give the rest back. That's what we did. The other two guys just wanted a shot. Pig and I gave the gear back to the girls waiting at Snooker Room. As soon as we walked in they asked, 'Did you get it back?'

'Yep,' we replied smiling broadly.

Pixie said, 'That's not all of it. There was more!'

'I could only catch one of them,' I told her. 'Maybe the pricks split it up.'

Pixie said, 'Hope you bashed him.'

Pig interjected. 'The cunt's laid out in the loo. Won't be around here again. You gunna give us a shot for the hassle?'

Dixie kept saying, 'No. Don't. We can't afford it. We'll give 'em one when we pick up again.'

If we hadn't already taken a shot I'd have been pretty pissed off but I did start thinking, *Why did I even give it back?*

They sold the rest of their deals while Pig and I played snooker. At about five in the morning they invited us to come back to their place. We did and later that day they got a delivery.

They bought half an ounce. Pig's eyes and mine lit up when we saw the stuff on the mirror.

We weren't about to rip them off because they sold for a heavy weight who was well known to the police. They shouted us a shot.

I was back on the streets twenty four hours a day. The only time I wasn't was when I slept. People I'd known and cared about and people who cared about me were now giving me a wide berth.

I don't know how many months had passed since I left Langton Clinic, but I knew I needed to go back. My habit had got worse with each day. I was doing things I knew were wrong, rorting everyone and using as much gear as I could possibly get. I felt I was one shot away from death. Each day was like rolling dice with my life. I was popping pills like they were lollies. I was getting a bottle of Rohypnol from a doctor on Victoria Street every week and went through them really fast. Parts of my days got lost and I couldn't remember what I'd done. I'd get so off chops I'd do the most brazen things. I learnt from others what to say to the Doctors to get Valium, Serapax and Rohypnol. The pills made the effects of heroin stronger but also increased the likelihood of overdosing.

People started telling me, 'You need help or you're going to die.'

So I rang up Langton Clinic to see if I could go back.

'Hello, it's Glen Fisher here and I want to come back to detox,' I said when they answered my call.

'Sorry Glen but we haven't got any places at the moment. Tell me what's been happening with you.'

I mumbled off all the shit I'd been using and that made me want to detox even more.

They told me that, given the amount of pills I'd been using, it would be unsafe for me to withdraw at Langton. They gave me a list of places to try.

Westmount in Katoomba could take me. I'd been to Katoomba as a child with my dad on the back of his motor bike. He took us to the Cascades and my feet got wet and freezing cold.

I complained to him and he yelled at me to be quiet.

On the train trip up I dozed and when I got to Katoomba I walked down a long hill to the little terrace that was Westmount. It had a reputation for sedating you for almost two weeks until your symptoms passed.

They welcomed me and told me to strip off and have a bath. That was to ensure I didn't have any drugs with me. I felt very uncomfortable as a man searched my clothes, searched me too then watched me bathe. He was a resident too and he'd been clean for a relatively short time himself.

The front of the terrace housed people who'd been through the withdrawal part of the program. The back had a dormitory. There was a table and a little kitchen where residents who had more clean time, one male and one female, watched over us and encouraged us to stick it out. Watching over addicts in withdrawal could not have been a popular job with them wanting to leave the place and acting out.

I struck up a friendship with the girl who was observing us. We just seemed to connect easily and we were attracted to each other. Our friendship became physical but my addiction got the better of me and I decided I needed to get on. With heroin, not with an attractive girl.

A doctor came and asked about my drug use and then he gave me some medication. I was there a few days and we were given meds several times a day. It was day five when I had deliberately waited until after meds to announce I was leaving. I wanted to take them so I wouldn't be hanging out on the trip back to Sydney.

As soon as I took my medication I said to the two watching me, 'I'm outa here.'

'You're not allowed to leave. You've just had meds!' Apparently the rules were that you couldn't leave for four hours after taking meds because they were so strong and you wouldn't be safe. 'You signed on to that when you arrived!' they said, getting alarmed.

My head just kept telling me to leave. I had stuck it out longer than the time at Langton, more because of the fact I was so far from the Cross and it would take a couple of hours to get back. They kept telling me that I wasn't allowed to go and that got me angry. I didn't care about rules. I'd made my mind up to leave and no amount of talking would stop me.

A man tried to physically stop me going out the door. I became aggressive. He wouldn't move so I shoved him into the door.

'I am fucking leaving and no cunt here is going to stop me,' I screamed. I think it was like a skinny, six foot tall, two year old child having a tantrum.

The long haired boss, who I could tell had taken something, I assumed heroin, came out. He tried to explain that I couldn't go. He failed to make any impression so I had to sign a paper to get my things back.

'We have no legal right to force you to stay, Glen. But we cannot be held liable if anything happens to you under the medication you have taken,' he said.

I was going anyway and I was becoming more volatile.

'You are being told to leave now because this violence is unacceptable.'

I laughed. 'Justify it however you want dickhead. I'm fucking going.' I couldn't resist a jibe. 'Do your mates know you're smashed?'

It seemed to take forever to get back to the Cross. Walking up the steep hill back to Katoomba station was hard work. I was still in withdrawals and the two hour train trip after waiting forever for the train to come, was hell.

I rang Peter from Katoomba to tell him what I'd done. He was so disappointed but he agreed to meet me under the clock at Central. Together we walked to the platform where Cross trains pulled in.

'Tell me what happened up there,' Peter said.

'They're all on drugs,' I said, once again shifting the blame away from myself. It was everyone else's fault, not mine. 'How am I supposed to get clean when they're all using?' I exaggerated but I had to make my point. Well, there had been one person using but not all of them.

Peter gave me money and we went our separate ways.

At last I was back in the Cross. It was late at night and I ran into a dealer, found a syringe and water then headed to Woolloomooloo to have my shot. I am not sure why I walked so far from the main street. Perhaps I just wanted to have my shot in peace. Usually when I used I had to get up and moving straight away before someone saw me. At least late at night in Woolloomooloo I could relax.

I mixed up my shot, put it in my arm. That was the last thing I remember doing. The medications I took at Westmount increased the risk of an overdose but I didn't really pay attention to that. I must have been blessed that night. This is how the story was told to me by Dez, the guy who escaped from the bull wagon.

He was walking home from the Cross, taking a route he never ever took. He took a drag on his cigarette then he flicked it and watched it float through the air and land. Was it coincidence or divine intervention? Whatever it was the butt landed on me. I was out cold, sprawled out on the ground, overdosed and with the needle still in my arm.

When Dez recognized me he did everything we'd been taught, to bring someone around. He slapped my face. No response. He pinched a nerve in my shoulder. No response. Then he ran flat out to his place and rang an ambulance.

Dez said they came quickly. He said my face had turned blue and he thought, *Glen's dead.* The ambulance people gave me Narcan but I didn't wake up straight away. I gained consciousness slowly and they got me on my feet. Like all ungrateful addicts I turned on them and said angrily, 'I was just fucking sleeping! What the fuck have you done? I'm hanging out now.' I wasn't. I was still very groggy from heroin and pills.

The ambos insisted that I go to hospital.

'No mate. I just got out of detox. They reckoned the pills in my system make the smack hit hard.'

'You need to come with us. You might drop again if you use. Those pills are still active in your system.'

I got up and tried to walk away. I staggered and knew I could not walk so I went with them. I woke up in the morning with a drip in my arm and charcoal coming out of my backside. They used some sort of charcoal stuff to take all the pills out of my system.

If Dez had not walked home by a different route, not flicked his cigarette away, not enjoyed watching it and not seen me as a result, I would be dead, without question. I couldn't have picked a worse place to use. I usually went to Junky Lane and several times I found bodies or overdosed people who I got help for.

Chapter 17.
Falling Down

One day I ran into Peter in the library where he spent a lot of time. It was right near his work and he said that it was the only place that had the books he liked.

I'd still go to the library sometimes to read Asterix and Obelix. I loved the stories of the little man and his fat side kick with super human strength. I'd go there sometimes to sleep safely too. The staff had known me for years and they never asked me to leave. They'd get Asterix in from other libraries especially for me and let me know when they were there. I think I must have made them sad. They'd known me since I was that innocent, lively kid running around everywhere with a group of mates. Now they saw the lonely addict, badly dressed, unclean, hair all over the place and just one shot away from death.

I was reading when I looked up and noticed Peter walking through the park like the Pied Piper. He was well known to the kids as the man who always carried coins for the kids to buy food.

He came into the library and spotted me straight away. He was always lecturing me to try to better myself. He didn't understand addiction. How could he? Peter had become like a father to me and we often introduced ourselves to others as father and son. He genuinely cared for me and I cared for him but my main focus for care was where I could get gear and how soon. That and my memories that tortured me and sometimes comforted me.

We went to the Castoria Café where they served full meals for five dollars but patrons had to share tables with whoever was there. Chicken Schnitzel that came with spaghetti, vegetables and two slices of bread was my usual choice. They included a dessert which was usually jelly and ice cream. They moved people in and out really quickly. Peter and I stayed for about forty five minutes then we left and sat outside to talk more.

He would quietly tell me stories about people he'd had to interview at work. I could listen for so long but then I would be desperately hanging out. He was always giving me money and deep down he knew every time I was using it for heroin. But I had to always make up stories about why I needed the money.

'I need money to get somewhere to stay,' I told him.

He babbled on about how many places he'd put me in but I never stayed. He gave me money and I saw a dealer with Pink Rocks. Peter stood to one side as I bought the heroin then we went to a chemist to get needles and water. There was a chemist who did a very good trade making up kits for addicts to buy for a dollar. It was handy to be able to get clean using equipment quickly: a vial of water, a blue plastic medical spoon and a syringe.

We walked up to Junky Lane but Peter stopped at the corner. He didn't want to know or see me do what I needed to do. He waited there pretending he didn't know.

He would tell me what happened next many, many times over the next ten years.

'I saw you walk down the lane the way as you always did. I stood at the corner of Victoria Street. Usually you'd come straight back but you didn't this time. A few minutes passed and I got concerned so I walked up to the bend in the lane to see if I could see you. Well, there you were! Out cold on the ground! I thought to myself, *He's in trouble!* I deduced that you must have overdosed. Yet again!'

Overdosing had become a theme, especially now that I'd added pills to the mix.

'I didn't know what to do so I ran to the house on the corner and banged on the door. When they opened it I told them that a kid had overdosed in the back lane. I asked them to please call an ambulance,' he said.

'Do you know what they said?' Peter always asked me. 'They said, "The best thing you can do is let the junky die. Do us all a favour. One less junky." Then bang. They slammed the door in my face! Outrageous!' That part always stunned Peter.

Peter got angry then and desperately banged on the next door. That person responded pretty much the same way but Peter had put his foot in the doorway to stop them shutting him out this time. He demanded that they ring an ambulance. 'I wasn't taking no for an answer this time,' he said.

When he heard them ring for an ambulance and was satisfied that help was on the way, he ran up Junky Lane where I was still motionless. He stood over me dressed in his work suit, looking very out of place and he had no clue what to do. All he could think of was talking to me to try to get me to respond. He was so worried about being found in the back street with a dead addict. It wouldn't look good on his resume.

It took a while for the ambulance to come. In the meantime two other addicts came around the corner to have a shot. They saw Peter and kept coming up the lane. When they saw me out cold they almost attacked Peter. They knew who I was and suspected that Peter had done something to me.

'What the fuck did you do to Glen?' one of them demanded.

'I found him like this. I've just rung an ambulance,' Peter replied. He quickly added, 'and I've called the police.'

He hadn't actually rung the police. He would never have done that. He felt threatened by these guys and said it as a safety measure. The guys had their shots quickly. That was all they were concerned with really.

Peter stayed kneeling beside me trying to get a response and as the two guys went he said, 'Stand on the corner please and tell the ambulance where to go.'

They did as he said and the ambulance came hurtling down Victoria Street. The two addicts directed them into Junkies Lane and I was given Narcan. Peter went back to work after this I think.

A sad thing was that the kid who introduced Peter and I all that time ago, Darren, had since died of an overdose.

Had it not been for Peter I would be dead rather than here

telling my story. I became reckless to the point of almost killing myself so many times over the years and Peter saved my life many times. If not for him I'd have had to move on to serious crime to support my habit. When I got into desperate situations Peter would give me money rather than have me ending up in prison. Another perspective could be that if he hadn't enabled me to feed my habit, I may have got the help I needed much earlier.

Cocaine started to hit the streets of the Cross and two rival groups were selling it. In a pinball parlour I could buy a cap of heroin for sixty dollars. Or Cocaine. There was a little hole in the wall where I told the person on the other side what I wanted. Out through the little hole would come either heroin or cocaine.

Peter drove me to Cabramatta one time. He had given me two hundred dollars that I spent on gear that was meant to last a few days. I'd heard that after the Vietnam War Australia took in refugees who congregated in the Cabramatta area and almost overnight that became the new heroin capital of NSW. Rather than addicts going to the Cross to score, many went to Cabramatta where the heroin was much cheaper, purer and easier to get. A very small minority of Cabramatta people sold drugs. Most people there were hard working families trying to make new lives and they hated the traffic of countless addicts wandering the streets to buy heroin. A politician tried to clean up Cabramatta and was killed. There was a lot of gang activity at the time much like the Cross.

When Peter drove me there I bought my stuff and I stayed in his car to have my shot. Peter sat outside the car and kept watch. I don't know what happened next but I awoke in the Royal North Shore Hospital. Peter would have had trouble explaining the presence of an unconscious addict in his car. Is that why he took me so far from Cabramatta? I still don't know.

I was revived. 'I wasn't dead!' I told them, angry that yet again they'd spoilt my ride. 'I was just on the nod.'

I hadn't used all the gear in that shot, so I asked Peter where the rest of it was.

'It's in your pocket with your needles,' he told me.

I had another shot in the hospital toilets. I dropped again, was revived again and released.

'Come on man, please. Get me to Cabramatta,' I pleaded when Peter picked me up. 'That stuff Narcan, it puts me in withdrawal. Please Peter, I need to use. I'm in agony here. Are you going to just watch or are you going to help me.'

I convinced him to take me back to Cabramatta to get on again. I used in his car again. Would you believe I dropped again! Peter drove me back to the Royal North Shore Hospital.

This time the doctor was really angry with Peter for enabling me to use. He said, 'If you actually cared for this kid you wouldn't be driving him anywhere to buy heroin!' It was my third overdose that day and Peter didn't know what to say to the doctor who went on. 'If you really want to help him, piss off. Just leave him alone!'

They kept me in the Intensive Care Unit, handcuffed to the bed until I was in a safer state. When I was released I went straight to the toilet and had a small shot. I didn't drop this time but I was so off my face as I walked out to the main street and I was angry that Peter had left me.

I walked out onto the road and I was hit by a car. The driver had managed to slow down enough to avoid a full force impact. I was so far off my face that I didn't feel anything at all. I stood up and stumbled off as if nothing had happened. I was too off my face to know I was hurt. The driver must have been stunned. I knew I'd been hit by something the next day when all the bruises came out up one side of my leg and body. That whole side of me was black and I could hardly walk. I had a broken rib too.

Often when I was tired and had nowhere to sleep or nothing to eat I'd catch the last train out of the Cross to Central then get the train to where Peter lived. It took an hour to walk from Hornsby station to where he lived.

I'd get to Peter's in the small hours of the morning. Peter's beautiful dog would bark but, as she knew me, I could get around the back and knock on Peter's bedroom window without disturbing his old mother. I'd climb through the window, say hello then go into the kitchen where I'd help myself to a huge bowl of ice cream with a heap of Milo on it. (Addicts have a sweet tooth.) Or I might heat up two cans of Irish Stew. I'd sleep in the end room or next to Peter. Nothing sexual went on anymore.

In the morning I'd eventually got up, had a shower then got something to eat. Peter's mother was very old and every time she saw Peter, she'd call to Bob. Bob was her husband who had died a while ago.

Sometimes she'd ask, 'Bob, who's this kid? Where's his family? Doesn't he have any parents?'

Peter would try to explain but his mum was in the early stages of dementia. She was a really lovely lady but her memory was going.

One time I saw a pair of binoculars there.

'Wow, can I have these?' I asked Peter.

'You can use them but you'll have to return them to me,' he replied. I saw dollar signs and thought I could sell them at the hock shop and get them back out later.

Peter made a lot of promises to me about his will and how he would leave me different things: his house, his mandolin and so on. I knew it would never happen because I was Peter's secret. To leave me anything, he would have to expose the fact that I was his only friend. He'd spend ages looking for jobs for me to apply for and trying to get me to get an education. He didn't understand the hold that drugs and the Cross had on me. He thought that if I'd just decide to stop using, I could get a job and all would be well. The reality seemed hidden from him.

Any nights that I stayed with Peter were single nights only. He made me leave when he left the following morning. I never ever stole from him but Peter always behaved as if he thought I might, especially in the first five years of knowing him. It hurt that he treated me that way. He even went as far as to install alarms in his home and make sure I knew they were there. I don't think he knew how much that hurt. Everywhere I went I was treated like a leper or thief. I didn't want to be treated like this from the one person who supposedly cared for me.

In the morning we'd get up early and get the train to Chatswood where he now worked. He'd give me some money and I'd catch the train to the Cross and score as soon as I could.

A new hock shop had opened in the Cross and I went in to have a look around. 'How much are these binoculars worth?' I asked, showing him the ones Peter had loaned me. Detective Roger Rogerson, scumbag from Darlinghurst, was talking to the guy who ran the joint as if they were best buddies.

This was first time I'd seen Rogerson since his demotion from the Armed Holdup Squad to general duties on the streets. He was well known for killing the boyfriend of Sallie-Anne Huckstep, one of the locals of the Cross. I'd met Sallie several times and she was so kind to me. She took me to the Cosmopolitan to eat once. Sallie bravely publicly exposed the corruption of police in the Cross, mainly targeting Rogerson. She had been subjected to corruption even more than I had. Sallie was killed later and Arthur Neddie Smith boasted about killing her. He denied that he had and was acquitted in court.

Well, there was Rogerson in the hock shop. I went to leave but he saw me.

'Where did you get the binoculars from,' Rogerson asked.

'They were given to me,' I told him. 'My friend Peter let me borrow them.'

'Yeah. 'cause he did,' Rogerson said. 'You're under arrest, dirtbag.' He reckoned I'd stolen the binoculars.

He handcuffed me and took me to the new Sydney police Centre behind Oxford Street. We came to the lift.

'Press the button,' Rogerson ordered.

'Yeah right. How the fuck am I supposed to do that with my hands cuffed behind my back?' I replied rather agitated.

'Use your fucking nose, you dirt bag.'

'My name's Billy Punt not Silly Cunt,' I blurted out, realizing as I said it that I was provoking him.

I'd been assaulted so many times by detectives of the Cross who believed they had the right to put hands on anyone they chose. Rogerson pressed the button himself and when we were in the lift he slapped me across the head. I was ready to spit abuse at him but he punched me hard in the guts before I got started. He had me charged with Possession of Stolen Goods. I got bail.

I went to see Peter after I was released to tell him what had happened. I asked him to go and tell the cops about the binoculars. He flatly refused. I pleaded again and again.

'I can't!' he exclaimed. 'I'm a Head of the Department. How do I explain my relationship with you?' He knew that the police would know he was a punter and he would be subject to blackmail or something else that let them take advantage of his position.

By coincidence a well-known corrupt Kings Cross detective lived in Peter's street. I saw him there once and told Peter how much of a scum bag he was. Peter said he was a good man and that I only had this perception of him because I was an addict. (Many years later I saw that place with police tape around it. Perhaps during the Wood Royal Commission when he turned and gave evidence against the police.) I often told Peter about corrupt police at the Cross and he didn't believe me.

Peter would not confirm that he'd loaned me the binoculars so I went to court. I got a fine. Easy for an addict to pay a fine! Once again I'd been in trouble for something I didn't actually do. I was defenseless against the police lies. An addict's word would never be believed over a police statement. They cleaned up their books by putting their own crimes on local addicts. An addict could cry blue murder and no one would listen.

A dealer named Davo opened a café where he could sell heroin for the police. The café was opposite Kings Cross Station. Everyone knew he sold for the police and the police were often in the café but I could walk in and walk out with my shot in minutes. Sweethearts cafe was another place I could buy heroin. Dealers use to sit in there drinking coffee. You would have to go in an order something then get your deal. One time a guy was shot at Sweethearts. I was walking up the main street to go to Sweethearts to score that day until I heard a local say, 'Someone got shot at Sweethearts!' I remember standing outside trying to hear what was going on. Just another day at the Cross.

I went to Davo instead. Another person walked in and we both scored. As we walked out I looked back and I saw Davo motion to two officers and indicate that the guy I was with had just scored. They arrested the guy as he left. The Police supplied the drugs then their dealer provided them with the occasional bust. Word got out on the street Davo was not just dealing but was also dobbing.

Every year near election time the police used to do a blitz. They'd arrest addicts left, right and centre. They seemed to have a target of forty people or so. They'd arrest the target number and charge them with Possession, Supply, Resist Arrest, Offensive Language and other shit charges. They made front page news the next day for cleaning up the streets. They'd fool the public into believing that they were solving the problems when they were actually creating them. The front page would read *Kings Cross Police clean up the streets of the Cross.*

There were fights on the streets every day. Often an addict would be in a fight with someone he'd ripped off. There was a man called Ian who was always being beaten up. He was a big guy with a heart the size of a pea. He had very little courage. One time I saw a man half his size chasing him with a knife. Pig and I ended up standing in and taking the knife away from the guy. Ian broke the main rule regularly. Don't rip off locals. Ian and Sharon would rip off any one.

Walking up and down main street one day, trying to score, I saw Peggy, a local dealer. She made everyone go through Sharon to get her stuff. So we all handed our cash over to Sharon then Peggy supplied her.

I gave Sharon a hundred dollars and she got the deals from Peggy. Sharon came back and gave me my gear. I started to go off but I turned back and saw that Sharon had a heap of deals. I grabbed her hand and she let the deals fall on the ground. I grabbed some and took off, thinking I'd got away with more than I'd paid for.

When I mixed a deal I found it fucking floated. Quinine! I was pissed off. Sharon had done the old the switcheroo on me! I ran up the street and saw her buying from another dealer. I didn't go near them. I watched. She scored then went to the back of the Chicken Spot where there's a toilet that only locals know about. There was a doorway that led to Kellet Street. We could rort people and disappear there. Sharon obviously knew about it.

I waited about a minute then I went in. She had the shot in her needle.

'Ah no Glen. Please don't,' she begged when she saw me.

'Don't?' I replied angrily. 'You have just fucking ripped me off a hundred bucks!'

I grabbed her syringe.

'There's a half in there. Please, give me some. I'm hanging out real badly,' she pleaded.

I thought about just putting it all up my arm but part of me understood how it was for her.

'What's the fucking golden rule Sharon?' I yelled at her. 'Don't rip off fucking locals.'

She looked pretty desperate.

'Oh, go on. Get another fit out,' I said.

I gave a third to her. She bustled for more.

'Mate, you stole a hundred bucks from me,' I told her angrily. 'You didn't give two shits about me hanging out. You're lucky I'm giving you any.'

We had our shots. Both of us got enough to stop us hanging out. We left as if nothing had happened. Just another day using and hustling and bustling. Every day brought new adventures, none of them good.

One time a pregnant woman was walking up the main street of the Cross trying to score. Her other babies were in a pram. Some addict mums left their kids in cars but these kids were in a pram. Two women saw her and they tried to get her to hand over her money.

'We'll just go in there and get it for you love,' they said but the mother was having none of it.

One of the con women grabbed a child from the pram and put a syringe to the child's throat. 'This needle is infected with AIDS. If you don't give me the money, I'll stick the kid.'

The mother was petrified but still didn't give up the cash. The street came together and helped her and the kid. No-one touched kids. You don't cross that line, junkie or not. People were angry with the mum, up there pushing a pram about trying to score but they were more angry at the scum bags who threatened a baby with a dirty needle. Threats of AIDS injections became common after that disease was identified. Syringes became weapons.

Most people wouldn't get involved if they saw a rort going down. Sometimes people stole other people's rorts. I've done it myself. I'd signal to someone that they were about to be rorted but what they didn't know was that I was going to do the same thing.

There was a woman who lived in the flat near the corner of Junky Lane. Women who were addicts and worked on the streets were sometimes beaten, raped and robbed by punters so the woman with the flat took them in and gave them a safe place. She also introduced a buddy system so when a girl went on a job she showed her buddy who she was going with and told her buddy about the punter's car. The buddies agreed on a place to meet up after the trick and the alarm would be raised if one did not turn up.

The girls all knew me and sometimes I was allowed to stay in their house. Most nights I had nowhere to go. I was the only male allowed to stay there. This same caring woman who started the buddy system got the idea of starting a free needle exchange a bit later.

She'd go out each day buy boxes of syringes, clean water and other things an addict might need. I think she was a diabetic and she could buy needles in bulk. I would sit up with her at night making up brown bags of things that kept the girls safer. We put condoms, lubes, waters, filters and even spoons into the bags. All of this was paid for with that woman's own money. Other women gave her money too so she could stay at the flat.

When I stayed I slept in a bed with two or three women. They all treated me like their little brother. Nothing ever happened sexually.

New needle exchanges started to pop up but long before that, this woman was saving lives through her own caring. She was an unsung heroin (excuse the pun) and the world needs more people like her who will care without recognition or applause.

Chapter 18.
Jenny

Darting up and down the main street, hanging out, looking for a quick earn, I passed the Snooker Room. I suddenly stopped. Although I was an addict I still noticed gorgeous girls and the girl standing there was stunning. We glanced at each other for a moment and off I went.

I'd had only had two relationships with girls. Linda was my first and she had died. Nadine was my next love but she had her own life apart from me now. I thought those were real love but it was more like puppy love. Not a day passed without me stopping and thinking about Linda. I would often think about Nadine too and wonder what her life was like. We had made a pact that if ever we were at the Cross on New Year's Eve, we would be at this spot opposite the Pink Pussycat. I went to that spot many years later and Nadine was there.

After I saw that girl I went back to my current serious relationship with heroin. My urgent love of heroin made her the mistress of my time, my resources, my body and soul.

A few days later I saw the girl again. She had dark black hair, big beautiful brown eyes and olive skin. All features I really loved. She was in the Snooker Room playing pool with her friend Candy. I walked around the room talking to the other locals. I knew most of them. I kept glancing over at this beautiful olive skinned girl and each time I looked at her she was looking back at me. The two girls were talking with a local pot dealer so I didn't talk to them this time.

There she was another day, standing outside an ice cream shop where her friend was working, chatting with another girl and Mad Dog and some other guy.

After she left I went to the friend behind the counter.

'G'day,' I said to her. 'My name's Glen. Who's the beautiful girl who just left?' Someone had already told me her name was Jenny but that was my way of starting the conversation.

'Hello,' she said. 'I'm Candy and that was Jenny.'

Candy was a lovely person. We talked for a few moments and I told Candy that I'd like to meet Jenny. The fact she had been out with Mad Dog didn't put me off at all. I knew in my heart Jenny and I were meant to meet.

'You like her?' Candy asked cheekily.

'Yes, I do,' I said. 'Is she with Mad Dog?'

'No! That was just a date. It's nothing serious. I'll tell Jenny you want to meet her.'

Days passed before I saw Jenny again. It was hard to focus on Jenny when my addiction demanded such a lot of time out of every day. At least I wasn't taking pills as often. Going to the doctor was hard work because I was impatient and I needed everything to be done fast. I only saw the doctor when I needed to get pills. I was trying to cut back on them so I wouldn't keep overdosing.

It was days later that I saw Jenny again, playing a game of snooker. This time when our eyes met, I smiled. She gave me a cute half smile then went on with the game. She kept looking up at me as she played so I strolled around talking to people while coming closer to my good mate Pig who was playing at the table next to Jenny's.

She was with a pot dealer who I thought was about forty and showed too much interest in eighteen year olds like Jenny. He made out he was her big protector but I suspected his real intentions were far less honourable.

I managed to muster up the courage to talk to Jenny that night and our connection was easy, like it was meant to be. From then on we were together every minute of the day except when we both went to work each day. Jenny worked in a restaurant in Oxford Street five days a week and my job was getting money for heroin seven days a week then injecting it.

I must have looked quite a site, given the amount of drugs I was using. How could a heroin addict link up with a girl like Jenny? She'd been raised well. She came from a beautiful Seventh Day Adventist family who adored her. She spoke well, was educated, had a good work ethic, a full time job, didn't do drugs and was very attractive. Why was she even at Kings Cross? Jenny was the most out of place person I'd seen there.

As she finished work each day I'd meet her outside the restaurant and spend time with her. I don't recall telling her straight away I was an addict but I did tell her I lived on the streets and I had no place to live. This didn't seem to put her off.

I didn't live anywhere so when the first time we wanted to sleep together came, I took her to an older bloke's house where heaps of street kids stayed. I didn't know him that well but I knew kids there.

I knocked on the door, 'Mate I need somewhere to crash for the night. Can I sleep in one of the spare rooms?'

He let me bring Jenny in with me. I suspect he was similar to other adults I had met who housed young street kids, a paedophile.

Jenny and I spent the night there. We had sex then fell asleep. Sex was good when I had drugs. If I hadn't, my senses would be heightened and it wouldn't have lasted very long. I'd be hanging out badly. On heroin it was the opposite, I'd last for a long time but reaching climax was difficult. After our first night together Jenny had to get up to go to work, and I had to get up and find heroin.

The intensity of our attraction grew rapidly. I was torn between thinking Jenny and I were meant to be together because being with her felt so right and wondering if it was wrong for someone like me to have her. We were polar opposites. The well raised girl and the street kid addict.

Did Jenny understand what an addict was? Or did she think she could save me? I had once thought that all an addict had to do was stop using. Problem solved. I was wrong and it would take years for me to understand it and sort out the complexities of my addiction and my demons.

Jenny had dreams for her future. She had been taught that dreams could come true if you worked hard. Her parents were good role models for her. My parents taught me that I was nothing. I had raised myself by copying what I'd seen and liked in others. My role models were drunks, addicts and people on the streets. I took a little piece of every one I liked and I reflected whoever I looked up to at the time.

At this point, a couple of adult sex offenders and heroin addicts were the only role models I had apart from people on the streets like Scar Face Ray who I admired for his *Take no shit. Fight first. Ask later* attitude. I tried to be a 'don't mess with me' type of man but I was still a wounded boy. I copied some things from my foster family too although I felt ambiguous about them for giving me an ultimatum that led me to the streets of Kings Cross.

One afternoon Jenny finished work and said, 'Let's find somewhere to live.'

She had just been paid and she was not happy with me having to sleep on the streets. She wanted a place for us to be together. I think she had been living with her dad at West Ryde before this and he and her mum had separated. Jenny had a better relationship with her dad than with her mum.

We found a flat behind the Pink Pussycat that looked out onto Kellet Street. It was a small, modest place but it met all our needs. It was ours and that's all we wanted. It had a little kitchen, a share bathroom and a lounge room that was also the bedroom. We didn't mind. Jenny needed it more than me as she had to go to work.

I call this part of my life Fletcher Christian meets Ned Kelly. Jenny had some Spanish blood and she was a direct descendant of Fletcher Christian. My mother told me once that we were related to Ned Kelly.

Once we started living together Jenny learnt about my using heroin and she saw daily how bad my addiction was. I tried to explain it to her and I told her that I wanted to stop. Jenny was my reason for wanting to stop.

Gavin, a guy I didn't really know well, turned up in the Cross one day on a brand new motor bike with all the trappings that went with it. He had just got a huge compensation payout for an accident he'd had. He wanted heroin. I scored for him then we went back to the flat to have a shot.

'How bout we go for a ride on the bike?' he suggested.

'Yeah, all right,' I said forgetting to factor in that we were both off our faces.

Jenny kept saying, 'I want to have a shot too.'

I said, 'No fucking way!'

'You just don't want to share,' she pouted. 'You just want to control everything.'

How could I explain that it wasn't greed that stopped me letting her get in the mess I was in? How could I watch someone so beautiful destroy herself?

Jenny couldn't grasp what addiction was or what hanging out was like. I think she saw using as glamorous or cool and she was curious about all the fuss. I had been there too when I was younger but now all the myths were debunked by addiction. Jenny got very upset with me when I refused to give her a shot.

Gavin said, 'I'll give her a shot.'

'No! No way mate. No fucking way.'

That started an argument with Jenny and I. She wouldn't accept that it was not cool or glamorous or that I was not trying to control her.

Later Gavin and I got on the motor bike and rode, as fast as the bike would go, to the Central Coast where Gavin's parents lived. On the way back Gavin was so off his face and reckless that it's a miracle he didn't kill us. He was showing off, speeding but every time we stopped at a set of lights he nodded off.

I kept yelling, 'Drop me at the station. I'm not going one more click with you.'

He kept saying, 'Nah, I'll be right mate. Just hold on.'

The scariest motor bike trip I'd ever had ended at the flat after so many close calls I lost count. I had spent many hours on the back of a motorbike with my dad and all of those times I was afraid we'd come off. This was a whole new level of fear.

In the flat we had another shot then I went up the street for some reason. When I got back Gavin was gone but Jenny was on the nod. She'd had a shot! I lost my shit.

'What the fuck are you doing?' I yelled at her. 'Who gave you that shot? It was that maggot Gavin wasn't it!'

Jenny wouldn't tell me at first, but eventually she admitted that it was Gavin.

I flipped a switch, lost my temper.

'That cunt's going down!' I stormed away to find him.

Jenny followed me. 'It was my fault. I asked him for it.' She pleaded with me, trying to stop the inevitable.

She probably had asked him but he knew I'd told him not to. I'd explained why and he'd agreed not to. He said he admired that I was protecting her from ending up an addict like I was.

Men were always hitting on Jenny, sometimes right in front of me. I became suspicious about what the shot had cost her. I viewed everything in the Cross with suspicion remembering my own childhood and adults exploiting me.

Gavin was a few years older than me. He was bigger, stronger and much more capable too. I didn't care. I had right on my side so I was at my best. I felt that I'd failed to protect Jenny. I was falling in love with her, enough to want to free myself of my habit and make a life with her. The last thing I needed was a shit bag putting Jenny on the same trajectory that I was on.

I walked up the street steaming inside. Jenny followed but she was not sure what to do. She was off her face too now so she didn't understand why I was so angry. She didn't want the fight to happen. Gavin was sitting in Sweethearts talking to a dealer when I caught up with him. A large group of people I knew were outside. I was ready to explode by the time I found him.

'Maggot! Get out here,' I screamed from the footpath.

The guy who ran Sweethearts said, 'No! Go away. Don't bring your fucking shit in here.'

I knew better than to mess with him. Gavin just sat there in the café while I went off my head outside.

'This fuckwit maggot,' I announced to all and sundry, 'has just given my girl a shot of heroin! My girlfriend who's not a user and I don't want her to become one.' I raved on and on until at last Gavin finally came out.

'I gave it to her. So what? She asked me for some so I shared with her. Who are you to tell her what she can and can't do!'

I was taken aback for a minute. That part was right! I had no right to tell anyone what they can or can't do. However, Jenny was my girlfriend, someone I was starting to love and that's why I was fucking fuming. I didn't know how to respond to Gavin.

I screamed at him, 'You're a fucking maggot. Who gives someone their first shot?'

I had plenty more to scream out but at that point the street turned on him. Local users, girls and some of my mates start berating him. Then Bunny a stripper from the Pink Pussycat told Gavin, 'Get on your fucking bike and fuck off out of the Cross you putrid Maggot!'

I was ready to fight him and I probably would have come off second best. It wasn't about winning the fight though. It was about standing up to someone who puts it on you. I felt morally right. An older man had tried to seduce Jenny with the hideous gift of heroin.

He got on his bike to leave.

One of the funniest things I ever saw happened later that day. Gavin was riding up and down the main street showing off doing wheel stands and being a fuckwit. Each time he passed we'd hurl abuse at him. He did a wheelie up the main street then pulled up. A biker was also riding along the same street. The biker pulled up beside Gavin and kicked him off his bike! The whole street erupted into laughter. The biker just road off while Gavin pulled himself up slowly, righted his bike and road into the sunset. I never saw him again. I was told about two weeks later that he had been killed in a terrible accident on that bike. I thought about our ride to the Central Coast and wasn't surprised.

'That, sir, is fucking Karma at its best,' I said nastily. I feel bad that I said that, especially when I thought about his mother who seemed like a lovely lady. Gavin was another victim to the disease of addiction. Heroin had taken another soul.

After we had been together for a few weeks, Jenny lost her job. I was bustling every day doing rorts and Jenny started to learn how I spent my days. One day she got it in her head to try a rort. She succeeded and she came home proudly announcing, 'I got a hundred dollars worth of gear for you.'

She was so pleased that she had ripped someone off and scored the gear. Now she wanted to have a shot. Jenny was unusual in that she could have a shot occasionally and say, 'Enough. I don't want any more.' She was different from me. I felt two ways about what Jenny had done. One way, I appreciated that she had gone to such lengths to get heroin for me when I was hanging out. But the other was fear about her being in a world she didn't belong in. One shot was enough to get me through four hours. Then I'd need more. I had the shot and then we went out to the main street to look for more cash.

Almost straight away a friend told me, 'Mate, watch yourself. Jenny ripped off one of the local gangsters. That Asian bloke that used to bet big money in the clubs.' Jenny looked frightened.

'Oh shit! He clicks a finger and someone gets killed or hurt.'

I didn't know the guy but I knew some people around him.

'He's got people looking for your girl,' my mate said.

'Go home now Jenny,' I said urgently. 'Don't open the door to anyone and don't leave the flat 'til I tell you it's safe. I've got to sort this shit out.' I felt protective and I wanted to fix this. A small part of me was angry with Jenny for stepping into a world she didn't understand.

I found the man who she'd ripped off to try to smooth things over. He was a small man and I thought he was in his mid-forties.

He wasn't flustered. He had plenty of money and I think he was more interested in Jenny herself. When he spoke it was obvious that he knew he had power and that I had better understand that. Chin, his side kick, worked at the Snooker Room and he was muscle for hire and protected the Snooker Room and the punters who brought huge amounts of cash with them.

The 'victim' of Jenny's rort said, 'I want my money back and I want the girl to deliver it to me and apologize to me.'

It took me some time to get the money which I attempted to return to him myself.

'I told you, I want the girl to deliver it herself,' he said, refusing to take the money from me. I got upset with him and I kept telling him she wasn't around. I said she was just a kid and she didn't know what she was doing. She thought she was helping me out. She didn't deserve to be stressed out with this.

He repeated his demand and assured me that no harm would come to her. If he did try to hurt her, I would have jumped all over him, gangster or not. He couldn't let a girl rip him off or he'd be walked over by everyone. Where would the respect and reputation be then? He had to be seen to hold us accountable.

I went home to get Jenny. 'I've got his money for him but he says you have to take it to him and say sorry.' Jenny looked scared. 'He doesn't want to hurt you. He just wants his money and an apology.' I reassured her that she would be safe. 'I don't care if he's the toughest, meanest cunt on the streets, I will protect you,' I promised.

I was pretty sure I could beat him up if I needed to. That was a bit worrying though but what if Chin set on me? He was a really big, nasty looking man with a big chin. I'd heard from other people that Chin had been a toe cutter before my time.

I took my trembling girl to the Snooker Room. Chin was beside Mr Big, the little Asian man. They acted all serious, as if they wanted to put the fear of a thousand dragons into us and save face.

The boss spoke sternly to Jenny about not ripping people off. She had already had two hours of that from me.

'What the fuck were you thinking?' he asked. 'Never rip off local people.'

Jenny said, 'I didn't know. I am really sorry. I didn't know.'

We gave him the money and Jenny explained that she just wanted to help me out and that she was sorry. It was all sorted out but that incident scared Jenny enough to stop her trying it again.

As we walked home, I told Jenny, 'Just leave that shit to me.'

Chin and Jenny struck up a friendship after that. There are some interesting stories about Chin. A girl I knew came to me very upset one day.

'I've been raped,' she said shakily. Gradually more of the event came out.

Two men who had just been released from prison drove up the main street. They had heroin but no needles.

They said to this girl, 'If you get us a needle we'll shout you a shot.' Rather naively she got in the back of the car so they could drive her to get needles. The grubs drove her out to La Perouse and both raped her. They said they were going to kill her but she broke free and ran to a house where she got help.

When Chin heard about it he found the mongrels and people said he hurt one of them on the beach at La Perouse. The other one got away.

One day Nifty (from Patches) and I went to a card machine to play Poker. I was using an electric lighter to click up heaps of credits on it. I had to put in five dollars then money was added by the machine.

Suddenly I was king hit from behind and I fell off my stool. I got up to find Chin had done the deed.

'Hey come out here you!' Nifty yelled at him. Nifty, a very good fighter, was now at the bottom of the stairs. 'Come out here Jolly Giant,' he kept yelling. I went down to Nifty to get him away from Chin. Did he know who Chin was! They didn't fight thank goodness.

Now that Jenny wasn't working and all my money went up

my arm, we didn't have money for the rent so inevitably we had to leave our flat. It had been more a place to sleep than anything, given my addiction but we really loved that little place. We had nowhere to go. I owned nothing but a few changes of clothes but Jenny had a few things. She always wore nice clothes and did herself up well.

'I am going to ring up my dad to come get us. We can stay at his place at West Ryde,' she said optimistically.

'Would he let us? I was reluctant to go stay with Jenny's dad. How would I be received. I didn't like adults, especially men.

Jenny's father, Keith, came to the Cross in his old blue Holden to pick us up. I was really nervous about meeting him. If I was her father meeting me, I wouldn't be impressed. I was not a bad person but a father would want so much more for his daughter. She had been raised well and had so much potential. To meet her with a heroin addict boyfriend must have been a nightmare.

Keith was a jeweller and he worked near Central station. He was older than I expected and he wore glasses. He was a very gently spoken man. I knew he earned a decent living and it intrigued me that he drove such an old car. He lived by his beliefs.

Jenny introduced us and he showed no reservations about me. He must have been horrified to see where we had been living. Whatever he felt he kept to himself although getting his daughter away from this was an obvious pleasure that he couldn't hide. As we cleared our stuff out, the addicts, stripper and prostitutes kept walking in and out and Keith said nothing negative.

He drove us to his flat. Not only did he drive an old car but he lived very humbly in a tiny one bedroom flat. He didn't care for worldly possessions. Keith was a good man and to this day I have never met anyone like him. Keith lived on his own and was very involved in his church.

We didn't stay long at the little flat. It was very cramped with three adults living there. My attempt to get clean failed. Every day I caught the train in to the Cross while Jenny worked. Although I hadn't gotten clean I was using much less than before I'd met Jenny. She was able to get short term jobs easily. When she wasn't working she came with me. A couple of times Keith drove me to the station.

Eventually Jenny and I got a flat in Croydon in a house divided into two residences. Peter helped us pay the bond and the first couple of weeks rent. Our flat was the back half of the house so we had the back yard too. It had always been my dream to have a home with a beautiful garden. The back yard was nice and spacious but the garden wasn't as beautiful as I wanted it to be. Now that I had a fixed address I went on the dole.

One night I was off my face and I said to Jenny, 'I want to make a garden.' I'd seen lovely gardens around the place and I wanted to make my own. I had not only used heroin but had taken a lot of Serapax also.

I got a shovel and went out around Croydon digging up all sorts of plants from other people's gardens. I didn't see it as a crime. They were just plants. No-one will care if I just take one or two. I helped myself to roses and all kinds of plants. The morning after I remembered what I'd done. Not only had I stolen about ten plants, put them all in a row across the back yard, I had taken ornaments too: a nice little bridge, a gnome with a hat, a gnome without a hat, and all sorts of things.

As we left the flat to walk to the station we could see the tell-tale dirt trails where I'd taken plants up our driveway. It wouldn't have taken a rocket scientist to figure out where the stolen plants had gone. No-one bothered me but now that I was a bit straighter I felt bad. If anyone called the police, I didn't see them. I was never home any way. Kings Cross was my home and Croydon was just where we slept. My addiction needed me to be close to the Cross, the drugs and the means to get them.

Late one night we got on the train at Central to go back to Croydon. We sat downstairs and cuddled up to each other. There was a large group of islander kids on the train too, about a dozen boys with a few girls. We got off the train at Croydon and they did too. I didn't pay too much attention to them. We just wanted to get home.

As soon as we got off the train one of the boys grabbed Jenny's handbag. She refused to give it up. I tried to stop him then all the boys turned on me at once. We were completely outnumbered. Preoccupied with the fight I didn't see what happened to Jenny. Another kid grabbed her bag and finally ripped it from her. Jenny was flung over and almost fell into the path of a moving train.

Suddenly a voice yelled, 'Hey!' The station master, an older man, was running down to help us. Who knows how this would have ended if he hadn't come. All that for the few dollars Jenny had in her purse! Neither of us was physically hurt but my pride was wounded. I hadn't understood the dangers I put Jenny in every day. All I saw clearly was my need for heroin. At the Cross I was always alert to danger but this was Croydon!

One night I was lying down with Jenny and I spoke to her about wanting to take a serious crack at getting clean. She was always afraid that I would die and she was especially afraid that I used alone in back streets where I might not be found if I dropped.

'There's a new drug they've brought out,' Jenny told me. 'It's called methadone and it's meant to help people get off heroin.'

That was the first time we had a serious talk about me getting clean. I didn't only want to get free from using drugs but I wanted to make a life for Jenny and me, away from the Cross. I had never felt the love I had for Jenny before. I wanted so much to express that love by getting clean and making a decent life for us.

Jenny suggested that I put away my scepticism about Methadone and at least go and check it out. I had to go to Chatswood to see a doctor to get into the program. Oddly enough my friend Peter was now working in Chatswood, close to the Clinic.

They were still trialling the drug so it was ridiculously difficult to get accepted into the program. There were rules to be followed, criteria to be met and appointments to be kept. For me, doing all that right would probably send me crazy. Luckily I had Peter and Jenny helping me to keep the appointments and do everything required by on the program. I thought it was mad to make it all so difficult to get onto the program but from their perspective I needed to show that I was serious about getting clean. If I was half hearted I'd keep a more committed person out of the scheme.

Jenny got herself a job in a café at Chatswood. Employers were usually keen to have her on their staff. She was attractive, lively and happy to work hard. She'd had experience as a waitress too. At first she came with me each day when I was trying to get on the program.

The assessment process included appointments with doctors, appointments with counsellors and jumping through so many hoops! At last I was accepted! Jenny now understood more about addiction and she knew that an addicts words were unreliable. I might say one thing and do the opposite. She would come to the clinic with me at first to make sure I actually went.

For the first three days I was given a small dose of Methadone and that was gradually increased. I would pick up my methadone, have breakfast with Peter, see Jenny at work then head off to get a hit. Jenny's boss didn't like me coming to the café. Well, she didn't like me at all.

About a week after being on the program I'd got my Methadone and caught a train to the Cross. I sat down near Slots. Then it occurred to me, *I haven't used today and I feel good. Dare I say normal! For the first time in years I'm not hanging out. Not even having a withdrawal.* I felt calm. I was no longer shackled to the Cross. I could leave and do anything I wanted.

I caught the train back to Chatswood and told Jenny then I went to the job centre to see if I could get myself a job. I spent hours applying for jobs and going to interviews. Over the next few days I went to the Salvation Army shop and bought some better clothes and Peter bought me some new shoes so I'd look presentable at interviews.

I was free. I thought I was free. I was free from rorting scams and chasing the dragon all day. However, I felt trapped by Methadone. It's five times more addictive than heroin. Unfortunately, it was administered by people who were very skilled at making me feel like a lesser being, letting me know that they could pull the pin and chuck me out at any time. It was just like my mother holding the threat of putting me back in home. It was abusing power over vulnerable people.

The program had very strict rules, especially in those early days. They were looking for success and if I made one little error they could and would remove me. I was told this a lot and it made me feel very insecure. I could be expelled for dirty urines, arguing, fighting, missed appointments or any indiscretion.

When I reached the forty mil dose level I found that was perfect for me.

I had to see a counsellor every second day. His role seemed to be to reinforce the rules. You must do this. You must do that. I'd always found it hard to accept authority so counselling was hard for me too when it was like that. Very off-putting. Especially in the early days of being clean and learning to adapt to a new life. One of the worst parts about the program was having to come every day with another 50 addicts. You are exposed to them every day. It makes it difficult to escape that life when you are forced to be around them.

The idea was stay on Methadone for six months then slowly be weaned off it and be clean and free from dependence on any drug at all. I really wanted that for me and my beautiful girlfriend. I wanted her to be proud of me too. She was. We had moved to a nice new flat in Campsie and each day we would get up, shower and dress nicely. I'd go to get my Methadone and Jenny would go to work.

I'd get my dose almost as soon as the clinic opened. There were always two other guys there as well. Todd, whose girlfriend was a drop dead gorgeous stripper from the Cross. Todd rode a motor bike and he was a very unattractive, long haired, skinny guy with a huge hooked nose. They seemed like such a mismatch to me. The other guy, Moose, was someone I knew from the Cross. Moose brought grief to so many people including me. He had no morals or care for anyone but himself. He was from Europe. He looked like a body builder. When I was with him I felt safe. No-one would mess with him.

We had just picked up our doses and were walking over the bridge to the other side of Chatswood. I was looking for work so I was nicely dressed. Moose bumped into an Australian bloke whose build was similar to mine: tall and skinny. He looked like a tradesman of some sort and he carried a toolbox.

'Watch where you're going,' the guy said.

Moose, big noting himself, took off his shirt and said, 'Wanna have a go mate?' He was strutting around like a rooster, flexing his muscles and poking out his chest, trying to intimidate the skinny guy.

'Let's do it,' the skinny guy said. He was ready for a fight and he turned to face Moose full on. The blood drained from Moose's face. His demeanour changed and he said quietly, 'Mate, you bumped into me.'

The other guy kept saying, 'You wanted to fight. Let's fight!'

Moose backed down, much to my disgust. He was well built and for-ever telling me how he could beat anyone on two legs. Now here was Pee Wee Herman in a Bob the Builder outfit asking to fight Muhammad Ali. Moose had morphed into Cinderella in seconds.

I jumped between them. The tradie was strutting now like a peacock and I felt embarrassed. 'Let's go,' I said but not to Moose.

That took him by surprise. It took me by surprise too. I wasn't into fighting. He would be an easy match for me though. We were the same build, the tradie and I, and I felt sure I could at least match him. It wasn't about winning the fight for me, it was about standing up.

I fired up and walked towards him asking him to fight me. I felt embarrassed by Moose and wanted to save face.

'I don't want to fight you,' the tradie said. 'I want to fight the mouth!'

Other people started to walk by so we ended it there. We walked away. I'd learnt a different side to my big mate. Up until that day I'd been a bit afraid of him. No More. He was all bluff.

Jenny and Nifty had told me to me stay away from Moose because he was into crime. Every day he told me how he'd done this or that. He said he met men, took them home, bashed them up and stole all their stuff. These days he picked up his dose each morning and latched on to me like a bad flu.

Moose knew a man, who owned a bakery. I went with Moose a couple of times when he went to get money from Gino at the bakery. I'd stand off to the side while Moose did business and then we'd leave. I never spoke to Gino but sometimes as he talked with Moose, Moose would point at me. I assumed he was just telling Gino who I was or maybe Gino was gay. In my early days on the program I'd go with Moose to the Cross sometimes after he'd got money from Gino. Moose would score and then we'd both use.

I been going to the Employment Agency every day and I applied for every job I could, every single day. No, was always the response to my application. It was so disheartening. I really loved Jenny and I wanted to be the man she needed me to be. She worked hard every day from early hours to late at night. I was on the dole and I hated it. I had no skills, no education and no history that would impress an employer.

At last I succeeded. I landed a job stacking fruit in Coles. Jenny could see that I was having a go. I had pulled right away from Moose by then. I dressed nicely and went to Jenny's café where I sat down for a feed.

'Guess what Jenny,' I said excitedly. 'I've got a job!'

Jenny was still trying to convince Nadia her boss that I was not as bad as I might look sometimes and that I was having a go at improving myself. Being seen with Moose hadn't helped my cause with Jenny's boss. Jenny was so proud to tell her that I was working. Nadia actually came closer to me and said, 'Well done on getting a job.' Yes, there was an underlying dig. I felt judged everywhere I went but I knew what I was capable off. I knew how vulnerable I was to people's judgment too.

Despite being on the program, having a job, a flat and a partner, I still had the constant memories of pain every day. I couldn't switch it off. I never spoke about any of it. I still didn't see that my past was having a huge impact on my present. That came much later. My long history with the police bothered me too although I knew most of it was lies.

When I wasn't wrestling with those demons, I felt pride as each day I got up and set off to work when Jenny did. I'd give her a kiss and say proudly, 'See you in my lunch break.'

I had a job and a lunch break! I was proud of myself.

I had always had the gift of the gab and it was mostly a great asset. However, I made the most stupid mistake one day.

'Coming to the Cross?' Moose asked. He adds an extra enticement. 'My shout.'

'No thanks. I can't. Got to go to work,' I told him.

I thought he might be decent enough to leave it at that. Maybe even be glad about it. Some addicts can be selfish and they'll go to any lengths to fuck up anything good that other people have. They sabotage others to keep them down at their level.

I worked at Coles for about two weeks, stacking and organizing fruit and doing whatever they asked of me. Every day Moose would come to my job and make an asshole of himself. I'd told him so many times to go away but he wouldn't. I almost lost my cool with him. He couldn't just come quietly, say hello and go. No, he had to make everyone notice him. One girl especially noticed him. She had let me know that she liked me but when I didn't reciprocate, she turned nasty.

At ten thirty I had a fifteen minute break and then a half hour break for lunch later. It was a boring job and I liked going to Grace Brothers every day to look at the fish in their aquariums. I got to know the people who worked in that section quite well. I bought my first fish tank and a book about cichlids there. I read everything I could about tropical fish and cichlids. Each day I went in and told the staff there what I'd learnt. I really loved fish. I loved how peaceful they seemed. I loved that when I watched them carefully I discovered that they have their own little personalities.

'If ever a job comes up here, please tell me,' I said one day. 'This would be so much more interesting than stacking fruit.' I put in an application to work at this aquarium and went back to stacking fruit.

Moose got worse. He'd get his dose then come down to my job and make a pest of himself. He'd throw fruit across at me just because he liked to be a dickhead. The boss called me into his office one day and said, 'Glen, tell your mate he can't come into the shop.'

I told him firmly and repeatedly not to come. He kept coming. I actually lost my shit with him one day. 'Just fuck off!' I yelled at him.

He did stop coming but the damage was done. Between Moose and the girl I'd apparently upset I was afraid I would lose my job. It was a shit job where I had to work really hard for crap money. Not that it was about money. It was about my self-esteem, about proving I could have a go. It had much more meaning to me than a pay packet.

One morning I was waiting for the Methadone clinic to open. As always Todd, Moose and I were lined up. This was unavoidable. I had to get there early to be at work on time. I had asked if I could pick up my dose later but they said I couldn't. Once the clinic shut at eleven in the morning they refused to give you your dose.

As we waited I noticed one of the girls from work going by. It was the girl who complained to the boss about Moose every day. Her eyes lit up when she saw me. I didn't know if she knew what the place was but it concerned me that she'd seen me there.

I was very loyal to Jenny and this girl couldn't accept it. She was attractive and probably not used to being rejected. About an hour after I got to work, there she was in the boss's office, talking seriously and pointing at me. I felt nervous. Was she trying to get me in trouble? What for?

She came down from the office and said with a smirk, 'Oh Glen, the boss wants to see you.

'Are you on Methadone?' was the very first thing he said to me. 'Are you a heroin addict?'

His question made me angry. 'What the fuck has that got to do with anything?' I replied abrasively. I don't think there were any laws that protected people on the Methadone program at the time.

Needless to say I suppose, I was sacked. I didn't know how Jenny did the work thing every day. She enjoyed her job and worked bloody hard. Feeling so defeated, I collected my pay packet and went to tell Jenny what had happened.

I had bought her an engagement ring and asked her to marry me only one week before. It wasn't exactly a romantic proposal. We'd talked about it often and I'd put a ring on lay-by. I'd been paying it off so I used my last pay packet to finish paying for the ring. Giving her the ring might distract her from the fact I'd been fired. I had planned a huge engagement party but there was no romantic dinner when I proposed.

'Don't worry,' I told her as brightly as I could. 'I'll find another job. I promise.'

Jenny tried to not look or act upset but I sensed her disappointment. I don't think she was as worried about my losing the job as she was about how I'd be spending my time now and how discouraged I was.

'Of course you will. People lose their jobs every day,' she said. 'Just keep looking until you find one.'

Was I destined to fuck everything up?

On Methadone I was having some crazy dreams. I dreamt about Linda and other kids who had died but in the dreams I was always afraid, not of anything physical, but just afraid.

I felt that, apart from Jenny, I was alone. Was there something about me? My parents hated me and I apart from my time at the refuge I had never really connected with anyone.

I spoke to my counsellor about the feeling of aloneness and about my constant dreams. He said, 'It's normal. They're called "Methadone dreams."'

I didn't think it was normal at all. I'd had so many traumas in my life that I'd never spoken about. My parents attitudes to me made me envious of Jenny having the father she had. Not one of my counsellors ever connected the early traumas in my life to my using. If they had I often wonder how things may have panned out had I spoken to someone about my abuse.

Jenny and I set a date for our engagement party. It was the sixth of June, 1987. We rented a hall in Ashfield. I didn't know about D Day, the day the Allies landed on the shores of Normandy. Was it ironic that we chose that day to get engaged?

We went to great lengths to make the party big and memorable. We ordered kegs of beer and Jenny's mother and family prepared the food. We had to set up two long tables. One was for all the Seventh Day Adventist, the so-called normal people. Table two was for friends from the streets.

Grant from the refuge came. I really disliked him and felt huge animosity towards him over the refuge but as an addict I'd needed to keep a kind of friendship with him and others, like Peter. They'd always helped me with money for heroin if I needed it. I was scared to let go of my connection with people like Grant and Peter. They were a crutch and I might need them again one day. Would I ever need it again though? The idea of being straight for ever seemed unlikely as much as I wanted it.

Grant brought flowers from his garden. They were miniature orchids. Not only that he brought Annie of the refuge. I hadn't invited her and was not pleased to see her.

Jenny put two tables together for presents.

'Bit optimistic there aren't we? You really think people are going to buy us gifts?' I had never received many gifts so the idea of people filling two tables seemed far fetched.

Gradually the tables filled with more presents than I'd hope to see in my life! People didn't usually invite people like me to celebrations so I didn't expect this. I felt embarrassed opening them in front of all our guests. I felt greedy too. Did we deserve all these gifts or this much happiness? People were clearly happy for us and wanted the best for us. I was still trapped in addiction even if it was Methadone. I had not addressed the underlying issues that had me using in the first place.

I'd invited two people from the Aquarium in Grace Brothers and they came. They handed me an envelope. I thought it was a gift card or money. Inside the envelope was a card that said, 'You have a job!'

I looked at them astounded and said, 'At the Aquarium?'

'Yes!' They were grinning and I was so excited.

My life was changing. I had a job doing what I loved doing, my girlfriend was now my fiancée, we had a place to live and life had never felt so good. It was normal but somehow it scared me. Was it all too good to be true?

At our party we had a lovely dinner first with all the niceties. Jenny and her mum had slaved away for hours preparing the food. It looked so generous and impressive. Then after nine o'clock we turned the hall into a disco and the stayers could drink if they wanted to. I wasn't a drinker but I had a few.

A group of drunks tried to gate crash the party later. My brother Michael was watching the door and he kept them out. A lot of people were from the streets and once a few of their heads popped up to say, 'Fuck off,' the gatecrashers left.

The night was wonderful. I was the happiest I had ever been and as stable. It was like someone else's world and I was there for a beautiful moment. Jenny seemed happy too. Her mother was there helping her and we both had a really great night.

It took the best part of the next day to clean up. Jenny, her mother and I worked like slaves. We'd paid a bond on the hall and we needed the money back.

My job in the Grace Brothers Aquarium was the best job I'd ever had, not that I had a long list of jobs. I really enjoyed it and I had a real passion for working with fish. I was earning decent money and I started buying things for our house. I found a really nice stereo in Grace Brothers. It was more expensive than I could afford in one pay.

'Can I put it on lay be?' I said.

'Yes or you might want to think about hire purchase. That means you put down a certain amount of money now, take your purchase home with you, then pay off the rest.'

So, the following morning I went up to pay for my stereo. I worked at the store so it was easy to make payments.

Unfortunately Moose found out about my job. We were both on Methadone so he could latch on and follow me. He turned up at work. He walked through an area that he wasn't allowed to be in, raising the eyebrows of the staff there. I didn't think it was such a big deal but I told Moose to pull his head in anyway. I went to pick up my stereo then went back to work. Moose followed me. I hadn't told him about our engagement party and we didn't invite him. No matter how many times I told him to go away he just wouldn't. He was such a fucking pest.

When he eventually left the aquarium one day, I went about cleaning out the tanks and doing my job. Later that day my boss, Carl, appeared and said, 'Glen, I'm sorry but we've been told to fire you.'

'What? Why?'

'Apparently you went into an area this morning where our staff are not allowed to go,' Carl said. He looked sad to have to tell me this news. Only weeks before this we had such as great night at that party and they saw how much it meant to me. I think it was more about Moose who brought attention to himself wherever he went.

One of the ladies said, 'Glen, just a hint. You might want to pick your friends better.'

I was absolutely gutted. This was my dream job. It felt like for everything I did right, I did three things wrong without even knowing it. I was trying so hard to improve my life. It felt like I lived in two worlds. One on the streets with loads of people around me and the other trying to create a new life with Jenny.

The hardest part was telling her I'd been sacked again. With every one of my failures I disappointed Jenny and she seemed to come to expect them. I was a fuck up. Was it even possible for me to live a normal life? What is normal anyway?

Chapter 19.
A Beautiful Gift

I got angry and upset at losing yet another job. I felt like everyone and everything was conspiring against me. I believed in my heart that I didn't fit in and no-one was ever going to allow me to. I didn't see that some of the people around me were reasons for my problems. It was going to get worse.

A few days later I was at the clinic at seven in the morning to pick up my dose as usual. Moose was there and not long after Todd arrived on his motorbike. The clinic opened and I walked in and sat down to wait until my name was called. Todd was called first and Moose starting yelling at him. I wasn't talking with either of them. I never spoke to Todd and I wanted nothing to do with Moose after losing my job. He was a dead set goose.

Todd walked up to get his dose when Moose says.

'I was here first dickhead!'

They began to fight and I didn't get involved except to break it up. I thought that was the right thing to do. After the melee settled down Moose and Todd picked up their doses and left. They took the fight with them out onto the street. Moose picked up Todd's bike and threw it on the road and they were yelling abuse at each other. I left them to it.

The following morning when all three of us got to the clinic we were each handed a letter that said that we were all to be kicked off the Methadone program. My dose would be reduced every third day and then I'd get nothing. They don't tolerate violence at the clinic and they referred to the incident yesterday.

I wish I could say I spoke with them calmly about my non-involvement in the fight, but I can't. I snapped. I knew that I had not been involved. I had lost two jobs because of that fuckwit Moose and now I was getting tossed off the Methadone program.

I knew what it meant for Jenny and I and it didn't look good.

In hindsight I should have got to the clinic after Moose had left.

Later that day I went to see my counsellor and explained what had happened. I complained about my being lumped in with the other two when I hadn't been involved. It fell on deaf ears.

The counsellor said, 'You might not have been involved in that situation but your behaviour when you received the letter is reason enough to remove you from the program!' I was off the program and that was all that was to be said. He had told me to surround myself with people who wanted me to succeed. I was learning that that was essential but I was learning this the hard way. I could have easily waited half an hour later to pick up my dose each day instead of arriving the same time as Moose.

Again telling Jenny about it was so hard. She knew I'd go back to using heroin. I knew that cold turkey was hard and my brain told me the only solution was to use. I picked up from the clinic two more times but I was too angry to go back for another dose.

Hanging out from Methadone was worse than it had been from heroin. I started selling things I owned and that led to fights with Jenny. She had been in charge of our money and I had agreed because we wanted a normal life. I was afraid I would be tempted to use if I had money. One morning she wanted to keep my dole cheque to pay some bills. She refused to give me any of my money at all. Jenny just didn't understand that I couldn't just stop using everything.

'Don't use. Easy.' That was her motto but I was hideously sick. We had a terrible fight. I was hanging out and seriously angry that jenny didn't understand or want to help me.

I stormed off to the Cross by myself. I stayed there for about two nights. I didn't come home or speak to Jenny at all. I hadn't been to the Cross lately. There'd been no need. I'd just gone a few times to see my mates.

Over the next few weeks while I waited to get into another

program I was going back to the streets every day to get money so I could use. The program policy was that if you were kicked out of a program, you had to wait twelve weeks before you could get into another one. That period was tough. I went from normal and working back to being a full on addict.

I managed to get into another Methadone program at Canterbury Hospital. Jenny and I sorted out our argument. Once I was back on the program I became stable and we could reason things through.

While we lived at Campsie I met a drug dealer called Mongo who lived on the same street as us. He had deliveries made to his house, opposite the Police Station. It was the best quality heroin I'd ever bought and it was much cheaper. Mongo was buying five weights from Baz, his dealer, for nine hundred dollars whereas you'd pay fifteen hundred in the Cross. I did not know this at first.

I bought deals from Mongo every day and I was getting on for many other addicts I knew from the streets. I would bring a lot of cash his way.

One day I saw Baz leaving Mongo's place so I approached him. 'Mate most of the money that Mongo's bringing you is coming from me,' I said. 'I bring heaps of people from the Cross to see him. I'd rather just come straight to you. Is that possible?'

'Yeah, we can do that. Give me a call.' He gave me his phone number. It didn't take long for me to work out that I could get five weights very cheaply from Baz and soon I was doing that.

'How much will you charge me for five weights?' I asked.

Baz said, 'What was Mongo charging? Nine hundred?'

'Yes,' I replied quickly, shocked at how cheap it was.

I was on the Methadone program, this time at Canterbury Hospital. Now that I had this great supplier I was dealing again in a matter of weeks. I knew so many addicts on Methadone at Canterbury Hospital who were still in the using stage. I could sell two five weight bags a day easily.

There was a bloke, a dealer from Newcastle, who came twice a week who paid me fifteen hundred dollars a bag and he bought two bags each time. I paid nine hundred so my profit was good. I went from being a street addict to being a supplier for Campsie, surrounding areas and the Cross. My objective wasn't to make a fortune. It was to always have heroin so I could avoid the pain of hanging out. I couldn't condone that now but back when I was an addict, it seemed like a pretty good way to make a living. I did not recognize that I was selling death. I just wanted my heroin.

I became addicted to being popular too, to the people who came to buy the gear. They were coming and going all day long so I had to ask them to ring me and I'd meet them in different places. I had never had friends, apart from the kids at the refuge, so I found my popularity overwhelming even though I knew it was only because of the money I had. That was new too, having money.

I was so excited when we were able to afford our first car, a blue Holden HG. It wasn't fancy and I loved it. So now with a license, a car, a place in the Methadone program and my heroin business, I thought things were picking up.

Jenny quit her job. She didn't need to work I guess. I'm not sure but together with my street smarts and Jenny's ability to manage money, we grew. We only sold to people we knew, if they were on Methadone. Most people who scored from us actually used it at our flat. So we knew that they were safe and they wouldn't get busted for Possession when they left.

We went from having few possessions in our flat to having everything we wanted, new. I had fish tanks everywhere. We had two six foot tanks and a couple of four foot ones. They held expensive exotic fish and the best equipment money could buy. One day we went out and spent fifteen hundred dollars in one go.

It felt like happy days but in fact I was still stuck in the dangerous life of an addict, risking robbery, overdoses, police raids and prison. I didn't see that. All I saw was free heroin, free cash and loads of friends. Best mates everywhere. I liked being popular. I liked being liked.

I was on Methadone. I was able to control the amount of

heroin I used and I never had to worry about having money to buy it. When the relationship with Jenny had started and I fell in love I really hoped I'd get straight and that seemed to be tracking well.

My passion for tropical fish and cichlids grew too. As with everything I did, I took it to an extreme. My addictive personality explains the preoccupations that grab me: the refuge, break dancing, drugs and fish.

There was a huge aquarium shop in the city, Mike's Pet Store, owned by its namesake. I was always talking to him about the fish.

'Mate, I've been in this business for so many years but you know much more than I do about fish!' Michael said. I was pleased to hear that. Then he said, 'You should come and work for me.'

I didn't take him up on the offer. My life was too hectic as it was. I told him about my addiction and that made him respect me more. 'When you do get your life on track and want a full time job come and see me and I'll hook you up.'

There were two sisters who hung out at our place a lot. Missy, one of the sisters, started selling for us when we were out. I'd swing by home, pick up the cash then ring up and buy more drugs. I'd make up the deals then we were free to go out again.

'Where's Glen?' That was the most asked question at our place now. I'd be picking up my Methadone each morning and there'd be half the clinic's clients asking each other, 'Where's Glen?' as they waited for me to score. The phone rang constantly and Missy or Jenny had to answer that question many times a day.

I didn't give much thought to Moose any more because I never saw him at the clinic where I now got my dose but one day, there he was.

'What are you doing over this way?' I asked him cautiously.

'Weekend detention,' he said sulkily. Then he reminded me about the baker he knew at Chatswood who used to give him money. 'S'pose to get it on Saturday but I gotta do this detention shit.' He hesitated for a second then said, 'Gino said he'd give the money to you to give to me if you went over there.'

I didn't want to have anything to do with Moose but he held out a sealed letter to me. 'All you gotta do is give him this and he'll give you some money for me. You can take fifty bucks out for yourself.'

Jenny and I sometimes went to church at Wahroonga with her dad on Saturdays so I agreed to do it if possible. I'd have to ask's dad to stop at Westfield Chatswood on our way to church.

Keith said he didn't mind stopping at Chatswood. He pulled up near the entrance to Westfield. I went inside to see Gino. I handed him the letter that he opened and read. Gino was polite to me but he looked anxious.

'Okay. But I don't have the money yet. Can you pick it up at one o'clock?'

'I have to go to church now. So yes, I'll see you on the way back.'

I never read the letter from Moose but I guess now, years later, that he was extorting money from Gino. The poor man must have thought that I was the king pin in the racket. I was dressed in good clothes because I was going to church. When I think of those times when the two men had talked and Moose had kept pointing to me, extortion made sense.

Jenny's father stopped there again on our way home and I went to Gino. When he saw me he looked so nervous. He looked back at two big men who were dressed like undercover police. I realised that something was not right. Gino handed me an envelope with about six hundred dollars in it and I walked outside. Then I ran. I didn't know what it was but I knew I'd got myself into something that wasn't good. The two big blokes chased me.

They yelled to people, 'Stop that man! Stop him!'

I ran past Jenny's dad's car. I outran the two blokes but more and more people joined the chase. No-one knew why they were chasing me. As I ran I thought to myself, *I have done nothing wrong. Why am I running?* So I went to Chatswood Police Station. The desk sergeant asked if he could help me.

'I hope so. Well, for reasons I'm not sure of, half of Chatswood is chasing me!'

Then through the door came all sorts of people who'd been trying to catch me. I spoke with the detective who had chased me when he arrived.

'You are going to be arrested for extortion,' he said.

'What?'

'We know it isn't you,' he said. 'You're not the man we're really after.'

I was being used. Had Moose played me? Had Gino threatened him with police action? I really did not know. Gino had apparently scared Moose off. He obviously had something over Gino so Gino must have decided to get me charged to warn Moose off again. I was charged with Extortion and three counts of Demand Money with Menace. Gino was willing to have me charged either because he really believed I was the person behind the scheme or because he was too afraid of Moose to have him charged.

Peter paid for a lawyer for me. Her name was Brenda and her office was in Edgecliff. She was well known to street people.

The police kept saying, 'We know it isn't you. Just tell us who the guy is and we'll let you go.'

Dog on someone I knew? I'd never do that. Setting me up to pay for his crimes was okay but for me to dog would be wrong! Such are the stupid laws of the street but I still lived by them.

I went to court and got bail.

One morning I picked up my Methadone and returned home. The police were at my door. They started asking me questions like where I was at such and such time on such and such a date. They were homicide police from Chatswood. Gino had been murdered! He'd been beaten to death with a hammer or something similar. To this day I believe Moose murdered Gino. I never saw Moose again after the charge of Extortion. He must have known I'd been charged. He didn't even come to get the money Gino gave me for him.

The homicide police searched our house and car tools and they took some items away, presumably for testing. I had to go to Glebe Coroners Court on the Extortion charge.

Brenda said to the judge, 'I demand all charges against Glen be dropped. Even if he were found guilty, we know that Gino cannot come to court. Glen must therefore be acquitted.'

The police knew I wasn't the extortionist but I was sorry not to get my day in court to prove I was innocent.

Later the police told me that they had eliminated me as a suspect for Gino's murder because witnesses had confirmed my alibi. Gino's murder had occurred when I was picking up my Methadone. Thank God for that.

The Chatswood detectives were furious and what I did next was more to be a smart arse than anything. I regret it now.

Brenda told me, 'The money the police took from you on that day is yours. You need to go to Chatswood Police Station to get it back.'

'Oh I don't want it Brenda,' I said. I didn't want to go and get the money but she thought I should. I had to pay the rest of her bill so I felt it was fair that I got the money.

The police messed me around for hours. They couldn't find the keys to the safe. They couldn't find someone to sign off on it. The paperwork hadn't come through. Every time I went there they had an excuse to not give me the money. Through Brenda I lodged a complaint and they had to hand it over. I really didn't want poor Gino's money. He had died in a horrible scenario and the money felt foul.

After I was cleared I heard that Moose was calling me a dog. That made me angry. I hadn't once opened my mouth about him. Partly through fear and partly through that warped loyalty I'd learnt on the streets. I wish now that I had spoken up about him at the time. There are many times in my life that I didn't speak up because I had been raised from birth never to tell on any one. 'Don't be a tattle tale.'

I don't know if Gino's case was ever solved. I hope it was.

Meanwhile after clinic in the morning, people would follow me home to score. Despite the fact that I asked punters repeatedly never to ask for me at the clinic and not to wait for me there, they still did. The staff must have worked out that I was dealing but the addicts didn't care if I got kicked off or busted. All they cared about was their fix. I understood that. It's normal selfish addict behaviour.

Rival dealers were unhappy that I was so accessible and sold the better quality heroin in bigger amounts. Most of them cut their gear but I didn't because I could make more money selling better deals. As our business grew we needed to have 'business hours.' I asked people to stop coming to our house but that didn't deter the addicts who were hanging out. They'd just turn up and buzz at the door. Being the ultimate people pleaser, I'd go off at them for coming then sell to them anyway. I set good boundaries but never maintained them.

Baz, my supplier who had been a soldier, hired a different car each time he came with my supply. He would meet me at pre-arranged places and was always quick and keen to supply a big buyer like me.

One morning I had four people make the same complaint to me. 'We got our shit from that Missy at your place and I tell you mate, the deals are smaller than they used to be. What's up?'

'No, they're not,' I replied. 'I measure them really carefully.'

'They are mate! Why do you think we come to you not her?

Many of my customers would ask for me specifically and I just assumed that they thought they could get a better deal. Heaps of customers started to complain that Missy was selling smaller deals for the same money.

At first I didn't pay much attention to the whining. I thought there was no way Missy would do anything wrong. We looked after her so well. But as more and more people complained about her ripping them off, I thought I'd better look into it. Each time I got home there'd be people who'd waited hours for me because they didn't want to buy from Missy.

Without telling Jenny, I arranged a set up. Some punters claimed that Missy's deals looked as if they'd been opened and taxed. I told them to ring me when they got to Campsie. I'd send

Missy to make the deal then I turn up to see what the deal looked like. I felt certain they were just trying to get more smack from me. I knew all the rorts.

They rang me and I made two deals up for Missy to take to them. As she was leaving Jenny said, 'I'm going with Missy.'

'Can you wait and come up the street with me later?'

'No, I'm going now.'

It was impossible to order Jenny about so I gave Missy the two deals and Jenny went out with her. I thought to myself, *I'll have to do it another time. There's no way Missy is going to tax the deals with Jenny around. I'll still go up and watch her though. I'll tell the guys we'll have to do the check another day and give them an extra deal to keep them happy.*

I opened the door to leave and I heard voices on the stairs on the next level up. Ours was a security block so there should not have been anyone there. So I went up to check it out.

There were Jenny and Missy taking the gear out of packets. I was really confused and pissed off too. We'd made sure Missy never had to hang out. So, why did she need this? Jenny wasn't using at all so what the fuck was she doing?

'What the fuck are you doing?' I asked them.

Jenny said, 'Missy's doing it for me.'

'You don't use … Oh fuck Jenny. You're using?'

She was. On the sly. Missy had been taxing deals so Jenny could use.

I loved this woman! I didn't want her to end up an addict like me. I was angry and confused. How had I missed this? Jenny had always made out that she never wanted heroin. I'd insisted that she stay away from the gear anyway. I was always so off my face and too caught up with being Mr Big Shot, that I didn't notice her using daily.

'How many people have you been cheating?' I demanded to know. They'd done it to at least three people who bought a lot at a time who wouldn't notice a little bit missing. But addicts do notice things like that. At least they'd only taxed the gear and not cut it to a lesser quality. I went to see the people who'd been short changed and I gave them a free hundred dollar deal with what they bought. I felt betrayed by Missy and hurt that Jenny was using and ripping other people off in the process.

I sacked Missy and that caused an argument between Jenny and me.

'She did it for me Glen. Why do have to sack her? That's just not fair.'

'Missy was selling for me, so even if you were a part of it, she's lost my trust. She's not staying.' Trust was so important to me. Any betrayal triggered my memories of abuses of my trust in the past and forced me to act to protect myself.

Two other sisters wanted to work for us when Missy was sacked. Both were good friends of ours. They were from the Campbelltown area.

'Yes. But we only need one person,' I explained apologetically to Stacey. 'We might need someone else soon, so I promise you'll be next,' I told her sister. It didn't help. She got really pissed off.

One morning I had my usual shot Jenny asked, 'Can I have some?'

'No way!'

'Please. Just a few lines?'

'No way.'

I didn't know she'd built up a little habit. I just didn't want to see her life go like mine. She was so beautiful and I was living proof of a drug fucked up life.

Jenny saw my refusal as me wanting to control her. That was true when it came to drugs in one way. I finished having my shot. Relaxing after it felt good. Without me knowing, Jenny went into the bedroom with a syringe of water and put it into the spoon I'd just used. The filter was still there so she could extract a shot from it.

After five minutes or so I realised that Jenny had not spoken for a while. I guessed she was just angry.

'Ba-jenna-bie!' I called out. That was my pet name for her. An amalgamation of her full name.

No reply. She must be really angry.

'Come on babe. I love you. I don't want you to be fucked up like I am, on Methadone, shooting up day and night.'

I kept calling out to her and I kept getting ignored.

'Come on Babe. Luke's on the run. This is the episode where they catch him and Laura.' I thought telling her a soapie we watched was about to start might bring her out.

Still no response. I sensed that something wasn't right. I walked towards the bedroom calling, 'Jenny? Babe?'

I opened the door. Jenny was lying on the bed. I knew straight away she wasn't well. I ran to her. She felt lifeless and her lips were blue. *Only dead people's lips turn blue.* I thought. I slapped her face. I pinched her shoulder. Nothing happened.

Don't be dead. Oh God! Please don't be dead.

I started mouth to mouth. I was panicking. The Medical Centre. Not far to there. I picked her up and ran down the stairs. Dead weight is hard to carry.

I sobbed as I carried her. *Don't Die. I love you Babe. Don't leave me.*

Twenty metres down the road I was struggling to hold her and almost dropped her. I kept going and sobbing to her, 'Don't you fucking die on me!' I screamed for someone to help me. Then pleaded to Jenny calmly, 'Babe? Please wake up.' Then reverted to screaming at her, 'Jenny! What the fuck have you done? Jenny, Jenny, wake up. Please! Wake up.'

I kept trying then I had to face up to it. I started talking to myself. 'I killed her. I've killed my fiancé. I am sorry Jenny. Jenny?'

Suddenly six foot six Adam is walking toward me. He saw me carrying Jenny and heard me yelling. Saw me staggering with Jenny.

'What's happened?' he yelled as he ran to me.

'Jenny's dead!' I tell him.

'Here, give her to me. I'll carry her,' he said.

Adam started running with Jenny. She started slipping out of Adam's arms too so we both carried her.

'What have I done Adam? She's fucking dead bro.'

Between us we got her to the Medical Centre. They were shutting the doors. We could see people inside so I screamed, 'Help. Help! My fiancé's fucking dead! Help me. Please.'

Finally a woman came to the door but she refused to open it. She called from inside, 'Call an ambulance!'

It was infuriating. She saw us as junkies and no hopers I think. I thought, *I'm a no hoper but Jenny isn't. No way are you letting her die without trying to save her.* I rushed to a back door. I could see a doctor inside. I started to kick the door in. He came to the door.

'Calm down mate. What is going on?'

Adam had come around with Jenny in his arms. He was desperate too. He yelled at them, 'For fucks sake man! Open the fucking door. Please. Help her.'

The doctor snapped into action, thank God. He opened the door and said, 'Bring her in here.'

We put Jenny's body on a table. Adam and I were shocked and frightened. I dropped to the floor with relief as I felt emotionally and physically exhausted. The doctor gave Jenny Narcan. Before long she sat upright as if she'd risen from the dead.

When I realised she was alive all the emotion came pouring out. I screamed at my beautiful, living fiancé, 'What the fuck did you do? Are you fucking stupid? You almost died!'

The last thing Jenny needed was abuse from me. She was still pulling herself together, trying to put the pieces back in place and comprehend what had happened. How did she get to be in the medical centre surrounded by a doctor, nurses and two very emotional men?

At that point I wasn't sure what she'd done so I questioned her angrily.

'Where did you get the heroin?' It was easier to put the blame on her than to shoulder it myself.

Jenny stood up and said, 'I washed out your shot. I put water in the filter.' She said it as if I should know that.

'I use half a fucking weight at a time Jenny! My filter would get a seasoned addict high!'

The doctor told us, 'You need to take Jenny to the hospital. There's a good chance the heroin will come back on.'

Jenny didn't want to go to the hospital so we went home.

Adam came too. Jenny was off her face and she kept nodding off. Adam and I spent the next four hours keeping her awake then she started to come good. The overdose scared her so much that she stopped using. Stopping was easier for Jenny because she hadn't developed a full blown habit. She was able to go cold turkey.

Another day I picked up a five weight bag from Baz. Stacey wasn't coming to work so I stayed home. I fluffed some gear up on the cover of a book. Fluffing it made it look bigger and although people got the same weight of drug, it looked like a more generous amount. I had a shot and felt groggy like I always did. I was half asleep on the lounge then I woke up with a sense of impending doom. A dealer often feels it when something is about to go wrong but so far I hadn't had it.

Why now? I wondered. The feeling sat with me for a while.

I got up and looked out the front window. Our flat was on the second floor and I could see a lot of activity outside. There were people hanging around who didn't fit the usual scene. A woman was standing there, apparently doing nothing. It all just seemed out of place on our street.

Alarm bells went off in my head. This was either police or a group of people who were about to rip me off. Three men and a woman walked to the doors of our building. They looked like plain clothes detectives.

We had security doors where people needed to use the buzzer to get in. I ran to the front door and looked through the peep hole. The woman I'd seen downstairs was waiting there with a piece of paper in her hand.

I dashed to the bathroom thinking I'd flush the gear down the toilet. No, couldn't do that. They'd hear the loo flushing. I spilt the heroin on the floor and rubbed it into the carpet as she waited to knock on the door. Any second now, I thought, the door would be kicked open. I walked back into the hallway, blew the heroin off the book and wiped the book clean. I threw the book into the bedroom and made sure the heroin was rubbed in well. Then I waited for the inevitable bang of the door being kicked in.

Knock, knock. That was the woman. No kicking it open yet.

I yelled, 'Coming.' I opened the door.

'Hello,' I said. As I greeted the woman I saw the shadows of other detectives on the stairs. One held a huge sledge hammer. I pretended not to notice.

'Hi. I am looking for these people,' she said showing me the paper she had brought. It was a list of names. I played along.

'Oh. Um. Okay. Smith you say?' As I look at her paper she turns around a bit trying to get me to turn my back on the action on the stairs.

I co-operated and there was a rush of the men up the stairs. They ran in yelling, 'Police! Drug Squad!'

'What the fuck's that for?' I asked the guy with the sledge hammer.

I stood around while they rifled through our place. The lead detective was a big man, heavy set, and although I was very tall, he towered over me.

He grabbed me by the throat and seethed into my face, 'I've just done a raid and I know you've got.' That's the expression they used when they reckoned you'd had heroin.) 'I know you're a dealer. I know that there are drugs here. I know you recently picked up. So where's the heroin?' He was spot on with every bit of information. Except one. He didn't know he was literally standing on the stuff he was searching for.

I replied, 'Heroin? What the fuck are you talking about?'

Our home was very clean and that was unusual for an addict. Jenny kept it really nice. She wasn't home for this adventure. Thank God.

I knew there were no drugs here so, despite feeling uncomfortable with the police presence, I wasn't overly concerned.

I'd given my bong away days ago and I kept my heroin needles in a toothbrush holder in the bedroom cupboard. We had digital kitchen scales that I used to make up deals but they were kitchen scales that anyone would have in their kitchen.

I said quite calmly to the detective holding me by my throat, 'No drugs here.'

The Drug Squad spent hours searching. They tipped out sugar, went through my fish tanks even checking the filters and they searched my car. I sat on the lounge, cocky but secretly afraid. Not having drugs on me didn't always translate to not being arrested. Would they plant something and arrest me?

Every now and then the lead detective said to me, 'I know it's here. I'll find it and when I do, I will charge you with a lot more than supply.' As he got more desperate he asked, 'Where are the drugs?'

'No drugs here mate?' I told him. 'It's the truth.'

Fortunately for me these were not corrupt police. They were getting frustrated as the search went on. What was more interesting was that they didn't know my name. I rarely told people my real name. I was Zac or Roach when it came to business. So I knew that whoever had dogged on me didn't know me. The search warrant had my address on it but not my real name. It had one of my nicknames. I would soon find out who it was but for now I just watched the show. That was between phone calls. That thing just wouldn't stop ringing. My door buzzer went off too.

The police would answer the phone.

'Hello. Who? Yes, Roach has just gone out but he said to come around.' Some addicts were naïve but others twigged.

Every person who rang was told to come to my place then the buzzer would sound. The police didn't talk when it did. They just pressed the button to let callers in. Some understood what was happening and didn't come up to the door. Those who knocked were grabbed as soon as the police opened it. They were dragged inside and questioned. I could hear the questioning.

'Who's Roach?' the police would ask.

Most people said, 'I don't know who Roach is mate. I'm here just to visit me mate.' Then they'd keep quiet or play dumb.

After hours of searching and questioning, the police had found just one needle.

'Well done mate!' said the lead detective. 'I know you're dealing. I know that somewhere here there is gear but I can't find it.' He was almost congratulating me. He threw the search warrant on the table and said, 'You might want to look at what friends you've got out Campbelltown way!' It amazed me that the police told me who dogged on me.

I knew it was Stacey's sister who was pissed off that I hadn't given her a job. I think the detective was very annoyed with her for making him and his people come all the way in from Campbelltown for nothing. She had probably made me sound much bigger than I really was. I spoke to Stacey and she confirmed the who and the why.

I was relieved that there was no police set up! Nothing but a seriously messed up house. I spent hours cleaning up sugar, taking out fish that had died because the heaters had been turned off and filters dismantled. I was pissed off at the condition they had left the place in.

Not long after the raid, I made an error. I told Baz about the raid because I wanted him to be careful. He got nervous and his face changed from cheerful to cold. Almost overnight he became less accessible or he'd arrive late where once he had been so punctual. He wasn't a heavy drug user who sold only to dealers.

For about a week I had to buy from the Romanians who had filtered into the area. Their gear was nowhere near as good and it was harder to get. I told them I usually bought three five weight bags every day. One of my punters was a guy who came from Newcastle. He brought two bags each time he came.

I said to Romanian John, 'If you get good quality gear and bring the price down, I'll buy a lot more from you.'

The Romanians just wanted quick sales. Scoring the below

par gear meant I had to tell customers that my new supplier had different gear and I made the deals a bit bigger to compensate for the lower quality. I wasn't making much money then. I didn't even get my money back and I used most of it myself. Although I was still on Methadone, I was still using a lot of heroin to get over the Methadone.

It didn't take long for me to slowly lose customers. They all moved on to the next dealer and even though I was on Methadone I still had a huge habit. So the money I'd made before was now going up my arm. At the Methadone Clinic I'd had several warnings about dirty urines. Every day when I went there there'd be a posse of addicts waiting for me or they had asked for me at the counter.

'We are not your secretaries,' the lady at the counter said sternly and coldly. 'Because you are dealing and you've had dirty urines, you are to be expelled from the program.'

I had pretty much stopped dealing a couple of weeks prior and the people who waited for me were hoping I had sorted the situation out. I could get on for them if they had money but I didn't have the gear myself any more.

The program took me down over the three day period and then I needed to use more heroin to compensate for the lack of Methadone. I was less motivated. My habit got worse without Methadone. I was very sick. I could get customers to come over but they lost patience having to wait for the new supplier I was using. They had been used to me having it at the ready.

Kings Cross bellowed at me to come back. I went there every day and I slowly sold off all the things we'd bought while I was supplying. I was supporting my habit that way.

One night I came home and Jenny told me she needed to speak to me. I sat to listen, thinking she was about to leave me or tell me I had to go to rehab.

'Glen, I am pregnant!' she said.

I was filled with so many emotions. On one hand I was ecstatic. I loved Jenny and I wanted a life with her. The idea of having a baby was something I had always wanted to do with her. But, I was a heroin addict and I seemed stuck in that. For the short time I'd been selling drugs everything was good but even then I suppose I'd known that it could end at any time.

'There's more news,' Jenny said less happily. 'We have been kicked out of our flat. We have two weeks to be gone.' My belly twisted then Jenny said, 'I managed to speak to someone at the Cross and they can put you back on Methadone at Kings Cross.'

Finally some good news.

'Oh babe! I am so happy. I can do it right this time and we can have a life together with our new baby.'

I was on an emotional roller coaster because the next thing Jenny told me was that the person who put me on the Methadone program was Annie. Annie from the refuge! The same women who I had told about Simon raping me all those years ago at the refuge. I had never told Jenny that story. I really wanted to, but would she understand? I bet she wouldn't think Annie was our saviour if she knew about her involvement in my life prior to my becoming a heroin addict. I blamed the refuge people for my abuse and for my subsequent addiction, for my bad dreams, my terrible memories and the anger I held deep down but never spoke about.

Annie, the drunk, had got me in the program Methadone clinic at Kings Cross! It took a little time to start the program and while I waited life was mayhem. I would spend any money I got on heroin.

Meanwhile Jenny had found us a place at Merrylands. We really wanted to get things right now. Jenny and our baby deserved me to be the best person I could be. I was ambivalent. I was nervous about that but excited too. *I don't even know how to take care of myself. How am I going to take care of a baby.* I was determined to get a job, make something of myself and most of all be a good Daddy. I was more stable again, having had a few weeks on the program.

I was in the city at Mike's Pet store. 'I've got a new store now,' Mike told me excitedly. 'Just bought it. Two storey place.

The entire top will be an aquarium. I've got birds too.' He was so enthusiastic and then he threw out the lifeline.

'How about you come and work for me? You know a lot and you've got passion. You're just the man I need.'

I was honest with Mike about my drug use and that I was on Methadone. He didn't judge me. He said, 'It doesn't matter where we've been mate. It's where we're going.'

Mike became a father figure and a role model to me. I had had Peter prior to this but he and I hadn't talked for some time. He did visit us but he seemed to resent Jenny. When she told Peter that he would probably kill me if he kept buying me drugs, Peter got upset and left. He was a strange man and I think he liked having me to himself as a dependent.

Mike was a wonderful man and our relationship was warm and uncomplicated. That did not make his son or his wife happy. They objected that he'd employed me. They objected when he made me manager of the Aquarium with the responsibility of setting the area up and doing the ordering of fish and equipment. I was so full of ideas and Mike entertained all of them. He gave me a lot of responsibility quickly and I believed I could handle it. I was confident and in time I excelled in my work.

A few months into Jenny's pregnancy I was stable on the Methadone program and Jenny got her old job back at Chatswood. We started going to a parenting program. I found that quite interesting.

Jenny's passion for her work had always been a mystery to me but now that I had a job I loved, I could see how that was. I felt pride in myself too. I was still on Methadone and Mike would let me take his car to pick up my dose. There were days when I got things wrong but they were rare.

Jenny and I had been collecting things for our new baby. Hush Bubba was a brand of baby stuff we liked. We had slowly been doing up a baby room and we had also been going with her dad on the weekends to church.

Time continued on happily and Jenny started looking as if

she was ready to pop. We went out one night for dinner and on the way home I was being a clown, pretending I was an ape and climbing up posts and stuff.

Jenny said, 'Stop making me laugh or I'm going to pee myself.'

As a man I didn't understand how hard it was to carry a baby on top of your bladder. I didn't stop my ape act and sure enough, what Jenny said she'd do, she did. Just a trickle and later we found out that was very common in expectant mothers.

Jenny looked really beautiful when she was pregnant. She seemed to glow. She was always smiling. We had really turned a corner and we were looking forward so much to bringing a new life into our world.

We had been going to baby classes at the health clinic. We had bought lots of beautiful things for our soon to be born baby. The best part about buying those things was that we had both worked for them.

We had never felt comfortable as drug dealers. It just wasn't us but this, yes, this felt very right.

We'd been told different ways to bring on contractions by the women at the health clinic. Jenny was due to give birth any time now so we went for a walk after dinner then we made love when we got home. I ran a bath for Jenny and put fragrant oils in the water. All these things that we'd been told would bring on the birth.

One night Jenny was in the bath she suddenly said, 'I need to go to hospital.' We didn't have our Holden any more so she said, 'Ring Dad.'

Keith came as quick as he could and took us to Merrylands Hospital. We waited for hours. I can't even describe the feelings I experienced that night. Jenny looked nervous yet excited. I was eager and anxious.

Then out of the blue the lift opened and out walked my brother Michael followed by Barry my father! I almost blew a gasket. I was fuming! What was he doing here! Barry started handing out cigars. 'I'm going to be a granddad,' he said proudly.

Had I rung Michael in the mayhem? (I still haven't a clue how they got the news.) I was happy that Michael was there but I didn't want Barry anywhere near us. I wanted to tell him to get out, among other things, but I didn't make a fuss. This was about Jenny and our baby.

Barry and Keith got on well. I'd never told Keith about my father or how badly he had treated me and then abandoned me. I hated the fact that Barry now inserted himself into this day. The birth of our child should have been totally joyful and there he was spoiling it. I tried not to let him.

In the wee small hours God granted us the beautiful gift of our baby girl. We named her Amber. I'll never ever forget the moment I first laid eyes on her. I adored that tiny girl more than anything. I cannot articulate the storm of emotion I experienced. I felt scared. I didn't want to let my little Amber down. She was so beautiful. I instantly learnt what unconditional love was when Amber was born. I was so fearful that the world as it was could hurt her. I kept thinking how I had to protect her from all that.

While I held our baby Keith said, 'You guys have a lot of work ahead of you now.' He was always so kind to me even after he'd seen me at my worst. I was now the father of his granddaughter. As uncomfortable as it was having Barry present, I felt some comfort at the presence of Keith. I knew that she had one good grandfather who would always love her and treat her right.

Keith had said how good it was that I was working. He always acknowledged the good things I did. He never talked down to me. What an incredible contrast he was to Barry. I often thought what life would have been like if I'd had a father like Keith.

How did Barry earn the right to be at the birth of our daughter? It made me angry that he got on so well with Keith and Jenny. If only they knew. Jenny was manipulated by Barry and she still defends him.

'Your mother wasn't well,' she argues. But Jenny only had Barry's version of our family.

When I told Barry our baby's name he said, 'Oh. You have a sister named Jade.' We had chosen Jade as Amber's middle name.

'What the fuck are you talking about?' I said to Barry. 'I've got one sister and her name's Tina.'

Barry said he had another family and two years before Amber was born he and his partner had a child.

Keith held Amber tenderly and his gaze at her shone with love. Michael held her and that was nice but when Barry held her I felt nothing but rage. There he was rocking and joking and charming everyone. *Liar! You lay one wrong finger on my daughter and I'll* ... I remembered when I was a child and people thought, *Oh what a lovely man. Raising a son on his own.* Then we'd go home and the real Barry would emerge. *Nope, Barry doesn't have the right to be here.*

Michael and I talked for quite a while, mostly about our beautiful gift. Amber Fisher. Born in September, 1988, in the Bicentenary year of Australia. Amber was given a special Birth Certificate as all children born in 1988 were. That only seemed right to us, as she was special to Jenny and I.

Jenny was only in hospital a few days then they released her to come home. Keith drove us home and eventually left. So, there we were. Two people who were very much in love with the most beautiful gift you could imagine. I had a job. Jenny was on leave. I felt the weight of responsibility come over me. I was a dad. I was the sole breadwinner.

There were so many positives but I focused on all the worries I had. As optimistic as I tried to be, I always felt that things were going to go wrong somehow. Trouble seemed to follow me. It had been that way since my birth. Now I felt like all this was too good to be true. It was just too good to last, was it?

I'd stopped putting needles in my arm but I knew that addiction was still very much a part of me. I just had to get things right for little Amber.

Every morning I got the train to the city, picked up my Methadone then got to work by nine o'clock. One day there was a train strike and I wasn't able to get into the clinic to get my dose. I rang them to explain. They said if I wasn't there by closing time, ten forty five, I would not get my dose and that was that. I went without my dose that day. It was hard but I managed. The following day I walked to the station but the strike was still running. Going without my dose for one day was hard enough but two! Could I do two? Jenny controlled our finances and when I saw that the trains weren't running I thought, *I have to go home and plead with Jenny for fifty dollars to get a taxi to the Cross to get my Methadone.*

Before I found a taxi I rang the clinic and told Margaret about the situation but that I was definitely coming. Margaret hated me because I spoke out about Annie one time and asked how the fuck she was allowed to be working there. They kept reminding me that she had put me on the program. As helpful as that was I couldn't forget the rest. Didn't they realise she was complicit in enabling the rape of children? Yes, Annette got me on this program but the more I thought about her the more her position at the clinic grated on me.

Back to the train strike day, I explained to Margaret that I was stuck with the train strike again but I had money for a taxi and that I should be there in time for my dose. I pleaded desperately with her to wait if I was a bit late.

'Yes, I'll do that Glen. Jump in the taxi and don't stress. Come in as soon as you can.' I had clean urines, was working and doing all I could to get there. I thought that would mean they'd try to accommodate me.

There was so much traffic on the roads. I kept telling the taxi driver back ways to go but he was determined to go his way. I got to the clinic at exactly ten forty five. As I dashed out of the taxi the clinic door opened and a man came out then they closed the door behind him. I knocked on the window. Margaret and the man she was talking to ignored me. They refused to open the door or even look at me. This was day two without my dose and I was agitated.

Thirty minutes later I was still standing outside knocking. The staff started to leave through the front door.

'Why wouldn't you open the door and dose me?' I asked.

'Dosing times are from seven thirty five to ten forty five,' Margaret said haughtily. 'If you don't get here, you don't get dosed.'

She enjoyed the power she had over addicts. This addict got angry.

'I've come from Merrylands. There's a fucking train strike and I have to go to work!' I yelled.

Margaret replied, 'If you say one more word I'll remove you from the program.'

I was silent for a second then I said, 'This isn't right,' and I walked away fuming.

I didn't go to work. I stayed on the streets all day bustling money for a shot. I rang Jenny to tell her what had happened and I rang my boss.

I didn't go home. I slept at the park that night and was awaiting the clinic to open first thing in the morning.

Along with my dose they gave me a letter. I'd been removed from the program for abusive behaviour. I could not believe this was happening again.

I went to work and I told Mike what had happened.

'It's just not right,' he said.

Mike rang the clinic and complained.

'This man came to me twelve months ago and he was a mess. He's made so many positive changes to his life since then. He works well for me and has a new baby and a place to live. And then you do this to him!' He spoke politely but firmly.

They didn't give a shit. Mike was mortified that they could be so callous. I reckon my comments about Annie had a lot to do with my expulsion this time.

Mike said, 'How about you take a month off the job and go to detox?'

Jenny was worried about my dismissal. She'd seen what my

coming off the program would do. I agreed with Jenny to go into detox and get this crap over with once and for all.

I went to Langton Clinic and checked myself in. Withdrawing from Methadone is much harder than coming off heroin. I was sitting in group one morning feeling very agitated when Judy, the facilitator who I'd met before and who was known as 'Dragon Lady', asked, 'Glen, why are you here?'

'To get off drugs?' I said. 'I love my fiance and my baby daughter and I want to get my life together. I'm sick of being trapped.'

Then she let me have it.

'Love! Ha! You wouldn't even know what love is!' Judy the Dragon went on and on and got me so worked up that I threw a glass at the wall smashing it to pieces. I walked out of Langton Clinic and back to the streets. I didn't want to go back to Jenny and Amber like this. I was in heavy withdrawals.

I went home every couple of days to see them but I spent about a month on the streets using every day. I didn't go home to see Amber or Jenny as much as I should have or would have liked. Heroin was in control again and this time it was worse. I had come off Methadone cold turkey and I needed to be on the streets every moment to get heroin.

I moved from using heroin to adding pills and cocaine to the cocktail. It fucked my head up badly. Paranoia ruled my days. I'd have a shot of cocaine and walk around for hours believing that I was being followed. I used heroin to come down from the speed I took. I started to get money from Giuseppe a Paedophile I had known in the past.

Giuseppe loaned me a car. It was a 1979 BMW. Talk about a flash car! I used it for about a month and I didn't take it back. He could have reported it to police but he didn't.

What a contrast to my other life. My habit was bad and my health was deteriorating. I had Hepatitis C and I weighed about sixty six kilos, very thin for a six foot three man. I was very sick. I started to sell again for dealers I knew on the streets of the Cross.

Chapter 20.
The Ultimate Betrayal

On the day before my twenty third birthday I went home to Merrylands to see Jenny and Amber. I wasn't in a good place with horrible withdrawals and feeling really unwell. I greeted Jenny with a hug and picked up our little Amber. I felt conflicted over having been away for so long. Then I saw Michael my brother sitting on a chair.

'Hello,' I said curiously. 'Why are you here?'

'Came looking for you.'

That made sense. I am his brother and this was where I lived. Jenny was acting very oddly. She hardly spoke to me but I didn't think anything of it because I was so sick. I thought she might still be upset that I'd been expelled from a program again and obviously using again. Not to mention my long absence.

On my birthday I walked about the house looking for clean clothes. I had a shower, not expecting my birthday to be happy because that rarely happened.

'I want to take you out for your birthday,' Michael announced.

'Yeah, all right,' I said reluctantly. 'I'll come if we go to the Cross.' I needed to be where heroin was. I had parked the BMW in the driveway and Michael and I walked to Merrylands station.

We went to the Cross and Jenny stayed home with Amber.

I scored heroin and we went to a pub in Woolloomooloo. Michael drank beer after beer while we played pool.

'Go on mate. At least have one beer. It's your birthday,' he kept saying. He seemed really keen on getting me drunk.

'I don't drink,' I told him. 'I fucking hate grog.'

I figured our parents, mainly our mother, had done enough drinking for all of us. I hated when Michael drank. There were two Michael's. Sober Mike was fun, talented and lovable. Drunk Michael was a dickhead, a douchebag and, like all piss heads, became aggressive, even violent. Jenny and I had told him not to come to our place drunk or drinking.

We stayed at the pub for hours. Every time I wanted to leave Michael insisted on us staying longer. He tried to provoke a fight with some guys in the pub but I wasn't having a bar of it. Something was troubling him but I didn't pick up the signs of it until later.

Eventually I said, 'I'm going home,' and I left. Michael followed me but I didn't want him to. On the train back to Merrylands he sat away from me and kept mumbling to himself. He followed me home. I walked ahead of him to warn Jenny that Michael was coming and he was drunk.

Jenny appeared nervous when I came in which I assumed was normal thinking she didn't like it when Michael drank alcohol. I picked up my little girl and made a few faces at her.

'My God you are beautiful,' I told her. I felt so sad as I realised I was so fucked up and sick and this perfect little girl needed a dad.

'Where's your brother?' Jenny asked.

Michael stumbled through the door, still mumbling.

'Glen, Glen, I need to talk to you,' he slurred.

'Okay,' I said. 'What's up?'

'No, no mate. No Glen. Talk outside.'

Odd, I thought but something was troubling him. I really didn't want to sit and listen to his drunken ramblings. Every time I smelt alcohol or saw a drunk, it reminded me of my mother. However he was my brother and if he needed me to, I'd listen. We went outside.

Michael couldn't hold in what he needed to say any longer.

'I slept with Jenny,' he blurted out.

I felt a stabbing pain inside my chest! Everything seemed to slow down.

'What? You slept with my fiancé? The mother of my

daughter? What the fuck are you talking about?' I couldn't stop. 'What's wrong with you? Why do you do this?''

He wanted to fight me then and there. He was so drunk that when he threw a big hay maker, he fell over. I was too sick to fight anyone but I was so fucking hurt. *Surely that was a lie. No way could it be true. Please God make it a lie. A drunk just talking shit.* Was Michael just trying to hurt me? Even that was more than I could understand.

I went inside. Jenny was holding Amber in her arms.

'What the fuck is Michael talking about?'

She looked everywhere but at me.

Then in stumbles the drunk and says, 'It's not her fault Glen. It's mine.'

What a dumb ass thing to say. How the fuck is only one person to blame. Two of the three people I loved most had betrayed me.

Jenny said, 'I've been lonely. I've hardly seen you for a month.'

The pain was more intense that I can describe. I was deeply hurt. I really can't even put into words what I felt about their betrayal.

I loved Jenny and our little girl. I loved Michael, my brother and my best friend. He was the one person who I'd been through so much with as a kid and teenager. Now we were adults. I was father and a soon to be husband. I was gutted. Couldn't think. I needed heroin. I'd used earlier that night but the shot was wearing off and I had started to withdraw again. My life was falling apart.

'Been lonely,' I said wearily to Jenny. 'Been lonely and your solution is to fuck my brother!'

Michael kept piping up as Jenny and I argued.

'Just get out of here Michael,' I told him.

He sat on the stairs outside the door, drunk, saying, 'Glen, I am sorry.'

'You're not sorry, arsehole,' I shouted. 'You always wanted what I had. You were always jealous of me. Linda, Nadine, the other kids at the refuge. You saw I had a good thing so you wanted to fuck it up for me!' I felt defeated, like there was no point to my even being alive. 'That's not a brother. That's one sick fuck.'

I still haven't forgiven Michael. That betrayal was a load too heavy for me to carry.

I went back to the streets. I didn't want to go home. I thought about suicide every day. I took heroin every day. Hanging out always made me really emotional. I thought daily about the abuse that had happened in my life, the lives lost, especially Linda's, Maxine's and other kids on the streets. Could life get more miserable and hopeless?

Jenny turned up at the Cross with Amber in the pram one day. She had money and she wanted to score. We scored and used but I couldn't speak to her. I left her and walked to the park. I sat down with a friend called Tammy. Jenny came up and asked, 'Are you coming back?'

'No.'

'Well, you can fuck off then. You have nowhere to live.'

Tammy said, 'You can stay with me.'

I walked off with Tammy and left Jenny at the park.

Mike, my boss, had given me time off work to detox and I hadn't been back to see him since the day I told him I was off the program. I'd found a friend to take over for me. I went to see Mike at work but bad news was waiting for me. Mike had died. I was devastated. His widow refused to let me come back to the aquarium but Mike's passing was far more heartbreaking than that was.

To say I was really lost would be an understatement. Not only did I have a raging heroin habit, I was taking pills again and withdrawing from Methadone. On top of this I was using cocaine and my mind was all over the place. I couldn't process the fact that Jenny and my brother had betrayed me. I couldn't process it in this mess but I think I wouldn't have been able to if I'd been clean either.

I stayed with Tammy for about a week, sleeping in her bed without anything sexual. Tammy had liked me for years. She was a street worker and worked in a brothel too. She made lots of money and was always trying to get me to go out with her. I only wanted to be friends with her. Despite what Jenny had done, I still loved her and I wanted to be loyal to her.

One day I decided I would just go back and talk to Jenny. We didn't really talk about it. We tried to carry on as if it hadn't happened. That wasn't easy for me to do. I was using again and needed to be where I could get hits. I had to keep selling drugs for the Romanians to support my habit.

I woke up one morning and one of my friends wanted me to drive him to Rockdale to score off the Romanians for him. I drove the BMW that Giuseppe had given me. I passed a car going too slow then I over corrected when I saw a car was coming head on. I slammed into a power pole.

Two tow trucks came even before the police got there. One convinced me that it was best for me to use his service as the place he was taking the car specialised in BMWs. I agreed. The smash repairs gave me a courtesy car to use while my car was to be repaired.

I still managed to get to Rockdale because the heroin was more important than the car. Screwed up priorities! I can see that now. I was using both heroin and cocaine and the cocaine made my mind do crazy shit. The idea of suicide was constantly in my mind.

About a week after the accident I went to the smash repairer for his quote to repair the car. Three thousand! Did I look as if I had that kind of cash!

'I'll give you five grand for it,' he said.

What choice did I have? I accepted the offer and took the money home to Jenny.

I told Jenny, 'I want to give this money to your dad to mind. I'll just spend it all on shit otherwise.'

Three hundred dollars is all I kept and I gave Jenny the rest, for Amber and bills then the rest was going to Keith for safe keeping. I caught a train to the Cross to buy two caps of heroin and one of cocaine. I hung around the streets for a couple of days and then caught the train back to Merrylands.

No-one was home when I got there. All our things were gone too. Jenny had packed up and disappeared with the money and with Amber.

I saw her a few days later at the Cross. She said, 'You're not seeing Amber unless ... 'She listed her conditions and that just made me more angry. Amber was not a possession! And what gave Jenny the right to take everything we owned? To hold Amber as if she was a bargaining tool who I had no right to see unless I met her conditions – it just was not right. Especially as it was Jenny who betrayed our relationship, she had no right in my view. I did not see my addiction as betrayal of our relationship. To be fair to Jenny I was in a relationship of my own – with Lady Heroin.

I wasn't surprised that Jenny had taken everything but I hadn't expected Keith to condone it. To be fair, he was looking after his daughter's best interests and those of Amber. But I had always got on well with him. He'd given me money sometimes and he liked me.

Jenny was using heroin occasionally and she would come up to the street sometimes to score. She had Amber one time so I refused to score for her. I went back to stay with Tammy. Most times Jenny came up she would leave Amber at her mother's place.

It was about this time that Jenny and I decided to go to Wisteria House in Westmead together to detox. We loved each other and knew that the biggest hurdle in our lives wasn't my brother. It was heroin. When I'd done the detox shuffle before, forty eight hours was usually the most I'd ever been able tolerate. Then I'd flee. I did last once almost a week at Westmount in Katoomba with medication.

Would I make it through with Jenny beside me? Amber was with Jenny's Mum. Although my father had befriended Jenny and her father, I was angry about that relationship and there was no way I'd let my child anywhere near him by herself. I'd often told Jenny about his convictions, and other things he'd done but Barry had charmed her so that she didn't believe me. I wish I'd had the proof I have now to have been able to show her.

Going to detox was a decision we had made together. We both wanted to be free from drugs, Kings Cross and the power they held over us. Well, me mainly.

We arrived at Wisteria House and we were sent into the detox section, a dormitory with about twenty beds. People were withdrawing from different drugs or alcohol. When we were coming up to our third day I wanted to run, as usual. This time I thought of Amber and how much I wanted to be her daddy. But I was deeply wounded. My first girlfriend Linda had been murdered. My second, Nadine, had slept with Chad the doormen and now Jenny had slept with my brother.

I decided I'd keep trying. Jenny and I needed different treatments in Wisteria House. Jenny was more rational because her habit was mild, not raging like mine. She had a family support system and had been raised normally so she knew how to fit in and behave. I was a bit like a wild animal. I'd raised myself and had skewed ideas about everyone and everything. I found trust difficult. Whenever I'd risked trusting someone my trust had been broken every single fucking time: my parents, an uncle, a family friend, foster parents, my own brother, my best mate the refuge, by people who ran institutions, by inmates, by police and paedophiles. By now I was unwilling to trust anyone.

After three days Jenny was moved into the rehabilitation section while I stayed in detox. She slept upstairs with the other residents who'd been through detox. I'd need between two and six weeks there before I'd regain a sleep pattern and be free of feeling ill. I stayed on but every time I saw Jenny, she was hanging off a guy who was also in rehab. I became so disturbed by this that I brought that to the attention of staff.

'Oh you're just seeing things that aren't there,' they kept saying. They tried to make out that I was paranoid and imagining things. I knew what I saw and, given what had happened with Jenny and my brother, I felt I had a right to the question. I saw Jenny flirting and it hurt every time I saw her.

The rehab patients went to N.A. or A.A. meetings every night. I wasn't able to focus on my stuff: detox and being Amber's dad. Each night I saw Jenny and the others go to meetings. I couldn't sleep and that enhanced my imaginings. After two weeks I was still in heavy withdrawals.

I didn't speak to anyone about another problem I was having - flashbacks to abuses that had happened in my childhood. I could not handle all these emotions as well as withdrawal and the secrets that I dared not speak about. I had tried to draw and even write poetry to express the things I felt I could not say. Thoughts of self-harm and suicide kept creeping into my head. I would lie in bed plotting ways to die.

I'm not sure exactly how many days I lasted in Wisteria before I left. I ran away from detox as I always did and headed back to the Cross.

Something inside me had changed. I was angry, hurt and I was more reckless now. All I cared about was Amber and Jenny and they had been taken from me by my brother. What was the use of anything? Of me and this life?

My behaviour on the streets was now different from any time before. I was more willing to rip people off, sell drugs in plain view of police and not care about being caught. I was shooting up as much heroin and cocaine as I could get. I was taking whatever pills I could get too: Serapax, Valium and Rohypnol. I was always overdosing. It's a miracle I didn't die within the first week. I didn't care who I hung with any more. Whoever had money or whatever it took to get drugs. I was even prepared to do crime now. In the past I hadn't been.

One night I had just taken a heap of pills and a shot of heroin when I decided to go to a meeting that I knew Jenny would be at. They were always at Westmead Hospital. I wanted to see Jenny and I even hoped to see our Amber.

When I walked into the meeting I saw a man sitting next to Jenny with his arm around her. He looked much older than her. He looked like a 'wanna be' biker. I went off my head and started raving. I was talking to another person who worked at Wisteria House.

'You have to leave the meeting, Glen,' she said.

I was walking off when all of a sudden someone punched me in the head from behind. He landed on top of me and kept trying to hit me. I wrestled with him a bit but I was too off my face to really defend myself. Someone broke up the fight. The attacker was Jenny's new boyfriend. He took it upon himself to dog shot me at Jenny's bidding I think. Coward! He was clean and I was drug fucked. If he had walked up to my face he would have possibly won. I could barely stand up.

I had blood in my mouth so I spat it at him. I said, 'Hope you like AIDS mother fucker,' and then I walked out. I know saying that was wrong, but I wanted to hurt him, if only for a few minutes.

I'd been using needles I found on the street every day. I didn't care and I had it in my head that I had HIV. I was always so sick. I knew that Hep C and drugs caused sickness but I was sure I had HIV too from needles. This only added to my being more reckless. Self care: zero. Getting clean made no sense. What was the use?

I heard many years later that Jenny had several relationships after this where the men where violent to her.

I couldn't see the part I played in any of the mess around me or inside me. To me, my choice to use heroin and give up getting clean for Jenny and Amber wasn't a choice at all. It was a necessity and it was Jenny's fault because she broke us up.

Late on a busy Saturday night I was walking up past The Wall towards the Cross when a car drove past me really slowly. Inside there were a group of men and I thought I saw a women holding a baby in there too. I couldn't see very well but I could make out a few middle eastern men. Suddenly the car stopped and a huge man got out.

'You cunt! Come here,' he says.

I legged it and he chased me. I outran him but he seemed determined to get me. I had no idea who he was or why he was chasing me but he shouted my name as he chased me.

'I know where you are every day cunt and you're going to die,' he shouted as he gave up chasing me.

Who the hell were they? Why were they chasing me? Maybe this had been someone I had ripped off? I didn't think much of it when they left. I had other things on my mind. Later that night I was walking down the main street and the same car went by. The big man jumped out again and tried to catch me. I outran him again.

Who was he? Why was he after me? My brain tried hard to process it all. Had I ripped him off? Had I ripped off someone he knew? It was very unnerving being an addict who depended on being on the street to support his habit. It was worse to be chased by someone I didn't know but who wanted me dead.

This cat and mouse game went on for weeks. I was using cocaine which just added to my anxieties. I slept in the daytime in the park behind the police station. Safety in numbers combined with safety in daylight. Normal people were about in the day when I slept and it was easier to get money and drugs at night.

Luckily the people who chased me only came out at night too. I was sitting at the fountain talking to my mate Scar Face Ray who I'd known and been protected by since I had first got to the Cross. As we talked the car drove past.

'Fuck,' I said.

'What's going on?' Ray asked. I told him as much as I knew.

'Listen. This is what I want you to do. Stand down the street a bit, on the main street. Let the bastards see you and wait 'til he gets out of the car. Then I want you to run past the fountain and I will take over from there.'

I did what Ray told me. I stood on the street and by the time the car came my nerves were ragged and I was shaking. The big guy got out and I started walking towards the park. When he got too close I ran and so did he, straight into Ray. Ray smashed him to the ground straight away. He got up and they fought each other. Ray was a street tough that no one ever messed with. They fought for what seemed like ages. Ray got the upper hand.

'Why are you chasing the kid?' Ray asked the bruised and bloodied man.

I wasn't a kid at twenty three but this wasn't the time to argue. He finally let on that Jenny had put him up to it. How Jenny even knew these people was beyond me. Anyway, after that night I never saw them again.

I went to Annandale to see Giuseppe, the paedophile who'd given me the BMW. He was a brick layer. He was seventy two by this time and owned many flats. I went to see him whenever I was desperate for money or somewhere to stay. This time I wanted to dry out and I stayed in one of his flats for a couple of days.

He would collect rents from his tenants on Tuesdays. I had gone with Giuseppe to collect the rent in the past so no-one was surprised to see me turn up and ask for the rent. I collected about four then I took a taxi back to the Cross and spent a few days off my face until the rent money ran out.

I felt bad so I went back to see Giuseppe to apologize and ask him if I could do odd jobs and cleaning for him to pay back what I'd stolen from him like I had in the past. I went into his flat and found him in bed with a boy about thirteen.

'You're a sick fucker,' I said angrily. 'I'm going to ring the cops!'

He had picked this kid up at The Wall, his favourite haunt. The kid got up and left. Giuseppe went out to his shed and he got his rifle. He aimed it at me. Someone must have seen all the commotion and the police pulled up as we argued. Giuseppe put the gun away. He knew the cops, so even after I told them that he'd just been with a boy they told me to fuck off. A drug addict is worse than someone who rapes kids?

As I walked down Johnson Street away from the police and Giuseppe I was walking past the church in Annandale and I heard music. The music reminded me of the Boys Brigade that I'd been to when I lived with Barry. It was my escape from the torture of home, a safe place. I liked the pastor's daughter back then and we would sit outside and listen to the music.

I sat outside of the church in Annandale and listened to the people inside singing Christian hymns.

As I listened I started to cry. The songs reminded me of a time when I was a drug free little boy, long before Kings Cross and all the loss of lives, the abuse and every other awful thing I'd seen. I was in an emotionally dangerous frame of mind. *I don't want to be on this planet any more.* The notion was stronger than it had ever been. *I want the pain to end. What's the point of living with it? No point. Not for me. I fuck up whatever I do.*

I had imagined ways I could suicide many times. There were dramatic ones like running in front of a train like my friend Troy had many years before. Or I could jump in front of a truck or off the Harbour Bridge. My most common thoughts were hanging myself or taking a shit load of pills and heroin and lying down to wait. Oh what peace that would bring!

I'd talk inside myself when I was down. *Fuck you Mum. I was never good enough. Why the fuck did you love Samuel and hate me so much? What could a little boy have done so bad to be hated so much? To be the target of every aggressive impulse you had.* I thought about my brother and about Jenny and Amber. *I have done to Amber exactly what my parents did to me,* I thought. *I've failed her. I'm a fucking blight. I killed Linda. If she hadn't met me she would not be dead. Or if I didn't go to South Australia she would not be dead. Or if I hadn't left her and gone off with Nadine.* I thought about the many others I loved or knew who had died. So many of them kids. I thought about the refuge, Simon and all the men who sexually abused me and my friends. How stupid they must think I am. How easy it was to rape a little boy using the word love. Buying him a shiny new BMX bike for his birthday.

'Revenge' and 'Retribution' were two words that often crossed my mind but it wasn't in my makeup to hurt others deliberately. I found it hard to physically hurt people, even paedophile's. The only people I ever hurt were people I loved and it was unintentional. Jenny, Linda, other friends and most often myself. I dedicated twenty four hours a day to self-harm. Shooting up, hanging out, withdrawing and having flashbacks to times of anger, hurt, betrayal, and confusion. I kept asking myself how I allowed these men to manipulate and abuse me. That I was only a child manipulated by men didn't occur to me. I blamed myself. I am stupid and so easy to prey on.

I was sitting there with my head in my hands when someone from inside the church came and sat next to me. They thought I might like to come inside. They told me that Jesus loves me. That made me angrier but I was too well mannered to say what I thought. If he loves me then why am I an addict? *If He loves me why didn't I get parents that gave two shits about me. No thank you. Thank you but please fuck off.*

'Thank you,' I said. 'I'm fine just sitting here listening to the music.'

After the music they had tea and coffee. I hate coffee. It brought back memories of my mother yelling out, 'Glen, make me a coffee.' Then when I brought her the sabotaged coffee she'd say, 'Fuck you're useless! You make shit coffee.' At least I'd got a laugh out of that but then the guilt set in because Tina or Michael were yelled at to make it then.

As I sat outside the church, every derogatory comment anyone had ever said to me washed around in my head. 'You're a nobody. You're worthless. You're in this home because society doesn't want you. Your family doesn't want you.' I had taken every word to heart and believed them all. The miniscule bit of self-worth I had had faded away completely. *Maybe I am not as smart as I think I am. Maybe I really am a piece of shit that no one wants. Anyone that does want me only does for sex. Or drugs. Not one person on the planet knows where I am. Or even cares where I am. Fuck this. I'll do the world a favour and end this shit right now.*

Finally the lights went off in the church and everything was quiet. My peaceful music had gone and all that was left was the noise in my head. Even my tears were all cried out.

Then my mind turned to biscuits. Were there any left? I tried the door and to my surprise it opened. I went inside. Some people were talking at the back of the church while others were saying their goodbyes and cars were driving off. I noticed a cross or something hanging on the wall and thought, *I'm going to hang myself right here in this church.*

I knew suicide was a sin. I'd been taught a lot about what I wasn't allowed to do in life. No-one ever said that I could do a lot of good things. Somewhere in my confusion I believed in God. Then I'd think about all the evil and pain in the world. This God of love, this God all knowing, this great miracle worker doesn't fix me, not to mention the world. Well, fuck you God. One part of me was screaming at Him, blaming Him for all that was wrong. The other was pleading with Him to take me to heaven. *Please. Please set me free. I want to be with Linda and Maxine and the other kids who've died.*

I saw a sheet that I assumed had been used for arts and crafts and I made a noose out it and attached it to the fixture on the wall. *I'm out of here.* I put my head through the noose and prayed to God to forgive me for what I was doing. I was scared but I'd had enough. I figured even God could see that my being here on the planet was futile.

Then the light came on in the church. Two men had come back in. They saw what I was doing. This had been my chance to end it all but fear delayed my taking of the final step. The men ran to me, lifted me up then talked with me for a while. The priest came in and spoke with me too.

Father Drake took me to his residence and made a cup of tea. Then I left and stayed in one of Giuseppe's rooms.

At about seven the following morning I turned up at the door of Father Drake's house. I don't know why I went there except that I'd found comfort in churches since childhood. Father Drake invited me in and offered me a piece of fruit and a cup of tea. As we sat and talked, he asked me what my plans were now. The longer I stayed talking, the more I wanted, needed heroin.

'I have to go. I'm hanging out. I need to get money and score.'

'How do you plan to get money?' he asked.

I didn't specify. I said, 'Whatever it takes but I've got to go.'

'Glen, I don't want you to do anything stupid. How much money do you need?'

I replied, 'The cheapest shot I can get's fifty bucks. I have to go.'

I kept telling him that I had to go. He looked conflicted when he took money from his pocket. He was going to give it to me. Relief! I can score. It was almost as good as shooting up, seeing that money coming my way.

Next he said, 'Oh, I can't give you money knowing that you're going out to use it for heroin.' He put the money back in his pocket.

The money vanishing really messed with my mind. Relief then suddenly no relief. Back to more desperate withdrawals. *Give me the fucking money for Christs sake*, I wanted to scream. I didn't though. Instead we back and forthed about whether he could help me and I got more and more desperate.

I grabbed a butter knife and held it against my neck. 'Don't you understand? I want to be dead!' I looked at him. Dropped the knife. 'I just want to die!'

'Calm down Glen,' he said. 'Look I'll give you fifty dollars and I'll drive you to the Cross.'

Father Drake drove me to Kings Cross then as I was about to get out of the car he said, 'Would you like me to wash the clothes in your bag?'

I had a bag of clothes that I had been carrying everywhere I went. I was stunned by his kindness. He asked where he could find me to return them, adding, 'I don't want to come back to Kings Cross.'

'I often go to Annandale. Can I come to your place in a few

days to grab them?' I thanked him for the money and promised to pay it back.

'Can I pray with you?' he asked.

I said yes and Father Drake prayed for me.

'Goodbye then,' he said when he'd finished.

I got out of the car and hurried off to do business. I spent a few days on the streets then I went back to Annandale one morning to get my clothes.

Father Drake opened the door. He was very polite and invited me in. Once again he made me a cup of tea. He gave it to me and said, 'I have to quickly do something. I'll be back in a minute.'

He disappeared and when he came back we sat and talked. Ten minutes later there was another knock on the door. Two uniformed police officers were invited in. He brought them into the kitchen.

'Glen Fisher I am arresting you for Demand Money with Menaces.'

I looked at the priest trying to understand what was going on and he looked at me apologetically.

They took me Annandale Police Station where I sat in the cells for hours. Then I was taken to Leichardt Police Station.

Eventually I was taken to the Sydney Police Centre where I was held for about three weeks in the cell. There had been riots at the prisons so they were not accepting new prisoners. I knew what the official charge was but I didn't understand what it meant. I had never been as sick as I was for those three weeks coming off heroin, cocaine and pills.

I didn't eat for the whole time I was there. There were other addicts in the cells and because the prisons were not accepting anyone, the cells were full. One guy who I knew had been on the Methadone program and desperately needed his dose. He wouldn't be dosed here so he pretended to hang himself. He was taken straight to Long Bay prison where a doctor would organise for his dose to be given there.

We were allowed to have about seven cigarettes a day. I didn't have any but the other guys shared. When a policeman brought me one from another guy in the cells, I asked him, 'When will I get bail?'

He said he'd go and look it up. When he returned he said, 'You can't get bail mate. You've been charged with Armed Robbery. You don't get bail on violent offences unless you go to the Supreme Court.'

'Armed Robbery? Are you fucking kidding me!'

I was building quite a resume! To the outsider looking in I was one mean tough man not the skinny addict I looked like who could barely function. I had previously had some big charges all of which had been dismissed: Assault and Robbery, Extortion. All dismissed.

Now Armed Robbery was added to the list. How, I wondered, did holding a butter knife to my own throat because I wanted to die become an Armed Robbery? I should have been sent to a Psychiatric Unit. I was very unwell physically and mentally. If I had understood mental health at that time I would have asked to speak to someone working in that area.

I spent nearly every minute of those three weeks in the cells going through withdrawals. Some of the other guys were on Methadone and none got dosed. It was really hard, to say the least. I'd lie on my bed while every bone ached, I had nausea, extreme hot and cold flushes, I became agitated, got jumping leg syndrome along with insomnia. And of course my head ran at a million miles an hour.

One morning a van came from Long Bay Prison and we were all bundled in and driven to Long Bay Gaol.

At Long Bay we were put in the Metropolitan Remand Centre (MRC). I was nervous. I'd heard about prisons all my life, especially Long Bay, and I had often been told I'd end up there. Here I was! Was it inevitable? I never saw myself as prison material. I was definitely not a violent person but here I was charged with Armed Robbery. I didn't understand why I couldn't get bail. Paedophile's, rapists and even murderers I'd seen on TV got bail.

We waited in a cell to go through reception one by one. Most of the guys had been there before. I went through and was given my prison number. When the officer handed it to me he said, 'This will be your prison number for the rest of your life. You are now 192704.' Reduced to six numbers.

Prison clothes were handed out. I was wearing a Tigers shirt and jeans that I had to exchange for a light green button up shirt, a green t shirt, a pair of trousers and a pair of boots. Some guys wore sneakers and some wore Dunlop Vollies. My shoes were too old and tattered to wear so I was given boots. Prisoners commonly referred to this outfit as 'Battle Gear.'

We were marched through the gates to 13 Wing. MRC was made up of two wings, 12 and 13. New prisoners went to 13 Wing, top landing.

I walked into 13 Wing and there was my old mate Nifty from Patches!

'Glen! Roach! You made it,' he called out from the top of the stairs. I was incredibly nervous but I felt some comfort seeing Nifty standing at the top of the stairs.

A screw (prison guard) took me to my cell and as we past Nifty he said, 'Love the battle gear mate!' Nifty was wearing green shorts, a Nike t shirt and a new pair of shoes. I didn't know it at the time but shoes and clothes showed your status within the prison. The only people wearing what I had on were either old men or Gronks (people at the bottom of inmate status.)

The cell was pretty bare except for my cellmate. We had a bunk, a toilet and a sink. Some of the other cells I saw were pretty flash. They had televisions, electric jugs, toasters, pictures on the walls and all sorts of stuff. I was still between shock and denial so I was not interested in making my cell more homely. I couldn't stand being caged. I'd never been able to stand still. I was always moving, talking or going somewhere.

I did my best to not show my feelings: anxiety, fear. If Nifty had not been there I might have struggled much more than I did.

After the screw gave me my towel and few other things Nifty came along.

'Hey bro. What happened? What's the charge?' he asked.

'Armed Robbery,' I told him.

'Fuck mate! What did you do?'

I didn't want to tell him that I'd tried to suicide and that this was all a fucking joke. I just waved my hand in the air and said, 'Fuck it.'

Nifty took me to a cell where he introduced me to his crew. He had about six mates. Their main guy was Colin. Nifty told them that I was okay. My head was spinning as he talked. I was still hanging out. Colin explained to me the rules of prison. 'Never dog on anyone. Don't ever take things from people. Steal from other inmates you're called Peter Thief. Just don't ever do it.' Colin told me about what not to do or say and how to act. 'Don't stand tall mate. Just stand up.' If you act tough people will go after you. If you walk around like a frightened mouse people will see you as a target. If someone puts it on you, don't speak. Just fire up. Fight. But don't provoke fights or bridge up. The rules were very similar to streets and the homes rules. The main difference from the streets was that you had nowhere to go if trouble started. People here had little to lose so could and would stab you if you did the wrong thing. I planned to just keep my head down and not buy into drama.

Colin decided I was okay. After I was back in my cell different guys came and dropped off different things for me: an old pair or runners, two pairs of green shorts and a white T shirt. I was told, 'Don't wear the battle gear.' I changed into the new gear and then I at least looked like I belonged.

At about three o'clock we were given dinner and sent to our cells. Spinner was my cellmate and he was a dead set spinner who paced the cell most of the night. In prison Spinner was the name they used for people with serious mental health problems. I was still withdrawing and his pacing made me agitated. I could see he wasn't normal. Within a few days I had a new cell mate who wasn't a spinner.

I had a serious Jack Rabbit, as they called a habit. Nifty told me that a golden rule was, No matter what, don't get into the drug scene in prison. It always caused fights and people even got killed. I stuck to that. I was still hanging out but I was three weeks clean. I didn't want to get back on again. One thing about addicts is that if there are drugs to be found they will find them if they want to. I chose not to even look or ask.

The rattling of keys woke me next morning. I'd managed only a couple hours sleep. (It took about six weeks before I could sleep a full night.) The cell doors were opened and we all went down to the dining area. Breakfast was Wheat Bix or porridge and a small carton of milk. As I lined up waiting for my meal I noticed ex Detective Rogerson serving behind the counter.

I said, loud enough for others to hear, 'Hey, that's Dodger, Roger Rogerson, fucking dog copper from the Cross!'

Nifty told me quickly to shut up. 'He's a Koala bear bro. A protected species!'

'How does a corrupt copper get in the main part of the prison and serve our food? Coppers are the enemy,' I said. I couldn't resist.

'Shut up man! He's got some heavy friends here,' someone said a bit more urgently.

Back to our cells after breakfast, doors were locked and we stayed there until we were let out into the yard about an hour later.

Walking outside that first morning felt good after spending so much time in my cell and, before that, weeks in the police centre at Surry Hills. An adjoining yard had demountable rooms that formed a make shift library. There was an awning that sheltered tables where guys played chess or cards. One section seemed to be used solely by old men and Gronks (people no one spoke to or were considered weak). There was a wall that people played squash against and a gym. There were many faces I recognized in the yard, including Viper, a huge stand over man who reminded me of Moose the troublemaker. I'd had an argument with Viper two months ago.

There were a few stand over men on the streets: Chicko, Big K John and Viper. I was friends with John. This day I had scored at the same time as Viper so we went and had a shot together. He said, 'You want to help me do some rorts?'

The plan was I would bring customers to him and he would sell them Quinine. I spent half the morning bringing people to him and sold about eight hundred bucks worth. Each time we ripped a person off they'd come back to Viper and he'd tell them to fuck off. His look was intimidating. I was tall and skinny and didn't look like much of a fighter. But I was an addict and I had learnt to fight. The more times I was hanging out, the more courage I got to do things I wouldn't normally do.

Viper and I got money then we walked up to Kirkton Road. I said to him, 'Can I have my half now? I want to get on?'

'Let's do a few more then buy a five weight bag,' he suggested.

I said, 'Okay, but give me my half.'

'I'll give it to you when I fucking choose!' Viper said.

'I want it now,' I told him. I smelled a rat and I started getting fired up.

He wasn't fazed by me at first. 'What the fuck you going to do?' he shouted back at me.

He pretended to pull out an eye lash and said, 'I lash.' That meant I'm lashing out of the deal. I'm not paying.

I saw a bottle, grabbed it and smashed it so I was holding a weapon. 'Give me my share or I'll stick this in your fucking neck,' I told him.

Viper was as shocked as I was. I wasn't that kind of person! But a desperate addict turns to desperate measures. I doubt I would have done what I said but he believed me. Maybe he knew I was a local who could get help from all corners if I needed to. Viper was a drop-in.

'Calm the fuck down,' he said. 'Here!' He handed me my

money. I saw him for who he really was that day: a gutless worm that seemed to get his way because of his size.

When I saw him in the prison yard with a group of other blokes from 12 Wing, he saw me too.

'Fisher,' he said loudly, 'Wait 'til you come to 12 Wing boy. You're gunna be my boy!'

I was afraid of him in this context where he had mates around him but I tried not to take him too seriously. He was spruiking in front of his mates. I looked at him and signalled with my hands, You talk shit.

I walked past him to see the gym. Skinhead Zac from the streets was there. We'd been mates and enemies at different times over the years.

Zac said, 'Hello,' and kept staring at me while he talked to his mate. It made me feel uncomfortable. I knew two kids in 12 Wing who were from the Cross and I'd heard they were constantly being raped. I didn't know if this was true or just made up to scare me. I knew both the younger guys from the Cross but hardly saw them.

I seemed to know about half the guys in there. They were my mates on the streets but prison is a different world. You had to stand up for yourself but it helped if you got into a group. I was in a group thanks to Nifty and I spent a lot of time with him. I didn't feel the same brotherhood we'd had in the streets though.

Big John, another guy I knew from the streets, was a sweeper in our block. The sweeper is the guy whose job it is to keep the wing clean. He got to be out of his cell when we were locked up. He usually ran the wing. He certainly was someone no one messed with.

I knew him because we'd been up the street late one night when two guys from western Sydney said, 'Want to get on?' They were in the Cross to make a quick buck and take off to wherever they'd come from.

'What have you got?' I asked them.

He said, 'Heroin, real good gear. I can do however much you want.'

I went to Big John and said, 'These guys reckon they've got good gear for sale.'

He said, 'Want to come with me and get it?'

'What do you mean?'

'Just follow what I do.'

John went to the guy and said, 'I want two of your hundred dollar deals. Can you do it for one eighty dollars?'

'Yeah. No worries.'

John said, 'What's the gear like mate?'

When he said it was good John said, 'I'll buy two off you bro but you come with me when I have it. I'm not getting rorted.' John had the money and he was looking to get on too.

'Okay,' the guy said. 'Car's parked down back. Come with me.'

We went to the car that was right down in Rosebay. The dealer pulled out a fair bit of gear. We sat in the car and John held it in his hand. The guy put two hundred dollars worth into a spoon. John mixed it and gave me half. I wasn't complaining! John was paying. I felt as if something was about to happen but I didn't know what exactly. John held the money in his hand while we both used the gear.

'Soon as I know I'm smashed, you'll get your money mate,' John said.

The guy must have been dumb. You always get the cash first then hand over gear. The gear was good and I was smashed straight away.

John asked me, 'What you reckon bro? Any good?'

'Yeah.'

Then John turned to the guy and said angrily, 'Who the fuck told you that you could sell heroin on my streets?'

The guy's face changed colour.

John said, 'Glen, get in the driver's seat.'

I did. We were parked at the bottom of a really steep driveway. I tried to reverse up and stalled twice. I finally just flattened it and got out. The guys had jumped in the back and John helped himself to all their cash and gear, about five hundred

411

dollars' worth. We drove to the main street and got out. John gave a final warning, 'Don't ever come back selling on my streets! If you do I'll take it off you again. You're lucky we're even letting you leave.'

John shared the spoils with me and then we went our own ways.

So we meet again in Long Bay. John was well known in prison and the few times I saw him, he didn't acknowledge me. He kept to himself mostly. No-one messed with him. I couldn't rely on John here because in prison you have to carry yourself. Knowing other guys can help but ultimately you need to be your own man.

I was held in remand for around eight months and in all that time I thought constantly about suicide. After a while I was in a cell on my own. I had nothing in it but what it came with: a bed and sink. Most people had friends or family who could get them a TV or whatever. I had no-one and nothing. Most of the battles I fought were in my mind. I saw so many things happen in prison I could write for days about it.

I became a bit of a recluse although I sometimes played chess with an Asian guy who was really skilled. Nifty ran around with his group. They amused themselves by giving Gronks and Spinners a hard time. I didn't want to be like that and that distanced me more from the group. I have a heart and except when I'm hanging out for drugs, I'd rather help someone than hurt them. For those months in remand my head was a mess and I was confused about who I was. Addict? Survivor? Prisoner.

When my head wasn't in confusion or thoughts of suicide, all I thought about was Amber and Jenny. I wanted to be a father to Amber so much and I hated that heroin took that away from us. I knew deep down somewhere that I was a good man who could have been a wonderful father.

I rang Jenny one day and her new man answered.

'Hey fuck wit,' he said. I could hear that he was drunk. Well, I was drug fucked and unhealthy when we'd met but each day I was in prison I got healthier and drug free. My mind was slowly getting clearer. I'd started doing physical training too. Every day I'd go into the boxing area and punch the bag.

'Can I speak to Jenny?'

Why was this drunk with the women I thought I loved? Is he bullying her? Why was he acting as father to our daughter? I am her father. He would eventually hand over the phone each time I rang and allow me to speak with Jenny.

Jenny came to visit me at the MRC. She brought Amber too. It surprised me that she had grown so fast. She warmed to me quickly and didn't mind when I held her. Sitting there with my beautiful, adorable child was special. I felt joy at seeing them both but I felt sad too that I wasn't with them every day. I was in prison and not being the father my daughter needed.

Then Jenny said, 'Daryl's hitting me. He's a drunk.' She sounded so dejected. I knew she still loved me and I loved her. I still loved heroin too, though I didn't understand why yet. It hurt me to know that Daryl was abusing Jenny.

'Want me to get someone to sort him out?' I asked her, thinking I could ask someone from the Cross. She didn't seem to be interested in that. I could see that she had grown fond of him despite his mistreatment of her. My treatment hadn't been good either, using drugs and disappearing all the time. I could not forgive Jenny and Michael for betraying me. I wanted to but it chewed away at me.

Not even my beloved baby could stop my suicidal thoughts. *There is literally nothing here for me. I've failed Amber. I've lost Jenny. I have no family.* I reminded myself constantly of every failure and of everything I felt responsible for that had failed. Being locked in a cell with my failures was torture. I spent hours lying on my bed thinking of ways to end my miserable existence.

I woke up one morning after a terrible dream. I can't recall what it was about. Beside my bed I had a photo of Amber with Jenny standing beside a horse. Jenny had written to me a few times and sent some photos. One was of Amber at Dream World in a fire engine. They were a comfort.

I made a noose with a sheet and hung it over something in my cell. I put my head in the noose and I prayed. 'Please Lord forgive me. I just can't do this anymore. Please look after Jenny and Amber. Please help my brother stop drinking.' I was about to step off the bunk when the cell door flew open. Fuck! *Can't I do anything right! I'm alone in this cell nineteen hours a day. The time I choose to do myself in is the exact time someone checks my cell.*

Coincidence? Divine intervention? Was this a turning point in my life?

I'd been serious that night at Annandale but I think maybe it was more a cry for help in my hopelessness. This wasn't. I felt absolutely defeated, useless and worthless.

The screws rushed in and got me. They took me to a dry cell. As we went passed other men yelled things like, 'He tried to slash up?' or 'Cunt tried to neck up.' or 'I'm doin' life ya weak cunt.' The noise got louder and louder.

I was stripped naked and sent into the cell. There was almost nothing in it: a mattress and one blanket put together in a way that I couldn't use them to harm myself. I was in that place, alone, for forty eight hours. People would walk past and taunt me. 'You're fucking weak!' I knew some guys who went by. They'd ask, 'You okay mate?' or 'What's going on bro?' or 'Why you want to end your life? You're only twenty three!'

I'd learnt not to respond to taunts in prison. To the caring questions I'd reply, 'I'm just sick of feeling sick every day.'

When they let me out of the dry cell, I was taken to the Superintendent. He made me speak to someone and convince them I wasn't going to harm myself if I was sent back to my cell. I was returned to my cell and was pretty much ostracized from Nifty's group. We didn't become enemies and if I walked past any of them they'd still say hello, but suicide was frowned upon in prison. That was a rule no-one had told me. I wanted to be alone with my thoughts so it didn't bother me a lot that I didn't hang with Nifty's lot any more.

One night on the news TV owners saw a story about an

inmate called Danny. He'd committed a crime against a child. All through that night men were yelling, 'You're dead Danny.' 'You dog.' 'You're a fucking dead cunt.' 'Soon as the cell opens we gunna run in on you.' 'Hey there Rocky. Hey Rocky watch me pull a baby out of my hat.' The taunts went on all night.

The screws came in the middle of the night and moved him to protection. I saw a lot of violence in prison. Men bashing into other men, men running into cells and beating the hell out of people.

Most of the day I spent playing chess or jogging around the compound trying to get fit. I thought a lot about Jenny, Amber and that fuckwit drunkard Daryl. *We will meet again Daryl and I won't be off my face or have my back turned.*

I didn't know when my court case would be. The date had yet to be fixed apparently. When someone got around to it, I was assigned a lawyer and saw drug and alcohol counsellors who said, 'We might be able to get you into Odyssey House, a rehab in Campbelltown. We'll have to see what the judge says.'

One morning I was woken up early and told to get into civilian clothes. A few other guys were too. We were taken to the Supreme Court in the city. I spent most of the day in court but not for my case to be heard. This was for a bail application. I was innocent but it took about eight months just to be able to apply for bail.

Men in wigs sat waiting as I walked into the courtroom. Had I time travelled back to the eighteen hundreds? I'd seen Jenny the day before this and she was in the courtroom with our beautiful Amber. I was told by the judge that I could only get bail if I agreed to go to Odyssey House. I didn't feel ready to go to rehab.

Before I left to go to the cells, I told Jenny, 'Meet me at Wynyard Station.'

'Glen, you're going to rehab. They won't let you just leave!'

I said, 'I'll meet you there.'

I was put back in the cells where I sat for hours. Finally it was time for me to go to rehab with a number of others in court that day. We piled into the bus with three big escorts. One drove the bus and two sat where they could keep an eye on us.

I said, 'Can I open my window please? I can't fucking breathe.'

The big burly man says, 'Sure? Just a little bit.'

I opened it and sat staring out the window. We drove for about two minutes then we pulled up at a red light. I jumped up and slid through the window and out.

I was free. The driver and another man got out and chased me but I'd been caged for too long and I wasn't going to be run down by some fat cunt dingo. I heard later that two other guys escaped as well. I ran through the streets and headed straight to Wynyard. I saw Jenny pushing the pram towards the station.

'Jenny! Jenny!" I screamed.

She turned and smiled. 'How the fuck … What the fuck? Fuck! You're so stupid!' she scolded. 'Now you'll go back to prison. You should have gone to rehab.'

'Yeah well. Have you got any money? I want to go and get on,' I said.

Here was my daughter, the love of my life yet all I wanted was to grab money and get on.

'Meet me at the Cross. I've got to get out of here.' I kissed my daughter and kissed Jenny.

She said, 'If you go now Glen, that's it.'

'Okay,' I said.

I'd known we were finished way before this. She was still with Daryl even if her heart was with me. We had been through so much together. But I wasn't meant for her and she wasn't meant for me. I was wild but Jenny was normal.

Wild needed to score. It hurts as I read this. I wish I understood properly the gift I had with Amber. I didn't feel me being around her was good for her. I am a fuck up.

Chapter 21.
Caged Runner

I watched Jenny walk to Wynyard station with Amber in the pram. I knew that I might never get to be a daddy to Amber but the addict in me had forty dollars and despite being clean for eight months I thought I needed to get to Kings Cross and score.

If I could turn back time, I would choose rehab over abandoning Jenny and my child. With that eight months of sobriety already done I might have made it. I might have been able to rebuild a relationship with the women I loved and I would definitely be father to my little girl. Amber had shown me, for the first time in my life, what love was. It was a feeling just for her. I hadn't felt the intensity or richness of it for anyone else. I still felt very conflicted about Jenny. I knew I cared for her but I also felt resentment over her unfaithfulness.

My addiction was no longer a physical thing but it was still running rampant, amplifying the insults of my childhood, nagging like a festering sore, insisting that I was worthless. My parents belief that I was stupid, abuse in the institutions and around the refuge all haunted me along with Simon's voice telling me I wouldn't live much longer. I felt ashamed of the sexual abuse. I wasn't aware yet of the depth of the impact these things were having on me. I just knew I needed to shut them up. The longer I was clean the more the demons of my childhood haunted me.

At this point I was a danger to the public and to myself. I was a wanted man who knew he'd be back in prison sooner or later. So I didn't give a fuck about anything. That's what made me dangerous. I had lost any hope and I was out of touch with my capacity to care for anything or anyone.

I ran to the Cross. I avoided the train because I thought they'd be looking for me there. Brett had called me The Runner and here I was, running again. But this time I imagined the police were chasing me.

When I arrived at the Cross I ran into two other men who had been on that bus heading to Odyssey. They took the opportunity to escape when I did. I felt responsible for them escaping instead of trying rehab. I wonder now who might have been impacted by their choices, who was hoping they would get clean.

I found a dealer and went into a back lane to have my shot. I was about to put the heroin into my arm but I burst into tears before I could. A voice inside said, *You are fucking stupid. You just spent months hanging out. You got clean and look what you're doing now!*

I'd been telling myself for years that if I could just get three months clean, I wouldn't ever use again. In rehab I'd learnt the saying, 'One is too many and a thousand is not enough.' I put that aside and used the addicts mantra, '*Just this one shot. I deserve it.*' I injected my self in my scar mangled arm.

The shot was strong. I sat on a bench nodding off but I kept thinking about Jenny and Amber. I had fooled myself into believing that if I left them they'd be better off. I'd forgotten that of all the abuse I experienced, the worst pain I ever felt was being dumped, discarded.

Later that day I was walking down the street when three detectives on the opposite side of the road noticed me. They made a bee line towards me and, thinking they knew I had escaped I bolted from them. They chased me but I lost them.

I went to see Jenny and Amber one more time. Daryl opened the door, stood aside and called Jenny. Their lounge room was strewn with motor bike parts. This was not the kind of housekeeping Jenny would choose. Amber was playing in a kitchen cupboard. Jenny and I talked for a while.

As I left Daryl came outside and I thought he might try to have a go at me. I half hoped he would because I'd spent eight months getting into a much healthier version of myself with boxing and training. Daryl didn't attack and I left.

I had nowhere to stay so I slept in the Manning Street Squat. I went to the street occasionally and detectives chased me whenever they spotted me. They never caught me. I knew that the more they chased me and failed to catch me, the angrier they'd become.

It was then I decided I needed to get out of Dodge.

Some time in 1989 I had heard that Tina was living in Mt Barker, South Australia. I knew I'd be going to prison again and I needed to get more clarity about my drug use and the direction my life might take. Going to South Australia would kill a few birds with one stone. I decided to hitch hike there to find Tina and make sure she was okay and I needed some time away from the darkness of the Cross. As usual I caught the train to Lumeah and walked to the highway. I got a ride with a weird man in a white ute. He seemed to be deep in thought as we drove but every now and then he'd turn his head to look at me very oddly. He started asking me a lot of questions and I wondered if he might be up to something. He asked me where I was from, where I was going. That was pretty normal but his questions felt like he was fishing for information. They made me uncomfortable, even unsafe. My instincts told me that something about this bloke wasn't right.

'I've got some friends waiting for me further down the road,' I told him.

He suddenly pulled up and told me to get out. It was late at night but I was relieved to be out of his car. I was on a desolate strip of road with bush on either side and I couldn't see a single light anywhere. The guy turned onto a dirt road and drove off. I didn't know where he was going because the road he took didn't seem to go anywhere.

I stood in the middle of nowhere to take it all in. Suddenly I heard a rustling sound in the bush when I moved. The noise stopped when I stopped. It sounded like someone was in the bush watching and following me. I started to walk up the highway in the pitch black. I was really afraid. I could sense someone there. I started running up the road that seemed like an endless ribbon of black. I came over a hill and, thank God, lights ahead! It was a roadside Stop, Revive, Survive place.

I bolted up to them and with enormous relief I told them what had just happened. I was still shaken and I must have been as white as a ghost. They gave me a cup of tea and while I was there I met a truck driver heading to Adelaide. He agreed to take me as far as Mt Barker.

Many years after this I was watching a story on TV about a man who had killed back packers who were hitch hiking. When I saw his photo and a picture of his ute I believed that he was the man who picked me up that night. I felt ill. I'm not a hundred percent sure it was him but everything about that night made me think there was a good chance it was him and I had dodged a bullet yet again.

The truck driver took me to Mt Barker where I found local people in the pub who knew my sister and where she lived. When I arrived to her place, no one was there. A lady who was best friends with Tina arrived while I waited and we had a friendly chat. We became friends as time went by.

It was good to see my sister again. I stayed with her for about six months then I stayed at her friend's place. I met a lot of people and a few became good friends. I met a group of blokes who were on the run too for various reasons. It was through one of them that I was able to help me get a job at the abattoirs. I was thankful that I had worked in the Homebush one when I lived with the Chambers family. I could put that on my resume and they liked that I'd had experience. I didn't tell them it was only for three weeks. At first I worked in the lard room making dripping all day. I hated that and later I moved to the chillers where my mates worked.

So I was able to support myself while I was on the run from the police in NSW. I became stronger, more healthy physically and I was more stable than I'd been for years. Thoughts of drug use were always on my mind but I had done well without drugs and I hoped to stay on that path.

We finished work at three in the afternoon then we'd go to the local to play pool, have a few beers and kick back. I wasn't a drinker but I joined the crew here. I was getting a good wage and I got overtime plus danger money.

One pay day we all went to a restaurant after work.

'Let's just run and not pay the bill!' one of the guys said.

We'd had a few beers and I said jokingly, 'Yeah, let's do it.'

I half staggered to the loo and when I came back, all the boys had taken off and left me there. The dumb thing was all of us were cashed up and didn't need to run. I walked to the door and the cashier tried to block me. I got around him and chased the others down the street. I had a fight of sorts with Michael as we ran down the street.

'Fuck man! You just left me there!' I said.

He said, 'I thought you'd already bailed.'

I said, 'Fuck you mate. I could have been pinched!'

My conscience couldn't handle this and the following lunchtime I asked a mate who owned a mad car if I could borrow it. I drove to the restaurant.

The manager recognised me straight away and came out fuming.

I said, 'Mate the boys were drunk last night and it was meant to be a joke. I didn't know they were going to not pay. I'm sorry.'

'Pay the bill now, no problem,' he said.

I paid it and apologized again.

'You're a good man. Thank you. But your friends? Bad men and can't come back here ever again.'

We often went to the Sterling pub or one in Hahndorf. Every October a festival called Oktoberfest was held to celebrate beer and all things German. We went to the festival, had some beers then went on to a pub in Sterling. A girl kept coming on to me and her ex boyfriend would bridge up every time she did. I ignored him and made out with the women on the dance floor.

At closing time I put money in the duke box and put on the song Money for Nothing. I stood drunk beside the machine, probably swaying out of time to the song. Suddenly it stopped. The manager had turned it of at the power. For some reason I flipped out.

'I just paid a fucking dollar to hear that song, arsehole,' I slurred. I was drunk and ready to fight the barman, the doorman or anyone else who wanted to fight. The boys got me outside and then as we stood beside the car, a drunk girl sidled up. She was really hot. She started kissing me and all the boys were wolf whistling.

'Take her home bro! Take her home.'

Her boyfriend bowled up with his mates. She said they weren't together any more but he wouldn't accept that. He wanted to pick a fight. He had tried to hit me but I backed away. Then something inside me snapped. I was still agile and knew some martial arts so I did a roundhouse and connected with his jaw. He hit the deck.

'Fuck it,' the boys said. 'Let's get out of here before cops arrive!'

The ex boyfriend stood up but he was pretty dazed. His mates try to fight but they were outnumbered. It nearly turned into a brawl. I got in the car and we left. I never would have been involved in that stuff if I'd been sober. That's why I don't drink now. I also didn't want to make out with a girl who was clearly drunk.

A week later we ran into the same guy in another pub when both of us were sober. We became good mates and he started hanging with us. But I was getting drunk every Friday and Saturday night, getting into fights and all the while I kept thinking about Amber.

One of the guys in our crew got a housing commission house in Murray Bridge about an hours drive from Mt Barker. The abattoir shut down and I had no way to make money. I'd been couch surfing between Michael and the other boys' places.

I was drinking one night at Murray Bridge when I said, 'I have to go to prison.'

'What are you talking about?' the guys said.

'I want to see my little girl. The only way I'll ever get to be in her life is to go back to NSW, face the music and do my time.'

I thought about Amber every day. I kept the photos with me and I pulled them out all the time and kissed them and told them, 'I'm sorry.' My mind was made up.

I'd lived in South Australia for about six months with the intention of spending time away from drugs. I knew that I had to go back to NSW if I ever wanted to see Amber again or even try to rekindle my relationship with Jenny. As unlikely as it seemed I held some hope. I had kept in touch with Jenny and Amber while in South Australia and I planned to contact Jenny as soon as I got back.

Leaving South Australia was sad. Tina and Christine came with me to the highway as I looked to hitchhike back to NSW. I became emotional as I said goodbye. The girls looked at me as if to say *Why are you getting so emotional about leaving us?* I always find saying goodbye difficult. Maybe because of all the people I had lost in my life.

I got back to NSW without any drama. I had been clean for the entire time I'd been in South Australia but the minute I arrived in Sydney, the streets and heroin called me by name. Eight months in gaol and six in Mt Barker had done me a power of good as far as using was concerned but here I was struggling again.

The very morning I got back I headed straight to the Cross. *Just one shot then I'll go to see Jenny and Amber.* I was unable to resist.

I went to the streets, scored one shot of heroin and had it in Junky Lane. I was smashed. Back on the main street a group of three Kings Cross detectives spotted me. They came towards me and this time I didn't run. They weren't aware that I was wanted. They remembered how angry they had been when I kept running from them all those months ago. All they wanted to do was search me but I'd been a smart arse and escaped them every time. After searching for me and not finding me, they decided to set me up for a crime I didn't do.

Two of the detectives took me to the interview room at Kings Cross Police Station while the third one checked my record. As I sat down ready to be interviewed a spring knife whizzed past me and landed on the table.

'The tobacconist was broken into last night and someone took a heap of these knives,' said the detective who threw the knife. He threw it across the table towards me then, hoping I'd pick it up and plant some fingerprints on it.

I was no fool and I was not going to touch that knife.

'You broke into the tobacconist's, didn't you,' the detective kept saying and I kept saying that I didn't. I didn't mention that I was still hitchhiking back when the break in happened. This set up could backfire on them if they pushed it. I hoped they would.

Things changed when the third detective walked back into the room.

'Mr Fisher is wanted for, get this, for Armed Robbery! Our Mr Fisher will be going to prison for a long time.' They all looked surprised as detective three went on. 'There is a bench warrant out for him.'

They arrest me and placed me in custody in the Darlinghurst Police Station cells then I was moved to Sydney Police Centre then on to Parramatta Goal. I had to go to court for the Armed Robbery charge.

The public barrister I was assigned to was about to retire and he was as useful as the tits on a bull. I was never going to win against a corrupt system. I was also assigned a lawyer who mumbled and fumbled as she spoke.

Father Drake appeared before the court and the story he told didn't match my memory of the incident. He lied. He came to the cells later.

'The police thought that was best for you,' he said, excusing his distortion of the facts.

'No mate, they wanted me off the streets and you were a puppet in their game.'

'You look really well,' he said. 'You look quite healthy.'

I was so angry with him! He was supposed to be a man of God but he embellished what I'd done and added a few fabricated details. He was never ever in danger from me. I'd gone to him because I needed help but he puts me in prison. I expected the police to be dishonest but not a priest who I trusted. I needed help, not prison.

I was sentenced to two years and eight months in prison. I had some time to reflect on my future. I felt let down by the system. I was no longer addicted physically to heroin and maybe this time would help me further towards staying clean. I thought, *I can use this time to write that book I had always promised I would write.*

After a few months in Parramatta Gaol I was reclassified to a B category prison. All A Classification violent offenders like me had to be moved to Long Bay prison. Violent Glen, the robber armed with a butter knife to hurt himself was transferred with murderers, rapists, arsonists and so on, to the more secure prison of Long Bay. I was there a few months then moved yet again to Bathurst prison. Long Bay is a particularly sad and dangerous prison.

On the day of our move to Bathurst we were shoved into a prison van with a jug of water. It was a sweat box and after what felt like hours travelling to Bathurst, they finally opened the doors to find us with our shirts off and gasping for fresh air. Still handcuffed and carrying our stuff we were marched inside to reception then to A Wing, the reception wing. Prisoners in A Wing were locked in their cells at three o'clock in the afternoon and we stayed there until breakfast at seven the following morning.

Breakfast consisted of two Wheat Bix and a small carton of milk. After that we went back to our cells for an hour then we were released into the main prison yard.

The screws didn't know the details of my case or anyone else's. All they did was put me in my cell, put a card on the door with my admin number, 192704, my offence and my sentence. I knew I did not deserve a sentence so I lodged an appeal. However, when I heard that if I went ahead with it I'd have to go back to

Long Bay, I withdrew the appeal. Waiting for an appeal can often take longer that your original sentence.

We were referred to by our surnames and we accessed everything through our admin numbers. You have to recite your number or show your card at every exit or entrance. While I was in Bathurst Goal I started to write my book but I was afraid another inmate might find it and read about the abuses of my childhood. Although that wasn't likely it was still a possibility and I wasn't prepared to take that risk. I wanted the account of my life to be honest. I didn't want to list my abuses in detail but I still wanted to show how a person goes from an abused child, to institutions, to the hands of predators and transforms into a heroin addict. I wanted to tell it and to be in control of who read it when I was ready. I've always been afraid of people knowing about my abuse and how they will view me because of it. Now I see that telling the truth serves to help others. More to the point is that I now understand that the abuse was not my fault.

The idea was to firstly expose the many abusers out there, but also to show the transition from abused kid into addict. I wanted to not only expose people but to educate others as to what addiction and abuse does to people.

There was quite a bit of thinking going on for the nineteen hours a day I was in my cell but mostly I thought about Amber. She has no daddy. She will never know me. That made me angry and sad. I wondered about her first words, her first step, her first day at school. I wondered if she ever thought about me or had memories of me.

I thought about Linda's death too and at times I'd blame myself. I thought about all the sexual abusers from Paul to Larry and then on the streets and that ogre Simon Davies. The more I thought about it all, the angrier I became. The more time I spent off drugs the more clarity I got. Anger burned and grew inside me but the real Glen, even when he was angry, was not mean. I have a very gentle spirit and I have a kind and caring heart. All that was still there between the layers of anger.

Prison life became the easiest part of my life so far. I was fed three times a day, had a shit load of mates, a roof over my head and plenty of time to train for hours every day. I had a routine and I ran for an hour a day and did boxing and weights. Fitness became my new drug. When I'd arrived at MRC I weighed sixty six kilograms, I was paranoid, scared, and I looked like death warmed up. I was now eighty four kilos and I worked my way up to ninety two kilos.

My cell now was my home so I set it up with my TV that I bought with money Peter had put into my account at a time he had visited me at Parramatta Gaol. About half an hour after I'd set up my cell I was walking down the stairs in A Wing and I noticed a group of men go into my cell and attack my cellmate. He was already there when I arrived in this place. I heard one of the thugs say 'Message from the Bay.' Then I heard them attack him again. Apparently he'd ripped off someone in Long Bay and word had come though to these guys to square up. I kept going, minding my own business. I didn't know my cellmate. Later that day he was moved to the Bubble in D wing for protection.

Walking around to see what there was outside I saw a tennis court and a group of men, mostly Koori, playing touch footy. The man organizing the teams was an inmate called Bruce. They had picked teams but they were one man short. I'd played at Parramatta and Long Bay, on concrete so I said to Bruce, 'I'll play.'

Bruce would end up being one of my best mates during my stay. He was from out west in NSW.

They probably thought I was shit at the game and I'd be a liability. They argued over whose side I'd be on then someone up the other end of the field said, 'He can play on your side.'

About ten minutes into the game I made a break through the middle and a man yelled, 'Hey long fella, stretchy fella, give me the ball!' I turned the ball in and the man who caught it ran and scored.

'This Stretchy fella has moves!' a guy on my side said.

'What's his name?' another yells.

Another one, hearing the comment yelled out, 'It's Stretch.'

From that day on I was known as Stretch in the prison. Every day I'd get up and run around the compound for an hour then I'd play touch footy with the boys. Running was like trying to outrun my thoughts but I never could.

I made friends with various inmates and one of them told me, 'You need to get out of A wing bro. In A wing you spend nineteen hours of the day in your cell and you have to share cells, right?' It was the reception wing or the place where short term offenders stayed.

One of my mates took me to see the screw in B Wing and asked whether I could take the empty cell there.

'Yeah, he can come to B Wing,' said the screw. 'No dramas or fights or you're back to A Wing.'

B Wing was an improvement. The inmates were serving longer sentences so their cells were nicely set up. One of the best parts about being in B Wing was that we were locked in the wing at three in the afternoon but our cells were left unlocked until seven at night. So I had an extra four hours out of my cell. Usually I spent that time playing chess or euchre with other inmates.

I'd played a lot of cards and chess as a kid. I was good at Chess. Who knew why but word got around and lots of guys challenged me. I won most games as I could work out people's strategies. Being good at chess meant I never had trouble finding someone to play.

I had taught myself to draw with all the hours I had spent in the cell in the various prisons. I didn't have a job, so I used to make gift cards for people's girlfriends. I would either draw a picture on the front of a card or on an envelope. I even helped people write letters. I had always been fairly smart and I had taught myself so much growing up. I have been able to read and write from an early age. I struggle in some areas like complicated maths but I did well with Basic English and General Arithmetic. During the times I did school, I never struggled with the work. I struggled more with the social side of school.

I spoke with the women who ran Education at Bathurst Gaol and I told her that I wanted to do my School Certificate. I told her that I wanted to use my time to better myself.

She said, 'Yes, you can do a GCE. That's a General Certificate of Education. It's the same as doing the School Certificate at school. It just has a different name.'

I did several courses. I learnt different skills and got some certificates. I completed front end loader, forklift, and backhoe courses. I did First Aid and a Senior First Aid certificates and also GCE. I did a couple of computer courses and joined in arts classes too. I spent most of my cell time studying for various courses.

All my certificates were issued by The Department of Corrective Services. That name is in large letters at the top of each one. So really they're of no value unless I need to advertise that I've done time. If I showed any to a potential employer it could stop them even considering me as an employee.

Every minute I spent locked in my cell I would work on my GCE. I would also write poetry and draw. I had stacks of my work. Most poems were about Amber and Jenny. Some were about Linda and I even wrote cryptic ones about my abuse. I found poems were a good way to express how I felt.

There were some well educated people in prison and I sought help from men who had done their HSC or School Certificate with subjects I struggled with. I was determined to better myself and they were willing to help me achieve my goal. I believe that some of the most talented people are in prison.

Prison was my home and I rarely thought about the outside. Guys with families, parents or other people who loved and cared for them really did it tough emotionally. They would need a few hours after their visitors left to bounce back into prison mode. I didn't have visitors.

For me, life had been tougher before prison. This was easier time with mates, Chess, cards, footy, training and now I could add studying to the list. It took me about nine months in prison to achieve that. Now I was clean, I had a routine and a purpose. I found life better in many ways than it had been for most of the years before getting here. How sad that the most stable and somewhat happiest time of my life up to age twenty four was in prison! Yes, the refuge had happy moments but they were accompanied by my saddest experiences.

The only people I thought about on the outside were Amber and Jenny. I used my allocated phone calls to ring Jenny but the calls got shorter as time went on. I knew that if I spent too much time thinking about them my time here would be so much harder.

I never acted tough in prison and I stayed away from the gangs or men who got into robbing other inmates or doing stuff that could haunt them later down the track.

Most guys had pictures of naked women hanging in their cells. They just reminded me of what we couldn't have so I didn't want that kind of decoration in my cell. I had a few trophies I won at touch footy in prison and I had a TV. I had my drawings too. I wasn't as good at drawing as some of the inmates who could draw anything they could imagine. I could only draw things I saw. The more I drew the more I learnt and the better I became.

One day I nearly got myself into bad trouble. I was at the card table playing Manilla. We were playing for match sticks that had value. They could add up to the value of tailor-mades, White Ox, even Noodles. At the table there were three long term prisoners. One of the guys was known as one of the most dangerous men in the system. He had persuaded his co-offender to come out of protection to the main. No one was going to mess with them. So we had three long termers, two lifers, me and a few others who were doing short term sentences.

Sean described in very vivid details an horrific crime he had done to a girl and it immediately infuriated me. As I stood up my chair flew back from where I had been sitting. I walked off trying to contain myself. As I went I said, 'What a fucking grub!' Bad choice of words or volume? I had just pissed off two extremely violent people who were doing fourteen years. Any way as soon as I said it I knew I had put my big foot in my big mouth.

'What did yer say cunt?' Sean demanded.

'Nothing mate,' I said. 'Just thinking aloud. I had something like that happen to a girlfriend. Opened my mouth without thinking.'

'Ah fuck you cunt,' said Bobby, recently out of Protection.

'I should fucking stab you right now, cunt.' Sean was still on the attack.

'Shut the fuck up Sean. What he just said was fucking sick and it upset me too,' said Edward who I was so grateful to. 'Stretch, sit down and don't open your big mouth again.'

Crisis averted. Kind of. They both played on but were highly agitated and kept staring at me. I started to feel unsafe.

That night I got my tooth brush and made a shiv. I had armed up. I spent the night shaving it down, ready to defend myself in case Bobby, Sean or both came at me. For the first time in Bathurst I was afraid.

The following day I played touch with the boys and at the end of the game Sean walked past us and said to me, 'Why are you playing touch with the Kooris? You're white aren't ya? You either hang white or hang black. You're hanging with the wrong colour bro.'

I didn't know what to say but I didn't want to appear weak.

'I don't see people in colours mate,' I told him. I didn't even look up at him.

We went back to playing. I gained the respect of the Kooris but I knew I had an enemy looking for any reason to start a war with me.

Every prison has a Chaplin and Bathurst had Father Howie, a good man who held a chapel service around lunch time every day. Most men who went did so because you got real sugar in the coffee and biscuits. One day I met up with Marty there. Marty had been at the refuge before me and now he was in Bathurst for the murder of the Greek Consul and a school teacher who hurt him as a kid.

Marty didn't seem tough but everybody knew not to mess with him. He was also a real gentleman though. I spent lunchtime that day listening to him and Father Howie talk. Howie got a lot of respect from the inmates and Marty really liked him.

There was a screws strike a couple of days after the incident on the footy field. We were locked in our cells for a few days. My next -door neighbour had dug a hole through our wall so we could talk. Power had been turned off but he had set up wire from the lights to power his TV.

I prayed a lot in my cell. There is a song that reminded me of my prayers: *I pray to a God that I don't believe in.* I believed there was a God. I was still angry with him.

When the strike ended and they let us out of our cells, I was back playing touch with the boys and Sean and Bobby were sitting together and watching me. I had my tooth brush shiv in my sock. I pictured myself, stabbing Bobby in the neck. Or him stabbing me.

Then I heard my name called with about six other guys to go to the office.

'You men are all transferring to X Wing,' we were told.

X Wing was in another part of the prison that was lower security. That was a relief because it meant I could get away from the bullshit that had just erupted. X Wing had a fence around it that allowed us to actually see the outside. Two friends, Bruce and Marty, were moving at the same time. Marty had been a resident at the refuge at the Cross though I didn't know that then. Marty and another kid had killed some men who had abused them.

X Wing had four sections. I found it a bit hard to settle each time I was moved because of the different dynamics and different people. I think that one reason they moved prisoners about so often was to prevent them becoming too settled.

At the end of our wing was a little dining area. I would keep parts of the food served up there and combine it with stuff from buy ups to make my own feeds. Sometimes a group of us had a combined cook up. We would mix vegetables, noodles, cheese and anything else we could get from the kitchen. Some guys got garlic or chili too. We'd split our creations evenly and eat them with bread.

The electric fry pan was the cause of so many fights. People wanted it overnight so it went from cell to cell. Long term prisoners thought that short termers could do without a frying pan for their time and let the long termers use it. Only about six cells were allowed to have it. I was fortunate enough to get access to it on certain days.

X Wing was a working prison so I had to get a job. Jobs were available in kitchen, electronics, sewing room and gardens or you could be a sweeper for the wing. I was lucky enough to get into electronics with Bruce and few other mates. We were paid forty dollars a week, one of the higher rates of pay for prisoners. We made cables for computers by soldering connections all day.

The further I got away from using drugs the more clarity there was to my thinking. My body was much healthier than it had ever been. Clear thinking did not erase the boiling pot of thoughts I had though. Amber and Jenny simmered and my childhood.

Sometimes I felt that my thoughts were still out of my control. Nights brought vivid, hideous dreams of abuses I had experienced. Often these dreams included faces I recognized and sometimes I dreamt about the many different people I had known, kids usually, who'd died on the streets. Other times I relived abuse and I'd wake up screaming which would be embarrassing and difficult to explain to my cellmate and others. I believe that some of this dreaming was an effect of withdrawals too because it can take two years or so for the body to adjust.

Other inmates would laugh next morning and ask, 'What was happening in your cell last night Stretch?'

I'd tell them, 'Not sure what the fuck that shit is man. I get these weird arse dreams that I'm being chased.' I'd try to play it down and laugh it off.

Another difficulty I had was that sudden loud noises still startled me. They'd send chills through my body and I'd freeze.

This was very difficult to hide. Years later it was diagnosed as a PSTD response but for now it was a bit of a disaster.

Cell mates came and went and I'd write my cell mates names in a book. The one I got closest to was Michael from Germany. He was very laid back and highly intelligent. He seemed to be a well adjusted person and we shared a love of chess.

I heard about Prisoners' Aid while I was in X Wing. They could help prisoners to get in touch with family and even arrange visits. I hadn't seen or heard from Jenny and I really wanted to see my little girl so I went to ask Prisoners' Aid to help with that. Jenny came to see me one time with Amber when I was in remand at Long Bay but this time I'd had no contact with her. I wondered if this had something to do with her new partner.

After some time they arranged a visit with Jenny and Amber. I was longing to see my little girl. The day they came wasn't a normal visiting day so I couldn't go out to the visiting area and I had to wear a white jumpsuit. They let us have our visit in a demountable on site. Jenny was still a stunner and got a lot of attention from the other guys who kept looking in on us. My God my baby had grown and she was beautiful. The visit seemed to pass so quickly. Amber was growing into a beautiful cheeky little girl and I had to say goodbye to her.

It was then that I finally understood why people were so crabby or down after visits. I had thought, *I don't even get visits so I have more right to be unhappy than you lucky bastards.* But I was wrong. Loved ones remind you of so much: freedom, their absence from your days and, especially for me, the fact that I wasn't a daddy to my little girl. She was nearly three years old and she didn't know who I was. I was missing out on her life. That ached in my very soul.

That was my only visit from Jenny and Amber. I wanted to write and ring them but I didn't know where they lived any more. I'd send my letters for Jenny to her mother's place and she would pass them on.

Just like the day I had been called to the office to move from

Bathurst main prison to X wing, I was called to the office again.

'Pack your things Mr Fisher. You're transferring to Oberon Correctional Centre.'

It happened so suddenly. No warning and no time to prepare myself. I was annoyed and I said, 'I don't want to go.'

I was told, 'You don't have a choice mate. We run the prison, not you. Get your stuff ready to go to Oberon or get it ready to go back to the Main.'

My time at X wing was over. I felt so frustrated. I had settled in there. It was hard saying goodbye again. I'd made some really good mates. One guy I found it particularly hard to say goodbye to was Michael from Germany. No more daily tennis and Chess for us.

I packed up my gear. The longer I'd spent in prison the more possessions I accumulated. Mates leave and give you stuff as they go. I had two televisions, one for renting out and the other for my cell. Everyone had his hustle in prison for survival, getting money or food and buy ups. I had accumulated money from working at electronics and making greeting cards, renting out a TV, tipping comps, playing chess, table tennis and so on. I had boxes of stuff to take to Oberon.

If I'd known more about Oberon, I'd have packed faster and bolted over there.

The same day I was being moved to Oberon, Bruce and Marty were too. That made it easier.

Chapter 22.
Doing Time

Into a prison van heading to Oberon prison on Shooters Hill Oberon. Looking through the small cracks in the back door we could see nothing but pine trees. They were everywhere. The facility was in the forest and there were no fences around it. It was fifty kilometres from the nearest town.

I had a sense of freedom as soon as I got out of the van. No walls. No barbed wire. Surrounded by beautiful, peaceful nature. Inmates were walking about freely. Having stayed in prisons closed in by giant walls and prison guards with rifles, Oberon felt like paradise. It was a prison farm with ten units that housed ten people in each. There were four single rooms and the others had two men in each room. The six main units faced in to a central compound. People in those houses were long termers or people knew men already there.

Each unit had one man as the sweeper. His job was to keep the unit clean and to prepare the meals. He was usually the person who had been there longest and had the biggest say in what happened within the unit.

I was assigned to H Unit. It was not a clean place but I didn't realise how putrid it was until I went into other units and saw how much cleaner and better they were.

A box of food was delivered to each house each day and the sweeper of each unit prepared our meals. It was good food and we ate well. It was far better than the food we got in max.

When a vacancy came up in a unit, guys would look for someone to move in before they had someone sent to them who they might not want. It only took a few days before I moved to F Unit. From filthy to a group of younger people who liked sport. It was easy for me to fit in there. I was now taking good care of myself and I took pride in keeping my cell clean and nice.

Each day we attended musters and then I spent the most of my time with the guys in our unit. Sport competitions were organised pitting unit teams against other unit teams. I put on weight in this prison and I trained every day and I jogged every morning for an hour. I played touch footy for an hour or more. I got very fit. I still smoked about ten a day but I was still drug free.

We were expected to work at Oberon and jobs were assigned to each of us. The men who managed the various workshops often were civilians who specialised in a particular area, like woodwork, mechanics and kitchen skills.

The worst job for me was pruning trees. Early each morning a gang of us set off and spent all day working on pruning pine trees. I hated it and I wanted to go back to X wing the first couple of days I was in the bush gang. Oberon is bloody cold. It snows most of the winter. Each morning when we got to the site we'd make a fire. Each of us was given a pole saw and we set to work removing branches. I was told that this had been a job done by locals but the prison was able to undercut them and took the work from the locals. Prisoners only had to be paid forty dollars a week. Some guys loved being in the bush gang but it was usually guys who couldn't land jobs elsewhere.

One day a few of us presented ourselves to the Timber Products boss to ask if we could work for him instead. I got the job of making pallets. I used a nail gun all day, producing pallet after pallet. The workshop had every tool imaginable. Guys were allowed to make their own stuff too and some were really clever. The man in charge would teach us skills and help with the making of these gifts. In their free time people would make jewellery boxes and other gifts for their partners. Marty worked his whole sentence in that area and he made furniture for his partner to take home when she came to visit him on weekends. Marty was a lifer. I was gradually given other jobs like furniture making and I liked that.

Eventually I got a job in Education. The manager, Jane, told me that sometimes they didn't have anyone doing the job I was given and I'd got it because I had a working knowledge of computers. I'd learnt about them in prison. She'd seen me in Education working on my GCE and maybe knew I loved art. This was definitely the most rewarding job I did in prison. Jane allowed me to teach a general introduction to computers to other prisoners. I had manuals for DOS and I read them repeatedly. Guys often asked me to set up games for them to play so I read as much as I could about that and we got games running. We had eight new computers there.

I created a prison newspaper called Wazza Happening. It was a weekly paper that detailed what courses were coming up in Education and other happenings within the prison, like touch footy comps, table tennis and a marathon that would be run sometime in the future to raise money for kids with HIV. I made up crossword puzzles for Wazza and I put in drawings, poems and items from other inmates. Any one from the prison could contribute. The paper after I would create it was first checked by Jane then sent to the Superintendent of the prison to make sure he was okay with it. That was the condition I had been given when I came up with the idea to create an inner prison paper.

I returned to my unit one day and Tom, another inmate who no-one messed with, came to my unit.

'Stretch,' he said. 'I need to see you in your cell.'

That made me nervous. What did he want with me? Did I do something wrong? He was rumoured to have stabbed people when he'd been in maximum security and had status within the prison.

Tom shut the door when we got inside my cell. That was not relaxing! I was ready to fight although I didn't want to.

'Mate,' Tom began reluctantly. 'Uh, I don't know how to read properly. I was wondering if you could help me.'

What a relief! 'Sure mate,' I said as I started to breathe again.

He was more comfortable when I told him, 'I never got to go to school much either. Everything I know, I taught myself.'

'Really? Jeez. I wouldna guessed that,' he said. 'I thought you must have been some really educated bloke. You know about computers and that.'

'Mate, I bluffed a lot and spent a lot of time reading,' I confessed. 'Before prison I never read a book but you know, you spend nineteen hours a day reading books. What else was there to do!'

I spoke to Jane and she set up a course specifically for Tom and he did very well. He wasn't totally illiterate but spending most of his life in an out of homes and prison gave him very little chance of getting a proper education. That was something I could relate to.

In our unit there was a guy called Tony. He was one of two extremely talented artists there. I could draw but not like these two. Tony could draw anything. He was a tattooist and every night after lock in he'd pull out the prison made tattoo gun and put ink on anyone who wanted it. I already had some on my calves, on my arm and a few names on my body. I was called to the office once and the officer pointed out that I had suddenly covered myself in ink. They knew we did the tattoos. In max it could land you in solitary but here the officers didn't hassle us much. There was one officer who went around the units at night, outside, listening for tattoo guns. To counter this we set up a lookout to watch for him or anyone else snooping about.

Marty and a few of the boys from E Unit decided to raise money for children with HIV. We learnt that many of the kids had contracted the disease through blood transfusions and we wanted to do our little bit. We wanted to raise money and we wanted to raise awareness of this cruel illness. The way we'd do that was to have a marathon run with participants from all the units. They got sponsors from McDonalds and we were allowed to use the phones in education to ring places to ask people for donations. Most people we asked agreed to donate and the money had to be sent to Oberon. One of the boys from E Unit even arranged from the star of E Street, Mr Bad, to come and present the trophy to the winner.

Our oval didn't have a proper track so the boys created one. We'd have to run ninety laps to equal a marathon distance. Did we do the maths right? I still believe we ran extra metres but I'm not going back to check it.

I ran every day anyway but leading up to the race I trained for two hours a day with Brett, one of two lots of brothers in our unit. I wasn't sure I'd be able to make the distance but my goal was to finish even if it killed me. The boys ran a book on the marathon and the odds on me were 13:1. Even the screws were in on the betting. About twenty five guys were going to run. I bet one packet of White Ox tobacco on myself and I was the only person to back myself to win. I didn't think I would win but I was determined to run the distance no matter how long it took me.

A few days before the race, Peter from Hornsby, who I had been ringing on occasions, came to see me. He bought a new pair of runners for me. We'd kept in touch over the years that Jenny and I had been apart and when I told him the particular shoes I wanted, he managed to get them. He had visited me once at Parramatta around nine months into my sentence and gave me money to get a TV. Prior to that I'd spent nineteen hours a day in my cell with nothing but books and my thoughts. Or cell mates who talked too much.

I had the biography of Robert D Costello, the famous Australian marathon runner. He had said that the night before a race he ate pasta and on the morning of the race he ate honey on toast. So I did exactly that. I didn't know that wearing brand new shoes was a bad idea. I had two pairs of shoes, both the same brand, Sauconies. One pair I played touch in every day and ran in. The other sat there shiny new ready for the big race.

The day of the marathon arrived. The boys got busy setting up the stalls and the trophies they had made in woodwork. There was a shield for the overall winner and trophies for the runners up. The local paper turned up and McDonalds set up a stall. Mr Bad didn't let us down and he was very popular.

I wasn't confident as about twenty five of us assembled at the starting line.

Bang! The starting gun fired and we were off. Brett and I jogged along together. A few people had decided to run in groups or in pairs. The guys from our unit were Brett's and my running crew. We all wore white shirts with a logo on the front that showed we were running for children with HIV. I was going to eat bananas while we ran and drink small amounts of water to make sure I stayed hydrated. Every time we passed a check point we were marked off on a board to keep a tally of the number of laps we had run.

About an hour into the race I started to notice familiar faces in the crowd. Barry, my father, had arrived. What the fuck was he doing here? He'd only seen me once at Parramatta prison but I hadn't been in touch with him since. How did he even know about this? His presence made me determined to do well. I'd show him how wrong he was about me being shit at everything. His words rang in my ears. Yes, I'd show him!

About half way through the race a pack of guys running together suddenly accelerated and overtook us.

Brett said, 'We better lift the pace mate. They're getting a lead on us.'

I said, 'No! No way. It's better if we just keep this pace for the whole race.' We were going at the steady rate I wanted to maintain from start to finish.

Brett didn't agree and he said, 'I'm going now.' He wanted to win whereas I just wanted to finish the damn race.

Should I go with him? What if he's right? What if I do need to lift the pace? I decided to stick with my plan.

Four laps later I passed Brett. He dropped to the ground. Other runners started to pull up or pull out. There were ten left. I kept running at my chosen pace and one by one I passed other men. I ran beside Marty for a while. His style reminded me of Cliff Young with his marathon shuffle.

As I ran I asked, 'You okay Mart?'

He said, 'Yeah mate.' He had a lot of pride and even if Marty knew he was going to die, he would still have kept running. I looked up to Marty. Everyone did. He was the man to beat. He was a few years older than I was. I was twenty four and despite my past drug use and my cigarettes I could still run.

I started to lap Marty and the others.

Three hours later I was still jogging along when I got the bell.

'One lap to go Stretch!' someone yelled.

Plenty of people were shocked that I was still going. None were as shocked as me. As I passed my father I said, 'Want to run the last lap with me?'

He said, 'No.' Just as I expected.

Nothing I'd ever done was good enough for him. But here in prison I was about to win a marathon. Would that impress him?

The track became crowded with people who were just having fun running around. As I came down the last lap, guys from my unit were running beside me chanting, 'Go Stretch! Go you good thing!' They wanted one of us to win but most of them had bet on Brett not me.

I was elated that for once in my life I was about to achieve something. I know it might be just some prison run marathon but I felt incredibly proud as I got onto the road for the final two hundred metres. At about a hundred metres out people were telling me, 'Sprint. Sprint!'

Scotty was filming the race. He didn't know that I was on my last lap and he kept the camera on another one of his mates. I wish he'd filmed me coming in so I could have it today to show to my children.

I sprinted the last hundred metres as best as I could. I collapsed over the finish line. My shins were aching. I'd developed shin splints, maybe because I wore the new shoes instead of relying on my old run in ones.

As I lay on the ground puffing and paining, people came and congratulated me. Scotty said, 'Aah Stretch, we didn't get you doing the last lap on film. Can you do one more lap so we can film it?'

My reply? 'Fuck that bro.'

I was lying on my back, sucking in air and trying to get my heart rate back to normal. I have a stack of photos of that day. One shows me lying on the ground with my hand over my face.

After about ten minutes I sat up and asked, 'Who else was left in the race?'

'There's five guys still running and Marty's one of them.'

There were about twenty other people on the track but they were people who went on and off at different times just to run for the cause.

There was an older guy who had just come to the prison and he came in second about fifteen minutes after me. The next person in was Marty. He was a popular guy in prison, someone we all looked up to, so everyone, including me stood up and cheered him in.

After the race was over Marty came along and said, 'You fucking crushed me mate! You jogged beside me and then just took off and I knew I wasn't going to catch you.' I felt proud to get admiration from Big Marty.

Then came the presentation ceremony. Mr Bad with his dyed blond hair presented me with the trophy. I'd never seen E Street but other guys knew who he was. Apparently at the time of the race he'd been doing the show in hospital with a bandage over his head. He spoke to some guys and confessed that it wasn't actually him in the bandages. They'd used a stand in.

When he handed me the trophy he said two things that I'll never forget.

This is the first thing I won't forget: 'Do you know who I am?'

'No fucking idea, mate,' I told him. I didn't give a shit either. I didn't much care for celebrities. Most I'd met when I was a kid were paedophiles.

The second thing I won't forget: 'This guy ran like a bloody greyhound.' He said as he handed me the shield.

That comment made me want to kill him! A murmur went around. Someone quickly explained to Mr Bad that one of the worst things you can say to a prisoner is that he is a dog. He meant it as a compliment but it didn't sit right in that context. I took the shield and posed for a photo with him anyway.

The local paper ran a story about the marathon and named me as the winner but the wrong time was shown. I ran it in three hours and one minute not the four hours they reported. Compared to a real marathon runner, it isn't fast. They run it in two hours, twenty minutes.

Receiving my award for winning the marathon.

The day was a great day for all the inmates as it broke up the mundane life of prison. Although this was a prison farm and was so much better than maximum prisons, I was still locked up, still had screws about and still had to deal with prison politics.

I went to my dad and his visitors for a barbeque. Brian and Carol had come. They ran the prison fellowship and belonged to a church at Bathurst. They had a lot to do with me as I attended all their Christian functions in the prison. Had they told Barry about the race? Had Jenny?

We had a B.B.Q and I spent time with my father, his girlfriend and her daughter who seemed to take a liking to me. I had been at this prison now for ten months or so and I was allowed to get day leave and even weekend leave. I asked my father if he would ask if he could get me out for weekend leave. Not that I wanted to be with him. It was a case of doing anything to have some time away.

He left without congratulating me on my win. He kept his word and asked about taking me out on weekend leave though.

I was called to the office and Mr Clarke called me aside. He said, 'Glen your dad cannot take you out on weekend leave.' He went on to explain the reasons for that. There had been some serious charges brought against Barry. Mr Clarke said he felt sad to have to tell me that but that was the way it was.

I rarely got mail so it was quite a surprise when my name was called for letters. A card! The front of it said,

I'm sorry for all the times I've been unkind …

It was a whole poem. Strange. It could only be from one of my parents. I opened the card and saw running writing that I knew was my mother's. She had written, 'To Glen from Margaret Evans.' Who's Mar oh, my mother must have married again. Margaret Evans, my mother.

At first I was ambivalent about her sorry. Did she mean it? As I lay on my bed thinking about it my emotions boiled when I remembered all her cruelty to me as a child. Unkind didn't actually cut it. All her hurtful words had scarred me more than any violent act. I dismissed her card as she had dismissed me.

Later in my life as I learnt about addiction, I saw my mother differently. I saw that perhaps she was more sick then cruel.

One of the perks of being at Oberon the longest was that you got to be in Room 1. My time had come to be there. It was at the back of the unit so it gave me a bit of distance from the crowd. I was now sweeper and cook as well as working in Education. In the middle of the day we broke for lunch and every day our unit had a cook up of mixed vegies, noodles, cheese and about half a loaf of bread each. One guy had recently moved out so we were down to nine people.

A bus just arrived with new inmates. Usually they were put into the back units and we'd go and check them out. If we spotted a guy we thought would suit our mix, we invited him in. About five of us were sitting in the lounge when a man walked in with his stuff and said, 'Where's the spare room. I'm moving in.'

I said jokingly, 'The fuck you are! Who told you that you could come into our unit?' I was joking and it was a thing we did all the time with new people. Most of them would have just walked to their room quietly, ignoring my banter. Not this guy. He went to the office and told them that the sweeper of F Unit told him to fuck off out of the unit.

Over the loud speaker in the office a voice says, 'Fisher, to the Office. Fisher to the Office.' The inmates I was sitting with started joking that I was in trouble.

Mr Wayne, a screw who everyone said was okay, was calling me. The men talked to him like he was their best mate but I never trusted him. Screws who tried to pal up with prisoners were the ones that I trusted the least. Mr Wayne would often say, 'I have never put anyone on paper.' I believed he told other screws what was going on and they would report the thing instead.

I heard him call me but I just sat there. The others said, 'Maybe you should go bro.'

I said, 'Nah. Fuck him. I was fucking joking mate. If some pea heart has gone there talking shit, that's his beef, not mine.'

Within the next ten minutes Mr Wayne called me about five times. Neighbours came to our unit and said, 'Stretch! They're calling you to the office bro.'

'Fuck them,' I kept saying.

I'd been at Oberon for a year and I was probably getting too comfortable and too big for my boots.

Soon Mr Wayne came in yelling, 'Fisher, I've been fucking calling you to the office!' He was furious. 'Who told the new inmate that he can't come into this unit?'

I said defiantly, 'I fucking did.' I was about to add that I was joking.

He got in before me and said, 'We run this fucking prison mate. Not fucking germs like you!'

He put me on show in front of my mates. I lost my temper and reacted in a way I didn't ever behave in. I jumped over the coffee table and got up in his face. I stood over him and yelled, 'Who the fuck are you talking to!'

One of the guys jumped in between us and the screw went back to the office. Next I could hear the superintendent calling my name. I got up at a leisurely pace and went to the office.

The superintendent called me in and asked, 'Did you just threaten one of my officers?'

The screw was in the room, visibly shaken.

I said, 'He put me on show chief.'

'You, Mr Fisher, do not run this prison. You are this close to being sent back to the main prison. Do you understand that?'

I didn't want to be tipped so I had to try to turn that around.

'Chief, I've been here for twelve months and I've never, not even once, been a drama of any kind. I do education and I run the prison paper. I help organise events everywhere. This officer put me on show in front of the entire Unit. What am I supposed to do?' I was getting so angry I could have blown a fuse. Yes, I should have come to the office when he called me and I own that part.'

'Go back to your unit Fisher. I'll call you down and talk about this later, when you have calmed down.

For the rest of that day I was stressed, waiting for my name to be called, to be tipped back to Bathurst.

I got lucky. It didn't happen.

Oberon was minimum security and there were lots of drugs around the prison. I never looked for them.

People came back from weekend leave and often had pot with them in our unit. I smoked with other inmates a couple of times. We'd sit around at night getting tattoos and guys with pot offered it to me. I found it hard to say no and that worried me. I was due for release in October, two months away and the thought that I might go back to the streets and use again scared me.

Our urine was tested constantly so I decided not to smoke

any more and mess up my day leave or week end leave chances, not to mention my release day.

I had befriended Brian and Carol, an older Christian couple who came with the chaplain on weekends and for different events at the prison. I got to know them really well and I had a lot of questions about God.

During one of our conversations I told them that I'd asked Barry to organise day leave or weekend leave for me. I told them that it had been refused and I told them why. Brian asked how I'd feel about coming out for day leave with them.

I was elated and Brian organised my first day leave. He said we'd go to the Three Sisters in Katoomba with Jenny, Amber and her new man who I assumed she had met at church while I was in prison.

Carol picked me up and I was really excited. I was going to see my little girl! During the drive from Oberon to Katoomba I stared out the window seeing nothing but those pine trees. As we got closer to civilization I talked to Carol about the nights in prison when a few of us inmates would disappear into the bush to a little river nearby and we'd catch trout there. She was amazed that we would risk getting caught for this little luxury. We just felt liberated for a short hour.

What a day in Katoomba! I had Amber on my shoulders most of the time as we went looking at the views of the Blue Mountains. Jenny's new partner was a Christian and seemed to me to be a really nice guy. He was very different from me but whatever made her happy, I guess, was okay. I was happy that she had a decent person around Amber.

The trip back from leave was hard. I'd seen life outside and what I was missing out on. To be healthy and not addicted to drugs made having to leave my daughter again unbearably difficult.

I went on two day leaves with this family from then on. One time we went to Cronulla beach and we invited the girl who was with my dad on the day of the marathon. I have photos of me that day, running on the beach looking so fit and healthy.

It was on the second weekend leave that I went to church at Bathurst and as we were sitting in church a very distraught man came in brandishing a knife. Most of the people in the church were really nervous and they threatened to call the police. I spoke to the minister. 'Do you mind if I talk to him.' Reluctantly he agreed.

I could see the man was young and I knew in my heart that he was more afraid and hurting than wanting to cause anyone any harm.

'Hi. I'm Stretch,' I said. 'I'm an inmate at Oberon Prison on day leave.'

I talked calmly to him and finally got him to give me the knife. Then we organised help for him. We contacted the hospital and they got him to see someone from a mental health team.

The minister and the congregation were amazed. I could see it must have looked impressive to them. I didn't feel threatened by this guy at all. I understood where he was coming from even though I didn't know details. I felt sadness for him and a genuine need for him to be understood. I briefly shared with him my own journey and how I ended up in prison.

I returned to prison. Carol and Brian discussed my going to live with them when I was released from prison. When they dropped me off they mentioned it and said they could get me a job too as a builders labourer. I felt humbled and grateful. I had only about five weeks to go. It was 1992.

Was I excited about leaving prison? I hadn't been excited at all prior to knowing I could go to Brian and Carol. In truth I was nervous about where I'd go and whether I'd start using drugs again. I actually liked being in this prison. It was safe and I had so many mates and things to occupy me. I didn't have to think for myself. I was fed three times a day, had no bills like rent and electricity to worry about and I had a comfortable bed to sleep in. I had a hundred other blokes who I got on well with and I played footy every day, cards, chess and had a job to do. If I was able to have had a girlfriend to be with me I would have been more than happy to stay put in Oberon prison.

So many times we heard about men with histories of drug use being released and going back to it straight away. I saw men leave prison and return a short time later with more serious charges against them. Others died out there. I believed that was the fate waiting for me – to use again and maybe die. Apart from Amber I had nothing and no-one waiting for me. I could see myself getting a train back to Kings Cross and then with nowhere to live, no income, no family or friends I'd resort to the only life I knew, drug use on the streets of the Cross with all anxieties and depression my main companions. Prison did not treat addiction or trauma. It simply added to it. Today they are moving in a better direction.

Now I'd been given a lifeline with Brian and Carol and maybe I could avoid what seemed inevitable. Although I was happier about leaving prison, the thought of going to stay with relative strangers was pretty scary. I'd be living in Bathurst, a town I knew nothing about, with two strangers and their daughter. I had got to know Brian and Carol over the last six months. Weekend leave with them helped a lot. I trusted them but I knew that things wouldn't be as easy once we lived fulltime under the same roof. I was scared I'd let them down.

About three weeks before my release I organised a talent competition in the prison. I'd been organizing events for some time including touch footy, soccer and table tennis competitions. Every time I came into our unit I was carrying a bluey. A bluey was a form inmates could sign that authorized me to take one dollar from their accounts and use the money to buy prizes. More often than not I put in the lion's share but I got prizes from the church groups too.

I did an act with three other friends. I wrote a song about the prison guards and we sang it to the tune of Mr Sandman. Brian agreed to be the MC and to help adjudicate. The loudest cheers determined the winner.

There was a guy in B Unit who sang a song he wrote and played guitar.

'I've been here sixteen years
And I've still got life to go …

He was really good and I thought he deserved to win. The applause for our group was louder though so Brian declared us the winners. I felt it was unfair. The other guys agreed that the B Unit man deserved to win because he showed real talent whereas what we did wasn't talent. It was just four men, dressed silly, making fun of the officers for a bit of a laugh. The B Unit man got the prize.

With three weeks to go I started to get excited about my release. I was counting down the days. I talked to Marty and he said to me, 'I don't want to see you back in here Stretch and I don't want to hear of you overdosing.' We had heard that one of our friends who'd just been released died of an overdose the very day he got out.

I told Marty I'd do my best and that I wasn't planning to mess up again.

The night before my big day a few boys got wind of the news. They decided that as a farewell gift to me, they'd catch me and throw me in the little river where we caught trout. I managed to stay hidden for a good amount of time and the guys gave up on it.

I felt some sadness about leaving. I knew that I wouldn't see most of the guys again. I had formed some good friendships and on top of that it was the first time since I was sixteen that I'd been clean, very fit and healthy. I went from unit to unit that night talking to everyone and saying good bye.

Most guys go back to their families when they leave but I felt like I was leaving my family by getting out.

After the morning muster I packed the stuff I hadn't given away the night before. I kept one TV and all my photos as well as my most treasured possessions: a book of poems I'd written and a portfolio of my drawings which included a huge mural of Jesus on the cross with two angels kneeling beside him. What did I wear for the big day? A Tigers jumper from the 1988 Grand Final, blue jeans and my joggers, the clothes I'd been wearing when I was arrested.

I walked to the office at around eight o'clock. I'd seen Carol arrive to pick me up. Did leaving prison make me the happiest bloke on the planet? I felt sadness as I prepared to turn away from the place where I'd had the best time of my life. Ever. I had achieved more in prison than I had in twenty four years of life.

My addiction had been doing pushups, waiting to assert itself when I was free, but I didn't see it. The prison system didn't treat my addiction. It just put it on hold.

I had stopped myself thinking about using and I told myself constantly I would never go back to Kings Cross or use again. I meant it too. As I walked to Carol's car several inmates came down to say goodbye and wish me well. This was my time to rebuild my life.

Out there in the free world, I'd get settled and get stuck into writing my book. A small inner voice was screaming out to me to find justice somehow, to hold all those abusers I'd known to account for what they did. I didn't trust the police but I had to find a way to get justice. I'd need to hunt them down and get my own brand of justice.

I found it hard to breathe as we drove away. I thought about Amber and Jenny. I wished it were Jenny picking me up, ready to start again now that I was drug free. But she had a new man with a Porsche.

In Bathurst on 28th day of October 1992 Carol showed me to my room and my adjoining ensuite. It felt like I'd be living in the Hilton Hotel! It was so different from the streets or boys homes or prison.

About an hour later I said to Carol, 'I'd like to go out and walk around the town for a while.'

I walked along the streets of Bathurst and I noticed pretty women everywhere. I was wearing my prison shorts and a t shirt and it hadn't dawned on me that the outfit wasn't the best. It felt strange walking freely and when I saw a police car go by I got so nervous. What had I done wrong? I'd never felt safe around police but my unease went beyond rational thought. It was instinctive for me.

A familiar voice yelled out, 'Stretch!'

Only guys from prison called me Stretch so I turned to see one Scott waving to me. Many guys from Oberon or Bathurst prisons stayed in Bathurst.

'Hey bro! I see you're finally free,' Scott says, beaming from ear to ear. We chat for a few minutes about prison, freedom and people we know then he says, 'How do you plan on celebrating your new found freedom?'

I didn't have an answer but Scott suggested a beer and a game of pool. I don't drink alcohol but I thought why not have a bit of fun with my mate? In hindsight I can see it wasn't such a good decision. Learning to readjust to life outside needed time. I'd learnt the mannerisms, behaviour and speech patterns of prison life and now I had to flip them. It took a few months for me to realise that I was speaking another language: prison slang.

Scott and I went to a local watering hole and played a game or two of pool. Scott shouted me two schooners that I drank too quickly. The beer gave me a light buzz and I liked how I was feeling.

I said, 'Let's go see what other pubs are here and have another beer.'

Bathurst seemed to have a pub on every corner. We arrived at 'The Eddy' and I ordered two more beers. It was my shout this time. I was cashed up with money I received when I left prison. We sat at the bar and I started my third schooner of the day. Two other blokes sat beside us and ordered beers.

One of the men started a conversation with me so I talked with him. I don't know why I said what I did but I have always been candid in chatting with people. I decided to share my excitement of just being released.

'What were you in for?' he asked.

'Armed robbery,' I tell him and I explain that I didn't actually do that.

'Congratulations on being free then mate,' he says and extends his hand for us to shake.

I happily shook his hand and reached out to his mate to shake his too. His mate wasn't as receptive or forgiving. He glared down at my hand.

'I'm not fucking shaking your hand mate! You're a fucking criminal!'

The person I became in prison might not have been normal but I was still him and this man had insulted me and put me on show. In prison I would arc up straight away but this is not prison. Scott saw the insult too. The guy had disrespected me and I felt angry instantly.

Scott said, 'Don't worry about it Stretch. He doesn't understand.'

I had lost all self-respect by the time I went to prison. I'd learned how to behave in prison and it was not the same as the way people acted in society. Now my prison behaviour got in the way of wise judgement. An insult in prison would be met with instant violence and that is how I responded to this guy in the pub. It wasn't appropriate. Scott could see my agitation growing so he tried to insert himself into the looming mess as the man's insults continued. His mouth just kept on running about people in prison and how it was their own fault they were there and they should ... 'Why do all the fucking crims have to come here when they get out?'

I snapped. I stood up quickly and knocked my bar stool over. I put my face in the guy's face.

'What the fuck did you say mate?' I asked through my gritted teeth.

He stood up to glare back at me. I hit him hard, much harder than I should have. He dropped to the ground. He got up and moved backwards to regroup. He was clearly stunned. I moved towards him but Scott grabbed me from behind to stop me throwing another punch. He didn't want me to risk going back to prison over some ignorant person's insults. Did it really matter what that man thought of me!

The questions I needed to ask myself was, *Where did all that anger come from?* And *Why was anger, followed by violence, my go to position now?*

I tried to calm myself. The guy I hit staggered towards the bathroom and as he goes in he lets out another barrage of abuse about me, more personal this time and of a sexual nature.

That triggered something in me. The alcohol didn't help I suppose but if I snapped before then hit him, this time I exploded. I ran at him. He barricaded himself in the bathroom. I pushed on the door screaming, 'Open the fucking door you weak cunt.' I kicked as hard as I could but he had his back up against the door.

Scott tried to intervene again. 'Stretch, calm down bro.'

The barman spoke up then. 'Listen mate, you just got out of prison and if you don't leave now you will be going straight back there.' He reached for the phone then he said to Scott, 'Put him in a taxi and call it a day eh.'

I walked outside with Scott who put me in a taxi. I am grateful to the barman who didn't call the police. I behaved badly and I regret it. I felt like a wild animal and I didn't understand my own anger or the depths of it.

I got home very drunk and later when Brian got home we talked about my day. He said, 'Well Glen, maybe alcohol just isn't your thing.'

He was so right. That one session of drinking was enough to assure me that I should not drink again. Prison had changed me. Some changes were for the better. It made me more willing to stand up for myself but if I stood up with raging anger it was counterproductive.

I still had not connected my anger with my past traumas so my responses to confrontation were still childlike.

Chapter 23.
Two Worlds Collide

I went to church with Brian and Carol the following Sunday. I noticed an attractive girl standing with other locals. I spoke briefly to her and she told me her name was Natalie. I didn't know it then but Natalie would become my wife. Natalie asked for minimum exposure of her and the kids' lives in the book and I agreed. We both want to protect our family.

It's been difficult to do because they are what I live for most. They are so much a part of who I became and who I am today.

I had intended to end the book with me getting out of prison then write the second book called the knock on effect. I decided though that people would want to know how I fought to get justice.

The day after I met Nat I dressed in nice pants, a dress shirt and a tie and went into Bathurst. I had enrolled in a course called Job Club in the local Job Network centre. Although I was to be working with Brian as a labourer, he didn't have any work for me yet so I took as many opportunities as possible to better myself.

I had a job and one day I decided to by a ring and ask this amazing woman to marry me. She said, 'Yes.'

We had a huge engagement party. Nat's mum came and so did friends and church people. We married a year after we met and our wedding night we conceived a child.

I was so happy to be married to Natalie but I failed to see my mistress lurking about waiting for her chance to seduce me again. Heroin is her name. At the start of my relationship with Nat we went to the Cross a few times to buy heroin to use recreationally. When we knew Nat was pregnant we stopped using drugs all together.

The birth of our baby in 1994, with no interference from

heroin addiction to skew my love, I now experienced what loving a child feels like full on. I chose his name to remind me, in a sense, of my boyhood hero and confidante, Zorro. We applied for and were successful in getting a Housing Commission home in Lithgow. I learnt also being straight what real love was, the love I have for Nat is real.

We really tried hard to be good parents to our little boy. It's difficult to be a first time parent if you have never been parented. Both of us came from broken homes and Nat had been a state ward. I was scared too. That I'd let our child down, that me, the addict would be back to take over my life and ruin everything. I was sure I wouldn't be the sort of parent my parents were. I never ever wanted to be like them and I had promised myself many times that I wouldn't. I hoped I would not fall into the trap that people do sometimes.

When I had come out of Oberon I was getting into fights all over the place but Nat had taught me to calm down. But who was the real me? The addict, the fighter or the me I wanted to be? A good dad. I didn't ever drink but when I first got out of prison there were a few incidents where I got drunk and looked for fights. I didn't understand the anger I had inside or where it began.

Regardless of all my questions we managed. We adored our little boy. I had always felt alone in my life but this was the first time I felt like I was loved and that I could love. Nat is the true love of my life. It was awesome having a mini-us with energy and joy and mischief, around us.

My little family inspired me to be a better man. I decided to create my own business and with Peter's help I was able to buy tools and everything I needed to start up. Peter had always encouraged me to find work and he was pleased to help. I called it Rustique's Reproduction Furniture. I would use recycled timber to build antique looking furniture from scratch. I had few skills but I'd seen guys in the workshop at Oberon using tools and making things so I managed to teach myself by trial and error. I made really nice pieces of furniture that I sold through antique shops.

Four years into our marriage I felt I needed to write this book. Then something happened to change our lives.

On the 30th day of October 1996 I was at home with Nat and our two year old when I heard a familiar knock on our door. I hadn't heard it for a while but I knew it so well.

Bang! Bang! Bang! Yes, police. Not just any police, this was Kings cross police.

I opened the door and there were two women and a man standing there.

'Hi Glen. We are from Kings Cross Police,' one said. Then without asking if it was a suitable time and place to talk they said, 'We're doing an investigation into some complaints against paedophiles from the eighties. You have been identified by multiple people as a victim of sexual assault.'

I felt like I was shrinking as they exposed me. I was angry, raw, embarrassed and deeply wounded by their words and their complete lack of tact. Nat was right there behind me. I had buried all that deep inside, as much as that was possible. I had not talked about it with Nat. I had told her that I had grown up on the streets and she knew I had been a heroin user and a prison inmate. She did not know that I was a victim of multiple sexual assaults. I still suffered from undiagnosed PTSD and flashbacks and I'd talk in my sleep and often wake up from nightmares. Sometimes I'd even wake up screaming and Nat would comfort me and ask me what was going on. I'd tell her it was related to my parents and leave it at that. Nat loved the man I was and didn't let the man I had been get in the way of her feelings. That's why I love her so much.

Now she was getting information that was my right to disclose when I was ready, not when the police chose to. In hindsight I can see it was not the best decision to keep it all from Nat, but I had seen no reason to tell her all of it. I was guarded in what I revealed. I just saw no need to give details.

I spoke briefly with the detectives that day. I was shocked at their turning up like that. I wanted them to shut the fuck up and leave. Reluctantly I agreed to go with them to Lithgow Police

Station and give a statement that day. From the minute the police came to my door until the moment I got back from the police station, I worried about how Nat had taken the news. Would she want to know more or would she be wishing she didn't know any of it. Would she still love me? Respect me? Want me in her life? It was unbelievably distressing to wonder about those things as well as to sit with the enemy and talk about the abuse.

At the police station I was questioned about two men, Ken and Paul. I knew them both. I gave a statement on each.

I told the police, 'I will help you on one condition.'

And what's that?' They asked.

'That you help me to put the men from the refuge in prison. Their names are Grant, Richard and Simon. They were the main ones.' I thought to myself, *If I have to relive all the memories and go down the court case path to justice, I want to include those men who I told that one day I would put you in prison and I would write a book.* The opportunity to make good on that promise was here and I was going to grab it with both hands. Heroin was still the only way I knew of to stop my feelings overwhelming me.

The police agreed to help. Did they ever intend to meet my terms and arrest those grubs? I made statements on the understanding that when these cases were completed I'd report to them about the refuge and about Uncle Paul raping me and what Larry did when I was in foster care.

Nat was angry one day when I got back from the police station where I'd been giving statements. I suspected she had read my statements I had kept in my room. No doubt this would have been distressing for her to read.

She yelled at me, 'How could you let somebody do that to you?'

I'd been beating myself up with that question all my life. I had not 'let' people do that to me. I'd been groomed for abuse as a child. It wasn't until we had children the same ages that I started to see how vulnerable a nine year old was. That came later. I had thought about telling Nat many times about my childhood but I got scared each time.

Over the coming weeks I had to go to Sydney several times to meet with the detectives and take them to various places where abuses had occurred and where I'd met people and so on. We went to Slots, to where I had lived with Derrick and to Petersham to show them the address where I had met my girlfriend Nadine and was abused by Paul. We went to Tempe to Ken's place and to a shop that was now a martial arts studio. When I walked in with the police there was a wall that I identified.

I said, 'Behind that wall is a staircase that goes up to the backroom.'

The owner verified all I said. He and the police were impressed with my memory. These things are hard to forget. We went up to an area that was very difficult for me to relive. I managed. I never really believed I'd get justice but here it was happening and I was helping. Once they finished this they'd help me to get the grubs from the refuge.

Ken pleaded not guilty to his charges and because the offences happened in the early eighties and laws had not yet been revised, the case was subject to the laws of the 1980s. I had to be at court every day and I could be called upon at any time to give evidence. The lawyers representing Ken could pretty much ask me anything they wanted to and drag me through the mud. They did just that. I was re-traumatised. Thank God Nat was not there. She was at home with our child.

A few months later I had to attend court. Every morning I had to wake up at six, get the train from Lithgow to Central and walk to the Downing Centre. A support person was assigned to me by the police. Sad to say the person assigned was the very man who ran another refuge in Paddington and was present when the 429 refuge was closed. I didn't like him back then and I didn't like him now with all this going on. I was angry that he failed to help us at the refuge at the time. I was angry with him over Linda's death too. If only he and others had tried harder to house us, she and many others may not be dead.

Reliving these memories was hard enough but the police

didn't make it any easier. They expected a lot from me and I was uncomfortable with them. In all the mire of memories, I made the almost fatal mistake of returning to Kings Cross to buy heroin. I couldn't cope with everything that was happening and it was just an easy quick walk away to get on. From then on I'd go to Kings Cross every day and get smashed before I went to court. The fact that my wife now knew about my past made it even more difficult. For both of us. I had no way to silence my head and I turned to the only thing I knew. Heroin.

The case with Ken went for around two weeks. Ken was found guilty and was given eighteen months prison. Were they serious? Kids' childhoods destroyed and he gets eighteen months gaol! I was furious! I got two years for a suicide attempt. I had been refused bail as it was a violent offence. Both of these men were given bail. What can be more violent than raping children?

The second case I had to go to court for came straight after the first. This time it was against Paul. There were multiple victims, most of whom came to court as witnesses. I knew just about all of them. Nadine came to help me as a witness for the Police and other friends too. I will not name them for privacy's sake.

Nadine was in trouble with the police again and she was in custody. She was brought before the judge any time they wanted to cross examine her and for the rest of the time she was kept in the cells. I was really grateful to her for being a witness. We hadn't seen each other since we were kids.

I mentioned the people who worked at the refuge as many times as I possibly could but the police just kept saying, 'Let's focus on these cases first.' They probably had seen my Mr Ombudsman police records and didn't like me much. I was just another number to help strengthen the cases they were working on. They cared little about me and treated me like dirt. The fact I was now going to the Cross each day to get smashed didn't help in my relationship with the Police.

I'd sit in court off my face. It was the only way I could cope with reliving painful memories. I wasn't allowed to see Nadine or other people involved with the case. The police kept promising me that I could see Nadine and the others but that never happened.

Paul pleaded not guilty and a couple of weeks into his trial an incident happened that could have put the case at risk. The court was adjourned for lunch. I went into a food court nearby to buy some food and use up time. I hardly ever saw my support worker and I think he spent most of his time with other victims in the case. As I ate my lunch, head down thinking about all that had happened over the last few weeks, I heard someone say, 'Glen? Glen!'

I was off my face so I didn't have a startle response. I looked up and standing beside my table was Paul Jones himself. The person I was giving evidence against.

Paul was standing there crying.

'Hi Glen,' he says.

I didn't answer. I was shocked to see him standing next to me and shocked that he was crying. Do I get up? Do I get angry? What do I do? I actually pictured myself getting up and flattening him. I was literally shocked that he would even approach me.

He says, 'Glen, I want to say sorry for what I did to you and your friends.'

He probably said more than that but I blanked out. Earlier that morning the police had yelled at me because when I was giving evidence I had left out a part that they had particularly wanted me to say. I wasn't in any condition to be giving evidence. I felt alone, very alone. I had my wife back home and our beautiful little boy but all I felt was fear and loneliness. I hadn't wanted anyone to know what had happened to me at the Cross. Going to prison and getting clean and breaking free from the Cross was a chance to start a whole new life. Now, my two worlds had collided.

Paul left as quickly as he'd come. I watched him go. A part of me wanted to chase after him and hurt him like he had hurt us.

His apology seemed sincere but I thought that it was easy to be sorry for abusing someone after you'd been caught. My reaction was mixed but I think the balance came down on the side of sincerity.

Paedophiles are very good at manipulating people. They can easily make you think you like them when inside you hate them. As a child I recall looking up to these men. Now I had spent years trying to repress the memories of all the abuse that I had lived with caused by these men, this man. It had wounded me so deeply that suicide had been my go to thought for several years. I feel sadness writing this, knowing that this happened to so many people who could not be here today.

Back to court. The police are excited. I heard one say, 'Paul has changed his plea.'

'What?' I ask.

'He has plead guilty. The case is over,' the cop said.

I didn't mention that he approached me and apologized.

I felt dead inside. The killers, heroin and confusion.

'Can I see Nadine now?' I asked.

'No! You can't. She's ...' More excuses so I leave.

I went to the Cross where it all began. I thought about us kids in innocent times, running around not caring about anything but each other. Linda, Nadine, Mike, Tommy and the others. I pictured the living faces of many who have died. The refuge, Simon, Grant and Richard. When will they charge Simon? I pray every night that that will happen. I remember sitting at the little wall where we had sat all them years ago as children. I felt sadness as each face came to me and I thought about them now. Many dead, in prison, lives destroyed. These are the things that the courts don't consider.

I scored heroin and went home to my wife and my child.

A few weeks later the police rang to tell me that Paul Jones got a sentence of eighteen months. Mixed emotions again. He gets a sentence but is eighteen months the value of my life in ruins?

'What about Simon Davies and the refuge?' I ask hopefully.

I heard a lot of what seemed to me to be excuses. I believe that the police never had any intention of investigating or arresting those people and that they altered statements related to the crimes I reported to them. In one part of my statements it says about Simon, 'Oh that was love. He just cuddled me.' I am absolutely certain I have never ever made that statement and I never will. Reading it enrages me. I had mentioned Simon Davies' abuses repeatedly to the police only to have it ignored. To them I was just a junky, not worth anything but an overdose. (Recent events may get me to a better opinion but only time will tell.)

In November 1994 the Royal Commission into Police Corruption began hearing evidence. I was interviewed by detectives when I was in such a bad state that I wasn't really able to give them the help I might have. I told them a few things but I was in such a bad way I was almost useless.

Nat was worried about my health and angry about my drug use and she confronted me. I got back onto a Methadone program and she was pleased about that.

In 1998 Nat and I had our second child, a beautiful daughter and in 1999 we had another son. I had no idea where Jenny and Amber were though I had tried to find them many times. I wanted to know Amber and be part of her life.

The Victims of Crime organization was able to compensate me with what others consider a large amount of money in 1998 ($165K). I personally think for a life that is very cheap. I hoped it would refresh our marriage and give us the life we so desperately craved. Our marriage was very strong despite the disruptions we were going through. I opened a skate shop and tried to make a new life. Sadly I went bankrupt in twelve months time, probably because I gave away more than I sold. I spent a lot of time with my son skating at the parks all over NSW. We played footy and cricket but I was still emotionally blank from reliving the memories that had now come out from where they'd been pushed down to prior to the police visiting me.

The disappointment of bankruptcy made me reach for

heroin again. My addiction had done what I feared it would. It really had been waiting to seduce me back into its grip.

We had four children now, one daughter in 98 another son in 99 and another little girl in 2004 but I had depression, I was on Methadone and my marriage hasn't got back to the place it was before the police knocked on my door. All I could think about was justice. The refuge people need to be held accountable but I have no idea how to make that happen. I am not going to share much more about my marriage because it involves two people, not just me.

My wife and I had different styles of parenting. I was hyper-vigilant and I had to know where the kids were all the time, who they were with and what they were doing. I had to go and see the people if they went to visit friends and I had to meet the parents and check the place out. I think I was quite suffocating. Nat often had to tell me to chill out and stop worrying.

I was generally very unhappy and I tried suicide. One time I overdosed and I was put into a mental care unit in Penrith called Piala. I stayed there for about four days and Nat came each day to be with me. I was given so many pills that I dribbled as I slept on Nat's arms each day.

I found myself in Katoomba at three in the morning and I was planning suicide again. I was standing aside a cliff when this old man appears from no where and says to me, 'They don't always die when they go over mate.' He convinced me not to end my life but to get help instead. I am very grateful to that man.

This was in 2009 and time for me to put myself in rehab. Nat who was now using too came as well and the kids went into care. We went to a rehab facility in Canberra to get clean for twelve months. I did go and use a couple of times when I first got out of rehab and actually overdosed once. That was it. I'd finished with heroin. I have not used since.

When I'd finished rehab Nat and I separated after sixteen years together. We didn't have a fight and we didn't ever say we were no longer married or breaking up. I went to live in

Parramatta and Nat took care of our kids back home.

When I had left Oberon I'd been feeling more fit and well than I ever had before. My health declined when the police intruded on our happiness and of course using heroin did absolutely nothing to help. I felt unwell again. My weight dropped to sixty kilos and so at six foot three I was very thin. My doctor told me to have tests and I was diagnosed with thyroid cancer. It is hard to treat Hep C and the cancer together but I had a Thyroidectomy followed by radiotherapy. Four years later the doctor told me that Interferon treatment can cure some Hep C. patients. We tried it and I was cured!

I moved to Parramatta into a place called Hope Hostel in 2012 and I had a counsellor who I spoke with about all the abuse I went through as a child and about how hard it was separating from my wife and our children. I still very much loved them all. I understood that my using drugs was not the best for our children. I was never going to resolve my relationships until I could get some closure on my past.

The counsellor listened while I told her about Uncle Paul raping me at age nine, then the stuff that happened when I was living in the Cross and finally the refuge, the thing that disturbs me most. I told her the Kings Cross police had promised me that they would pursue those people but they hadn't. I told her that I wasn't able to move forward in my life without getting closure around this. This is the time when I got the counselling I needed. I learnt to identify when I was angry and I learnt where my anger was coming from and why. I learnt that the abuses of my past were influencing my thoughts and beliefs about myself and others to this day. I gained new perspectives on my behaviour and on other behaviour too.

My counsellor took me to see a lawyer and then I was taken to Parramatta Police Station where I met with the Sex Crimes Squad. I spent hours trying to recall all the traumatic details of my abuse. I made a seventy five page statement outlining abuses from the day I arrived at the Cross. It was hard to remember it all in one go. The body language and responses of the police told me that they didn't believe what I was saying. How could all that happen to just one person? I went home feeling dejected and disturbed. Maybe nothing would happen if they didn't believe me.

Later that day many more details came to mind so I went back to the detective the next day.

'You can't change your statement now,' she told me.

'But I left so much out!'

'If you change your statement now,' she said, 'you'll be less believable.'

How frustrating! Surely a person would not remember everything in one sitting. I was so stressed about the omissions. I should have been allowed to list the men who abused me and then make a statement about each one separately instead of making just one statement that included what I remembered at that particular point in time. I don't think the police or any one believed or could believe all I had shared with them. I've often thought to my self if someone shared to me my story I would find many things hard to accept, so how to make the Police believe me.

A month later I went back to the police and they told me that they had been all over the country interviewing hundreds of kids and witnesses and that every single person they spoke to repeated the same story I had told them. I hadn't seen any of the other victims I knew since I left the Cross but apparently we were all saying the same thing. Now they believed me! Why not believe us then when we first report! Whatever the reason they were finally accepting what I told them as now every person they spoke to was telling them the exact same thing.

The Sex Crimes Squad created a special strike force called strike force Boyd to track down and interview the perpetrators. I suggested that they speak to Paul, the guy who had apologized to me at his trial. He might be willing to help given that he felt great remorse. He did help. I suggested that Grant would be a good person to track down too because I thought he regretted his crimes against children as well.

A plan was put in place where I was to help. The police gave me a phone that was bugged and would be used to help catch Grant. I was to 'accidentally' run into Grant in Parramatta.

I met with the Sex Crimes Squad officers early one morning. They introduced me to their technicians who put a wire on me and instructed me about what I needed to do.

Grant had to put his car in for repairs and they wanted me to meet up with him. I waited in a car with strike force officers while other detectives watched Grant. For a moment they panicked thinking he was going to rent a car or take a courtesy car and not walk where I could bump into him. He didn't though so as he walked up the highway I got out of the car and began my part. I could see Grant about a hundred metres ahead of me. A group of construction workers was between Grant and I and the noise of their machines was incredible. I walked quickly so we'd meet where there was much less noise and where the detectives could hear what I had to pick up on the wire.

'Grant?' I said when I was close enough.

He turned to look at me and I thought how much older he looked. I could still recognize him.

'Glen?' he said. I guess I looked older too. Grant was surprised to see me. We had a short conversation and I gave him 'my' phone number, the bugged phone.

'We should catch up soon,' I said.

I felt anxious doing that but I felt empowered too. I was helping to get this man and the others like him arrested and charged. I did it for all the kids whose lives they had ruined.

Two or so weeks passed and I didn't hear from Grant.

'Should I contact him?' I asked the detective.

'No. Just wait,' they advised.

Late one night, a month or so after we'd met, Grant finally rang me. He'd been drinking which was usual as far as I knew. He was keen to have a chat. We talked for over an hour. He talked for the entire time about the abuse. It was like he was reliving his past and he seemed to be getting off on it. It was a difficult call to take but I had to go along with it to get what we needed. When Grant had finished talking we said goodbye. I hung up and rang the police. They told me they had heard it all. As soon as I finished with the police Grant rang me again.

He wanted to meet up at a cafe a few days later. I met with the police to be wired up again. They introduced me to a young detective, Aaron, who I was to introduce to Grant as a paedophile. He was working on another case and he needed help about grooming and about how to get a child back from a predator.

I had asked Grant if he had any photos of us kids at the refuge and he told me that he did. I was excited to see them and I hoped he might have a photo of Linda.

Once again I was a bit anxious going to this meeting, especially at having to introduce an undercover detective to Grant. I was worried he might get suspicious and then everything would fall apart.

Aaron and I sat in the café waiting for Grant while other under cover police hid in places I could not see. I didn't look for them as I didn't want to be distracted. Grant eventually arrived and he immediately handed me a piece of paper. I opened it. It was a photo of two naked boys. I felt sick. Was that me? It could have been any two kids from the refuge or any other place. After looking more closely I recognized one of the kids.

I passed the photo to Aaron and introduced him to Grant. In no time they struck up a conversation. Grant was only too happy to teach Aaron how to groom and he made suggestions on how to get a kid away from his parents. Grant was happy to share his method of recruiting children. At one point he said words to the effect of, 'We looked for kids from broken homes that no one cared about.'

Maggot! What an absolute grub! Inside I was raging. I knew that was me he was talking about. Me and other kids no one cared about. Kids who no one bothered to come looking for.

'I need to go out and have a smoke,' I said.

I needed to breath, to calm down before I said something

that would ruin everything. Aaron was doing a really good job and Grant was only too happy to have a buddy to speak to about kids. Talking this way was normal for Grant. I recalled the times I was at the Colonial Café in Kings Cross when Grant, Richard, Paul and Simon would boast about their conquests and Annette and her friend would listen. The conversation Grant was having with the undercover was very similar to the conversations I overheard many times as a kid at the Cross.

As I stood outside smoking and fuming another detective from the strike force rang to check that I was okay.

"Yeah mate. I'm just trying to calm down. I'm so fuckin' angry from hearing all that shit from Grant,' I said. 'I'll be back in there in a minute.'

Grant was still chatting away to Aaron when I went back in. Stories of different exploits were told and I sat down and let them continue. We left eventually having made a plan to meet up again.

The second meeting was much like the first. I met with the police in a park the day before to discuss the plan. I'd meet with the detectives before Grant arrived to review what needed to happen. The three of us met again for lunch and Grant is as chatty as ever.

Not too long after Grant was arrested. The police also arrested his flat mate who had child pornography on his computer. Grant was charged with distributing pornography because he'd given me that photo. He was also charged with offences against me and another kid who didn't want to be involved in the case because he now had a new life. Grant had said enough for police to convict him without needing the other victim.

Grant pleaded guilty. His lawyer got the police to agree to what they called 'Agreed upon facts.' I felt helpless. I was never asked if I agreed to this. Grant was given two and a half years sentence. I was asked to provide an impact statement. When I was about to read it in court the judge said, 'I have read the statement. It's rather long.' I think she was trying to dissuade me from reading it.

It wasn't written for her. I wrote it for Grant to hear. I would not be put off. I understood Grant had read it and the police told me he was crushed. Well I was crushed by living it!

I stood in the dock and I read my statement. The Judge was not paying attention and I felt that I was reading to a wall. A guard was on the phone arranging an escort to take Grant to prison while I read. I felt angry and disrespected. I stopped reading and glared at the guard. The judge must have heard the silence and she told him to be quiet. I read on.

I'd spent hours choosing exactly the right words to make Grant comprehend that he had abused, not loved us kids, as he'd repeatedly told us. It was an abuse and betrayal of our trust and our vulnerability.

I had my own place in Parramatta now and my eldest son had come to live with me.

I had managed to find my daughter Amber on Facebook. I was able to speak with her.

The first words Amber said to me were, 'I knew you had been looking for me. It wasn't your fault you couldn't see me back then Dad.' I knew it was my fault because I'd had such a bad drug habit. I'm still finding ways to get to know Amber but I think she is a very impressive young woman.

Richard, the man who took me and the other kids to the refuge had disappeared. I asked the police not to go after Larry from my foster family because I didn't want to hurt the family. I had been told they had health issues and I didn't want to put them through it. Later they told me that they wished I had gone through with it. Police have been unable to get enough evidence to convict many other people I've reported and this frustrates me no end.

Simon Davies, C.E.O, (Chief Executive Ogre) of the refuge, has always been my main target. He fled to London. The police told me that he would be the easiest of all to convict because there are so many complaints against him by multiple victims. If only they could catch him!

After Grant was sent to prison I waited for the police to

make more arrests, mainly Simon. My depression came back in truckloads while I waited.

The police seem keen to pursue other perpetrators they've been made aware of discovered in interviews with victims. Every time I mentioned a perpetrator referred to in my statement they gave me what seemed to be an excuse about why they can't arrest the person. The case with Simon frustrated me most of all.

By 2016 the strike force had grown to around nine detectives. Two of the detectives arrived on my door that year.

'The Attorney General has given us a red notice on Simon Davies. That means he can't leave his current country of residence. That means we think that an arrest is imminent.'

I was speechless at first. I had been waiting so long.

'We have to rely on London police to make the arrest,' the detective told me. 'So let's hope they don't drag the chain. It's a matter of when he's arrested now, not if he's arrested.'

I was so excited.

Later I was told that Simon had left London and was now in Germany. He had been photographed at an outdoor café table, looking smug and healthy, happily sipping coffee. This was by 60 Minutes whom I did an interview with regarding the refuge. They later went to find Simon again and because they couldn't speak to Simon they decided not to air my story. They didn't want to air it with out speaking to him also.

Linda's passing still upsets me. I went to the Mitchell Library in Sydney to research her death and the refuge at 429. I came across an article about her death. It was written by David Hardaker. His portrayal of Linda had upset me. He described her as a fifteen year old heroin addict and prostitute. That was not who Linda was. She was vibrant, funny, intelligent, curious, beautiful, lovable and popular. She was a vulnerable child too. Her abusers portrayed her as a heroin addicted prostitute in their defense at court. The truth about her death was that she was given heroin by three drug dealers who wanted to rape her and Linda died of a heroin overdose. Instead of getting help for Linda, they left her to die.

I wanted to speak to this Hardaker person and tell him the truth about this beautiful girl.

A friend from a group of Forgotten Australians contacted him on Twitter and he agreed to meet me at the Mitchell Library the following day. I told him about Linda and he explained that he had reported the story from the court sheets. No other research was done.

I told David a little about the 429 refuge. David asked if he could read my statements overnight and get back to me. The next time we met he was almost excited.

He said, 'Do you know who Simon is?'

'Umm. Hello. Yes, of course I know who he is!'

'He is a big deal,' David said. 'He is very well connected, a professor now in a London university. This story has to be told by 60 Minutes. Do you mind if I talk to a few journalists to try and get this story told?'

He introduced me to two ABC journalists but after they read the documents they said, 'This is too big for us. Be better to take it to 60 Minutes.'

So I agreed to meet journalist Ross Coulthart from 60 Minutes. Another week passed and Steven Rice, a producer of 60 Minutes, wanted to meet with me. I met Ross and Steven at a supportive friend's place. They were keen to tell the story and they had a man in London who found Simon. They showed me a photo of him and I confirmed that they definitely had the right person. It made me sick to see that pompous demon. Ross and Steve asked me to come to the studio to be interviewed for their program.

By this time I had moved to the Blue Mountains. For the next week I debated with myself whether I should or shouldn't do the interview. I wanted Simon caught and exposed. I wanted the world to know what happened at the refuge. I just didn't want the world to know me. I rang Steven and told him I was having second thoughts.

'Can we do the interview without showing my face or my name?' I asked.

'Glen the world wants to see your face so they can see you're not lying.'

A few days later they sent a car to take me and a friend to a hotel in the city. This was a person I'd met years ago during a period of deep depression. They were set up to start when we arrived so I felt a little overwhelmed. The questioning started straight away. I found it quite confronting. Talking about my particular abuses is always uncomfortable and I was still wondering if this interview was the best thing for me.

Someone had found a video Annie had shot about the refuge. I watched it and there was Simon, drunk as usual. A kid was telling Simon and Annette that he would never go to the refuge because Simon abuses all the kids. Simon replied jokingly, 'Yeah but I give them five dollars.' As I watched the video I saw many kids I knew. I couldn't name every one but I knew most of them. A turmoil of emotions ran around in my head.

One of the first questions Ross asked me was, 'So your mother tried to cut off your fingers?'

'Yes, she did.'

'Can you show us the scars Glen?'

I show him and his face changes to incredulous. Mine must have changed to severe embarrassment. The interview went on and I was so uncomfortable.

When it was over I went home with my friend. I kept asking her, 'Have I said too much? I mean too much about me. I didn't want to share much about me. I wanted it to be about the men who worked at the refuge.' I couldn't stop thinking, *The world is going to know I have been sexually abused. The kids are going to be embarrassed by their dad.* I was afraid of that. I went deeper into depression. On top of that, the police seemed to be doing nothing to bring Simon back to Australia to face charges.

Countless victims of Simon had all given statements but the police kept saying that they were waiting for the Attorney General to act so the London police could make the arrest. That was in contrast with what they'd told me weeks before.

Is Simon Davies untouchable?

Many survivors of sexual abuse find trust hard and I found it hard to trust the 60 Minutes team and the police. I wanted justice so badly. I wanted the system to hear me and to validate my claims. Ross and the 60 Minutes team were very kind and considerate.

I often rang the police and asked, 'What's going on with the Simon Davies case?'

Each time they assured me that he is going to be arrested. It isn't a matter of if they say, but when. The Police spoke to 60 Minutes. The police did not want them to air the story yet so it was shelved. The police contacted me to tell me that Peter from Avalon had died. I'd been to his glass house with Nadine years ago. Larry from my foster family had also died. Uncle Paul is dead. Paul died too.

Early on I'd asked the strike force if they were going to pursue Annie. I feel adamant that she should be held accountable.

'No Glen. Let's focus on the cases we can win.' Then the detective said, 'We have a bigger problem. Simon wasn't living at Summer Hill when you were released from Bidurra.'

I hung up feeling gutted. I know I went from Bidurra to Simon's at Summer Hill. *They don't believe me,* I kept thinking. I was struggling with depression and PTSD but I was determined not to use drugs ever again to resolve my mental health issues. I had got a lot out of going to rehab and I started seeing counsellors about my abuse but I really felt defeated as far as Simon's case was concerned.

About two weeks after this the detective rang and said, 'Sorry Glen. We had the dates mixed up. You were released twice and the dates do match up with what you've said.'

He went on to tell me that they had spoken to Simon's sister and she confirmed everything I said. All was good again but the effect of having not been believed was hard to shake and it made it hard to trust the police. A lifetime of broken trust doesn't allow for me to trust anyone in a position of power.

Two more years passed and nothing happened. I went to the police again only to hear that Simon had fled London and was now in Germany. How? What about the red notice that was supposed to prevent him leaving the UK? I was told that if he goes to any airport in Germany now he will be arrested immediately.

More time passed then I rang the police again. Simon is sick. He is in Germany because he is very ill and he can't be brought back to Australia.

I am sick too. Sick of lies.

The 60 minutes team showed me a photo one of their team took recently of Simon at a café, looking very healthy. Did he hear he was going to be arrested and become ill suddenly? He will manipulate a doctor to support his lies about illness. Manipulation is his strongest skill. He has enough strength and energy to run a company called the Privacy Surgeon that has a website. His company teaches people how to avoid police attention.

In August 2018 the Attorney General gave police permission to go public with the story. David Hardaker is now a producer of 60 Minutes. I spoke with David about the police now wanting the story to go public. I messaged Ross who is writing for the Australian newspaper. Ross said it is madness if 60 minutes don't air the story. He may write a piece for the Australian.

There is to be a meeting to decide whether 60 Minutes will do the story. It is very frustrating for me. When I think of all the times I have made statements and reported abuse and tried to get justice, Simon Davies is still out there.

Today is the 1st of October 2018 my birthday. I am waiting for 60 minutes to contact me about our story, mine and the refuge kids'.

It is 2019 now. I first spoke up in 1996 and I spoke up again in 2013.

A Poem: Crippled by PTSD

A sudden noise, fight or flee?
My body freezes up on me.
I feel ashamed, fear rises
Living life with PTSD.

Who do I tell? What do I say?
I speak to a counsellor in another session
Low self-esteem, sleep all day
An abuse survivor, with deep depression.

Dark thoughts circle
Feelings, I try hard to hide
Repressing Memories
And constant thoughts of suicide.

Nightmares, pools of sweat
Flashbacks of heinous abuses
Sex crimes squad, royal commission
People offering up excuses.

Boy's homes, Yasmar, Daruk
Always marching in time
Locked up for running away
Absence of a proper crime.

Orphanages, YACS, the beak
Men in power with yellow streak
Constant tears, children dying
Heroin abuse, life on the street.

Little children who trust
Predators and paedophiles,
Families torn apart
Decades pass don't reconcile.

Overdosing, children raped
Predators of wealth
Doctors with their clip boards
Understanding mental health.

Lifeline, SAMSN, Are you ok?
The Black Dog, Beyond Blue
Reaching out to the pain
So we don't lose any more of you.

Twenty years chasing justice.
Four men in Prison for rape
Sentences of eighteen months
Hurt again by old red tape.

Damaged families
Many tears we have all cried
I cannot take another loss
Of a mate gone to suicide.

Epilogue

Here I'd like to summarise my life now. I will do so briefly because I will write another book showing more detail about my fight for justice and my continuing recovery. Friends say there are questions readers might want answered before my next book, so I offer this:

We hear so many times from all kinds of people that if you were an abused child, you'll probably be an abusive parent.

One of my daughters, Jess, had a habit of running straight out onto the road whenever she got into trouble or didn't get her own way. We lived on a busy road where cars sped along faster than the speed limit. One day when Jess was eight she did it again and I said to her, 'If you run out on the road one more time, I'll smack you.'

I never smacked and I think she might have thought I wouldn't follow through. Sure enough she ran out onto the road later when one of us had ticked her off. I walked to her and smacked her leg. She came inside and sat down on her bed. I came into her room and she looked at me and said, 'I can't believe you smacked me Daddy.'

'I'd rather smack you every day than have a car smack you down on the street sweetheart.'

We still talk about that incident because she remembers it as the only time I smacked her. So it's safe to say that abused children do not always become abusive parents. That doesn't mean I haven't made mistakes because I have.

Do I have a 'tribe' now? I joined many groups of Forgotten Australians and at first I found it really hard to fit in. Sometimes people made me feel I had no right to speak about our issues or my own issues so I stopped participating. That negativity made me decide to create a Forgotten Australians group where people can come and feel, safe, respected and not judged. I have formed some really good relationships in my groups.

I started going to Wattle Place, a service run by Relationships Australia. Going to Forgotten Australians events where people support each other rather than attack newcomers is helpful. At Wattle Place Forgotten Australians can get counselling, legal advice, all kinds of information and friendship. I have met so many wonderful people as I've been going to groups.

Do I use drugs? Definitely not. I used in the past to prevent my feeling overwhelming me. Getting clean along with taking counselling made me confront my past head on. I can't change my childhood. I have to accept that that is how it was. Now I have the tools to deal with what comes up and stay clean. Getting clean was the second hardest thing I have ever done. It's not just a matter of staying away from drugs. It's understanding why I needed them as a crutch. I have found resources within myself that I wasn't aware I had and these keep me stable and give me purpose and self belief. I have not put a needle in my arm for nine years.

I write poetry. I have done that for years. You have seen examples in this book. I have a collection that I share with other Forgotten Australians when it feels right.

I do art too. I draw my feelings and I like drawing pictures that I see in books but I put my own spin on them. Again, you have seen examples in this book.

When a child is abused his development can be arrested and he stays emotionally at the age he was when the abuse occurred. Looking back I can see that a lot of my responses were childlike. Thank God I have learnt to understand myself and I think I'm moving ahead to more mature behaviour. It could not have happened without counselling and being free of drugs.

Speaking of God, I was angry with Him for a long time. I blamed Him for my parents, my abuse and Linda's death. Deep down I needed Him to be real. I was baptized in Glenbrook in 2015. I have mixed feelings about faith when I see so many paedophiles attached to churches.

I want to finish this book with good news. I have five absolutely amazing kids and five amazing grand kids. They are so talented and I am so grateful that they live normal lives. I love them with all my heart and I know they love me. My kids are with me a lot and we spend a lot of time going to the footy and bush walking. It is so good that I now surround myself with people who will not show my kids the darker side of life. I am grateful to be a dad, a father. I am also proud to be a Survivor, a Forgotten Australian and a former Kings Cross street kid.

Nat and I will always be best friends. I made a promise to myself and to Linda after she died that I would never stop fighting for myself, the kids of the Cross and every Forgotten Australian.

My life now is not quite a bed of roses but there are far more petals than thorns these days. I still struggle with depression and fear but they will not defeat me. I am afraid of failure, of letting history repeat itself as it almost did before I went to rehab in 2009. I hate being scared so I hold my tools for healing tightly. They saved my life and they saved my kids from who I might have become again.

I need to be liked and I think others can see that I have likable qualities. I am learning to like myself far more than I used to. I am not stupid or a failure. I am smart and have skills and instincts that have kept me alive despite the odds.

Friends say readers might want to know about my mother. The last time I saw her was when I visited her in Whyalla. Then I received a card from her when I was in Oberon. I have always hated her but I always wanted her love and approval. She died a few years ago but I was not told until later. She had lived her final years in Iron Knob until she needed to go to hospital to die. The Golden Child knew her until the end but he did not let us know she was sick and dying. He robbed us of her in life and in her death. I would like to have gone to see her. I would have sat with her and maybe got some answers I needed. I'd have said goodbye at least. I feel cheated.

Her death upset me more than I had expected yet another part of me felt relief. She couldn't hurt me ever again. I am safe now. I do forgive her.

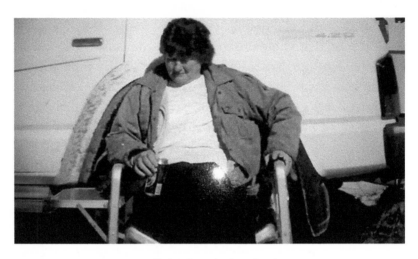

Mum, still drinking in her final years.

My father? I have nothing to say about him.

Strike Force Boyd is still actively pursuing Simon Davies and other cases relating to abuse from my days in the Cross. The Sex Crimes Squad is seriously understaffed and underfunded, especially after being loaded up with cases exposed in the recent Royal Commission at which I also gave evidence in a private hearing with Commissioner Murray. The hoops today's police have to jump through to extradite a person hiding overseas are so numerous they are almost unworkable. They have to approach the Department of Public Prosecutions first, wait for that decision, then the Office of the Attorney General, wait for a decision and then refer it to Interpol and then the justice systems in other countries. What is more the many branches and task forces within Australia's police service don't seem to be linked and each one reinvestigates details that others have already been confirmed but not communicated across the network. This is inefficient and stresses witnesses. It makes you wonder sometimes if they just want us to give up and leave the criminals to do their crimes uninterrupted. What sort of a society is that?

Who am I now? I have been defined by many people in my past by my addiction and the abuses I experienced. I refuse to let those things define me. They were part of my journey but they are not my destination. I am a survivor. I am a warrior.

As far as my search for justice is concerned, I have experienced some through the court system but the wheels grind so slowly. I've been able to help police put several paedophiles in prison but their terms are pathetically short and deeply hurtful to us victims. Some perpetrators have died and I wonder what they've said to their Maker. Simon Davies? Simon Davies is living large in Germany.

I keep remembering the words Simon said to me, 'You'll never see me arrested!' I pray fervently that I will.

I keep remembering Simon Davies saying, 'You'll never write a book. You won't live to twenty one.' Well here I am Simon. I am a proud survivor, father and grandfather and here is my book.

Acknowledgments:

My wife of sixteen years who showed me love and hope and gave life to our inspirational children.

Kate Shayler for helping me edit this book and showing me kindness.

Vivienne Tuckerman my good friend.

The men at 60 Minutes who tried to investigate our story. Ross Coulthart and Steven Rice.

David Hardaker for all his support and encouragement, and who took this book to a publisher. He also took our story to 60 minutes and other journalists.

Ray Leary who introduced me to Kate.

Every member of Survivors Safe Place and Tributes who keep me sane.

Shane and Nick from Parramatta Sex Crimes Squad and all of the Police on Strike Force Boyd.

Julia Gillard for caring enough to initiate the Royal Commission.

Every person who has supported me in my life. There are too many to mention.

Wattle Place for helping me through my abuse and introducing me to other Forgotten Australians.

Where to get Help:

Glen facilitates support networks on Facebook:
    The Survivors Wall (Tributes).
    https://www.facebook.com/groups/1644127599133970

Other available services are:
    Wattle place 8837 7000
    Lotus place 0747242559

National sexual assault support lines:
    1800 RESPECT: 1800 737 732
    Adults Surviving Child Abuse (ASCA): 1300 657 380
    Bravehearts: 1800 272 831

The following are State-based victim support lines that can help connect individuals with specialist counselling in their geographical area:
    ACT: 1800 822 272
    NSW: 1800 633 063
    NT: 1800 672 242
    Qld: 1300 139 703
    SA: 1800 182 368
    Tas: 1300 300 238
    Vic: 1800 819 817
    WA: 1800 818 988

Lifeline - 13 11 14

Suicide Helpline Victoria - 1300 651 251.

Kids Help Line (free call) - 1800 55 1800.

Mensline - 1300 789 978.

BlueKnot Helpline on 1300 657 380.

Geelong: 03 5222 4318.

Sexual Assault Crisis Line (24 Hours): 1800 806 292.

Safe Steps (24 Hours): 1800 015 188.

ACT - Canberra Rape Crisis Centre 6247 2525

New South Wales - NSW Rape Crisis Centre (24/7) Phone: 1800 424 017

NSW Health Sexual Assault Services (visit web page to find the number in your local area).

Northern Territory - Department of Health, Sexual Assault Referral Centres: 08 8922 6472

Queensland - Sexual Assault Helpline: 1800 010 120

South Australia - Yarrow Place Rape and Sexual Assault Service: (08) 8226-8777 or 1800 817 421 freecall

Tasmania - Sexual Assault Support Service 1800 697 877

Western Australia - Sexual Assault Resource Centre:

(08) 6458 1828 or free call 1800 199 888